"Mr. Estulin?" The voice belonged [illegible] of duty. An official representative of t[illegible] ing hard decisions where the meek a[illegible] gamble and the brain-dead travellers are concerned.

"You are looking at him."

He held my passport in his right hand, checked the seal on the cover, opened it to the corresponding page, looked at the photograph, and then at me.

"My name is –"

He gave me his name.

"You are from –" He told me where I was from.

"Look," I told him. "I know who I am, and I certainly know where I am from. Do you want an autograph and simply can't find a way to ask me for one, or is there a problem with my passport, my face or my name?"

The man cleared his throat.

"Mr. Estulin," he lowered his voice, "you appear on a certain list of people who are not allowed entry into the United States. We are checking once more to make sure. I am aware of who you are. In fact, I have read your book. Very interesting, if I might add." He clearly felt uncomfortable.

"I have made several trips to the United States over the past year, and I didn't have any problems getting into the country," I replied, trying to put the situation into perspective.

"These are troubled times, sir," he tried to reassure me in the most obtuse way.

"Troubled? How do you mean?"

"The War on Terror, sir."

"Don't insult me, please." I gave him my if-looks-could-kill stare. "I thought you said you had read my book."

"Sir, as far as the United States regulations are concerned, the airline is powerless to do anything," he replied apologetically. "We simply must comply with whatever directives they issue."

"So, the directive to preclude me from boarding my New York-bound plane was made by the United States government?"

"We assume so, sir. The airline certainly has no reasons to keep you here."

"At what level?"

"The computer doesn't offer that information."

"How would the US government know I was travelling to the United States?" I asked him.

"We, sir, well, I mean, the regulations and the requirements of international co-oper–..."

"Stop, please." I cut him off. "So, the European Union has caved in to the demands of the United States government, I asked him?"

"What?"

"Officially, the EU has categorically denied any inkling of the US government's access to European passenger lists.

"Officially," I repeated. "Unofficially, through several secret Europe-wide programs coordinated with the United States and Canadian governments, this information is available upon request."

Suddenly, it dawned on me. "All the right person needs to do is request information on potential terrorist subjects. Does that mean the airline willingly provided my name to the US government without being asked to do so in the first place?"

A look of horror registered on the man's face. He certainly knew who I was, he was well aware of my reputation in Europe as a first-class polemicist, knew that my books were read by millions, interviews and TV appearances were religiously followed by tens of thousands of zealous supporters. The idea of having all these people picket their company's offices on national television had crossed his mind. He was being most deferential, on purpose.

"Mr. Estulin, I cannot tell you more. You have to believe me. If I knew anything else, I would tell you. Even if I was forbidden by my airline, I would still tell you."

I listened to the tone, the intonation, to the cadences of his voice. There was a grumble in the man's voice, but not a trace of dissembling or guile. He was telling the truth. Those who tell the truth in ordinary conversation take it for granted they will be believed. Liars, on the other hand, more often than not instinctively look at you attentively after they speak, to see if you bought it or if they need to do more in order to persuade you. The airline representative took it for granted.

"What you people have done is illegal," I said. The man didn't reply.

"The Dutch representative for the Green party in the European Parliament, Kathalijne Maria Buitenweg, stated on record that this type of action was a clear violation of existing European privacy laws on data protection," I shot back, my jaws clenching.

(However, Kathalijne Maria Buitenweg should know better. The European Parliament, the only elected institution in the EU, is no more than an assembly, with no legal powers to initiate legislation: its sole legal recourse is to *ask* the Commission to do so. Moreover, the number of proposals is so large that Members have to vote on many with little or no knowledge of what they truly involve. Debate is virtually non-existent, and the strict, five-minute time limits favor most legislative proposals going through virtually unchallenged. The European Parliament has no control over moneys, nor can it impose taxes. The money supply is the domain of the synarchist-controlled European Central Bank, which orchestrated the 1922-1945 spread of fascism throughout much of Europe, and which exists today in the form of a network of private banking houses, such as Lazard Frères.)

"Mr. Estulin, you can lodge a complaint with your European representative."

Another lie, I thought to myself, not to mention a naïve way to try to unload this onto someone else.

He was about to speak again, but I interrupted: "Remember that these fine people do not, in any way, represent your interests, but rather interests of a supra-European state, regions on earth and not independent countries. This was made sure through the signing of the Treaty of Amsterdam in October 1997, which removed the border controls between EU states. The next step in the wholesale dismantling of independent nations comes in the form of the Nice Treaty. This is the foundation that is about to strip us, the people of Europe, of our basic individual human rights under the guise of a charter of fundamental rights."

For the record, EU Commissioners, all of whom, incidentally, have attended Bilderberg meetings in the past, campaign a great deal for the charter of fundamental rights, supposedly enshrined in the European Constitution, to protect all of its citizens from malice, until you read the fine print of the Constitution and realize that the only rights you are entitled to are the ones specifically mentioned in the charter. What you shall never hear from these malignant people is that *all rights*, under article 51 of the European Constitution can be suspended if "the interests of the Union" so require.

I watched with chagrin as my Air Europa plane taxied down the runway, waited its turn and took off without me, veering due north, and then northeast when it was out of the busy Madrid air corridor.

Use the situation to your advantage, I thought to myself. Adapt and improvise. I couldn't be in New York on Wednesday, August 12 as planned, which meant that Jesse Ventura and his crew had to be alerted, plans altered or changed or, in the worst-case scenario, cancelled altogether. A simple "no" from the airline in collusion with the United States government affected plans of at least twelve people.

Temporarily, I promised myself. I will get to New York one way or another.

I checked my electronic telephone directory, which has more than 500 names of people I can call on in times of emergency. This was an emergency. Luckily, a former journalist for *La Razón*, a national newspaper owned by the publisher of the Spanish edition of my Bilderberg book, had taken on a position as the US Embassy's press secretary. I looked up his phone number and dialed.

August is the worst month for business in Spain, as the entire country is on holidays. Unlike Canada and the United States, Europeans get thirty vacation days per year, plus national and regional holidays. In Spain, you can also add all the holidays of local and regional and provincial patron saints, not to mention people's individual patron saints. No wonder Spaniards work on average forty-three fewer days than the rest of Europeans, and two-and-a-half months less than North Americans.

"Whatever it is, call me in three weeks," came a blissfully lazy reply from the other end of the line.

"Where are you?"

"In your part of town?"

"Andalucía?" I asked.

"Very much so."

"Where?"

"Conil."

"Christ, you are five minutes from my house!" I exclaimed, suddenly remembering I was not there, but six-hundred miles north in Spain's capital.

"How about dinner tomorrow?" he asked.

"I hope to be in New York tomorrow," I replied.

"Hope?"

"I was denied access to my New York City-bound flight." I waited.

"Okay. If you wanted my attention, you have it," he replied.

I briefly explained to him what happened, emphasizing the responsibility of the United States government. No need to bring in a hapless guy from the airline company. He was simply following orders.

"What are you planning to do?" he asked, all traces of bliss erased from his voice.

"I would like you to call the US Ambassador and tell him that unless I am allowed to board that plane tomorrow, I will be on every Spanish mainstream and US alternative radio station talking about this incident. You can also tell him I will be back tomorrow at the ticket counter with a throng of Spanish journalists from television, radio and the print press, who will bear witness to what transpires. You tell him it will be more expedient for him, and whoever gives him orders, to let me be rather than to deny me access again."

"Give me one hour. I will call you back."

"Manuel," I said. "You and I have known each other for some six years. Please tell the Ambassador ..."

"I know, I know" he interrupted me. "Dealing with you is like wrestling with a pig. One might win, but one is going to get awfully dirty in the process."

"Exactly."

He hung up. There was little left to do but wait. Two in the afternoon in Madrid was eight in the morning in New York, and five in the early morning on the West Coast. I left a message with the A. Smith & Co people and called the hotel to change the reservation for the next day. The airline reservation would have to wait. There were too many unknowns even to consider booking another ticket at this point. As much as I hated to admit it, my bravado and grandstanding held little water with the United States government in Washington. The mainstream press made sure of that.

Spain, however, was different. I knew I could count upon at least two- to three-dozen friends in the mainstream national press to show up at the airport. I needed numbers to make a statement. Three journalists showing up wouldn't cut it. I needed a sizable enough force present to threaten the bureaucrats into action.

Nothing riles up a Spaniard more than seeing an underdog mistreated by someone in a position of power. In the underdog culture that is Spain, Cervantes and his knight of sad countenance still ride strong. Seeing the images of someone who had been done wrong on national television would force the Spanish Minister of Foreign Affairs into calling his American number, not out of duty, but necessity. To cover their backs. With the European Elections scheduled for the fall, I knew that phone calls would be made, and throats would be cleared and explanations requested. I was hoping *that* would be enough to sway someone's opinion to my favor.

Manuel called me back less than forty minutes later. "The Ambassador doesn't know what happened. He is out of the country, so the decision wouldn't have been his to make."

I thought about it for a moment. We had booked the tickets at the last minute, as the production company had trouble balancing Governor Ventura's schedule and mine.

"All right, Manuel. Let's say the Ambassador really didn't know. Who did? Who covers his back when he is away? Who is responsible for plausible deniability as far as the high-ranking members of the Embassy in Madrid go?"

"That's above my pay grade. They don't tell me much."

"But you shovel all their shit, don't you?"

"That I do. But not the good stuff."

He paused for a moment before adding, "I have been assured unofficially that you won't have any trouble should you decide to try again."

"I am trying again tomorrow, and I am bringing out the cavalry. Enjoy Conil de la Frontera."

August 13, 2009 Madrid 11:30 a.m.

The airline representative, a fifty-something man with red round cheeks, dressed entirely in company blue: blue-spatted, blue bow-tied, blue shoed, and with a fashionable goatee and a long patch of black dyed hair brushed over a "bald spot" the size of the Grand Canyon. He stood at Air Europa's reception desk, a glass of water in one hand, and a passenger manifest conveniently folded into a tube of documents in the other.

One of my companions spoke first. "My name is Pepe Arenzana. I am a senior editor with *ABC*." *ABC* is a conservative Spanish national newspaper.

The representative leaned over to an associate, who looked over my shoulder, squinted, and then whispered something in his ear.

"Do you know Mr. Estulin?" asked Pepe Arenzana, pointing in my direction.

As if in a trance, the representative stared pensively at the surface of the table, absently gripped the rolled-up documents, then raised his eyes, looking first at his associate, who was obviously in shock, his impressions a blur, his thoughts suspended, then at Pepe and then at me, studying us individually, and then collectively as a group. Cameras and flashlights were going off all around us. Inquisitive passengers tentatively craned their necks to see what famous film star was the center of all the attention.

"Were you aware that Mr. Estulin was denied access to the airplane yesterday?"

"Has the US government given the airline credible reasons for such exclusion?" came a question from somewhere behind me.

"Does the US government consider Mr. Estulin a terrorist?"

"Does Air Europa, a Spanish airline, consider Mr. Estulin a terrorist?" shouted a female voice to my left.

In that fraction of a second, the airline representative's countenance expressed both unmistakable resignation and crystalline contempt. For me? For the system? For himself? For the United States government and their misguided zeal? Madness.

The assistant who sat next to the official representative tried to take some of the heat off his boss. "We assure you that Mr. Estulin will be allowed to fly."

He tried to sound calm and collective. Except for his shifty eyes, his external demeanor was calm. "There is no problem with his visa," he tried to assure some twenty-plus reporters who had gathered around the airline's stand.

"Since when do Canadian citizens need visas to enter the United States?" shot back a journalist from *Tiempo* national magazine.

"There has simply been a misunderstanding. We were led to believe ..."

If there is such a thing as baptism by fire, I thought to myself, the assistant was getting the real treatment. Live and in real time. What better way to learn the nuances of the trade? And once again, Daniel Estulin was at the center.

"Why do you always have to be a skunk at every garden party?" my ex-wife had asked me once, what now seems like centuries ago.

"Because injustices, sweetheart," I said rather self-righteously, "need to be paid back in kind. That's the only way, short of violence, that goons learn."

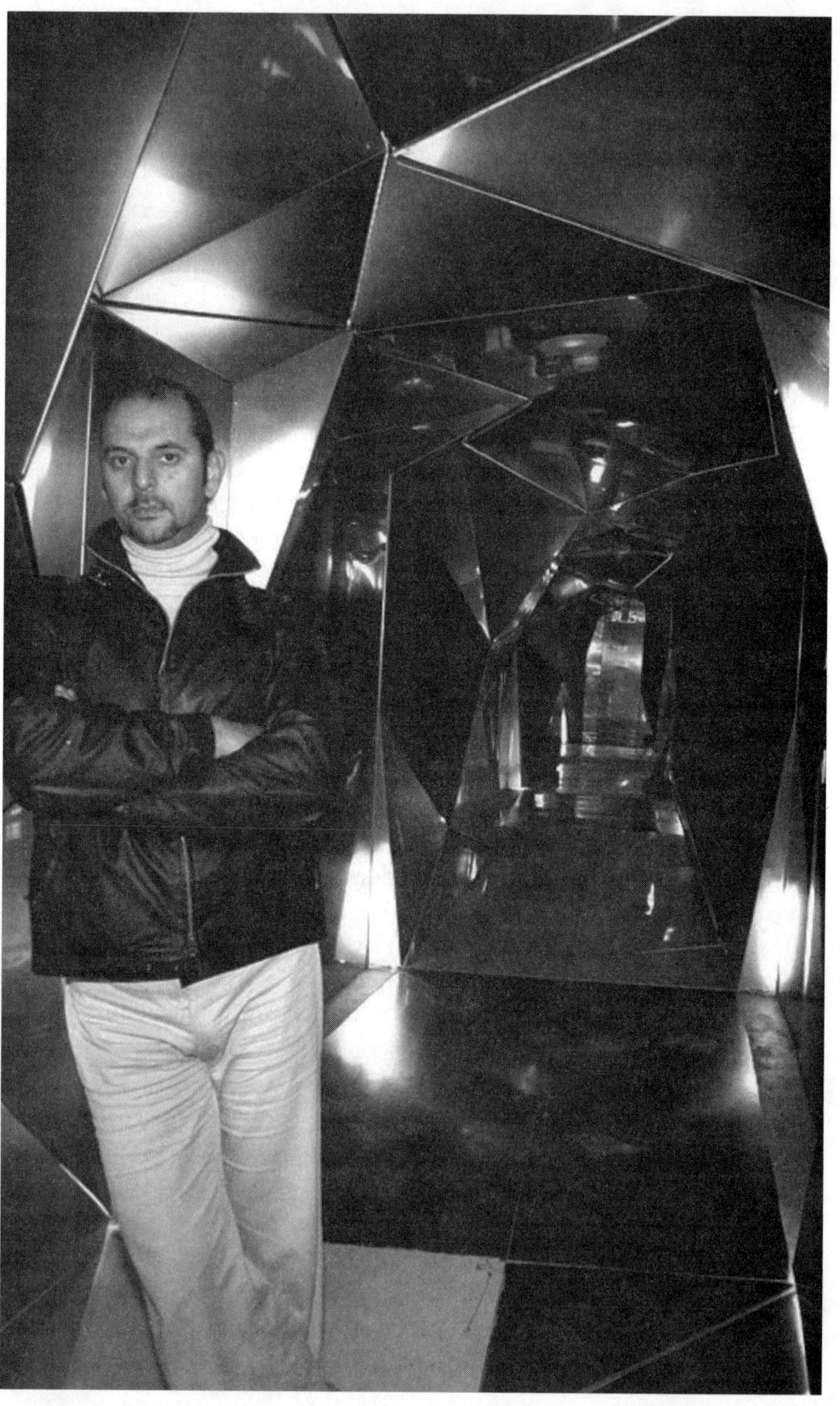

Chapter One

Conspirators

That one may smile, and smile, and be a villain ...
William Shakespeare, *Hamlet*, Act 1 Scene V

Into the Wilderness of Mirrors

By chance the final touches to this book were made during the 20th anniversary of the fall of the Berlin Wall in November of 1989. It didn't actually fall, rather the East German authorities announced on November 9 that access to West Berlin was open, and jubilant Berliners simply disassembled most of it over the next days and weeks. Since then it has become emblematic of the end of the Cold War and the beginning of the "post-history," "unipolar" world touted by American neoconservatives. The benefits from removing the expense of the arms race and from the spread of Western capitalism and finance – the "peace dividend" – would lead inevitably to a new golden age, a New American Century. It wasn't meant to be.

Beyond the significant specifics, the fundamental message of this book is that on the world stage, *things are rarely as they seem*. Leaders meet at G-20 meetings, national legislation is enacted, UN resolutions are passed, NATO forces are dispatched, and only rarely do the real reasons for these actions even approximate their justifying rhetoric. Such is the reach of the Shadow Masters.

At the time I watched the party in Berlin – for that is surely what went on – with as much pleasure as anyone who had experienced Communist rule firsthand. But my meeting with Vladimir was years ahead, and I took the events at face value: as a vindication for Ronald Reagan's carrot-and-stick approach to better relations with the USSR. It would not be long before the USSR was no more, and Muscovites would be partying like the Berliners, albeit on a tighter budget. It seemed as if the wildly popular Boris Yeltsin would be leading a no-longer-belligerent Russia into a new age of free enterprise and progress. It wasn't meant to be.

Instead, Yeltsin presided over years of decline and economic disaster, all the while himself clearly declining into a world of alcohol and illness. When he abruptly left office, naming the ex-KGB officer Vladimir Putin as his successor, Yeltsin was the most hated man in Russia. Yeltsin, who had sold off state assets at bargain prices to oligarchs and foreign interests, was seen clearly as the West's stooge, and US-Russian relations have cooled considerably since.

The answer to "what went wrong?" depends on who is asked. The Shadow Masters' answer is another question: "What's not to like?" Their world of deception thrives on conflict, both real and imagined. They consistently play both ends against the middle, and vice versa.

They relish a war in Afghanistan precisely because it can be sold to the publics among the "coalition of the willing" as the defense of Western civilization against the forces of Islamo-Fascism, whatever that may be. In fact it appears to be an occupation to protect and control the most lucrative drug trade in the world while stationing powerful military forces on the high ground between America's potential rivals Russia and China. It has the added "benefit" of further destabilizing the Indian subcontinent while appearing to threaten Iran. As I said, what's not to like?

Few Americans took much notice of the June 2001 formation of the Shanghai Cooperation Organization (SCO), a mutual security concord including Russia, China, Kazakhstan, Uzbekistan, Kirgizstan, and Tajikistan. The Shadow Masters noticed. The invasion of Afghanistan took place in less than six months. A glance at any globe will show the immense swath of Eurasia that these six states comprise. In an effort to gain greater influence, the SCO has granted observer status to Mongolia, India, Pakistan, and Iran, which applied for full membership in March 2008. These ten nations together comprise over 25 percent of the world's land-mass and over 45 percent of its population. Among other activities, which have included military exercises, the SCO has stated its intent to curtail the drug trade. Western dominance of Afghanistan is viewed as essential in limiting the power of the SCO.

However, the current global financial crisis, though largely engineered, does provide an opportunity for more and more people to see through the veil of deception. This is particularly true outside the US, a phenomenon discussed by F. William Engdahl by way of an ancient Chinese concept:

> The problem for the US power elites around Wall Street and in Washington is the fact that they are now in the deepest financial crisis in their history. That crisis is clear to the entire world and the world is acting on a basis of self-survival. The US elites have lost what in Chinese imperial history is known as the Mandate of Heaven. That mandate is given a ruler or ruling elite provided they rule their people justly and fairly. When they rule tyrannically and as despots, oppressing and abusing their people, they lose that Mandate of Heaven.
>
> If the powerful private wealthy elites that have controlled essential US financial and foreign policy for most of the past century or more ever had a "mandate of Heaven" they clearly have lost it. The domestic developments towards creation of an abusive police state with deprivation of Constitutional rights to its citizens, the arbitrary exercise of power by non elected officials such as Treasury Secretaries Henry Paulson and now Tim Geithner, stealing trillion dollar sums from taxpayers without their consent in order to bailout the bankrupt biggest Wall Street banks, banks deemed "Too Big To Fail," this all demonstrates to the world they have lost the mandate.
>
> In this situation, the US power elites are increasingly desperate to maintain their control of a global parasitical empire, called deceptively by their media machine, "globalization." To hold that dominance it is essential that they be able to break up any emerging cooperation in the economic, energy or military realm between the two major powers of Eurasia that conceivably could pose a challenge to future US sole Superpower control – China in combination with Russia.[1]

The world has discovered that *risk* has been globalized far more than either democracy or prosperity. The US bubbles in housing, banking and insurance have led to economic ruin even among America's traditional friends like Ireland and Iceland. Their publics have been awakened by another type of "shock-therapy," applied by the same culprits who used that as a justification for the "reforms" necessary to devastate the Russian economy.

But again, none of this seemed likely, or even possible, when the Berlin Wall was crumbling. It had been not yet thirty months since

President Reagan had issued his famous injunction during a speech in Berlin: "Mr. Gorbachev, tear down this Wall!" The irony was lost on me at the time, but if I had known in the wake of the Cold War's end what I do now about spycraft, I would have noticed a significant portent. November 9 marks the anniversary of a number of other important watersheds in German history, to the extent that it is called *Schicksalstag*, "Fate's Day": The 1848 Vienna arrest and execution of German liberal parliamentary leader Robert Blum, seen as symbolic of the failure of the Revolutions of that year in the German states. The 1919 abdication of the Kaisar and the declaration of both the Weimar Republic and a "Free Socialist Republic" in Berlin. The 1923 Munich Beer Hall Putsch, which failed but marked the beginning of the rise of Adolph Hitler and the Nazis. The 1937 *Krystallnacht* rampage against the Jews, leaving well over one thousand dead and marking the onset of the full-blown Holocaust, which (ironically) helped lead to the creation of the modern state of Israel.

I also noted recently the 30th anniversary of the seizure of the American embassy in Tehran on November 4, 1979. The ongoing "hostage crisis" did more than anything to discredit the Democratic Carter administration and usher in the Reagan era, with its attendant Reaganomics, Iran-Contra, etc. Nearing the presidential election of 1980, rumors began to swirl of an "October Surprise." The Carter administration was negotiating for the release of the hostages before the election, with the very reasonable expectation that this would ensure the president's reelection. It wasn't meant to be, and Reagan was elected in a landslide on November 4, 1980, the first anniversary of the onset of the crisis. The hostages were released *six minutes* after Ronald Reagan was sworn in.

The timing naturally raised a lot of eyebrows, and rumors now began to swirl of secret meetings with Iranian officials prior to the election by Reagan operatives, most notably spymaster William Casey, Reagan's campaign chief and his future Director of Central Intelligence, and an ex-head of the CIA, then-VP candidate George H.W. Bush. Charges and denials flared at various times via books and articles during the decade of the '80s and beyond. In the wake of persistent Iran-Contra revelations that had for years been vigorously denied by administration officials, a US House task force had been established to investigate the October Surprise story. By late 1992, with a new Democratic administration on the horizon, it was evidently time for the outgoing leadership to be exonerated, and the task force's report was released on January 13, 1993, one week prior to Bill Clinton's inauguration.

Republicans then lauded it as complete vindication, especially after the task force's Democratic co-chairman, Lee Hamilton (yes, the same Lee Hamilton of 9/11 Commission and Iraq Study Group fame), provided the *New York Times* with an op-ed piece titled "Case Closed," in which he recited the various "solid alibis" of the alleged evildoers. The powers-that-be were eager to apply the whitewash, lest the Reagan/Bush victory in 1980 be seen more as a coup d'etat than an electoral triumph. It is now apparent that Hamilton knew better, and that the report wasn't worth the paper it was written on. But the disinformation campaign nonetheless succeeded, and subsequent revelations have never pierced the veil of the mainstream media.

It turns out that Hamilton was withholding key information from the public. In the course of its investigation, the task force had in October requested the Russian government to supply any information it might have on the affair. The thaw in US/Soviet relations now produced some inconvenient results. The Soviet reply was received on January 11, just two days before the reports already at the printer's were scheduled for dissemination.

Based upon its extensive intelligence gathering, the Soviet report declared unequivocally that both William Casey and G.H.W. Bush had met secretly with representatives of Ayatollah Khomeini before the presidential election to urge delaying the release of the hostages. It named specific individuals and provided the specific locations in Paris and Madrid and dates. Also present, according to the Soviet report, was Robert M. Gates. (Yes, *that* Robert Gates, who would become Director of Central Intelligence under George H.W. Bush and Secretary of Defense under both George W. Bush and Barack Obama.) None of this information was made public, and the report was quietly buried among the task force documents. To this day, the Russian report remains "classified," and its contents have never been officially released.

It was discovered in 1994 among the stored raw documents of the task force by a Washington journalist, Robert Parry, who had broken a number of the Iran-Contra stories for the Associated Press and *Newsweek*. His 2004 book *Secrecy and Privilege: Rise of the Bush Dynasty from Watergate to Iraq* discusses the matter in detail. A succinct account, including a discussion of the flimsy alibis, missing passports, etc. that provided the "rock solid" evidence of the principals' innocence for the task force, is given by Parry in a recent Internet article, "The Crazy October Surprise Debunking," for *ConsortiumNews*.[2]

I am not suggesting that the Soviet report should be taken at face value; that would be naïve in the extreme. The point is that the information should have been investigated, not suppressed. And the fact that it *was* suppressed, and for the most part exists "below the radar" of public awareness, illustrates the very important fact that warfare in today's world is primarily *information* warfare. Control of the very terms in which discussions are framed, and more so, even the "facts" which underpin the discussions, yields control of the outcomes of those discussions. The ritual drama of democratic process proceeds, while John and Jane Q. Public haven't a clue.

This phenomenon is discussed in depth in another highly-recommended recent Internet article, "Beliefs: The Power Behind Unending War" by Jeff Gates for *Veterans Today*.[3] Consider the following excerpts:

> In unconventional warfare, manipulated beliefs are used to displace inconvenient facts. When waging war by way of deception, false beliefs are an oft-deployed weapon. Recall Iraqi weapons of mass destruction? Iraqi ties to al-Qaeda? Iraqi mobile biological weapons laboratories?
>
> Iraqi meetings in Prague with al-Qaeda? Iraqi purchases of yellowcake uranium from Niger? All these claims were reported as true. All were later proven false or, worse, fabricated. Yet all were widely *believed*. Only the yellowcake uranium was conceded as bogus before the invasion of Iraq. As the US crafted its response to the provocation of a mass murder on US soil, those widely shared beliefs shaped a consensus to wage war on a nation that had no hand in it....
>
> First and foremost are the consensus shapers and thought manipulators who target perceptions and opinions until a critical mass of agreement is reached. Then comes war. Those skilled at such duplicity induced coalition troops to war in Iraq. Knowledge was their target. Manipulate thought and all else was downstream.
>
> Unconventional warfare is waged "upstream" with the assistance of those with the means, motive and opportunity to massage consensus opinion. Where are modern-day battles fought? Not on the ground nor in the air nor on the seas.
>
> The mindset is the primary theater of operations. The first battlefield is the public's shared field of consciousness. The death and destruction come later.

> Deceit is not new to warfare. What's new is the reach of the technologies–including modern media technologies–that now enable deception on a global scale

Jeff Gates outlines how American neoconservatives manipulated public opinion toward war through such organs as the Council on Foreign Relations' journal *Foreign Affairs*, where "The Clash of Civilizations" theme first appeared in an article in 1993. By the time it appeared in book form in 1996, Gates maintains, over one hundred non-government organizations (NGOs) were on board to promote it.

But again, Gates' more general point is the one to keep in mind.

> When waging [information] field-based warfare, timing is everything. That's particularly the case when, as here, a belief-manipulating adversary is faced with the greatest danger of its six-decade life: facts that conflict with the narrative required to sustain *The Clash* storyline. ...
>
> With consensus beliefs the upstream target, democracy becomes the downstream casualty. When manipulated beliefs displace facts, the rule of law degenerates into a faith-based parody of self-governance. To protect the informed consent essential to freedom requires that those waging war on the public's shared mindset become transparent so that those complicit can be made apparent.

As I said, in the world of geopolitics, things are rarely as they seem. This will become more *apparent* as the narrative proceeds.

Who killed Litvinenko?

On November 1, 2006, London became the site of the world's first nuclear terrorist poisoning. The former KGB agent, Alexander Litvinenko, a major conspiracy theorist, was poisoned with radioactive polonium. He had launched a barrage of damning accusations at the KGB's successor, the Russian Federal Security Bureau: It had masterminded 9-11 ... was an accomplice in the Danish cartoons mocking Muhammad ... was directly implicated in a series of Moscow apartment block bombings in 1999 that killed more than 300 people ... and the 7/7 London train bombings of 2005 ... and the 1999 shooting in the Armenian parliament ... and so on and so forth. The former-Soviet/Russian intelligence service, by Litvinenko's account, was the guiding force behind most world troublemakers, especially Carlos the Jackal, Yassar Arafat, and Ayman al-Zawahiri.[4] On his deathbed, Litvinenko pointed his accusatory finger squarely at Russian President Vladimir Putin and the Russian intelligence network.[5]

The western media was rabid in proclaiming that Putin had ordered the poisonous hit, even though there was not a shred of evidence implicating the Russian state. To me, none of it made sense. Putin would have to be mad to make such an attack. Litvinenko's demise initiated a tsunami of Russophobic hysteria. How would Putin benefit from such massive antagonism? And why choose the highly unusual method of eliminating a target with polonium 210? It's a highly radioactive and very rare metal, about 250 million times more toxic than cyanide, and its production requires a nuclear reactor to bombard the element bismuth with neutrons.

I recalled the words of a former US ambassador to the Republic of Seychelles, David Fischer: "The whole game of intelligence is called a wilderness of mirrors. You look at it, but what you see isn't reality, it's always changing." I had a feeling that none of what I was seeing was real.

What looked like a clean and simple narrative, a morality tale pitting a heroic "human rights" crusader and former KGB agent against a tyrannical leader of Russia – a rough nation of lawlessness and corruption doomed to imprisonment by its bloody past – has, on closer examination, turned into something quite different, and far more complex. Again, why would the President of Russia, at the peak of his popularity and awash in oil revenues, risk a breach with every Western nation by ordering the protracted public murder of a man who, at worst, was a nuisance to the regime?

Was this a concerted attempt to discredit Putin's administration? After all, according to Zbigniew Brzezinski's assessment, an independent Russia stood in the way of America's plans for global hegemony. The grand strategy of the neoconservatives was revealed in a leaked 1990s Pentagon document written by Bilderberg Group attendee, Paul Wolfowitz. It too identified Russia as the biggest future threat to US global designs.

Though Putin allowed the expansion of American influence in former Soviet republics, the Russian president's limited efforts to defend his country's interests evidently irked America's new imperialists. Bruce P. Jackson, director of the neocon Project for a New

American Century (PNAC), wrote in 2003 that Putin's partial re-nationalization of energy companies was a threat to what he called the "democratic objectives" of the west.[6]

With Litvinenko withering and wilting away in pain and anguish in front of millions of television viewers, I kept asking myself a single question: Who would benefit most from his dramatic demise? Although the Cold War was over, it seemed the wilderness of mirrors stretched on.

There were a number of individuals, organizations and countries, I thought, who would benefit greatly from Putin's removal: big western oil companies barred from an unimpeded access to Russia's energy reserves; former and now expelled or jailed oligarchs who looted the Russian economy and stashed the stolen billions abroad, men such as Boris Berezovsky, Mikhail Khodorkovsky and Leonid Nevzlin;[7] Chechen "freedom fighters" and their supporters in the American Committee for Peace in Chechnya (ACPC). The list of the distinguished individuals supporting that organization is a who's-who of conservative America.

Supporters of the ACPC include Zbigniew Brzezinski, the architect of the "Grand Strategy" against Russian interests in Central Asia; Alexander Haig, former US Secretary of State and a close confidant of KLA terrorist Hashim Thaci, the current prime minister of Kosovo; Richard Perle, US representative of a pro-Israeli lobby; Kenneth Adelman, the former US ambassador to the UN who eagerly supported the Iraq invasion; Michael Ledeen, of the right-wing American Enterprise Institute and a former admirer of Italian fascism; and James Woolsey, the former CIA director and a leading advocate of remodelling the Muslim world along pro-US lines.[8]

One of the connections between Chechnya and the American Committee for Peace in Chechnya is oil, involving a powerful interplay of economic, political and strategic interests. Chechnya and Georgia share a border, and Georgia, like Russia's big neighbor Ukraine, is on the fast track to join NATO. "There are hundreds of US troops in Georgia, training the local forces," explains renowned and well-respected political analyst John Laughland in the investigative journal *Global Research*. "They are there for two reasons: first, to protect the US-built Baku-Tbilisi-Ceyhan pipeline; secondly – and this follows from the first – to assist Georgia in recuperating its two secessionist territories, South Ossetia and Abkhazia."[9]

For the ACPC principals, it will not do to have Russia anywhere close to the pipeline, and it has troops in both those areas. Pushing Russia out of the Caucasus, as Brzezinski outlined in his revealing 1997 book, *The Grand Chessboard: American Primacy and its Geostrategic Imperatives,* requires victory for the Chechens. An independent Chechnya may also be the prelude to the long-term breakup of Russia itself; after all, the CIA predicted that oil-rich Siberia might escape Moscow's control in its *Global Trend 2015* report.[10]

These strategic interests were further supported by, and are interlocked with, the private interests of powerful people lobbying for this anti-Putin policy. They included people like David Owen, representative in London of now-defunct Russian oil conglomerate Yukos, along with Henry Kissinger and Jacob Rothschild, members of the board of Open Russia Foundation, a Yukos front. Cheap oil is a matter of life and death for the US. Maintaining its dominance in a unipolar world, especially in monetary matters, is also considered absolutely essential. Putin's Russia stands in the way of both of these imperatives.

But these suppositions distract from the real reason for Litvinenko's murder: he had joined with the Russian oligarchs in a bid to retake the Kremlin after their expulsion by Putin.

Boris Berezovsky, who is wanted in Russia on charges of murder, extortion, and massive theft, had taken Litvinenko under his wing. He found Litvinenko useful, and thus posthumously published Litvinenko's book blaming Putin for practically every ill under the sun.[11]

In 1998, Litvinenko had called a press conference. In it he claimed that a year prior he had been given instructions by a high Russian security official to kill Berezovsky. The press conference was one of the strangest things I have ever witnessed. With other members of his unit beside him, one sporting a black balaclava, Litvenenko said his refusal to carry out the hit led to violent threats from his superiors. Still, as the *Guardian* of London put it in an obituary article, "The truth of the accusation would remain disputed. Critics said it was fabricated to help Berezovsky blacken enemies in the FSB [Federal Security Bureau]. Litvinenko claimed it was just one manifestation of the corruption and violence inside the FSB that he wanted to expose."[12]

Investigative journalist, Oleg Sultanov, who allowed himself to be "recruited" by the Berezovsky network-in-exile, was commissioned by the oligarch to write a book on Putin's Russia, with the one requirement that it must be "as scary as possible." Says Sultanov, "It was meant to be some kind of 'foundation study' of the horrors of contemporary Russia and the criminal role of the special services." The core of Berezovsky's theory was "the special services, and Putin the former KGB agent, are responsible for everything that's happening in Russia – all the contract murders, terrorist attacks, frauds." Litvinenko's books had been a flop,[13] so Berezovsky, says Sultanov, "urgently needed to create some hot new reading material, which would prove Berezovsky's case was just and Putin was the enemy of the human race."[14]

When Sultanov turned out to be an undercover investigative journalist, Berezovsky decided that he needed another approach. He contracted the services of a security firm called RISC, (formerly known as ISC Global UK). According to independent British journalist Martin Kelly in his December 12, 2006 blog, documents seen by the *Sunday Times* of London, confirmed that the firm worked on plans in 2003 for a worldwide operation to "discredit Putin and those around him.... Clearly, the best possible outcome would be for Putin to be removed from power at the earliest opportunity."

Everyone is assuming, I thought to myself, that the Russian government was behind Litvinenko's assassination. But this was too easy and extremely counterproductive. There were several alternative theories to the "KGB agent Putin and his old-buddy goons doing it" scenario.

Some surmised that a rogue element of Russian intelligence or some other part of the military-security apparatus did it out of revenge, or as part of the struggle for power in the post-Putin government. The problem with this theory is that there is no evidence for it whatsoever, and one should not work with suppositions that do not meet the rigorous test of investigative journalism. Furthermore, it is very improbable that something of this magnitude and planning would go undetected for very long. And certainly, the only people who would benefit from Litvinenko's assassination would be those seeking to undermine Putin's legacy and his chosen successor.

Others suggested that Ahmed Zakayev, Berezovsky's right hand man did it. But the *Times* of London seemed to indicate otherwise: "On the morning of November 1, Litvinenko was given a lift by Zakayev into the center of London by car. Zakayev is a close associate of Berezovsky and considers himself the Chechen's 'Foreign Minister' in exile. However, no trace of polonium was found in that vehicle – an indicator that Litvinenko had not yet been poisoned. Given the high radiation he suffered, he would have fallen ill rapidly. 'It would have been within hours, a day at most,' said a source at the Health Protection Agency (HPA). It was the evening of November 1 that he first became sick.[15]

There were claims that ex-KGB cadres Andrei Lugovoi, Dmitri Kovtun and Vyachenslav Sokolenko, who met Litvinenko hours before he fell ill, poisoned him. There is nothing remarkable to tell about the lives of former KGB agents Kovtun and Sokolenko. Andrei Lugovoi, however, is another matter. He is both a former KGB agent and a former bodyguard to Yegor Gaidar, once Russia's Prime Minister in the pre-Putin days, and has also been in charge of personal safety for the President's administration Head, Sergey Filatov, and of the Minister of Foreign Affairs, Andrei Kozirev.

His story was not difficult to track down. Lugovoi became front-page news in Russia in connection with the escape from custody of former national airline Aeroflot chairman Nokolai Glushkov, jailed on charges of money laundering. Glushkov and several others were charged with stealing over $252 million of Aeroflot's cash and depositing it in Swiss accounts. To whom did the Swiss accounts belong to? To Boris Berezovsky.

After Glushkov was incarcerated, Lugovoi, the prison's warden, helped him escape to neighboring Georgia, a favored destination for Russian Mafia on the run. Lugovoi's role became known when he was compromised by phone calls overheard by the FSB while investigating Glushkov's role in the crime.

There was something else about Lugovoi's past that caught my attention. He and Litvinenko both worked in the 1990s in a private security service for Boris Berezovsky.[16] You might want to call it another coincidence, but one of Lugovoi's clients at the time was Badri Patarkatsishvili, Georgian oligarch and longtime associate of Berezovsky. A small world, indeed. Patarkatsishvili was found dead in February 2008 at his English manor house, of an apparent heart attack, at a ripe old age of 52. His personal detail counted over 120 bodyguards.

Let's see. Glushkov is Berezovsky's protégé. Glushkov is jailed for laundering $252 million of Aeroflot's money. Lugovoi helps Glushkov escape. Lugovoi is jailed, but released. If Lugovoi had anything to do with Litvinenko's murder, then the assassination dressed up to look like a KGB hit was far more likely to have been a Berezovsky job than one of Putin's.

And how does one explain the rather expensive method used to eliminate Litvinenko? Berezovsky is a multi-billionaire. His estimated fortune is believed to be some $3 billion. With this kind of money, he would have had enough resources to procure the polonium, hire the assassins, and make it look like a cucumber-eating-KGB-goons-did-it job.

A peripheral look at some of the other minor characters in the story line nets an entire platoon of former KGB types. One of them is Oleg Gordievsky, the highest ranking KGB officer to escape from Mother Russia. He is under the protection of British MI6. Another is Michael Trepashkin, arrested in 2003 and charged with divulging state secrets to British intelligence. From his jail cell, he claims to know everything about Litvinenko's death and to have vital information for investigators. A May 19, 2004 *Moscow News* story reported that Trepashkin, Litvinenko and Berezovsky are old friends.[17]

Another player is Yuri Shvets, a former KGB major who in 2002 landed a $400,000 contract from Berezovsky to transcribe a set of audiotapes that appeared to implicate then-Ukrainian President Leonid Kuchma in the killing of journalist Heorhiy Gongadze and in sanctions-busting arms deals. Then there is Yevgeni Limarev, to whom Alex Goldfarb said he gave a $15,000 grant in 2002 for running an anti-FSB website. Goldfarb is the executive director of the International Foundation for Civil Liberties, established by Russian oligarch-in-exile Boris Berezovsky. Goldfarb presides over the information flow coming out of the Berezovsky camp. According to Goldfarb's himself, he also has links to the CIA and the State Department.

So, I thought to myself, Putin does not preside over this mysterious web of former KGB operatives: Berezovsky does. Virtually all of the suspects in the Litvinenko murder are somehow tied to Berezovsky. The principals Litvinenko met with the day he became sick are all stridently anti-Putin. The common thread is exiled oligarch Boris Berezovsky, who by his own admission is on a campaign to discredit Putin and the Kremlin.

I examined Litvinenko's movements on November 1, 2006, the day he fell ill. One of the visits made by Litvinenko was to the security firms Erinys and Titon International, which shared offices. We are told that the occasion of Litvinenko's visit was to see a "friend," but I wonder if it really was just a social call. On the day he was effectively killed, Litvinenko paid a visit to the world headquarters of a major mercenary operation actively involved in security for oil infrastructure in Iraq. Given the brief interval it would take for Litvinenko's poisoning symptoms to appear, one must ask when precisely this visit occurred. The timing could be a coincidence, but then again ...

In SourceWatch, I found a detailed description of Erinys' operations. The company was established by a pair of ex-Apartheid-era intelligence officials, Sean Cleary and Jonathan Garratt. Cleary was closely linked to Jonas Savimbi, the leader of the UNITA rebel movement in Angola. After reviewing some of the press clippings about Erinys' Iraq operation, I found a reference to a certain Francois Strydom, who was killed in action. I knew Strydom personally, and believe me, he was someone you would wish to avoid at any hour of the day or night. He had been a member of Koevoet, a known brutal counter-insurgency arm of the South African military active in Namibia during that nation's fight for independence from South Africa. To say he was right-wing would be a significant understatement.

Both Erinys and Titon International are headed by the same CEO. Titon claims to be engaged in confidential computer forensic investigation, whatever that is. What caught my attention is its logo – an iceberg floating in the sea, with the great mass of it underwater and only a tip jutting through the surface. Might this imply that much of Titon's clout is unseen?

I found myself thinking back to one of the more startling anomalies surrounding 9/11: Many of the clues lead in the direction of Saudi Arabia and its uninhibited support for jihadist terrorist networks, but *some links also lead in an opposite direction*, towards Israel. One such link was unexpectedly confirmed by the *Washington Post* in its reporting on the counterfeiting of US $100 bills by a South Ossetia-based organized crime ring operating with Russian-Israeli mobsters based in the Republic of Georgia and Israel: On October 27, 2004, a courier for the counterfeit ring, Hazki Hen, met with an undercover Secret Service agent at a hotel in Linthicum, Maryland, near Baltimore-Washington International Airport. Hen, who had just arrived from Tel Aviv, offered to exchange $230,000 in counterfeit $100 notes for $80,000 in real currency. He also discussed the potential of delivering as much as $100 million on counterfeit bills in the future. Hen was finally charged by the US government in November 2005.[18]

The same linkage is seen with al-Qaeda financier Yehuda Abraham, a US-Israeli diamond dealer who was laundering money for the Russian-Israeli mob and a Malaysian linked to al-Qaeda affiliate Jemaah Islamiya; Asher Karni, a South African-Israeli who was shipping nuclear triggers from the US to the AQ Khan network in Pakistan; and various Israeli spies caught around sensitive US facilities posing as art students, movers and tourists prior to 9/11.

What do avidly pro-Israel neocons and radical Islamists have in common? Hatred of Putin and his Russian nationalism. According to one commentator, "Putin is hated by Western elites, not because he aspires to be a dictator, but because he is defiant in the face of an all-out assault. He destroyed the power of the Russian oligarchs,"[19] and, with it, the unadulterated, in-your-face theft and destruction of his country.

The prejudices of the media lead us down one path, signalling Putin and the KGB as scary nuclear murderers, but the facts, at least as they are known to me, take us down quite another. The *Times* of London's suppression of Litvinenko's conversion to Islam is a case in point. According to the *Times'* parallel universe of smoke and mirrors: "Litvinenko was a loyal servant of the state ... who grew disillusioned with the corruption of the FSB."[20]

Yes, and I am a cucumber. Litvinenko's career at the FSB was dead once Berezovsky, his *krysha* (Russian Mafia slang for "roof and protection"), was forcibly removed from shaping the government's gangster capitalism. One thing is certain in Litvinenko's case: he wasn't killed for something he knew and was about to reveal. Berezovsky invested a lot of money over a five-year period into Litvinenko's "sensationalist" accusations. The results, to say the least, were underwhelming. Alex Goldfarb, Berezovsky's right-hand man, clearly stated that when Litvinenko tried to run to the United States, he had nothing to offer in terms of information in exchange for settlement of his immigration case. Only the UK was willing to take him unconditionally, thanks in large part to the personal intervention provided by MI6's Director of Security and Political Affairs, John Scarlett. He had wrongly assumed that "Litvinenko would be able to fill in the gaps, and details in Vasili Mitrokhin's KGB Archive which he had been instrumental in bringing to Britain, especially more information about unidentified Soviet spies."[21]

* * *

Another possibility in the murder of Litvinenko, although it first seemed quite remote, was the involvement of the Italian "academic"

Mario Scaramella, who has been acquainted with dead Russians since 2002. Scaramella is one of those goofy characters that populate the outer rings of the lunatic fringe of would-be spies. He has claimed to hold a professorship at the University of Naples; the University apparently has never heard of him. He was caught on tape bragging that Silvio Berlusconi, the once- and future-Italian Prime Minister, was considering him for a top job at an unnamed international organization. He later admitted they had never even met.

This history requires that his claims be accorded an extra degree of scepticism. Nonetheless, in an interview with the *Independent* shortly after the poisoning became public, Mario Scaramella said that Litvinenko told him he had masterminded the smuggling of radioactive material to Zurich in 2000. Was this mere bragging? Or was Scaramella in a position where an operative like Litvinenko would be willing to divulge this information? Or might they have simply been swapping "war stories"?

One of Scaramella's chief tormentors has been the wonderful Italian periodical, *La Repubblica*, one of Europe's best sources for hard-nosed investigative journalism. Throughout the Litvinenko affair, I compiled quite a collection of its articles. One of them specifically discussed a January 25, 2006 conversation between Mario Scaramella and a mysterious ex-CIA agent from California, named "Perry." In the conversation, Scaramella stressed to Perry that his activities were not "just my activities, but the activity of the organization." What organization? I jotted down my question and pinned it to the Litvinenko puzzle board.

The latter portions of the conversation were even more revealing. Scaramella discussed political "dirty tricks" against his opponents, who included the campaigning center-left Prime Minister Romano Prodi. The conversation made clear that Perry gave Scaramella his orders. When Scaramella went off on a tangent about his international activities, Perry merely replied, "You must work on the Italian politics." When Scaramella presented a list of the possible future options open to him, Perry very curtly suggested, "You could be part of the cabinet of the minister [Berlusconi]." But Scaramella was pessimistic: "Most probably Prodi will win, even if we will launch our attack."

But what did Scaramella mean by launching an attack? Was it a political attack, a personal attack, a dirty-tricks operation? What if, by "our attack," he was referring to an attack for geopolitical gain, like the 3/11 (2004) train bombing in Madrid or the 9/11 attack in the United States? Could the deeper links of the Scaramella-Litvinenko affair have to do with a dirty-bomb plot gone awry, which the Russian intelligence services may have actually derailed?

Something else in the transcript drew my attention. *La Repubblica* was reporting that, while talking to Perry, Scaramella declared that he had obtained taped testimony against Prodi from Oleg Gordievski, the highest-ranking officer to have ever defected from the KGB, and that the testimony was given in the presence of Lou Palombo. Who was this person, evidently involved in the reported attempt to tarnish Prodi?

I checked the Italian press for clues. According to *La Stampa* and *La Repubblica*, Louis F. Palombo was a 22-year veteran of the CIA and a managing partner of Florida-based Incident Management Group (IMG). Palombo's biography at the IMG website stated that, in 1977, he had founded the security consulting firm Ackerman & Palombo. I scanned the list of IMG partners. They included Daniel Donohue, a former CIA clandestine services agent in Southeast Asia and India; Harley Stock, a "forensic hypnosis" expert with the FBI and US Secret Service; and perhaps most intriguing, Christopher Hagon, a 21-year veteran of the London Metropolitan Police, better known as "Scotland Yard."

Hagon told *La Stampa* that another individual associated with IMG is Filippo Marino. The IMG site was quite clear on Marino's credentials: "Filippo Marino, senior consultant, has 10 years of international experience in the areas of security and environmental crime prevention. He is one of the founders of Special Research Monitoring Centre (SRMC) and a founding member of the Permanent Intergovernmental Conference for Environmental Crime Prevention." LexisNexis confirmed Scaramella's links established by Italian investigators to Filippo Marino.

With great interest, I went back to IMG's website. One of the consultants whose name was listed on the site was Curtis Perry. According to IMG, "Curtis Perry, senior consultant, has 27 years experience in government and private sector security and was stationed with the CIA throughout the Far East." I skipped a paragraph. "Previously, he was employed as a Senior Consultant by a security firm of Ackerman & Palombo and was a managing director for Kroll Associates in Manila 1992-1996."

Egad, Kroll! I made a note. I would need to check that link further.

Another IMG consultant was Robert Wager, whose biography claimed he managed security for the US Embassy in Bogota, Colombia. Scaramella has also claimed to have worked in Bogota, I thought to myself.

The Internet biography of another consultant working for IMG, Ned Timmons, stated, "for two years Timmons directed an international import/export corporation related to environmental issues operating undercover in Colombia, Venezuela and Central America." Another Colombia-IMG link describes John Stanton as a "senior consultant with 17 years experience in security management and 13 years of specialization in Colombia. He has designed security in hostile locations in Colombia, Panama, Ecuador and Chile."

So, IMG is comprised of a number of former US intelligence officers in Colombia, in addition to Mario Scaramella's colleague, Filippo Marino. Along with Afghanistan, Colombia is one of the world's epicenters for international drug trade. In both of these locations, the CIA controls the routes and the profits, which are laundered through Wall Street. I knew that the Colombia-CIA-IMG link was no coincidence. I had no idea where I would end up, but experience taught me that the seemingly endless connections would eventually lead to an opening, if I could stay the course.

An SEC EDGAR search revealed a stockholders' agreement between Harrison-Kroll Environmental Services, Inc. of Louisiana and Palumbo Partners, dated December 31, 1992, in which Kroll acquired Palumbo Partners.

Kroll Associates is a renowned security company with extremely close ties to the CIA. Kroll, a very active player in private military contracting in Iraq, was also responsible for the security of the World Trade Center on 9/11. According to my "community" sources, Jules Kroll, who founded Kroll Associates in 1972, in the 1980s obtained much-needed cash from Foothill Capital when his firm fell on hard times. Foothill was deeply mixed up in the Savings & Loan collapses in the 1980s, but somehow miraculously managed to survive by becoming a part of Wells Fargo Bank.

In addition, IMG chief Lou Palombo, while working with Kroll at his Miami vantage point, reportedly tracked the activities of Colombian drug cartels, including the Medellin Cartel, according to investigative journalist and former NSA analyst, Wayne Madsen, in his highly respected online investigative journal, *WayneMadsenReport*, on January 13, 2007. One final note on Palombo: he is linked to Avram Shalom, a former member of Israel's Shin Beth domestic security service. My Mossad contacts told me that Shalom was fired after a scandal involving the massacre of Palestinian civilians. Subsequently, Shalom joined Kroll as a security consultant.

Mario Scaramella's link to Colombia intrigued me, including his association with IMG. Scaramella had claimed he was a professor of environmental law at Externado University and the University of Nuestra Señora del Rosario in Bogotá. But, we know that his Naples University credentials were a smokescreen and an empty promise, and his Berlusconi links were also a figment of his imagination. There is no evidence that these Colombian affiliations were any less imaginary.

I went back to the Scaramella archives in *La Repubblica*. According to numerous reports in the Italian press, the so-called "professor" ran an organization called the Environmental Crime Prevention Program (ECPP) from his home base in Naples in the region of Campania.

Naples holds an interesting connection to both Scaramella and Litvinenko. Not only were traces of polonium 210 discovered in the office of Britain's deputy ambassador at the UK embassy in Moscow, but Britain's Deputy Consul in Naples, Frederick Brian Keeves, signed a false passport for Alexander Litvinenko with a fictitious identity: Edwin Redwald Carter. According to insider accounts, Keeves also countersigned a document prepared by Litvinenko concerning a meeting with a Russian Mafia member who worked for the Russian Federal Security Bureau. He was to have transported a "nuclear suitcase" from Moscow to Zurich for onward shipment to the Middle East.

The document, "authenticated" by the British authorities, ended up in the Mitrokhin Commission archives in the Italian Parliament. The Mitrokhin Commission is a controversial Italian parliamentary inquiry set up by right-wing politicians during Silvio Berlusconi's prior time in power to investigate links between Italian politicians and the KGB. Vasili Mitrokhin himself was the senior archivist for the First Chief Directorate of the KGB from 1972 to 1984. In 1992, after the collapse of the USSR, he had defected to the UK with his extensive files about agents and operations of the KGB and its predecessors, from the Bolshevik revolution of 1917 onwards.

In addition, the British consulate in Naples dovetailed neatly with Mario Scaramella and the Italian consulate in Miami, Florida, which

Scaramella used as a major base of operations. In fact, all of the forged documents passed by Scaramella to the Mitrokhin Commission were authenticated and officially marked by the Italian Consulate in Miami.

Scaramella's ECPP website listed a number of officials whom he claimed to be affiliated with his program. On November 15 and 16, 2000, the ECPP conducted what it called its "Fourth Intergovernmental Plenary" in New York City at the Environmental Protection Agency, where former Environmental Protection Agency Criminal Enforcement legal council Michael J. Penders was named Assistant Secretary General of the ECPP. The Scaramella-Penders link is quite interesting.

Penders is President of Environmental Security, Inc. (ESI), located in downtown Washington, just one block from the White House. The ESI website states that "ESI conducts investigations, implements environmental management and security system ... and training to improve environmental performance." According to the Berlusconi-owned Italian magazine *Panorama*, Scaramella has boasted of his contacts with Penders.

Scaramella's conference biography stated that "Dr. Mario Scaramella is Secretary General of ECPP, whose mission is to provide environmental protection and security through technology on a global basis. ECPP has used aerial surveillance and the remote sensing capabilities of satellites to detect environmental crimes and eco-terrorism."

Through a friend working for the US government, I got in touch with an official in the Environmental Protection Agency. What's going on? I asked him. Why are all these questionable characters with links to security companies also involved with environmental issues?

The insider told me that the EPA criminal investigative branch has access to NASA's sky-viewing geographical information system. "It means," he continued after a brief silence, "they know where every ounce of bad {nuclear} stuff is in the world, and they can get access to it. The EPA enforcement center's data import/export database system has the capability to identify suspect shipments of nuclear material."

I went back to Scaramella's biography, which described what ECPP does: "ECPP has used aerial surveillance and the remote sensing capabilities of satellites to detect environmental crimes and eco-terrorism." I scanned the list of officials named as officers of the

ECPP. One name jumped out at me: Toni Popovski, the Environmental Minister of Macedonia. In January 2000, Popovski was named as the director of the Regional Environmental Centre for Central and Eastern Europe (REC), which also happens to be the nexus for the smuggling of nuclear and radioactive material from the former USSR and Warsaw Pact nations. Other REC members included Albania, Bosnia and Herzegovina, Bulgaria, Croatia, the Czech Republic, Macedonia, Malta, Serbia, Slovenia and Turkey, along with Germany, Canada, Austria and Switzerland. Many of these nations are part of the nuclear and narcotics smuggling trade.

So what do we have so far? IMG "environmental" consultants with long-lasting links to Colombia and the CIA; Kroll Environmental Services and their CIA links; ECPP environmentalists and Mario Scaramella; Michael J. Penders and his ESI environmental management and security system. If the Environmental Protection Agency has been infiltrated by some of these people or their organizations, then it raises some extremely troubling issues. The compromise of agencies in the United States and Europe that are tasked with monitoring the location and transport of nuclear material represents an immense danger to public safety around the world, and the implications of Russian-Israeli, Chechen and/or Camorra Mafiosi penetrating environmental regulatory agencies are enormous. If compromised, the regulators are in an ideal position to enable the shipment of radioactive waste materials around the world.

Might the "attack" Scaramella mentioned in the telephone transcript, for instance, actually be referring to a dirty bomb? If the answer is affirmative, then the Litvinenko affair may be merely the tip of a "Titon iceberg" of huge international nuclear smuggling operations and global false-flag terrorism: one with hooks into the EPA and possibly the White House, but aimed at the United States and its allies.

London's *Observer* surmised as much in a December 3, 2006 report: "Among the theories that remain open is that the poisonings were an accident that happened, while Litvinenko tried to assemble a dirty bomb for Chechen rebels. Those who know him believe he was crazy enough to attempt such a thing and, in the past week, some have implicated him in the smuggling of nuclear materials from Russia." This makes one wonder whether the November 24, 2006 press release on *Chechenpress.org*, with its ominous reference to "the weapon," may have been hinting at a Litvinenko project to build a purported radioactive "dirty bomb."

According to nuclear physicist Alexander Borovoi, former consultant to the International Atomic Energy Agency in Vienna, quoted in a December 14, 2006 UPI report, "The worst part of the Litvinenko story is that it was like a rehearsal for a dirty bomb. The incident shows that something dangerous is cooking in the terrorist kitchen, with menacing ideas and plans that can generally be described as a crime.... Litvinenko or one of his close friends have somehow got hold of polonium. From them, we can trace a connection to those whose dream is to get hold of a dirty bomb – terrorists."[22]

I now thought back to *La Repubblica*'s revelations of that January 25, 2006 conversation between Mario Scaramella and the mysterious ex-CIA agent named Perry. In the conversation, Scaramella stressed to Perry that his activities were not "just my activities, but the activity of the organization." It was becoming clear that the "organization" to which Scaramella was referring to was a private and global intelligence organization involving former members of the KGB like Litvinenko, private military contractors, intelligence companies, as well ex-CIA and ex-British intelligence officers.

The more confusing the Litvinenko affair became, the more it appeared to be yet another example of a nefarious worldwide network of spies, weapons smugglers, far-right politicians, Russian-Israeli Mafia businessmen, and Islamic mujaheedin false-flag provocateurs. If anything, Litvinenko's death helped to expose this international network.

Far from being a sympathetic figure, as the corporate media would have us believe, Litvinenko was a player in a global crime, disinformation, and terrorist networks, with links to all the shady characters who played such a key role in Russia's disintegration, through ill conceived "loans-for-shares" theft of billions of dollars of the International Monetary Fund's money, and also via gangster capitalism. Litvinenko also had contacts with the United Kingdom Independence Party, a right-wing British political party; the mujaheedin movements of Chechnya and Dagestan; and the Russian-Israeli criminal organization of wanted Russian oligarch Boris Berezovsky and his accomplices. Many Litvinenko contacts, including former KGB colleagues whose loyalty to Berezovsky has been proved beyond any reasonable doubt, have strong ties to the criminal world. And we have noted his connection to two British mercenary firms operating in Iraq: Titon and Erinys.

With geopolitical fault lines erupting everywhere and the latest energy crisis then making itself known in earnest, it was no surprise to find Zbigniew Brzezinski and his ilk returning to familiar stomping grounds – the original "geostrategic" battle plan for control of the "Grand Chessboard," with Russia as the key. Of course Russia, like the United States and Britain, is deeply enmeshed in the world of Deep Politics, which are, in the words of academic Peter Dale Scott, "Political practices and arrangements, deliberate or not, which are usually repressed rather than acknowledged."[23]

Notes

1. F. William Engdahl, "America's Phoney War in Afghanistan," *Global Research*, October 21, 2009, http://www.globalresearch.ca/index.php?context=va&aid=15761.

2. Robert Parry, "The Crazy October Surprise Debunking," November 6, 2009, http://www.consortiumnews.com/2009/110609.html.

3. Jeff Gates, "Beliefs: The Power Behind Unending War," *Veterans Today*, November 9, 2009, http://www.veteranstoday.com.

4. Trowbridge Ford, "Why and how Alexander Litvinenko was murdered," *Spy News*, July 2008; http://codshit.blogspot.com/2008_07_01_codshit_archive.html.

5. There is little doubt that Litvinenko did not write the "deathbed" letter. The letter exists in only one form: a typed, stylistically perfect English text. The problem with the letter's credibility is that Litvinenko hardly spoke English at all. If the letter was dictated to Alex Goldfarb, who then transcribed it for the world, there has to exist a Russian original, be it in written form or in a taped conversation. Yet neither a Russian version of the letter nor any audio record appears to exist, and none have been offered to the public.

6. Neil Clark, "In Bed with Russophobes," *Guardian* (UK), December 4, 2006; http://www.thetruthseeker.co.uk/article.asp?ID=5625.

7. Nevzlin was one of the senior men in the business empire of the jailed Russian oil tycoon Khodorkovsky. Nevzlin fled Russia after authorities launched a campaign against corruption and tax evasion in Yukos. He also has been embroiled in a criminal investigation by the Israeli police into the alleged laundering of at least $500 million through a branch of Bank of Hapoalim, Israel's largest bank. His alleged co-conspirator is Russian-Israeli billionaire, Arkadi Gaydamak. In December 2000, Gaydamak fled France, where he was wanted for illegal gun running, tax evasion, money laundering and corruption. French authorities had alleged that Gaydamak – who holds Russian, Canadian, Angolan and Israeli passports – was hiding behind Israel's financial privileges for immigrants to protect his assets and avoid prosecution.

8. John Laughland, "The Chechens' American Friends," *Guardian* (UK), September 8, 2004.

9. John Laughland, "Gaining Control of Russian Oil," www.globalresearch.com, October 25, 2004.

10. Ibid.

11. Alexander Litvinenko and Yuri Felshtinsky, *Blowing Up Russia: The Secret Plot to Bring Back KGB Terror* (Encounter Books, 2007).

12. Tom Parfill, "Security Agent Sucked into a World of Russian Power Games and Oligarchs," *Guardian* (UK), November 25, 2006.

13. Brian Brady, "Death in Londongrad," *Scotsman* (UK), November 26, 2006, http://news.scotsman.com/international.cfm?id=1751882006&format=print.

14. Chris Floyd, "Pale Fire and London Fog," www.lewrockwell.com, December 2, 2006.

15. "Focus: Cracking the code of the nuclear assassin, *Sunday Times* (UK), December 3, 2006; http://www.timesonline.co.uk/tol/news/uk/article658487.ece.

16. http://www.axisglobe.com/article.asp?article=1176.

17. http://www.mosnews.com/news/2004/05/19/trepashkin.shtml.

18. Peter Finn, "Probe Traces Global Reach of Counterfeiting Ring," *Washington Post*, November 26, 2006; http://www.washingtonpost.com/wp-dyn/content/article/2006/11/25/AR2006112500963.html.

19. Justin Raimondo, "The New Cold War," Antiwar.com, http://www.antiwar.com/justin/?articleid=4120.

20. "Focus: Cracking the Code of the Nuclear Assassin," op. cit.

21. Trowbridge Ford, op. cit.

22. Tatyana Sinitsyna, "Outside View: Dirty Bomb Trial Run?" UPI, December 14, 2006; http://www.spacewar.com/reports/Was_London_The_Site_Of_A_Dirty_Bomb_Trial_Run_999.html.

23. Peter Dale Scott, *Deep Politics and the Death of JFK* (University of California, 1996), pp. 6-7.

Chapter Two

The Economic Rape of Russia

Transparent national borders, fewer trade restrictions, and truly global financial and telecommunications systems provide significant opportunities for criminal organizations to expand operations beyond national boundaries.
Office of International Criminal Justice, *Bulletin*, Winter 1996

The way of the world?

With the passage of time, the degree of corporate theft, the outrageousness of the cruelty, and the absurdity of the lies we are being fed as part of a daily news diet can only increase as financial resources dwindle. In the post-Cold War world, Russia's role has been fundamental, for whosoever gains Russia's resources holds the key to global supremacy. Thus, destabilizing the Russian state became the goal of the Shadow Masters after the collapse of the Soviet Union in December 1991.

The United States undertook a massive effort to help the former Soviet Union make a transition to capitalism. As it turned out, the effort was intended to remove large amounts of wealth from the country. According to an internal FBI memo by Treasury Special Agent Philip Wainwright, but signed only as "Mr. X," the Russia objective was quite simple: "There would be a possibility of a Western privately orchestrated economic Jihad that could help crush the Communist ruling powers by destroying their unstable rouble."

In other words, the Soviet Union – possessing the world's largest mineral wealth, a vast reservoir of gold and gemstones, the world's largest oil reserves, untold quantities of nickel, platinum, and palladium, and more timber than the Amazon, *not to mention an immense stockpile of Soviet-era weapons* – was to be asset-stripped. The strategy was intended to topple the country into anarchy, to the point Russia could not oppose US military operations designed to secure control of the oil and gas reserves in Central Asia. The plan developed, as echoed by former National Security Adviser under President Carter, Zbigniew Brzezinski, in his 1997 book, *The Grand Chessboard: American Primacy and Its Geostrategic Imperatives,* became a part of the most spectacular criminal coup ever devised.

In the period leading up to its collapse, floods of movable wealth left the USSR. Truckloads of Soviet roubles motored down autobahns. Many were used in complex swap operations in which billions of narco-dollars were laundered on behalf of the Calabrian Mafia, Ndrangheta. Numerous prime western banks such as the US Treasury using the Harvard Endowment, Bank of New York, Goldman Sachs, Massachusetts banking giants Fleet Financial and Bank of Boston looted up to $500 billion. Also participating was the CIA, whose chief goal was to destroy the Soviet currency. Ndrangheta, one of the most feared criminal organizations in the world, is financially interlocked in its drug-running business with Colombian and Mexican criminal cartels. Since the dismemberment of the Soviet Union, the Russian Mafia has joined Calabrian operations, providing an eastern root to the already lucrative cocaine and heroin business.

In one operation, 280 billion roubles[1] – with a market value of hundreds of billion of dollars at the official commercial rate of exchange – were being auctioned to leading figures in the world of organized crime. In January 1991, shady Russian dealers were offering "140 billion clean, clear, good, legal, bundled, counted, verified, packed and stamped Russian roubles" for an estimated $7.7 billion from a dubious Liechtenstein-based company, but the transaction was foiled by a KGB sting operation. Six months later, another transaction with a market value of 140 billion roubles netted $4.5 billion, demonstrating how quickly the currency had been devaluing.

The entire Russian government apparatus was gripped with panic as cash was draining out of Moscow at an astronomical rate.

At the time, no one could understand why Colombian cartels, the Mafia and the world's criminal fraternities were lining up to purchase with hard cash (albeit at a fraction of the official rate, sometimes for as low as eight cents on the dollar) vast quantities of what was in effect little more than colored paper. These were hard-nosed criminals with keen business minds honed by "decades of greed and power, and were not known for squandering their wealth."

In a murky cloak-and-dagger operation, western intelligence services worked with black market profiteers, leading banking houses, the Italian Cosa Nostra, the American Mafia and the Russian Thieves' World, former KGB officers, veterans of the Afghan war, and unemployed military officers to expedite illegal alliances on a colossal scale meant to destabilize, and eventually to destroy, the USSR. On the one hand, you had criminals preparing to launder their dirty narcotics revenue, while on the other, opportunists expected to garner a giant profit when the rouble became repatriated. They bought bargain-basement priced commodities with devalued currency as "inward investments" and financed crooked joint venture companies mushrooming in the meantime. In 1990 and 1991, the rouble proved to be the currency of choice.

Fearful of plunder, Prime Minister Valentin Pavlov announced in a February 12, 1991 interview in a Russian daily newspaper, *Trud*, that the government had uncovered a "plot by Western banks in Switzerland, Canada and Austria to flood the country with billions of rouble bank notes." Such a move would create instant hyperinflation and, in turn, destabilize the Soviet Union financially. Pavlov saw this plot as a quiet and bloodless annexation of the Soviet Union's economy in order to eventually topple the government.

According to British investigator David Guyatt, "It became clear that the massive quantities of exported roubles weren't just coloured paper. Almost worthless on the international market, they were repatriated through some of the 260 Mafia-controlled banks that sprang-up around the country.... Wasting no time, the now rouble-rich Mafia set about plundering Russia's abundant natural treasures: platinum, gemstones, oil, lumber, strategic raw materials, non-ferrous metals such as cobalt, copper, bronze, titanium, and even caterpillar tractors and other high value equipment; all went under the hidden hammer."[2]

Robert Friedman, in the January 1996 cover story, "Money Plane," for the *New Yorker* magazine explained how the process worked: "Russian assets, such as oil, are stolen by underworld figures or corrupt plant managers and sold on the spot market in Rotterdam. The proceeds are wired through front companies on the Continent and deposited in London banks. Gangsters place an order for, say, $40 million in US currency through a bank in Moscow. The bank wires their bank of choice, placing a purchase order for the cash. The bank of choice buys the currency from the New York Federal Reserve. Simultaneously, bank of choice receives a wire transfer for the same account from the London bank. Bank of choice pockets a commission and flies the cash from New York to Moscow. It is then used by mobsters to buy narcotics or villas, or run political campaigns."[3]

A Wall Street brokerage or investment bank may also go "offshore" in order to legally borrow once-laundered drug money to finance a corporate merger or leveraged buyout (LBO). Why do this? If you were a major investment banker or securities firm and could arrange to borrow laundered drug money at say five percent rather than the ten your bank wants, and you are in a cutthroat competition to buy a company, would you be willing to lower your cost of capital in this way? It is hardly surprising that such practices are becoming "business as usual."

In December 1989, the First Directorate (PGU – *Pervoe Glavnoe Upravlenie*, First Chief Directorate – Foreign), and the Sixth Department (which dealt with international economic programs) realized that the chaos about to overwhelm the Soviet Union in the wake of its political crises would leave the country without an economic structure to perform the tasks needed by the Russian state. They concluded that the survival of the entire nation was at stake.

The Communist Party leadership gave the KGB responsibility to embark on a perestroika campaign of mass pilferage of state property and natural resources, and commissioned it to dump roubles abroad, illegally sell vast quantities of raw materials for hard currency, and launder the hard currency proceeds in the West.[4] Weeks after the Soviet collapse, a parliamentary investigative commission reported the following:

> ... realizing as irrevocable the loss of then-authoritative and ideological priorities in society, the Politburo of the CPSU CC [Central Committee] made several secret resolutions toward direct concealment in commercial structures of property and monetary resources actually accumulated at the expense of the nation. Based on this, at all levels of the party hierarchy, there was a mass founding of party banks, joint enterprises, and joint stock companies in 1990 and 1991.[5]

A Central Committee resolution titled "On Emergency Measures to Organize Commercial and Foreign Economic Activity of the Party," passed in 1990, details how the Party intended from the start to conceal its holdings in the embryonic market economy. The resolution called for numerous actions, including:

> • preparation of proposals to create some new "interim" economic structures (foundations, associations, etc.), with minimum "visible" ties to the Central Committee, which could become focal points of the "invisible" Party economy;
> • immediate preparation of plans for using anonymous organizations to mask direct links to the Party when launching commercial and foreign economic Party activity; in particular, consideration of the possibility of merging with already functioning joint ventures, international consortiums, etc., through capital investment.
> • consideration of ways and means of establishing a bank controlled by the Central Committee with the right to conduct hard-currency operations, the investment of the Party's hard-currency reserves in international firms controlled by friends of the Party;
> • creation of a consulting firm with the status of a legal entity, but without direct links to the Central Committee apparatus, for the practical organization of economic cooperation and the provision of brokerage services for foreign economic activity of various Party organizations and the commercial firms of fraternal parties.[6]

In their 1991-1992 probe, parliamentary investigators found that the External Intelligence Service (*Sluzhba Vneshnei Razvedki*, SVR) was a key player in large-scale money laundering between 1989 and 1991 (when it was known as the KGB First Chief Directorate) and that the SVR had covered up the entire operation since that time. According to investigator A.P. Surkov, describing a highly sophisticated arrangement of phony agreements, ghost companies and offshore accounts throughout Europe in 1992:

> ... the Party moved abroad at least 60 tonnes of gold, eight tonnes of platinum, 150 tonnes of silver, and in the safes of Western banks are stored resources of the Communist Party amounting to from 15 to 50 billion dollars. There are significant violations with valuable metals, which have shown up in the State Repository for Precious Metals. Gold bullion, for example, was provided to the KGB. On October 30 of [1990], the KGB was given 502 kilograms of valuables. Among this were gold bullion, gold American dollars [coins] stored for some special operations, and they were not returned in time, a gold brooch with 31 diamonds, a gold ring with 20 diamonds, a gold brooch with 12 diamonds and two emeralds, a gold

> necklace with 104 diamonds, a gold brooch with 60 diamonds, and so on ... and there is a basis to think that the Moscow Special Alloys Plant did not fall outside the KGB's attention, and naturally, that of Party functionaries.
>
> The new money would be stored in one of the newly created banks, 80% of which, according to the US State Department and BBC News report of November 21, 1998,[7] were under the control of organized crime. In the pre-Perestroika Soviet Union, the banking system basically consisted of a single bank, Gosbank, rudimentarily run and owned by the government which the Russian people instinctively did not trust. This "instinct" had more to do with a fatalistic nature of a Russian soul than any concrete evidence to the contrary. Because wages were paid only in cash, and households used cash exclusively for making payments, Russians rightfully had a penchant for stuffing money in mattresses and socks, something the KGB planners realized was not feasible.

One of these "new banks" established by the Party and the KGB apparatus was Bank Menatep, set up to handle the fund transfers. Men in their late 20s and early 30s were given authority, and the money flowed. The system hadn't changed, nor the beneficiaries.

Former KGB Colonel Viktor Kichikhin, who served in the First Chief Directorate responsible for ideological enforcement, witnessed the process firsthand: "In 1989-1990, most of the Soviet-Western joint venture enterprises were created by our directorate, except those which were established directly by the Central Committee of the CPSU."[8]

The process was so integrated that former KGB general Timofeyev commented, "The market will be occupied by the ruling apparatus and the KGB, because they have the opportunities to control the process of privatization and the creation of new enterprises. They have the licenses, they have the influence. This is not so much for the party's sake as it is for self preservation," and added, "There is undoubtedly an element here of an organized retreat ... under which the retreating force tries to maintain some element or order and the possibility of preserving a nucleus, and then perhaps, in time, returning to the past."[9]

There may be as many as six thousand of these "retreating" KGB Chekists in powerful positions.[10] "Chekists," by the way, were the Soviet Secret Police under Felix Dzerzinski in the 1920s; since then the term has been used pejoratively to refer to any secret service *apparatchiks*. The list of KGB/Putin appointments reads like a who's who of KGB elite: Vladimir Putin, Prime Minister of Russia, former Colonel of the KGB; Nikolai Patrushev, current secretary of the Security Council of Russia; Igor Sechin, head of second biggest oil producer, Rosneft; Valery Golubyev, a former KGB general appointed to the top position at state-run energy giant, Gasprom; Yuriy Zaostrovtsev, FSB deputy director; Viktor Ivanov, Director of Russia´s Federal Service for Control of Narcotics; Boris Gryzlov Minister of the Interior; Sergei Ivanov, Defense Minister; Prosecutor General, Vladimir Ustinov; Sergei Stepashin, chief of the Audit Chamber; Sergei Pugachov, president of Mezhprombank Bank; Nikolai Negodov, deputy transportation minister; Vladimir Yakunin, first deputy president of the Russian Railways Co.; Konstantin Romodanovsky, chief of internal security at the Ministry of the Interior; Viktor Cherkesov, head of the Tax Police; , and a current chairman of the national airline Aeroflot.

The Russian mob, known as the *Vorovskoi Mir*, or "Thieves' World," a loose federation of Soviet mobsters, immediately grasped that the "retreat" of Communism heralded a glorious new world criminal order for them.

Within one year of Mikhail Gorbachev's ousting, over 2,600 "crime clans," employing more than three million criminals, had appeared and spread like wildfire throughout the former Soviet empire, according to a research paper written by a group of Fellows for the prestigious Hoover Institute.[11] Forty of them equal or surpass the size of both the Sicilian and American Mafias. Taken together, they comprise the most powerful criminal enterprise on earth.

In fact, the CPSU's secret directive emphasized the need to forge a link with the *mafiya* through the vast resources of the former KGB. That was in the beginning of the 1990s. The early stages of the Yeltsin reign.

By 1997, the Soviet Union had been dead for six years. A new world had emerged in which the United States alone ranked as a superpower. Yet Russia still remained a threat – a potential block to the complete imposition of US economic and military will. In Zbigniew Brzezinski's *The Grand Chessboard*, published in 1997, "Russia" and "vital energy reserves," as it turns out, are mentioned more frequently than any other country or subject in the book.

Once again, energy imperatives and geopolitical control would come to play a key role in the lives of hundreds of millions of people.

It was in Russia's backyard, the central Asian republics of the old Soviet Union, where Brzezinski saw that the move would have to be made to corner the world's energy reserves. The history of mankind has always shown that controlling the heart of Eurasia was the key to controlling the entire globe. Azerbaijan, which contains the riches of the Caspian Sea Basin and Central Asia, is key. The independence of the Central Asian states can be rendered nearly meaningless if Azerbaijan becomes fully subordinated to Moscow's control.

Though motives have changed over 20 centuries, this area's strategic importance remains essentially the same. Brzezinski spelled out the compelling issue driving American policy: "A power that dominates Eurasia would control two of the world's three most advanced and economically productive regions. A mere glance at the map also suggests that control over Eurasia would almost automatically entail Africa's subordination, rendering the Western Hemisphere and Oceania geopolitically peripheral to the world's central continent. About 75 percent of the world's people live in Eurasia, and most of the world's physical wealth is there as well, both in its enterprise and underneath its soil. Eurasia accounts for 60 percent of the world's GNP and about three-fourth of the world's known energy resources."[12]

Again the energy theme appears later in Brzezinski's book: "The world's energy consumption is bound to vastly increase over the next two or three decades. Estimates by the US Department of Energy anticipate that world demand will rise by more than 50 percent between 1993 and 2015, with the most significant increase in consumption occurring in the Far East. The momentum of Asia's economic development is already generating massive pressures for the exploration and exploitation of new sources of energy."[13]

With the Middle East safely but implicitly included, but minimized in his discussion, Brzezinski stressed the importance of central Eurasia, particularly for the critical goal of diversification of energy supplies: "Moreover, they [the Central Asian Republics] are of importance from the standpoint of security and historical ambitions to at least three of their most immediate and more powerful neighbours, namely Russia, Turkey, and Iran, with China also signalling an increasing political interest in the region. But the Eurasian Balkans are infinitely more important as a potential economic prize: an enormous concentration of natural gas and oil reserves is located in the region, in addition to important minerals, including gold."[14]

Could the eventual dismemberment and weakening of Russia to the point it could not oppose US military operations that have now successfully secured control of the oil and gas reserves in Central

Asia been part of a multi-decade plan for global domination? One of the terms I have come to hear when referring to Russia is "Weimar Russia." This is a reference to Germany after WWI, when reparations and plundering by the Allies destroyed Germany's economic base, created hyperinflation and ripped the social fabric apart. Some experts have described the economic jihad against Russia as a deliberate attempt to revert the tottering superpower to Third World status.

First came the chicken, then the egg, then the ubiquitous Russian cucumber, then the Bolshoi, and finally *oil*. With oil, came *market reforms* orchestrated by some of the best and brightest of world financiers such as Jeffrey D. Sachs and Anders Aslund. Market reforms in an unconsolidated and sluggishly developing proto-democracy, such as Russia, inevitably created the collapse of the Russian economy. Its population was rendered desperate, and its ability to support a world-class military establishment destroyed, which inevitably invited colonialism. This colonization, masked as reforms, destroyed the basic institutions of Russian society along the following basic lines:

> 1. Destruction of the financial system of the state, by means of an endless build up of the state-debt pyramid, shrinking of the tax base, deepening of the non-payments crisis, and disorganization of the monetary system.
> 2. Destruction of the scientific and technological potential of the country, achieved by means of a many-folded reduction in state financing of science, the collapse of technological cooperation and scientific production integration, in the course of mass privatization, and the refusal of the government to have any scientific and technical, industrial, or structural policy at all.
> 3. Sale of controlling blocs of shares in the leading and most valuable Russian firms, in industry, electric power, and telecommunications, to foreign companies.
> 4. Transfer of the right to exploit the most valuable Russian raw materials deposits to transnational corporations.
> 5. Establishment of foreign control over the Russian stock exchange.
> 6. Establishment of direct foreign control over the shaping of Russian domestic and foreign economic policy.[15]

Among the policies of the Yeltsin government, none did as much to discredit the notion of reform as the thoroughly corrupt "loans-for-shares" program. It was devised by a former Soviet trade official turned banker, Vladimir Potanin, and further developed by a consortium of the new Russian banks. "Loans-for-shares" was run by Anatoly Chubais, key ally of the Clinton administration, who is primarily known for his role under Yegor Gaidar as the vice-premier of the Russian Government under Yeltsin. Gaidar and Chubais, in the mid 1990s, were credited with "shock therapy" privatization and the creation of the Russian oligarchs that overnight left 40% of Russians penniless and starving. The term "shock therapy" refers to the sudden release of price and currency controls, combined with the withdrawal of state subsidies, and immediate trade liberalization within a country, all the necessary ingredients for impoverishment of the Russian society.

In failing to oppose "loans-for-shares" and continuing to endorse Chubais strongly after its shock therapy, scandal-ridden failure, the Clinton administration tacitly endorsed means that fundamentally undermined America's publicly stated objective: to help the former Soviet Union, and in particular Russia, make a "successful transition" to capitalism. As it turned out, the US efforts were intended to remove large amounts of wealth from the region and debilitate Russia. What happened was that Russia, in the words of Yeltsin himself, became a "superpower of crime," a "mafiocracy," not merely because of the absence of adequate laws (or the supposed robber-baron period which some apologists say is a natural stage of economic development), but because of the inherently corrupt nature of its law enforcement, security organs, and intelligence services.[16]

Though the seeds had been planted by the outgoing George H.W. Bush administration, the US assistance program to facilitate Russia's transition to capitalism took off under the new Clinton administration in 1993. A task force headed by Vice President Al Gore, Treasury Secretary Lawrence Summers and Deputy Secretary of State Talbot involved an exclusive US Treasury contract with Goldman Sachs, the Harvard Institute for International Development, the International Monetary Fund (IMF), and the World Bank. Their partnership with the government of Boris Yeltsin remade the Russian economy.

One of the clues to this remake was given in Zbigniew Brzezinski's 1997 book, *The Grand Chessboard.* As far as Russia was concerned, the imperative was clear: "Understandably, the immediate task has to be to reduce the probability of political anarchy or a reversion to a hostile dictatorship in a crumbling state still possessing a nuclear arsenal. But the long-range task remains: how to encourage Russia's democratic transformation and economic recovery while avoiding the re-emergence of a Eurasian empire that could obstruct the American Geostrategic goal ... But, in the meantime, it is imperative that no Eurasian challenger [Russia] emerges, capable of dominating Eurasia and thus of also challenging America.[17]

Both economic and strategic considerations drive US interests in the oil and gas reserves of Central Asia. After the decline of the Ottoman Empire in the 19th century, Russia faced another colonial power on one of its southern flanks, separated from British India by wild Afghanistan. Their struggle over Asia's high ground became known as the "Great Game," and they played it for a century, not only to gain control of important resources for themselves, but also to deny them to others. Today, US world domination is based largely upon its near hegemony in the world oil economy. Official US policy in Central Asia, as an NSC official told Congress in 1997, was to "break Russia's monopoly control over the transportation of oil and gas from that region, and frankly, to promote Western energy security through diversification of supply."[18]

One of the first steps towards breaking that monopoly took place in mid-December 1999, when US officials participated in a formal meeting in Azerbaijan in which specific programs for the training and equipping of *mujaheedin*, Muslim guerrilla fighting forces, from the Caucasus, Central and South Asia and the Arab world were discussed and agreed upon. "This meeting led to Washington's tacit encouragement of both Muslim allies and US private security companies to assist the Chechens and their Islamic allies to sustain the ensuing jihad [against Russia]."[19]

The Taliban's rise to power in Afghanistan can be linked to the same, single, golden theme of denying oil to your competitor – in this case, Russia – by pushing Russia out of its natural sphere of influence. Armed conflicts on the southern frontiers of Russia's territory in Nagorno-Karabakh, Abkhazia and Chechnya "represented a distinct, tactical move, crucial at the time, in discerning which power would ultimately become master [of the energy supply]."[20]

The Crowning of Boris Yeltsin

Acceptance of Boris Yeltsin by the Western press was a key ingredient in the equation. Once the mainstream press followed the lead of the Clinton administration and defined the former hard-line

Communist apparatchik and alcoholic Boris Yeltsin as a 'democrat,' the looting of Russia began.

Journalist Anne Williamson was for many years a leading expert on Russian and Soviet affairs, writing for among others, the *Wall Street Journal* and the *New York Times*. She lived in Russia, spoke the language, and saw firsthand what was done to Russia in the 1990s. Her testimony to the US Congress on how the Russian Federation was dismembered and pillaged forms part of the historical record.[21]

What Williamson described before the Committee on Banking and Financial Services of the US House of Representatives on September 21, 1999, is the creation and installation of a whole new set of elites, the oligarchs, whose motives – personal enrichment at any cost – were already known. The oligarchs were loved in the West because they were rather unsophisticated and also could be readily controlled with money. In her testimony before Committee on Banking and Finance, Anne Williamson said, "Western assistance, IMF lending and the targeted division of national assets are what provided Boris Yeltsin the initial wherewithal to purchase his constituency of ex-Komsomol [Communist Youth League] bank chiefs, who were given the freedom and the mechanisms to plunder their own country in tandem with a resurgent and more economically competent criminal class."[22]

The new elite learned everything about the confiscation of wealth and the stripping down of assets, but nothing about its creation. In a sense, modern Russian political life cannot be understood without reference to the very Russian phenomenon of "political technology,"[23] which in Russian understanding of realpolitik involves both manipulation of individuals and large-scale deception. As Peter Reddaway explains, "Part of this process, was the growing non-accountability of the Yeltsin regime and the taking of most real decision-making out of public sphere and into the privacy of the bath houses and tennis courts used by Yeltsin, his confidant Alexander Korzhakov, and their cronies. This increasingly secretive method of government involved the manipulation of parties, social groups and public opinion, both through the media and through a wide range of deceptions and dirty tricks during election campaigns."[24]

Indeed, with the presidential election of 2000 fast approaching, an "advisory group," made up of committee chairmen of the US House of Representatives, issued a report on the mess Clinton and company had made in Russia. Of course, with the majority Republicans holding all the chairmanships, the report must be read in the context of US politics. Nonetheless, and perhaps because their party was uninvolved in the affair, I find their report to be candid and largely on target. Certainly the title of their September 2000 report leaves little room for misinterpretation: "Russia's Road To Corruption: How the Clinton administration Exported Government Instead of Free Enterprise and Failed the Russian People." Here is a bit of what they had to say:

> In 1995, Russia was under considerable pressure from the IMF and the Clinton administration to implement the IMF-Clinton troika program of increasing tax revenues to meet arbitrary budget deficit targets.... Russians' real income had dropped to the lowest levels since Soviet days. The Russian government [under Yeltsin] desperately needed cash, but a new IMF loan at the moment seemed impossible since Russian government borrowing in 1995 had already soared to over 350% of the prior year's.
>
> To meet the IMF and Clinton administration demands for more government revenues, Potanin, Chubais, and their colleagues devised a secretive plan in the spring and summer of 1995 for the Russian government to borrow money from Russian banks. As collateral, the government would offer stock in premier state-owned industries.[25]

In exchange for the stock, the government issued bonds. Bonds represent debt. As with any debt, if it can't be paid, then the collateral used to secure it is forfeited. The report continued:

> The key feature of the "loans-for-shares" scheme was the proviso that if the government were unable to repay the loans, the banks would have the right to auction the shares – primarily in the energy, natural resources, metals, and manufacturing industries. Given the banks' ability to rig such auctions, and the fact that the loans were heavily over-collateralized, default by the Russian government would yield a bonanza for the banks' owners.
>
> A number of observers [including such qualified observers as Chrystia Freeland, a former Rhodes Scholar and Deputy Editor of the *Financial Times*, Joseph Stiglitz former chief economist of the World Bank and Anne Williamson] believe the "loans-for-shares" scheme was actually designed with the intention of turning over these enterprises to the select insider group who were allowed to participate, and that from the inception the government neither intended nor was able to repay the loans.[26] The government need-

> ed money, and this was a way of getting at least a small amount of it while simultaneously accomplishing two other objectives: "privatizing" industries without Duma [Russia's legislature] approval, and providing political friends with enormous new wealth through a non-competitive process. Some Russian officials apparently believed that the beneficiaries of "loans-for-shares" could then be counted upon as a powerful political constituency in favor of market reforms.
>
> In its execution, the "loans-for-shares" scheme failed to produce a constituency for reform – the bankers' real interest was in increasingly lucrative sweetheart deals – but did succeed in winning the support of a powerful group of businessmen for the Yeltsin government in the upcoming elections. It is not difficult to see why: exceptionally valuable government assets were virtually given away at a fraction of their true worth. As one of the oligarchs commented with significant understatement, "each ruble invested in one's own politician yields a 100% profit."[27]
>
> When the shares pledged as collateral were eventually sold after the government failed to repay the loans they secured, the winning bid was almost invariably submitted by an affiliate of the bank managing the auction – and typically exceeded the minimum bid by only a nominal amount. Thus the "loans-for-shares" program essentially offered a select group of Russian bankers an opportunity to acquire cut-rate shares in prized state enterprises.

Since then, a number of the oligarchs have been brought before the courts for their misdeeds. Russian state prosecutors initiated corruption investigations in 1999 against both Boris Berezovsky, at one time Russia's leading oligarch, and Vladimir Gusinsky, an oligarch and one time Berezovsky associate. Both have fled rather than stand trial. Mikhail Khodorkovsky, the target of a similar probe, was arrested on October 25, 2003. He is currently in prison camp number 13 in – where else? – Siberia. Security operations in Yukos and other Khodorkovsky companies had been run by Mikhail Yosifovich Shestopalov. Shestopalov, ironically, is a former head of the Division for Combating Thefts of Socialist Property and Speculation of the Ministry of Internal Affairs, and an intimate friend of Yuri Primakov, former director of the KGB. In the end, the system, controlled by the ruling apparatus and by the KGB, hadn't changed, nor had the beneficiaries. There were secret service agents loyal to the Party at every level of Bank Menatep. In the fall of 1995, Khodorkovsky's Bank Menatep was given the right to conduct an auction for a 45% stake in the state-owned oil giant, Yukos.[28] It was clear to informed observers that a monumental rip-off was brewing, but it turned out to be startling, even by the standards of 1990s Russia, in both its simplicity and audacity.

As the representative of the seller, Khodorkovsky had sold Yukos to himself! The Soviet Union's third-largest stockpile of oil came along with the title and deed to the company, and Yukos was generally regarded as one of the crown jewels of the Russian economy. According to the murdered, former-*Forbes* senior writer Paul Khlebnikov, Khodorkovsky and his partners, Leonid Nevzlin, Mikhail Brudno, Vladimir Dubov and Platon Lebedev, "ended up with a 78% stake in Yukos – for which they paid $309 million. How absurd was this sum? In the summer of '97, two months after this deal was finalized, Yukos was trading on the Russian stock exchange at a market capitalization of $6 billion."[29]

Clinton and the IMF Rescue of Yeltsin

Desperately afraid that Yeltsin, with a 3% approval rating perhaps the most unpopular politician in history, would not be reelected in 1996, the Clinton administration pushed through a new $10.2 billion International Monetary Fund loan in March of that year, which provided liquidity not only for the Russian central government also but for Yeltsin's campaign.

The 2000 report from the US House group condemned this loan in no uncertain terms:

> By December 31, 1995, the Russian central government had borrowed over $10 billion through the IMF. When on March 26, 1996, the IMF and Russian central government reached final agreement on a new loan of $10.2 billion – the second-largest loan ever made[30] to any borrower by the IMF – many outside observers were dumbfounded.
>
> In a single commitment, the IMF was preparing to flood the Kremlin with more money than it had disbursed in the more than four years since the end of the Soviet Union. The extension of such significant new credit was surprising because there was little in the way of basic free-market reform legislation in place to justify it. There was still no market in banking services, no reliable protection for private property rights, no mortgage lending, and no honest system of commercial dispute resolution.
>
> On its merits, there was little economic justification for extending the IMF package in March 1996. The loans-for-shares ersatz

> "privatization" of major Russian industries into the hands of a few insiders was already notorious. The poor state of the Russian Federation's official budget and finances made it implausible to assume that the government would ever repay the latest IMF loan. Worst of all, the loan did not effectively stipulate economic conditionality: in the first year alone, the IMF granted three waivers for "nonobservance of performance criteria."[31]

In fact, President Clinton had endorsed the loan a month before the details of the commitment were even agreed upon. The president could do this because the United States was the largest contributor – about 18.25% or $35 billion – of the IMF's total quotas. With such heavy US influence on the IMF, Clinton's endorsement left little doubt that the loans would be made, and the Clinton administration turned the IMF into an agent of US policy in Russia.

In reality, the Clinton administration's decision to extend yet another IMF loan was nothing short of a sophisticated form of bribery. "When Clinton was pushing the NATO Expansion Treaty through the Senate, which Russia looked upon as provocative, the US President defused Yeltsin's opposition by assuring his re-election with a $10 billion IMF loan front-loaded with a billion dollars in cash."[32]

Immediately following the accord with the IMF, explained Simon Pirani and Ellis Farrell at a symposium in Moscow in 1999, "the Russian Central Bank began to place funds, including much of the money Russia had been loaned by the IMF, into the accounts of its offshore subsidiaries Fimaco and Evrobank."[33] This money was then recycled back in to the Russian financial markets to buy short-term treasury bonds [GKOs]. This pump-priming with funds from Fimaco and Evrobank inflated the GKO market, and western investors and financial institutions then caught the GKO mania, without understanding what was really going on, thereby both betting for and helping assure a Yeltsin victory at the polls.

The Central Bank fixed the rouble exchange rate, interest rates rose and the yields on the GKOs increased to insane levels – nearly 200% by the time of the election. "The result was that the state was able to use the proceeds from the sale of the GKOs to pay off pensions and wages in arrears shortly before the election; it also let private employers know that they should pay off wages arrears rather than pay their taxes. This, together with completely fictitious promises that (for example) army conscription would be abolished, enabled Yeltsin to be re-elected."[34]

The alleged threat of a Communist election victory had been ludicrously overblown. The Communist Party was way out of its league. The combination of oligarch millions and western marketing panache had dazzled the primitive Russians into voting for the corrupt and criminal Yeltsin regime. The votes had been in effect purchased with IMF money that had been converted to roubles and then recycled through the GKO market to boost its value. A gigantic bubble was forming.

The 290-percent yields (on three-month paper at one point) on Russian GKOs were paid with US taxpayers' money via IMF loans. It isn't difficult to surmise the investments' final destination. "By yielding those kind of non-market returns," reported Anne Williamson, "the bond market insured that all the country's resources and all that it was capable of attracting went to the support of the state, just as Czarism and Communism had done previously."[35]

Compounding the pillage, a number of investment schemes sponsored by the Export-Import Bank of the United States, the Overseas Private Investment Corporation, and a number of congressionally mandated funds were designed for individuals, Russian corporations, and banks. These initiatives created nothing other than huge money laundries. The Russian bond market's unscrupulously leveraged returns, sustained by IMF loans, were a magnet for investors, and soon developed into a classic pyramid scheme. As fast as the IMF, the World Bank, and institutions lent money to Russia, providing astronomical returns to favored players, just so quickly was the money taken right back out of Russia. Those huge sums, initially provided by taxpayers, returned to Wall Street, US banks, and Harvard, according to Anne Williamson's US House of Representatives testimony.[36]

As debt analyst David Riley put it in London's *Observer* on October 17, 1999: "All this was part of the build up to the Russian financial crash in August 1998." Russia was literally a free lunch for American institutions and non-profit organizations. Eventually, of course, the Russian economy collapsed so badly that it was necessary to secure a total bailout from the IMF: the ultimate kiss of death for any country, and all funded by American taxpayers.

To get the Russian nation out of its quagmire, the country desperately needed "direct investment, not speculative debt traders."[37] Why then did international lending and bilateral aid programs work overwhelmingly to the international debt merchants' benefit? All aid programs form part of the IMF's liberalization policy. They are meant first to advance globally the Federal Reserve's money monopoly through IMF lending and the private banking sector, and secondly, to subsidize expansion of US firms into foreign markets thus improving conditions for speculative finance capital to operate.[38]

In the aftermath of the August 1998 meltdown, an editorial in the *Financial Times* suggested that the IMF should stop lending to support currencies (i.e., the rouble) at unsustainable levels. To its credit, the *Financial Times* on December 31, 1998 published a scathing rebuttal in a letter from economist Harry Shutt. Such a suggestion, he argued, "indicates a failure to grasp that such support [from the IMF] is driven by a desire *to give priority help to foreign short-term speculators* investing in emerging markets at the expense of the real economy" [emphasis added].

"Combined with the absence of exchange controls (also insisted on by the Fund)," Shutt continued, "it [IMF support for currencies at unsustainable levels] ensures that domestic interest rates are kept at astronomic levels in order to defend the overvalued parity. This in turn ensures that, as long as the exchange rate is kept more or less stable [through IMF-funded intervention in the market], holders of government treasury bills at interest rates ranging from 40% to 100% make super profits, while local enterprise is strangled, government debt is pushed to ever more unfundable levels, public servants and pensioners go unpaid and *millions more are subjected to destitution and premature death*" [emphasis added].[39]

The Final Days

The US House report succinctly tells the story:

> The disaster that began on August 17, 1998, spread immediately throughout Russia. Millions of ordinary men and women who had deposited their money in Russian banks lost everything. ATM and debit cards ceased to work. Dozens of banks became insolvent and disappeared. Angry depositors besieged Russian banks, only to learn they had been wiped out.
>
> Millions of senior citizens, whose meager pension income had been suspended for months, were cut off completely. When the dust finally settled in March 1999, the ruble – and with it, every Russian's life savings – had lost fully 75% of its value.

> The devastation of Russia's economy was worse than what America experienced in the Great Depression. By 1932, the US gross national product had been cut by almost one-third. But within just six months of the 1998 crash, Russia's economy, measured in dollars, had fallen by more than two-thirds. From $422 billion in 1997, Russia's gross domestic product fell to only $132 billion by the end of 1998.
>
> At the end of 1929, following America's disastrous stock market crash, unemployment in the United States reached 1.5 million, representing 1.2% of the total population. The 1998 collapse of the Russian economy was far worse: 11.3 million Russians were jobless at the end of 1998 – 7.7% of the nation's total population.
>
> In the Crash of 1929, stock prices fell 17% by year end – and 90% by the depth of the Great Depression four years later. By contrast, the Russian stock market lost 90% of its value in 1998 alone.

By March 1999, billions of dollars backed, as usual, by the US taxpayer had disappeared into the secret bank accounts of both Russian and American gangster capitalists. Then the IMF washed its hands of any responsibility for what happened to the enormous sums of money it had poured into Russia so quickly, and were so quickly siphoned off by government crooks into their foreign bank accounts.

With the collapse of the economy and the banking system, ordinary Russians froze, starved and drank themselves to death. According to the House report, more than 500 billion dollars had been looted out of Russia.[40] And that wasn't stockholder equity. It was real hard cash. Within a decade, the population of Russia had shrunk from an estimated high of 160 million in 1991 to 145 million people. According to the Hoover Institution Policy review, life expectancy of a Russian male had dropped in the year 2000 to around 48 years.[41] Those living below the official poverty line, defined as income of less than the rouble equivalent of $500 per year, now formed 41.2 percent of the population.

By the dawn of the new century, Russia was a basket case, as badly ruined as it had been at the worst part of World War II. Dmitri Vasiliev, former chairman of Russia's Federal Security Commission, confirmed the unimaginable: "The $10 billion IMF money is all spent," he told the *Los Angeles Times* a month after the devaluation. "It went to foreigners and Russian speculators, including the Central Bank. They got payments for their GKOs, converted the roubles into cheap dollars, and took the money out of the country."[42]

None of this was accidental or circumstantial. It was "profit taking" on a grand scale. Interpol money-laundering investigators have been quoted as saying that the IMF money just visited Russia briefly before returning to the US, leaving all of the debt, with no evident benefit to the economy. One Interpol source, whose name I cannot cite due to security reasons, even hinted that they did not really know whom to trust for accurate information in Russia, because the highest levels of government were part of the looting.

The more I studied the circumstances of the case, the more one thing became absolutely clear: someone at the highest levels of power deemed this money expendable. I needed to find the reason. I have been investigating money laundering by organized crime for over a decade, and none of this made any sense. You see, criminal money, dirty money is different from clean money. Money that is not criminal has to go through regulations and banking systems. It has to go through taxations. It's tracked. The lawyers follow it. The government follows it. The regulators follow it. The secret services follow it. Legal money is slow money.

There is absolutely no way that all this IMF money could have vaporized into thin air. The billions in IMF loans had collapsed the currency, insuring a banking crisis, which wiped out Russia. Someone, somewhere knew where it was and how it got there. Moreover, this held the key to the rest of the mystery.

How do you lose so much money, I kept asking myself again and again? I re-read several dozen articles from the American, European and Russian press appearing around the time the money disappeared. The IMF blamed the Russian government for incompetence, the Russian government blamed the IMF for trying to destroy the country, and financial analysts were blaming HIID (Harvard Institute for International Development) and the Clinton administration for short-sightedness in their handling of the "loans-for-shares" scam. Yet, none of them dealt with the consequences of the loss. When the money used to bankroll the luxurious way of life of the Russian oligarchs disappeared, Russia went belly up. Ordinary people froze, starved and drank themselves to death by the millions. And no one seemed to have been concerned.

Major western corporate media groups who picked up on the story blamed Russian gangster capitalists, Mafia bosses and ruthless oligarchs. But there was no follow-up and no hard-nosed investigative journalism to uncover the money's whereabouts. It was as if the mainstream press was in collusion with the US government, the IMF and major banking institutions in sweeping the entire episode under a rug, I thought to myself. Why? As far as I knew, the money was still missing, and the hunt was still on.

The *Wall Street Journal Europe* had mentioned that the Swiss Federal Prosecutor's Office was involved. That was a very good start. I have done business with the Swiss secret service in the past, and I knew that they were very professional and extremely tight-lipped. The Swiss were my ticket to getting it right.

I weighed my options. In some tough investigations when leads are sparse, there are times when it becomes necessary to "shake the trees" and see what falls out. It was 2006 and the year 1998 was far removed. Most of the leads had gone stone cold. Some of the witnesses and perhaps even the perpetrators had been rubbed out, or "suicided" as the CIA likes to call it. I called on a few acquaintances at the *Wall Street Journal* and the *Financial Times* who, it turned out, had long ago lost interest in the story. With the Iraq quagmire front-and-center and Iran dangerously looming in the background, you couldn't blame them.

Yep, this would have to be a major "tree shaking." Only one person could help me: an old and trusted contact at the world's largest international police organization, Interpol.

A little-known fact about Interpol is that the organization grew out of anticipation of the Second World War. It was organized by the House of Rothschild in Vienna in 1923. The family felt it needed a special intelligence organization to watch over the interests of bankers, who were financing both sides of the war. In order not to make things look too suspicious, they had earlier in 1914 called on Prince Albert I of Monaco to invite lawyers, judges and police officers from several countries to discuss international cooperation against crime.

Today, Interpol is staffed by agents from MI6, MI5, the CIA, Mossad, the former East German Stasi and the KGB, to name just a few of the more famous organizations.

My contact listened silently and told me he would be in touch. When he got back to me, the information was worth the wait. According to him, the case was "XD-Top Priority Red Tab," meaning of utmost importance. Interpol has special files bearing different colored tabs. Red tabs get first priority. These meant that an investigation was in progress against individuals whose immediate arrest was sought by Interpol. Furthermore, the Swiss Prosecutor's Office was not working alone. They were assisted by the Money Laundering Reporting Office (MROS) for Switzerland, which functions as a relay and nexus among financial intermediaries and the law enforcement agencies.

If this case was "XD-Red Tab," I speculated, then Interpol must have named suspects. Color tabs are applicable to people, not to organizations. If MROS was involved, then this was a major international investigation into money laundering involving at the very least four or five international crime prevention agencies working in tandem and being coordinated out of Switzerland. My Interpol contact gave me his source's name at MROS, with very specific prearranged instructions of what must be said to indicate an outsider coming from a friendly source. I dialed and waited.

According to the source, the only way money could be transferred from account A to account B was on direct orders from an official in charge of foreign loans. By a process of elimination, it appeared that this mysterious official could only be Mikhail Kasianov, then Russia's Deputy Finance Minister, whose authority could move 100 percent of the 1998 IMF loan.

Enter Edmond Safra

My MROS contact, in turn, supplied me with a source at the Swiss Prosecutor's Office. What I then learned staggered my mind: the $4.8 billion IMF loan was formed under "account No. 999091 at the US Federal Reserve Bank on August 14, 1998." The FBI, the Swiss told me, had confirmed that information. From there, the money should have been transferred to the Central Bank of Russia. It never got there. Instead, the entire amount was moved to account No. 608555800 at the Republic National Bank of New York, owned by the self-acclaimed "world's greatest banker," Edmond Safra.

When I saw Safra's name mixed into this, I began to realize the sheer scope of what I was on to. Edmond Safra, one of eight children of a Syrian Jewish banker whose ancestors were gold traders in the Ottoman Empire, was one of the most colorful characters in the financial world and certainly more than just a banker. He was a gold trader. No, take that back. He was the greatest clandestine gold trader in the history of mankind, suspected at the time, by the FBI, according to Interpol, of being the principal conduit for Russia's criminal money laundering.

According to my FBI contacts, the laundered money, in turn, was transferred through the Swiss Creditanstalt Bankverein branch, to banks and accounts in no way related to the Russian budget. One of these sums, $2.35 billion out of the $4.8 billion was transferred into the accounts of the Bank of Sydney.

Through the Sydney, Australia city directory, I checked for the bank's address. To my surprise, there was no "Bank of Sydney." I called MROS for the second time. I learned that the Bank of Sydney, which had functioned from July 1996 to September 1998, was an offshore entity unrelated to Australia.

The time line was clear enough. The IMF loan was approved in August 1998. One month after the loan was transferred, it disappeared and the account closed. Period. Yet, nobody seemed to have been too concerned. My source at MROS confirmed my suspicions. "When have you ever heard of a case of vast financial conspiracy against your [Russian] government, and the government itself never following up on it?" he asked.

"Unless, *you* stole the money in the first place," I added sarcastically. There was more to learn.

When the money was transferred into the Swiss Creditanstalt Bankverein branch, Italian money-laundering experts and Russian government investigators out of the Attorney General's office got involved. What they discovered were connections to the usual suspects. Part of the money transferred to the Bank of Sydney was placed in an account of a company which was 25 percent owned by Tatiana D'yachenko, former President Boris Yeltsin's younger daughter. D'yachenko and a small group of opportunist people such as Boris Berezovsky, the then-richest Russian oligarch, Valentin Yumashev, head of the Russian Presidential administration, and Roman Abramovich, principal and most aggressive ideologue of the "family,"[43] ruled the country in the name of the President while Yeltsin faded from the political scene due to his rapidly declining health.[44]

According to the Swiss Prosecutor's Office, $2.115 billion of this money was converted into British pounds and transferred to the National Westminster Bank, where any trace of the money disappeared. A much "smaller" amount of money, $780 million, was transferred on August 14, 1998 to the Credit Suisse bank, followed by $270 million transferred to the same bank four days later. These two transfers attracted the attention of Swiss investigator Loran Casper-Anserme, who together with Geneva prosecutor Bertrossa and Russian investigator Nickolai Volkov joined the investigation.

The last $1.4 billion was transferred to the notorious Bank of New York and then to its Geneva branch, Bank of New York-Intermaritime. However, this was far from being the end of the story. The money was deposited into the account of a Russian United Bank owned by Boris Berezovsky and Roman Abramovich, the current owner of the Chelsea Football Club. At that time, these two oligarchs were the best of friends.

Subsequent events transpired with breathtaking precision. The investigation concluded that the IMF money was immediately transferred to the account of the Swiss RUNICOM company. Through my Interpol contacts I found out that RUNICOM was registered in Switzerland at No. 1 De Mulen Street. Company owner? Chelsey Football Club president, Roman Abramovich.

British Special Services had the best report of nefarious RUNICOM activities. They published their report on the *Compromat.ru* website, categorically stating, "As a result of RUNICOM SA Director Roman Abramovich's swindling in the course of privatization of the state-owned Sibneft company in 1995-97, the Russian state received $2.7 billion less," contributing significantly to the devastating economic crisis in the country.

The investigation, however, was not without casualties. While visiting Russia, the magistrate who launched the Swiss investigation, Laurent Kasper-Ansermet, was found bleeding and unconscious after an attack in St. Petersburg. Investigator Nikolai Volkov, who had joined the Swiss investigation concerning the loan, was immediately dismissed from the Prosecutor General's Office by the Swiss government and blacklisted.

Murder in the Gold Market

Born in 1932, Edmond Safra was working in finance and trade by the age of sixteen. After World War II his family moved first to Italy and then Brazil in 1952, where he was in business with his father. In 1956 he settled in Geneva, where he launched the private Trade Development Bank. In 1966, he began the Republic National Bank of New York. For many years, Edmond Safra was listed among the richest people in the world.

His family's banking and precious-metals empire was built primarily after the creation of the state of Israel in 1948, with the Safras acting as the savvy money-managing experts for wealthy Sephardic Jews, the descendants of those who initially fled the Spanish Inquisition in the 15th century. Mostly Middle Easterners, whole families desired to extract their fortunes before they moved to Israel.

With its base in Lebanon, the original Safra bank catered to many of Syria's and Lebanon's richest Sephardic Jewish families, who trusted the Safras' care and discretion to manage their financial interests. "Mr Safra, has been able to win their loyalty, gathering 30,000 wealthy investors from the Sephardi Diaspora from not just Syria and Lebanon, where they began, but Iraq and Iran, and the Jewish communities of Latin America. In this very tribal group, which has at times felt politically isolated from more westernized Jews, investing with the Safra bank was a link to both the past and a secure future."[45] To the day of Edmond Safra's death, his every financial transaction was conducted in a rare Judaeo-Arabic script, used only by the Sephardic Middle Eastern communities.

He died in December 1999, under what were "suspicious circumstances" to say the least – in a fire that engulfed his Monte Carlo residence after, an ex-Green Beret nurse/bodyguard claimed, it had been started by two intruders he had fought off, leaving him wounded. The nurse, Ted Maher, eventually confessed to inflicting knife wounds on himself and setting the fire in what he hoped would turn into an opportunity to "rescue" Safra, and thus enhance his hold on very lucrative employment. Maher served several years in a Monaco prison for the offense.

At the time of his death, Safra was finalizing the sale of his entire banking empire to a British banking conglomerate. What is less known about Safra is that he was likely the premier clandestine gold trader in the world, financing covert operations for intelligence agencies such as the Israeli Mossad. Additionally, Safra was evidently the key man in the gold-for-opium trade, supplying very large quantities of gold to the Hong Kong market via the Trade Development Bank. The sources for this sensational information will, I am sorry to say, have to remain anonymous at this time.

Realizing that he might well be accused of laundering billions from the IMF-Russian loan, and being aware that his life was in danger, either by those who stole the money or from Russia's security forces, the billionaire became extremely alarmed. Safra understood that the evaporation of the funds had caused the financial crisis in Russia. To save his life, he sought the protection of the US Federal Bureau of Investigations. He told authorities he was ready to show how Russian officials were laundering $4.8 billion of the IMF stabilization loans. In the summer of 1999, Safra started giving the FBI concrete evidence of how the money was laundered and who did it, revealing the names of Russian top officials and tycoons.

Given the problematic nature of his demise, it is no surprise that it has invoked its share of notoriety, even in the mainstream press. The following is from a 2004 article on the missing IMF funds in London's *Times*:

> A sinister footnote to the investigation came in the fate of the banker Edmond Safra, 67.
>
> Swiss investigators noted Mr. Safra had been questioned by the FBI in connection with unusual movements of funds originating from the IMF. After Mr. Safra began cooperating with the FBI, he hid in a penthouse flat in Monte Carlo. He died when an inferno turned his fortress-like retreat into a pile of cinders.
>
> The official explanation, that his nurse started the fire with a candle, failed to explain how an unknown man's DNA was found under Mr. Safra's fingernails. There was speculation that he had tried to fend off an attacker. The nurse was sentenced to ten years' imprisonment for arson.[46]

Connecting Drugs, Money Laundering and Big-time Banking

According to a US Congressional Investigation conducted in 2001, "US and European banks launder between $500 billion and $1 trillion of international criminal proceeds each year, half of which is laundered by US banks alone. It is estimated that half of that money comes to the United States," claims Michigan Senator Carl Levin. In other words, during the 1990s, between $2.5 and $5 trillion (laundered criminal and corrupt money) had been laundered by US banks and circulated in the US financial circuits.

What does it all mean?

Without its illegal money, the US economy would collapse onto itself. As it stands, the US trade deficit is close to $900 billion. Now, compare it to the laundered money of between $250 and $500 billion per year. Dirty money covers part of the US deficit in its balance of trade. "Without the 'dirty money,'" stated James Petras, a professor at Binghamton University, "the US economy external accounts would be totally unsustainable, living standards would plummet, the dollar would weaken, the available investment and loan capital would shrink, and Washington would not be able to sustain its global empire."[47]

Tough banking disclosure laws could put an end to the multibillion-dollar flow literally overnight. How much is $500 billion of criminal and dirty money flowing into and through the major US banks? It exceeds the net revenues of all the IT companies in the United States as well as all the net transfers by the major US oil producers, military industries and airplane manufacturers.

Intimately involved in the money-laundering business are the most important banks in the US, sustaining America's global power through money laundering and management of illegally obtained overseas funds. Again quoting James Petras in the same source, "Washington and the mass media have portrayed the US as being in the forefront of the struggle against narco trafficking, drug laundering and political corruption: the image is of clean white hands fighting dirty money. The truth is exactly the opposite. US banks have developed a highly elaborate set of policies for transferring illicit funds to the US, investing those funds in legitimate businesses or US government bonds and legitimizing them."

There are two methods that premier banking institutions use to launder money: through private banks and through correspondent banking.

Private banking caters to extremely wealthy clients, requiring minimum deposits of $1 million. Private banks are very attractive for money laundering because more than financial advice, they sell confidentiality to dirty-money clients. Private banks routinely use code names for accounts, establish "concentration accounts" which co-mingle bank funds with client funds (cutting off paper trails for billions of dollars of wire transfers), and set up offshore private investment corporations (PICs) in countries with strict secrecy laws, such as the Cayman Islands, the Bahamas, etc.

The second, and related, route that the big banks use to launder hundreds of billions of dirty money, is through "correspondent banking," a financial technique wherein illicit money is moved from bank to bank with "no questions asked," thereby cleansing funds prior to being used for legitimate purposes. In correspondent banking, one bank simply provides services to another in moving funds, exchanging currencies or carrying out other financial transactions. Since this is what banks do, why would a bank incur additional cost by hiring another to do the work? According to US Congressional Hearings, these accounts "give the owners and clients of poorly regulated, poorly managed, sometimes corrupt foreign banks, with weak or no anti-money laundering controls, direct access to the US financial system and the freedom to move money within the United States and around the world."[48] Needless to say, some of these customers would include drug dealers and others engaged in criminal activity.

It is no surprise that most of the offshore banks laundering billions for criminal clients have accounts in the US. Some of the biggest banks specializing in international-fund transfer process up to $1 trillion in wire transfers per day.

According to reports from the Associated Press, Reuters, Interpol and Agence France-Presse, one of the banks involved in laundering as much as $15 billion worth of Russian organized crime and capital flight money was the Bank of New York [BoNY]. BoNY was founded in 1784 by Alexander Hamilton, the first Secretary of the Treasury of the United States. It is one of the oldest banks in the world, and the sixteenth largest bank in the United States, based on total assets. According to a class-action lawsuit brought on behalf of shareholders of the Bank of New York Company, Inc. and its wholly-owned subsidiary, the Bank of New York, BoNY "acting as primary Western correspondent bank for the Mafia-controlled Inkombank, earned as much as $250 million a month in fees,[49] and certain of its officers earned illicit income, in exchange for wrongfully providing the Russian 'oligarchs' with powerful connections to the Kremlin and to Russian-organized crime factions in control of Inkombank, with unrestricted access to the Western banking system, thereby knowingly facilitating money-laundering, multi-billion dollar conversion of assets and capital flight."[50]

Apparently, BoNY became the US correspondent bank of choice for at least 160 gangster Russian banks. In the weeks leading up to the August 1998 Russian financial crisis, which led to the devaluation of the rouble, BoNY generated an average of $3.7 billion in daily transactions with those banks. The class action complaint categorically states, "This laundering process was substantially enhanced by passing those funds through a major bank in the US banking system, because the size, speed and efficiency of that system helped immeasurably to 'cover the tracks' of the laundering operations."[51] In addition, BoNY's stature in the banking community would cloak the unlawful transactions with a veneer of legitimacy.

I checked the full Board of Directors list of the Bank of New York at www.sec.gov using the EDGAR data base. Then I cross-referenced it with the Federal Elections Commissions databases at their respective websites. The interrelationship of those directors, as well as BoNY's investment stake/loan exposure in many other firms, helped me understand these convoluted relationships much better. Many of the major corporate donors of the Republican and the Democratic Parties, as well as leading financial institutions and Wall Street corporations, were interlocked with the very individuals under criminal indictment. For example, BoNY Board member John C. Malone sat on many other boards including those of Tele Communications, Inc., where he served for years with former chief Al Gore fundraiser, Tony Cohelo. Malone also had connections to Viacom, which bought CBS television, whose financial expansion was supervised for a long time by Brown Brothers Harriman and its senior partner, Prescott Bush: father and grandfather to future presidents and a major sponsor of Nazi Germany.

For a waiver of any further US liability in the money-laundering affair, BoNY settled in late 2005 with federal regulators for $38 *million*, roughly 1% of its value calculated shortly thereafter, in April 2006, in a complicated swap of assets with J.P. Morgan Chase. In May 2007, Russia sued the bank in its own courts for $22.5 billion on charges of money laundering.[56]

The financial finagling of course has not been restricted to the BoNY affair. The post-perestroika, post-Yeltsin Russian Federation, not exactly unschooled in the way of corruption, quickly took advantage of the new system; call it *glasnost*, openness, opportunism or money laundering. Overnight, thanks to Clinton and the IFM policies, Russia was awash in dirty money, dirty politics and dirty political vendettas. It didn't take long for the government bureaucrats, the politicians, the KGB-controlled Mafia and a newly wealthy clique of oligarchs to join in the Shadow Masters' agenda of turning Russia from a superpower into a cleptocracy.

Is it any wonder that the Russian people would find the austere autocracy of a nationalist like Vladimir Putin to be a change for the better?

Notes

1. As Claire Sterling, author of *Thieves' World: The Threat of The New Global Network of Organized Crime*, put it, "On January 23, 1991, a British 'businessman' named Paul Pearson was picked up at Moscow's Sheremetyevo airport. In his briefcase was a signed contract, endorsed by the government of the Russian Federation, proposing the illegal exchange of 140 billion roubles for US$7.8 billion. The two noteworthy aspects of this deal were (a) 140bn roubles was more than all the cash then physically circulating in Russia and (b) at the then official exchange rate, this sum was worth not $7.8bn but $224bn. British-born 'businessman' Colin Gibbins, based in the then pariah-state of South Africa, was also involved in the 140 billion rouble contract whose signatory on the Russian side was an A.A. Sveridov, a high official from Chelyabinsk, at the centre of Russia's military-industrial complex in the Ural mountains. He signed on behalf of the 'Ekho Manufacturing Ecological Company' [*sic*] and a dubious charity called 'Eternal Memory to Soldiers.' Russian Federation deputy Prime Minister, Gennady Filshin, had arranged to provide the roubles from the state budget. Yeltsin in person authorized such black market swaps, as the only practical way of luring foreign capital to his bankrupt country."

2. David Guyatt, "Gangster's Paradise," Deep Times News Service, 1997, http://www.copi.com/articles/Guyatt/GangPar/; DeepBlackLies, http://www.deepblacklies.co.uk/gangsters_paradise.htm.

3. Robert Friedman, "The Money Plane," *New Yorker*, January, 22 1996.

4. S. Sokolov and S. Pluzhnikov, *Komsomol'skaya Pravda,* January 22, 1992, trans. in *Soviet Press Digest.*

5. Report of January 22, 1992, trans. in *Soviet Press Digest*. *Ponomarev Commission Hearings*, February 10, 1992, English text, p. 167.

6. Jeffrey Surovell, "Ligachev and Soviet Politics," *Soviet Studies* vol. 43, no. 2 (1991), pp. 355-374; http://www.jstor.org/pss/152113.

7. BBC News special report, November 21, 1998; http://news.bbc.co.uk/1/hi/special_report/1998/03/98/russian_Mafia/70095.stm.

8. J. Michael Waller and Victor J. Yasmann, "Russia's great criminal revolution: The Role of the Security Services," *Journal of Contemporary Criminal Justice* vol. 11, no. 4 (1995).

9. Ibid.

10. Jonathan Stern, a expert on Russia at the Oxford Institute for Energy Studies, in an interview in Britain's *Independent*, December 11, 2006, noted the changes since the Yeltsin era: "Putin appointed people he trusted because in the 1990s there were young unprincipled cowboys who got very rich at everyone else's expense – and you can't have that again."

11. Annelise Anderson, "The Red Mafia: A Legacy Of Communism," in Edward P. Lazear (ed.), *Economic Transition in Eastern Europe and Russia: Realities of Reform* (Hoover Institution Press, 1995).

12. Zbigniew Brzezinski, *The Grand Chessboard: American Primacy and Its Geostrategic Imperatives* (Basic Books, 1997), p. 31.

13. Ibid., p. 125.

14. Ibid., p. 124.

15. Sergei Glazyev, *From a Five-Year Plan of Destruction To a Five-Year Plan of Colonization*, EIR Bonn Symposium, 1997.

16. J. Michael Waller and Victor J. Yasmann, op. cit.

17. Zbigniew Brzezinski, op. cit., p. 87.

18. Ahmed Rashid, *Taliban: Militant Islam, Oil and Fundamentalism in Central Asia,* Yale University Press, p. 174.

19. Peter Dale Scott, "The Global Drug Meta-Group: Drugs, Managed Violence, and the Russian 9/11," *Lobster: The Journal of Parapolitics*, October 29, 2005.

20. Michael Griffin, *Reaping the Whirlwind, the Taliban movement in Afghanistan* (Pluto Press 2001), p. 115.

21. Anne Williamson testimony before the Committee on Banking and Financial Services of the US House of Representatives, presented September 21, 1999.

22. Ibid.

23. Peter Reddaway, *The Tragedy of Russia's Reforms*: *Market Bolshevism against Democracy* (United States Institute of Peace Press, 2001), p. 636.

24. Ibid.

25. *Russia's Road To Corruption: How the Clinton administration exported government instead of free enterprise and failed the Russian people*, Speaker's Advisory Group on Russia, US House of Representatives 106th Congress, Hon. Christopher Cox, Chairman, September, 2000. The Speaker's Advisory Group on Russia consisted of Christopher Cox, Ben Gilman, Porter Goss, Jim Leach, Floyd Spence, C.W. Young, Tillie Fowler, Jim Saxton, Spencer Bachus, Sonny Callahan, Curt Weldon, Roger Wicker. The entire report may be read at http://www.fas.org/news/russia/2000/russia/.

26. For further discussion, see Natalia Dinello, "Bankers' Wars in Russia: Trophies and Wounds," *Post-Soviet Prospects*, Vol. VI, No. 1, Feb. 1998, p. 3.

27. Ibid., p. 4.

28. Paul Klebnikov, Moscow editor for *Forbes*' Russian edition and author of *Godfather of the Kremlin: The Decline of Russia in the Age of Gangster Capitalism* (Harvest Books, 2001), summarized the situation in the November 17, 2003 issue of the *Wall Street Journal*. He was murdered in Moscow in 2004.

29. Quoted at http://michael-hudson.com/interviews/040227_counterpunch.html.

30. Michael Gordon, "Russia and IMF Agree on a Loan for $10.2 Billion," *New York Times*, Feb. 23, 1996, Section A, p. 1.

31. The House report cites "Approach Used to Monitor Conditions for Financial Assistance," General Accounting Office Report to Congress, June 1999 (GGD/NSIAD-99-168), pp. 144-145.

32. Phyllis Schlafly, "Clinton's Post-Impeachment Push for Power," *Phyllis Schlafly Report* vol. 32, no. 8, May 17, 2000.

33. Simon Pirani and Ellis Farrell, "Western Financial Institutions and Russian Capitalism." Presented at *The World Crisis of Capitalism and the Post-Soviet States* conference held in Moscow, October 30-November 1, 1999.

34. Ibid.

35. Anne Williamson, "An Inconvenient History," *WorldCity Essays*, September 1999.

36. Ibid.

37. Ibid.

38. Ibid..

39. Harry Shutt, "The real cost of supporting speculators in emerging markets," Letters, *Financial Times*, December 31, 1998

40. *Russia's Road To Corruption*, op. cit.

41. Nicholas Eberstadt, "Power and Population in Asia," *Policy Review* no. 123, February & March 2004; http://www.hoover.org/publications/policyreview/3439671.html.

42. Richard Paddock, "Russia Plays Loose with IMF Billions," *Los Angeles Times*, Sept. 24, 1998, Section A, p. 1.

43. RFE/RL Newsline, May 27, 1999.

44. Lilia Shevtsova, *Putin's Russia* (Carnegie Endowment for International Peace, 2003), pp. 25-27.

45. David Vital, *A People Apart: The Jews in Europe, 1789-1939* (Clarendon Press, 1999).

46. Dominic Kennedy, "Mystery of the IMF cash trail to Russia," *Times* (UK), August 16, 2004.

47. Quoted in Pratap Ravindran, "US' war on funding of terrorism – Trailing the dirty money," *Business Line*, February 11, 2002, http://www.blonnet.com/2002/02/11/stories/2002021100100900.htm.

48. Minority Staff of the Permanent Subcommittee on Investigations, US Senate, Report on Correspondent Banking: A Gateway for Money Laundering, February 5, 2001.

49. Johanna McGeary, "Russia's Ruble Shakedown," *Time*, September 19, 1999.

50. United States district court southern district of New York, re. Bank of New York derivative litigation, Case No. 99 Civ. 9977 (DC), (Case No. 99 Civ. 10616 (DC) (Con.).

51. Ibid.

52. http://en.wikipedia.org/wiki/Bank_of_New_York

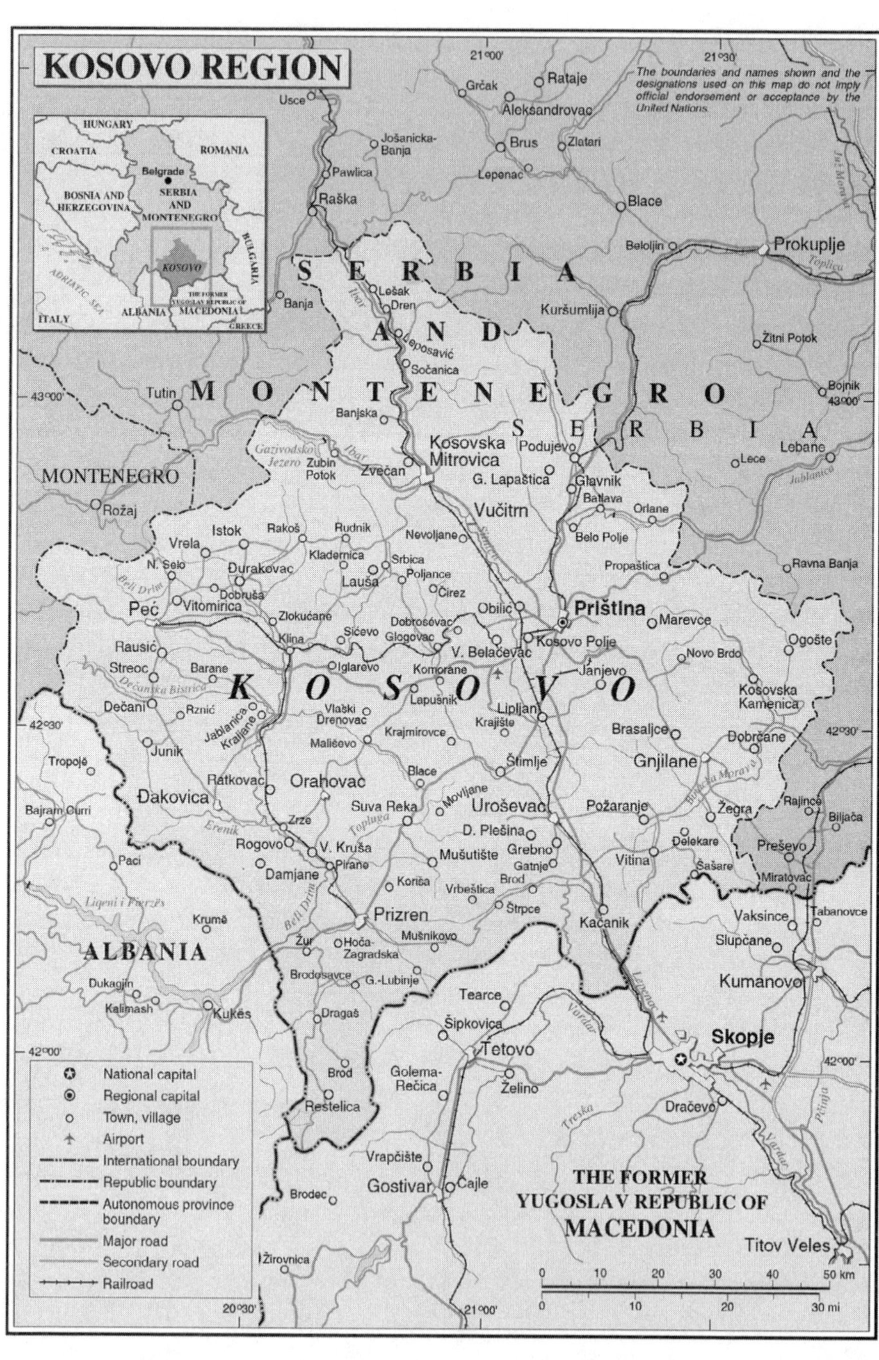

KOSOVO REGION
The boundaries and names shown and the designations used on this map do not imply official endorsement or acceptance by the United Nations.
SERBIA AND MONTENEGRO
SERBIA
KOSOVO
MONTENEGRO
ALBANIA
THE FORMER YUGOSLAV REPUBLIC OF MACEDONIA
Priština
Peć
Prizren
Kosovska Mitrovica
Uroševac
Đakovica
Gnjilane
Skopje
Tetovo
Kumanovo
Prokuplje
National capital
Regional capital
Town, village
Airport
International boundary
Republic boundary
Autonomous province boundary
Major road
Secondary road
Railroad

Chapter Three

The Bilderberg War in Kosovo

Miloševic was a brute; he was also a banker once regarded as the West's man, who was prepared to implement "economic reforms" in keeping with the International Monetary Fund (IMF), World Bank and European Union demands; to his cost, he refused to surrender sovereignty. The empire expects nothing less.

Australian journalist John Pilger, *New Statesman*

Slobo rules?

In 1996, the Bilderbergers decided to get rid of then-Serbian president Slobodan Miloševic. Their master plan was put together during the 1996 meeting in King City, a small luxury town about 35 kilometers north of Toronto in Ontario, Canada. The Kosovo War and the subsequent overthrow of the Yugoslav president occurred because of political strategies secretly conceived at this Bilderberg Group conference. Their agenda was clear. When the time was right, they intended to implement their plan to solve the "political problem" that Miloševic's political survival and continued socialist policies created in his rejection of their capitalist goals: to turn all of Europe into a "free market."

In the article quoted above, John Pilger revealed how the US and Germany had begun supporting secessionist forces in Yugoslavia after the collapse of Communism in the former Soviet Union, when the Yugoslav federation refused to be brought wholly into the Western orbit.[1] Neil Clark, who specializes in Middle Eastern and

Balkan affairs, provided specifics: "Over 700,000 Yugoslav enterprises, at the time, remained in social ownership and most were still controlled by employee-management committees, with only 5% of capital privately owned."[2]

Sara Flounders, an activist and journalist aligned to the Workers World Party, reported on this as early as 1998: "Throughout the '90s, as the capitalist market has swept over the former socialist countries of Eastern Europe and the Soviet Union, socialist Yugoslavia has attempted to resist privatization of its industry and natural resources. To break this resistance, the Western countries have played a major role in the break-up of socialist Yugoslavia.... The lending and credit conditions of the International Monetary Fund and the World Bank require the break-up of all state-owned industries. This is true for the oil and natural gas wealth in the Caucasus and the Caspian Sea as well as the diamond mines of Siberia. The decision on who will own or have controlling interest ... will be made by whoever wins the armed struggle raging in Kosovo. NATO domination on the ground would have put US corporations in the best ownership position."[3]

Tim Marshall, a British reporter, had impressive connections in the former Yugoslavia among secret service agents who were planning its overthrow. In Marshall's book, *Shadowplay*, Mark Kirk, a US Naval Intelligence officer, is quoted on the conflict in Kosovo: "Eventually, we opened up a huge operation against Miloševic, both secret and open. The secret part of the operation involved not only things like staffing the various observer missions, which were sent into Kosovo with officers from the British and American intelligence services, but also— crucially – giving military, technical, financial, logistical and political support to the KLA [Kosovo Liberation Army]," The KLA is a terrorist organization which, according to Marshall, "smuggled drugs, ran prostitution rackets and murdered civilians."

In late 1998, Miloševic, in an effort to stave off the destruction and later splintering of what was left of Yugoslavia, agreed to let the Kosovo Diplomatic Observer Mission enter Kosovo to monitor the situation in the province. The Kosovo Diplomatic Mission (KDOM) was an undercover CIA operation staffed with 2,000 specially trained British and American intelligence agents, Special Forces and "deep surveillance" operatives. The KDOM was run by a Bilderberg-controlled body, the Organization for Security and Cooperation in Europe. This is a regional security organization, founded in 1975 and supervised by the CIA, that prides itself on conflict prevention, conflict resolution and post-conflict reconstruction. The Yugoslavs knew perfectly well what was going on, but were powerless to stop it.

The Bilderberg organs insisted upon prosecuting, in a new international court, alleged war criminals among the Serbian populace, fully expecting to incite enough violent response to justify military intervention. The Serbs cleverly defused the situation by persuading the less important suspects to surrender voluntarily. Something more was needed. To further enrage the Serbs, the US-controlled Hague Tribunal resorted to illegal kidnappings ("Snatch Squads," as Henry Kissinger referred to them at the 1996 Bilderberg conference) to bring about the war.

After the 1996 Bilderberg Conference in King City, Ontario, Canada, we warned anyone willing to listen: "If the Bilderbergers could not get such a war going by inflaming the Serbs through the use of NATO 'Snatch Squads' to seize suspected war criminals for trial at The Hague, their plan was to use Kosovo as the flashpoint to ignite a regional conflict, which would ultimately embroil the Yugoslav federation, Bosnia, Russia, Greece, Turkey, Albania, Macedonia, the Western European military powers, the United States, and by extension – as allies of Turkey and Greece – Israel and Syria."

A knowledgeable Greek source present at the meeting, not as a member of the Bilderberg Group but rather as one of the support staff, had drawn my attention to the vast pool of oil reported to underlie the relatively shallow Aegean Sea. He suggested that this, in fact, is the primary reason why the US is furthering a "peace" policy in the region that actually increases the chances of war between Turkey and Greece: such a conflict might well then give the Bilderbergers an excuse to garrison the disputed area with UN peacekeepers and thus ensure their ultimate control over the exploitation of this treasure-trove of untapped oil reserves. If so, that would explain why the US Ambassador to the United Nations from 1999 to 2001, Richard Holbrooke, "father of the November 1995 Dayton Agreement," which ended the Bosnian war, was busy upsetting Greeks and Greek-Cypriots, why the US was still busily feeding weapons to both sides, and why Bilderberger Bill Clinton was so eager to link the Cyprus issue with an Aegean settlement.[4]

It would also explain why Holbrooke, a Council on Foreign Relations (CFR) and Bilderberg member as well as a recipient of six Nobel Peace Prize nominations, inserted a clause in the final Bosnia agreement regarding Kosovo. What did Kosovo have to do with Bosnia? Nothing. Except that Holbrooke's agreement was to become a blueprint for further Bilderberg expansion in the Balkans. In a column titled, "Dayton Sellout," in the Dec. 7, 1995 *Arizona Republic*, journalist Bob Djurdjevic – an internationally renowned specialist on the Balkans and a frequent contributor to the *Washington Times*, a newspaper with close military ties to the Pentagon – called this expansion a "Green Interstate, an ethnic/geopolitical highway with a dual carriage and a dual purpose": on the one hand, "connecting NATO West with NATO East (Turkey)," and on the other, "projecting the Islamic influence into the soft underbelly of Christian Europe." Historically, both the Albanian and Bosnian populations consisted of Serbs who had forcibly or voluntarily converted to Islam to avoid Turkish persecution.

In another article, Djurdjevic described ominous signs "provided by the Kosovo Albanians themselves. They have been boycotting all Serbian elections since the fall of Communism in 1990. This sent a clear signal that they were planning to achieve their political aims by bullets, not ballots. A steady flow of arms into Kosovo, financed in part by the Albanians' drug trafficking operations ... reinforced the assessment that it was just a matter of time before Kosovo exploded in violence."[5]

Michel Chossudovsky, Professor of Economics at the University of Ottawa in Canada, details the secret German and American plan to re-colonize the region following the Kosovo War: "The fate of Kosovo had already been carefully laid out prior to the signing of the 1995 Dayton agreement. NATO had entered an unwholesome 'marriage of convenience' with the Mafia ... the narcotics trade enabled Washington and Bonn to 'finance the Kosovo conflict' with the ultimate objective of destabilizing the Belgrade government and fully re-colonizing the Balkans."[6]

But I am jumping ahead of myself.

The Snatched Succomb

The *Truth in Media Global Watch Bulletin* of July 1, 1998, reported a number of untoward events occurring to Serbs unfortunate enough to fall into the hands of the "peacekeepers": "Slavko Dokmanovic, the former Serb mayor of Vukovar who was tricked, kidnapped, and shipped off to the 'NWO Bastille' in the Hague a year ago, committed suicide in his prison cell on June 29, a year after he was abducted by 20 masked New World Order commandos.... In February 1996, two unindicted senior Serb military officials were similarly kidnapped and whisked off to The Hague, where they were held illegally without charges. Gen. Djordje Djukic was later released on account of his poor health. He died in April 1996 of cancer.... In January 1997, Dr. Nikola Koljevic, vice president of the Bosnian Serb Republic and one of the chief Serb negotiators at Dayton, also committed suicide. His motives were unclear."[7] Neither Dokmanovic nor Gen. Djukic nor Dr. Koljevic had been on the published list of people indicted by the War Crimes Tribunal. Yet all of them are dead now.[8]

When illegal kidnappings failed to incite a Balkan war, our sources within the Bilderberg Group said, they were prepared to utilize Kosovo to accomplish that objective. The alleged massacre at Racak began the process. This was followed by the bogus settlement negotiations at Rambouillet.

The head of the undercover CIA operation dubbed the Kosovo Diplomatic Observer Mission (whose outward assignment was to monitor the situation in Kosovo) was William Walker, a former ambassador to El Salvador (whose US-supported government ran death squads) and a CFR member. In 1985, as deputy assistant secretary of state for Central America, Walker was a key operator in the Reagan White House's operation to overthrow the Nicaraguan government, run by Lieutenant Colonel Oliver North and Assistant Secretary of State Elliot Abrams. North had been assigned to the National Security Council staff beginning in 1981 until he was fired on November 25, 1986, and was the White House official most directly involved in secretly aiding the Nicaraguan Contras,[9] selling arms to Iran, and diverting Iran arms sales proceeds to the Contras. North claimed to have taken much of his direction from Central Intelligence Agency Director William Casey, who died at the height of the investigation from a cancerous brain tumor.

In 1991, Abrams, a disciple of Bilderberger Richard N. Perle, was investigated by the Iran-Contra special prosecutor for giving false testimony before Congress in 1987 about his role in illicitly raising money for the Contras. Avoiding indictment, he entered into a plea agreement on two misdemeanor charges of withholding information from Congress. He paid a $50 fine, and was sentenced two years of probation and 100 hours of community service. In December 1992, as he was about to leave office, President George H.W. Bush pardoned Abrams, along with five other Reagan administration officials involved in Iran-Contra.

With this track record, how could George W. Bush not have jumped at the opportunity of bringing Abrams into his administration? The odd thing is that it took almost a year. On Dec. 3, 2002, Elliot Abrams was appointed Special Assistant to the President and Senior Director for Near East and North African Affairs, which included Arab/Israel relations and any US efforts to promote peace and security in the region. What is even more curious about this adjudicated criminal is that he served as President of the Ethics and Public Policy Center from 1996 to 2001.

According to court records, CFR member Walker was responsible for setting up a phony humanitarian operation at an airbase in Ilopango, El Salvador. The airbase was secretly used to run guns, cocaine, ammunition and supplies to the Contra rebels in Nicaragua.[10] It was also Walker who "discovered" the "massacre" in the village of Racak in January 1999, the event that led to NATO's decision to commence bombing Serbia on March 24th.[11] Although the mainstream press, represented by the *New York Times*, *Los Angeles Times* and the *Washington Post*, were aware of Walker's illegal actions in Nicaragua, they decided against bringing his past activities into the open. In fact, lack of media interest in getting to the bottom of what happened isn't new, and should surprise no one reading this book.[12]

A January 20, 1999, *New York Times* editorial observed that the Racak "massacre" followed "a well-established pattern: Albanian guerrillas in the Kosovo Liberation Army kill a Serb policeman or two. Serb forces retaliate by flattening a village. This time they took the lives of more than 40 ethnic Albanians, including many elderly and one child."

George Szamuely described the scene: "On January 15, 1999, following a military operation by Yugoslav armed forces against a KLA stronghold at Racak, KLA leaders had led observers of the Organization for Security and Co-operation in Europe (OSCE) to a gully where 45 bodies were piled on top of each other. Without waiting for any investigation, the United States, through Ambassador William Walker, immediately announced that the Serbs had carried out a massacre of unarmed Kosovo Albanian civilians."[13]

William Norman Grigg, writing in the *New American* on March 15, 1999, reported that "rather than a pitiless attack on helpless villagers, the unedited film depicts a fire fight between police and encircled KLA guerrillas, with the latter group getting by far the worst of the engagement." Further complicating things about the "official" account are the number of "journalists who found only very few cartridges around the ditch where the massacre supposedly took place."

"What really happened?" asks Renaud Girard in *Le Figaro*. "During the night, could the KLA have gathered the bodies, in fact killed by Serb bullets, to set up a [phony] scene of cold-blooded massacre?"

Christophe Chatelot, in a January 21st dispatch from Kosovo, expressed similar scepticism in *Le Monde,* an *anti*-Serb publication. "Isn't the Racak massacre just too perfect?" inquired Chatelot. "How could the Serb police have gathered a group of men and led them calmly toward the execution site, while they were constantly under fire from [KLA] fighters? How could the ditch located on the edge of Racak [where the massacre victims were later found] have escaped notice by local inhabitants familiar with the surroundings who were present before nightfall? Or by the observers who were present for over two hours in this tiny village? Why so few cartridges around the corpses, so little blood in the hollow road where twenty-three people are supposed to have been shot at close range with several bullets in the head? Rather, weren't the bodies of the Albanians killed in combat by the Serb police gathered into the ditch to create a horror scene, which was sure to have an appalling effect on public opinion?"

According to George Szamuely, writing in 2004, "On March 17, 1999, a week before its onslaught on Yugoslavia, NATO organized a press conference at which Helena Ranta, the leader of the Finnish forensic team hired by the OSCE to investigate Racak, announced her findings. Though the Finnish team's report was never published, the US government, with the *New York Times* in tow, touted her inconclusive findings as confirmation of William Walker's initial statement that a massacre had taken place at Racak.[14]

Walker, accused gun-runner turned peace observer, had screamed to the world press that Serb police were guilty of "the most horrendous" massacre imaginable. The Serbs, who had very skillfully avoided NATO/Bilderberg provocations up to then, were "had." The supposed "massacre" triggered a pretext for intervention. On January 30th, the NATO Council authorized Secretary General Javier Solana to "use armed force to compel Serbian and ethnic Albanian delegates to 'peace' negotiations in France to discuss a framework for Kosovo 'autonomy.'"

In fact, as skilled as the Serbs were in side-stepping armed confrontation with NATO, the plan of attack was drawn long before the Racak incident. The US Senate Republican Policy Committee in its secret report released August 12, 1998, noted that "planning for a US-led NATO intervention in Kosovo is now largely in place.... The only missing element seems to be an event – with suitably vivid media coverage – that would make the intervention politically sellable."

Anyone observant enough could have easily guessed this was the pretext the Bilderberg-controlled NATO needed to intervene. The August 4th *Washington Post* (the newspaper and its owner are Bilderberg full-time members) quoted "a senior US Defense Department official who listed only one thing that might trigger a policy change [toward intervention]: 'I think if some levels of atrocities were reached that would be intolerable, that would probably be a trigger.'"

Helena Ranta evidently revealed the pressure she was under to make her findings conform to NATO requirements. George Szamuely quoted an interview she gave to the *Berliner Zeitung*: "KLA-fighters [were] buried around Racak. At that time I received information that proved that several Serb soldiers had been killed as well. Unfortunately, we will never know the exact number of Serb soldiers that died that night. When Ambassador Walker said that there was a massacre at Racak, this statement had no legal value. I declared at that time that the OSCE-observers forgot to take all steps necessary to secure a crime scene: isolating the area, refusing admission to all unauthorized persons and collecting all material evidence.... A bunch of governments were interested in a version of Racak that blamed only the Serb side. But I could not provide this version."

Among the confusion there is at least one certainty: William Walker's role in the affair was so important that the country road in Kosovo which leads to Racak has now been renamed after him.[15]

Ethnic Cleansing – Truth or Falsehood?

The question of mass murder cuts to the heart of the intervention in Kosovo. The Serbs were guilty of murdering innocent civilians, as were the Croats, Bosnians, Macedonians and the KLA. Intentional provocation of racial tensions in a land that has been the epicenter of two world wars can hardly be a positive occurrence. In WWII, entire Serb villages were burned and their inhabitants buried alive by the Croat sympathizers of the Nazi regime. Serb partisans had also done their share of raping and murdering of Croat and Bosnian villages. War causes massive movements of threatened populations. And in the Balkan wars, there were plenty of those.

But these dislocations were not in themselves the alliance's justification for military intervention. The justification was the apparent "discovery" of secret and detailed plans worked out by the Miloševic regime in 1998 for the ethnic cleansing of Kosovo-Albanians by the Yugoslav regular army and paramilitary groups. According to NATO, the war would cut short this operation. The German military took the lead in promoting the deception.

But the German Section of the International Association of Lawyers Against Nuclear Arms (IALANA) saw through the smokescreen, simply because the "plan" first became known only *after* March 24, 1999, that is once the bombing campaign had gotten under way: "In its press statement, even the Foreign Ministry admits that it had become aware of the existence of such a plan only on April 1, 1999."[16]

And there was at least one chink in the media's wall of indifference, appropriately enough in Germany itself:

> The existence and content of the Horseshoe plan was – like so many other elements of NATO's war propaganda – generally treated as fact by the media. Its content and sources were hardly checked. The only exception I found was an article published on May 19 by the foreign editor of the German daily *Frankfurter Rundschau*, Karl Grobe.
>
> Grobe makes clear that the origins, sources and content of the Horseshoe plan are very mysterious, and that even if such a plan actually existed, it could hardly be interpreted as a blueprint for the expulsion of the civilian population from Kosovo.
>
> The press was informed about the plan in the third week of the war by general inspector Hans Peter von Kirchbach, the highest commander of the *Bundeswehr*, the German army. Kirchbach refused to give any information on the sources of the plan, because they were "too sensitive." The news agency AP later quoted "experts" who "thought" that it was leaked by a deserter or originated from secret service sources.
>
> German defense minister Rudolf Scharping claimed that the plan had been agreed on by Yugoslav President Slobodan Miloševic and the Yugoslav military leadership in December 1998. Its main aim was, according to Sharping, to "smash or neutralise" the Kosovo Liberation Army (KLA) *and* to expel the Albanian civilian population from Kosovo.[17]

Any credibility this story may have had was further undermined in a book by a retired German officer, *Der Kosovo-Konflikt. Wege in einen vermeidbaren Krieg* [*The Kosovo Conflict: Road to an Avoidable War*] (Baden-Baden: Nomos, 2000): "Heinz Loquai, a retired brigadier general, has claimed in a new book on the war that the plan was fabricated from run-of-the-mill Bulgarian intelligence reports. Loquai, who now works for the Organization for Security and Co-operation in Europe (OSCE), has accused Rudolf Scharping, the German defense minister, of obscuring the origins of Operation Horseshoe.... Loquai has claimed that the German defense ministry turned a vague report from Sofia into a 'plan,' and even coined the name Horseshoe. *Die Woche* [a German news weekly] has reported that maps broadcast around the world as proof of NATO's information were drawn up at the German defense headquarters in Hardthöhe.... The Bulgarian report concluded that the goal of the Serbian military was to destroy the Kosovo Liberation Army, and not to expel the entire Albanian population, as was later argued by Scharping and the NATO leadership."[18]

Peace Conference at Rambouillet

In February 1999, to avoid being bombed into oblivion by a vastly superior combined NATO forces, the Serbs were compelled to participate in negotiations at Rambouillet, near Paris. US Secretary of State Madeleine Albright (Bilderberg, CFR) led the negotiations. "The Serbs were confronted with the choice of either accepting the text of the agreement unconditionally, or of being dragged into a war against NATO. The manner in which the negotiations were set up made it almost impossible to avoid the latter alternative," wrote journalist Bo Pellnäs in the Swedish newspaper, *Dagens Nyheter*, February 8, 2004.[19]

Under the terms presented at Rambouillet, Kosovo would have virtually become a NATO colony. But, according to Michael Parenti, the West was evidently fearful that Miloševic might yet accept these difficult terms "to avoid a full-scale NATO onslaught on the rest of Yugoslavia." Therefore, to insure that war was inevitable, the American delegation added a "remarkable stipulation," known as Annex B: "NATO forces and personnel were to have unrestrained access to all of Yugoslavia, unfettered use of its airports, rails, ports, telecommunication services, and airwaves, all free of cost and immune from any jurisdiction by Yugoslav authorities. NATO would also have the option to modify for its own use all of Yugoslavia's infrastructure including roads, bridges, tunnels, buildings, and utility systems. In effect, not just Kosovo but all of Yugoslavia was to be subjected to an extraterritoriality tantamount to outright colonial occupation."[20]

John Pilger's conclusion? "This demanded the military occupation of the whole of Yugoslavia, a country with bitter memories of the Nazi occupation. As the British Foreign Office minister Lord Gilbert later conceded to a Commons Defense Select Committee, Annex B was planted deliberately to provoke rejection."[21]

The government of the sovereign state of Serbia, although fully recognizing the consequences of its actions, had no recourse other than rejection of the humiliating proposal, as expected.

Enter the KLA

The Albanian underground group Kosovo Liberation Army is, without any questions, a terrorist group.

Agence France Presse, 2/23/98

The Clinton administration's then-special envoy for Kosovo, Robert Gelbard, made this statement before the KLA became a US geopolitical asset. From virtually nowhere, the well-financed Kosovo Liberation Army had sprung into the limelight, and once again the Balkans were being prepared for a war of great carnage.

On the heels of the 1996 Bilderberger meeting in King City, near Toronto, Canada, I had predicted this. Furthermore, a number of respected media sources in the US and Europe have documented the Kosovo Liberation Army and their Albanian sponsors to be heroin-financed organized-crime groups hoping to dominate the flow of Middle Eastern heroin into Europe and the US.

As the *Christian Science Monitor* had reported on Oct. 20, 1994, "Disrupted by the Yugoslav conflict, drug trafficking across the Balkans is making a comeback as Albanian mafia barons carve out a new smuggling route to Western Europe, bypassing the peninsula's war zones, according to United Nations and other narcotics experts.... For example, just 6 kilograms of hard drugs were seized by Hungarian police in 1990, but by August this year [1994] the figure had risen to 600 kilograms."

Great Britain's *Jane's Intelligence Review,* one of the world's foremost investigative journals, went even deeper in predicting the coming crisis in an article entitled, "The Balkan Medellin," published February 1, 1995. It included the following:

> A great deal of revenue is thought to derive from Albanian narco-terrorism as well as associated gun-running and cross-border smuggling to and from Albania, Bulgaria and the Kosovo province of Serbia. Although its extent and forms remain in dispute, this rising Albanian economic power is helping to turn the Balkans into a hub of criminality.
>
> Previously transported to Western Europe through former Yugoslavia, heroin from Turkey, the Transcaucus and points further east is now being increasingly routed to Italy via the Black Sea, Albania, Bulgaria and Macedonia. This is a development that has strengthened the Albanian Mafia, which is now thought to control 70% of the illegal heroin market in Germany and Switzerland....
>
> If left unchecked, this growing Albanian narco-terrorism could lead to a Colombian syndrome in the Southern Balkans, or the emergence of a situation in which the Albanian Mafia becomes powerful enough to control one or more states in the region.

According to a report marked Top Secret that I was shown by a deep undercover "Q" Clearance CIA officer stationed in Europe (Q clearance permits the holder to have access to documents dealing with atomic energy, restricted data, formerly restricted data and national security information at the Confidential, Secret and Top Secret levels) in 1996 the Bilderbergers used the CIA and the German Federal Intelligence Service (the *Bundesnachrichtendienst*, or BND) to covertly recruit, arm and train the Kosovo Liberation Army through a series of front companies located mainly in Germany. The companies were used to pump money into accounts in Switzerland held by Albanian sympathizers, in preparation for their planned Balkans war.

The choice to involve Germany in order to destabilize the Serbs and supply the KLA with arms and training has its roots in German-Serb enmity going back to before the World Wars of the last century. The Serbs blocked the Berlin-Baghdad railway project (for oil) before World War I, and predominantly Serb Yugoslavian forces valiantly held off the Nazis for quite a while at the outset of World War

II. In 1941, Nazi Germany finally took control of the Trepca mining complex, insuring a supply of minerals essential for German U-boat batteries.

Hidden Origins of the Kosovo Liberation Army

According to a US Department of Defense briefing of July 15, 1998, "initial contacts" between the KLA and NATO took place in mid-1998, during the first part of CFR member General Wesley Clark's mandate as NATO Commander in Chief: "... the realization has come to people [in NATO] that we [NATO led by Wesley Clark] have to have the UCK [acronym for KLA in Albanian] involved in this process because they have shown at least the potential to be rejectionists of any deal that could be worked out there with the existing Kosovo parties. So somehow they have to be brought in and that's why we've made some initial contacts there with the group, *hopefully the right people in the group*, to try and bring them into this negotiating process."[22]

I emphasized that phrase because, of course, "the right people" are those who will follow orders. As professor Michel Chossudovsky, in an article titled "Kosovo freedom fighters financed by organized crime," observed in 1999, "The west was relying on its KLA puppets to rubber-stamp an agreement, which would have transformed Kosovo into an occupied territory under Western administration."[23]

The framework for KLA operations was designed at the 1996 Bilderberg Conference, whose Kosovo intervention forum debate was attended, among others, by Henry Kissinger, US Secretary of Defense William J. Perry, Lord Carrington, the Queen of Spain, Richard Holbrooke, George Soros, George Stephanopoulos (representing President Clinton) and Vice President Gore, as well as David Rockefeller, who has attended almost every Bilderberg Group meeting.

The job of carrying out its detailed plan of operations fell to Hansjoerg Geiger, who was appointed that year at the insistence of the Bilderbergers as the new head of Germany's BND. In order to set the entire operation in motion, it was first necessary to establish BND regional stations in Tirana, the Albanian capital, where a pre-selection process enlisted useful recruits for the KLA terrorist organization's "command structure from the estimated 500,000 Kosovars in Albania," reported the *Truth in Media* weekly news bulletin for October 24, 1998.

Yet, the Germans weren't the only ones involved in the concerted effort to provoke a full-scale war. The CIA's covert participation was reinforced with Britain's Secret Intelligence Services MI6 and SAS Special Forces, as well as the US Defense Intelligence Agency (DIA), together with "former and serving members of 22 SAS [Britain's 22nd Special Air Services Regiment], as well as three British and American private security companies," stated Scotland's national newspaper, the *Scotsman*, on August 29, 1999. The paper was very specific about the role the US government played: "The rag-tag Kosovar Albanian rebels were taken in hand by the Virginia-based company of professional soldiers, Military Professional Resources Inc. (MPRI). [MPRI was paid by the Albanian government.] An outfit of former US marines, helicopter pilots and special forces teams, MPRI's missions for the US government have run from flying Colombian helicopter gunships to supplying weapons to the Croatian army."

The involvement of the Albanian government isn't surprising. Tomislav Kersovic, a member of the Belgrade-based Institute for Geo-Political Studies, has publicly produced documents that demonstrate finances to subsidize the KLA were provided through an Albanian foundation known as "Fatherland's Call," with active offices in Dusseldorf, Bonn, Stockholm, Bern and other European capitals, according to Anthony Wayne, reporting in April 1999.[24]

Returning to the *Scotsman*'s report: "The US DIA approached MI6 to arrange a training program for the KLA, said a senior British military source. 'MI6 then sub-contracted the operation to two British security companies, who in turn approached a number of former members of the (22 SAS) regiment. Lists were then drawn up of weapons and equipment needed by the KLA.' While these covert operations were continuing, serving members of 22 SAS Regiment, mostly from the unit's D Squadron, were first deployed in Kosovo before the beginning of the bombing campaign in March [1999]."

Secret agent Michael Levine, formerly of the Drug Enforcement Administration, made the following disheartening observation in the *New American* magazine, on May 24, 1999: "Ten years ago we were arming and equipping the worst elements of the Mujahideen in Afghanistan – drug traffickers, arms smugglers, anti-American terrorists ... Now we're doing the same thing with the KLA, which is tied in with every known middle and far eastern drug cartel. Interpol, Europol, and nearly every European intelligence and counter-narcotics agency has files open on drug syndicates that lead right to the KLA, and right to Albanian gangs in this country."[25]

The Bilderbergers needed their war, and they weren't going to let grass grow under their feet waiting for one to start. MI6, SAS Special Forces, and the US Defense Intelligence Agency, together with three British and American private security companies, were busy training the KLA terrorists in Northern Albania. In addition, Chris Stephen reported in November 1998 in Britain's *Sunday Times* that military instructors from Turkey and Afghanistan financed by the "Islamic jihad" were providing the KLA with guerrilla and diversion tactics: "Bin Laden had visited Albania himself. His was one of several fundamentalist groups that had sent units to fight in Kosovo.... Bin Laden is believed to have established an operation in Albania in 1994.... Albanian sources say Sali Berisha, who was then president, had links with some groups that later proved to be extreme fundamentalists."[26]

Bin Laden and the Kosovo Liberation Army

Although, President Clinton and his Secretary of State, Madeleine Albright, tried mightily to build a political legitimacy for the KLA terrorists, the group's links to international terrorism and organized crime were well-documented by the US Congress. The Bilderbergers, however, needed the KLA to spearhead the long desired war against the Serbs. So, the paramilitary army's drug-running gang of assassins in Kosovo, supported by al-Qaeda, literally overnight was elevated to the status of "freedom fighters" (and renamed the Kosovo Protection Corps) directly supported by NATO and the UN.

What's more, NATO's Supreme commander from 1997 to 2000, General Wesley Clark (also a Bilderberg and CFR member), was squarely in the center of the whole mess. The evidence against him, and consequently against the Clinton administration, compiled in the Congressional transcripts, news reports and intelligence documents became overwhelming. When asked during the US Presidential primaries in 2004 about some of the allegations, Democratic candidate Clark could only shrug without ever, not once, confronting any of them. Clark, a useful Bilderberg dummy, had complied to the letter with his obligations.

According to a 2003 investigative report on *www.globalresearch.ca*, Clark had developed "close personal ties with KLA Chief of Staff Commander Brigadier Agim Ceku and KLA Leader Hashim Thaci," who directly collaborated with NATO during the 1999 Kosovo campaign.[27] According to Agence France Presse on October 13, 1999, Thaci also had the distinction of being recognized by the Hague ICTY Tribunal "for alleged war crimes committed against ethnic Serbs in Croatia between 1993 and 1995."[28] There is a famous photograph of the handsome, 34-year-old KLA leader Hashim Thaci kissing US Secretary of State and CFR member Madeleine Albright, with her loyal stooge General Wesley Clark looking on: a picture that is indeed worth more than 10,000 words.

According to an article by Alex Todorovic and Charles A. Radin in the *Boston Globe* on August 2, 1999, "Terrorists with ties to Osama bin Laden running around with AK-47s and anti-tank weapons is bad enough. Worse, Hashim Thaci's boys aren't just killers and kleptomaniacs, but mafiosos who are neck deep in the drug trade." During the war, the *Washington Times*, an organ with close military ties to the Pentagon, quoted an unnamed US drug enforcement official commenting on the KLA: "They were drug dealers in 1998 and now, because of politics, they're freedom fighters."

In 1999, Bill Clinton's administration got a boost from Senator Joe Lieberman, an unofficial representative of the Israeli government in America and soon to be Democrat Al Gore's Vice-Presidential running mate in 2000, who stated authoritatively that "fighting for the KLA is fighting for human rights and American values." Was he misinformed, or might that have been a "Freudian" slip of the tongue?

Shortly after the US presidential election, Ralf Mutschke of Interpol's Criminal Intelligence Division testified to the US House Judicial Committee on the relationship between the KLA and Osama bin Laden: "The US State Department listed the KLA as a terrorist organization, indicating that it was financing its operations with money from the international heroin trade and loans from Islamic countries and individuals, among them allegedly Osama bin Laden. Another link to bin Laden is the fact that the brother of a leader in an Egyptian Jihad organization and also a military commander of Osama bin Laden's, was leading an elite KLA unit during the Kosovo conflict."[29]

Why would the KLA be attracted to Osama bin Laden and vice versa, in a fight that apparently pitted Serb nationalists against a US-backed terrorist organization, the KLA? According to military affairs analyst Ben Works, director of the Strategic Research Institute of the United States (SIRIUS), "The KLA is not rigidly ideological. The Maoist ideology is an important element, but the selling point for recruits is the group's militant Albanian nationalism.... Its chief appeal is to the ethnic Albanian Muslim population, and so its nationalism is couched in Islamic terms."

So, you have an international terrorist (Osama bin Laden) trained and funded by the CIA, an international terrorist organization (the KLA, excuse me, the Kosovo Protection Corps) trained and funded by the British, American and German Secret Services and Special Forces, and an American establishment (Clinton, Gore, Clark, Albright, Holbrooke, Lieberman – all Bilderberg and CFR members, who represent the interests of the New World Order) fighting to re-establish "democracy" and bring justice to a long suffering and oppressed people.

Truth, when unravelled, in many instances is indeed stranger than fiction.

Reason for War – KLA, Albania and the Drug Trade

What was largely hidden from public view was the fact that the KLA raised part of their funds from the sale of narcotics. Albania and Kosovo lay at the heart of the "Balkan Route" that links the "Golden Crescent" of Afghanistan and Pakistan to the drug markets of Europe. This route is worth an estimated $400 billion a year and handles 80 percent of heroin destined for Europe.

Frank Ciluffo of the Globalized Organized Crime Program, US House Judiciary Committee, December 13, 2000.

The KLA, an internationally recognized terrorist group is funded, in large measure, by Albanian organized crime – particularly heroin trafficking, and is also associated with a major drug smuggling ring that runs from Turkey into Europe via the Balkans.

Recall that Michael Levine, a highly decorated former undercover, counter-narcotics agent for the Drug Enforcement Administration (DEA), and an author of the exposés *Deep Cover* and *The Big White Lie*, stated that "Interpol, Europol, and nearly every European intelligence and counter-narcotics agency has files open on drug syndicates that lead right to the KLA, and right to Albanian gangs in this country [the US]."

What Michael Levine almost certainly did not know is that the KLA-Albanian drug trade is controlled from "top down," by the same group that tried to orchestrate the break-up of Canada and started the wars in Afghanistan and in Kosovo. To understand NATO, and consequently Bilderberger, involvement in Kosovo, we must understand the principles of drug trade.

It is likely that the actual amount of profit generated annually by the drug trade is among the world's most closely guarded secrets. However, a high-ranking expert on money laundering within the US government agency charged with monitoring global cash flows once told me, "The round off figure is somewhere around $700 billion in tax free cash flow per year." In fact, drug money became "an essential part of the world banking and financial system because it provides the liquid cash necessary to make the 'minimum monthly payments' on huge stock and derivative and investment bubbles in the US and Britain," explained Michael C. Ruppert, former LAPD narcotics officer, in his best-selling book, *Crossing the Rubicon.*

The Spoils of Empire

Corporations trading on Wall Street all have stock values that are based upon annual net revenues. Known as "price to earnings," this multiplier effect in shareholder equity may be as much as a factor of thirty. Thus, for major firms, say like Chase Manhattan Bank, General Electric or Brown Brothers Harriman to have an additional $10 million in revenues from the drug trade, the net increase in the firm's equity could be as much as $300,000,000. These large firms and others have held ownership positions in America's three main news networks, with thousands of affiliate stations around the country). Why don't these networks provide accurate reporting on the drug trade and the CIA's involvement therein? Might they be integral to the enterprise?

Another thing often overlooked in the lucrative illegal drug trade is the fantastic amount of money corporations can earn from borrowing illegal money from drug dealers, and drug-dealing nations, at a lower interest rate and laundering it into astronomical benefits. When 100 billion dollars of useless illegal money is loaned at five percent to a giant corporation, the money, in turn becomes legal and liquid:

> The drug trade now has power because it is underwriting the investments of the largest corporations in the world. It underwrites politicians. It has hooked the gringos on Wall Street whose own children sometimes die from its drugs. Wall Street cannot afford to let the drug barons fall. Congress cannot afford to let the drug barons fall. Presidents and their campaign finances cannot afford to let the drug barons fall. Why? Because our top down economy, controlled by one per cent, cannot take the risk of letting competition (business or political) have the edge of using drug money. And for every million dollars of increased sales or increased revenues from a buyout, the stock equity of the one percent who control Wall Street, increases twenty to thirty times.[30]

Thus, the obstacle to a more direct, profitable and efficient route from Afghanistan and Pakistan through Turkey into Europe "was a cohesive Yugoslavian/Serbian government controlling the Balkans," continued Ruppert in *Crossing the Rubicon*. With the destruction of Kosovo and Serbia and the installation of the KLA as a regional power, the Clinton administration opened a direct line from Afghanistan to Western Europe.

Christian de Brie and Jean de Maillard, in an exposé article titled, "Crime, The World's Biggest Free Enterprise," for *Le Monde Diplomatique's* April 2000 issue, described a tangible "operating system" of international drug capital flow, estimating the total annual drug trade at $500 billion:

> By allowing capital to flow unchecked from one end of the world to the other, globalization and abandon of sovereignty have together fostered the explosive growth of an outlaw financial market. It is a coherent system closely linked to the expansion of modern capitalism and based on an association of three partners: governments, transnational corporations and Mafias. Business is business: financial crime is first and foremost a market, thriving and structured, ruled by supply-and-demand. Big business complicity and political *laisser faire* is the only way that large-scale organized crime can launder and recycle the fabulous proceeds of its activities. And the transnationals need the support of governments and the neutrality of regulatory authorities in order to consolidate their positions, increase their profits, withstand and crush the competition, pull off the "deal of the century" and finance their illicit operations. Politicians are directly involved and their ability to intervene depends on the backing and the funding that keep them in power. This collusion of interests is an essential part of the world economy, the oil that keeps the wheels of capitalism turning.

After the 1996 Bilderberg meeting in King City, Toronto, Canada, through the information provided to us by our very, very deep sources within the Bilderberg Group, we warned that "to ensure the conflict's deadly and rapid spread, discussions are already underway concerning the posting of a small and hapless force of NATO troops on the border between the Yugoslav Federation and Albania, ostensibly to prevent Albanian gun- and drug-running into Kosovo. This will hardly impede the steady flow of weapons coming through that rugged terrain, but it will succeed in protecting the drug shipments being used by the KLA to raise the necessary funds for a continuous armed struggle and hostilities against the Serbs, necessary conditions for a full-scale war in the Balkans."

We can draw a stunning parallel between today's Kosovo and another distant land that occupied the minds of the then-world rulers – the British crown. Every English child is raised in awe of the immortal name Khyber Pass. Hundreds of thousands of pages have been written about the British army's adventures in this no-man's land, battling the natives and local tribesmen to protect a meaningless chunk of land, which no one in his right mind would want to die for ... *unless*, there was a more sinister reason for sending young officers to their death in distant lands.

Why was the British Army stationed in the Khyber Pass? For the vile opium trade, the so-called "spoils of Empire," frivolously talked about in the educated, elegant and well-washed upper-circles of English society, of course. What Rudyard Kipling neglected to tell you is that the tall tales of valor in the Khyber Pass covered a vast trade in opium. Just as NATO troops were stationed on the border between the Yugoslav Federation and Albania protecting the drug shipments, so was the British Army stationed in the Khyber Pass to protect caravans carrying raw opium from being robbed by the tribesmen.

Did Clinton, (Bilderberg, CFR member) the US President who had CIA intelligence at hand, know what was happening? Did Secretary of State Albright (Bilderberg, CFR member) know the KLA boys were drug-running assassins? Was Richard Holbrooke (Bilderberg, CFR member), the "father" of the Dayton Peace Plan, not informed of the comings and goings of the drug-running terrorist assassins associated with Hashim Thaci? Did NATO's Secretary General at the time, the "pride of Spain" Javier Solana (Bilderberg member) not know what was going on?

Did the British Crown know why soldiers were stationed in one of the most hostile regions of the world? After all, the costs to the Exchequer were prohibitive. The lucrative opium trade was practically the only thing of value in the region at that time. It stretches credulity to think that the highest levels of Her Majesty's Government, if not Her Majesty herself, were ignorant of why the Redcoats were being sacrificed. Unfortunately, humankind has not changed one iota, and what drove them to kill then still keeps millions dying in distant lands for the benefit of a small, privileged group of world rulers.

Another Reason for War – The Mineral Wealth of Kosovo's Trepca

Kosovo, loosely translated as "land of blackbirds," (*Kos* is a Serbian word for "blackbird") was often portrayed in the media as an isolated and poor mountainous region. It had been a cradle of the Serbian civilization ever since King Stefan Nemanja threw out the Byzantines from Kosovo in 1180 and established control over the territories of neighboring Serb tribes. All in all, Serb tribes have lived in Kosovo for over 1,000 years. Ancient Christian monasteries dotting the map of Kosovo keep records of their history. In fact, up until 1945, the Serbs constituted a majority of Kosovo's population; that is before the purges and repressions under Communist rule decimated Christian Serb inhabitants. In 1929, Serbs constituted a bit less than two-thirds of the population, ethnic Albanians, about one-third, and others just over five percent. In 1961, the percentage of "others" was the same, but the ethnic Albanians accounted for two-thirds and the Serbs for twenty-seven percent.

Trepca, situated in northern Kosovo, is a conglomerate of not only its three key industries: the Stari Trg9 mine, the Zvecan smelter and the Mitrovicë, an industrial complex, but also of 41 other mines and factories. Collectively they are capable of producing up to £3 million worth of vital industrial minerals per day. The *New York Times* called them the "Kosovo War's glittering prize."[31] The Stari Trg mine has been yielding precious metals for over two millennia, having been worked initially by the Greeks, then by the Romans, etc.

The only article on the Kosovo Trepca Industrial complex to appear in the mainstream press was a 1999 piece by Balkan correspondent Chris Hedges. It was surprisingly frank: "This huge complex of mines, refining, power and transportation in Kosovo may well be the largest uncontested piece of wealth not yet in the hands of the big capitalists of the US or Europe. The industry, natural resources and transportation of all the former Soviet republics, the socialist countries of Eastern Europe, and the secessionist republics of Yugoslavia are now being rapidly privatized. No one within the region has the wealth or connections to finance capital to buy controlling shares of these vast state-owned industries. The major Western corporations are gobbling these industries up."[32]

Could this "uncontested piece of wealth not yet in the hands of the big capitalists of the US or Europe" be reason enough to invent a war? As Trepca's Director Novak Bjelic emphatically stated, "The war in Kosovo is about the mines, nothing else. This is Serbia's Kuwait – the heart of Kosovo." One observer compared the conventional mainstream description of Kosovo to describing Kuwait and the oil-rich Gulf states as "barren deserts."[33]

To get control of the mines, the Bilderbergers introduced the International Crisis Group (ICG), a high level Brussels-based think tank supported by financier and regular Bilderberg attendee, George Soros. The ICG crew consisted of all the regular New World Order globalists dedicated to dismantling independent nations for the benefit of the global elite. Zbigniew Brzezinski was one. So was General Wesley Clark, once the NATO supreme allied commander for Europe, and neoconservatives Richard Perle and Paul Wolfowitz, as well as former congressman Stephen Solarz, who was once described as "the Israel lobby's chief legislative tactician on Capitol Hill." Perle, Wolfowitz and Solarz became famous for their 1998 letter to President Clinton calling for a "comprehensive political and military strategy for bringing down Saddam and his regime." Ironically, this was the same regime they had helped put together.

The outward reason for the International Crisis Group's existence was "to provide policy guidance to governments involved in the NATO-led reshaping of the Balkans." The hidden reasons were far less humanitarian. On November 26, 1999, the ICG issued a secret paper called "Trepca: Making Sense of the Labyrinth." It advised "the United Nations Mission in Kosovo (UNMIK) to take over the Trepca mining complex from the Serbs as quickly as possible" – not for the purposes of returning it to the Kosovars, to whom, according to the ICG, the mines belonged, but rather for passing the valuable assets into the waiting hands of Bilderbergers, including Soros.

The ICG report also detailed the timing of the theft. Conscious of political repercussions of Trepca's explosiveness, the ICG urged UNMIK to hurry up with the game plan for taking over the valuable mining complex "before Serbian elections so that a new government more to the West's liking cannot be accused of losing Trepca." They intended to put the blame at the feet of Miloševic for "losing" this property, vital to Yugoslavia, so he would be denied re-election by an outraged populace.

The under-handedness and greed of these people flew in the face of the description on their website, www.crisisgroup.org: "The International Crisis Group is now generally recognised as the world's leading independent, non-partisan, source of analysis and advice to governments, and intergovernmental bodies like the United Nations, European Union and World Bank, *on the prevention and resolution of deadly conflict*" [my emphasis]. With friends like these, who needs enemies?

The Serbs, however, had sensed the trap thus laid for them and had confined themselves to short, repressive police actions against the Kosovo Albanian population, none of which had been sufficient in duration, extent or intensity to provide the pretext necessary for the Bilderberger elite to rally Western European and American public support for a full-fledged military engagement against the Serbs. So, their methodical preparation, kidnappings and the Bilderberg-friendly Hague Tribunal – funded in part by billionaire financier George Soros, who had a long history of underwriting programs to destabilize countries whose markets were closed, or partly closed, to Western investment.[34] Financing and arming of the newly-revealed Kosovo Liberation Army provided the Bilderbergers with no dividends at all ... and the clock was running out on their schedule. They needed this war, and they needed it soon.

The justification for intervening, or to use ICG's terminology the "game-plan of measures," was given as, of all things, Zvecan environmental hazards, that is dangerous atmospheric lead pollution! The ICG advised UNMIK to instruct a "Zvecan environmental assessment team" to report on the status of the equipment, and determine the measures to be taken."

UNMIK was further advised to issue a statement wherein "the mines would remain closed until repairs could be made to reduce emissions." Furthermore, according to the ICG secret report, "Stari Trg, one of the richest mines in Europe, must be potentially profitable again and should be a priority for donors interested in setting Kosovo on its feet." In other words, "You donate money, which we will use to channel into our Bilderberg-controlled corporations that shall reap handsome profits from the rebuilding process, all supervised by the World Bank and the International Monetary Fund, and we will have taken over the crown jewels of Yugoslavia for a song and a dance."

The last morsel of the Kosovo Trepca Industrial complex still in the hands of the Yugoslav government, the Zvecan smelter, was seized by NATO forces on August 14, 2000. The ICG instructed UNMIK, headed by France's former Minister of Health and the Founder of Doctors without Borders (*Médecins sans frontières*), Bernard Kouchner, to "take over management of Trepca itself," even though the true ownership of the mines was, at the time, a hotly contested issue worth billion of dollars to the eventual winner. Kouchner, "whose mandate was to channel humanitarian aid under UN auspices, worked closely with NATO officials including Wesley Clark in providing support to Kosovo's terrorist paramilitary army.[35] Kouchner is also a member of the Bilderberg Group.

A License to Steal

How was it possible to plunder virtually all of Kosovo? On June 10, 1999, Dr. Bernard Kouchner, pursuant to authority given to him by the UN Security Council as Special Representative of the Secretary General, issued the following edict: "UNMIK shall administer movable or immovable property, including monies, bank accounts, and other property of, or registered in the name of the Federal Republic of Yugoslavia or the Republic of Serbia or any of its organs, which is in the territory of Kosovo."[36]

Think about that. And remember that the power to "administrate" implies the power to redistribute.

Financier George Soros invested heavily in Kosovo, spending perhaps $100 million to help oust President Miloševic. The George Soros Foundation for an Open Society opened a branch office in Pristina. It established the Kosovo Foundation for an Open Society (KFOS) as part of the Soros network of "non-profit foundations" in Eastern Europe and the former Soviet Union. On November 16, 1999, the World Bank issued a press release that confirmed that, together with the World Bank's Post Conflict Trust Fund, the KOSF provided "targeted support" for "the development of local governments to allow them to serve their communities in a transparent, fair, and accountable manner."[37] But, as Michel Chossudovsky observed wryly, "Since most of these local governments are in the hands of the KLA, which has extensive links to organized crime, this program is unlikely to meet its declared objective."[38]

Neil Clark left little in doubt with the title of his article on Soros' activities for the *New Statesman* of June 2, 2003: "The billionaire trader has become Eastern Europe's uncrowned king and the prophet of an 'open society.' But open to what?"

Karen Talbot, in her review of Neil Clark's article for *www.globalresearch.ca,* quoted him in this excerpt: "Soros' way is to use a few billion dollars, some NGOs and a 'nod and wink from the US State department' to bring down foreign governments that are 'bad for business' to seize a nation's assets, and even get thanked for your benevolence."[39]

The Russian paper *Nezavisimaya Gazeta* reported in its issue for August 9, 2005, that former Georgian President Eduard Shevardnadze had personally warned Uzbek President Islam Karimov about spying activities of George Soros's Open Society Institute in Uzbekistan, Georgia, Ukraine, Kyrgyzstan, Kazakhstan, Abkhazia, Adjaria, South Ossetia, Turkmenistan, and Tajikistan. Shevardnadze had been ousted in a coup by a neocon ally of the Bush administration in November 1993.

Soros' well-known animus for US President George W. Bush may seem puzzling given their similar New-World-Order objectives. Neil Clark speculated in the *New Statesman* that Soros was angry, "not at Bush's aims – of expanding Pax Americana and making the world safe for global capitalists like himself – but with the crass and blundering way Bush is going about it. By making US ambitions so clear, the Bush gang has committed the cardinal sin of giving the game away. For years, Soros and his NGOs have gone about their work extending the boundaries of the 'free world' so skillfully that hardly anyone noticed. Now a Texan redneck and a gang of overzealous neocons have blown it."

Meanwhile, an incarcerated Slobodan Miloševic had resigned the Yugoslav presidency shortly after the disputed election of September 2000. He was arrested on March 31, 2001 by Yugoslav federal authorities on a variety of charges relating to corruption and abuse of power. When their investigation failed to reveal hard evidence, the Serbian prime minister shipped him to The Hague to stand trial for war crimes, where he languished for years. "Yet the organizations that are normally so vociferous in their indignation about human rights violations have been remarkably silent," observed George Szamuely for the *New York Press*. "Fraudulent NGOs that are really agencies of Western governments, like the George Soros-financed Human Rights Watch, have been positively gleeful at the treatment meted out to Slobodan Miloševic. Amnesty International anguishes about the plight of al-Qaeda prisoners at Guantanamo, yet stays silent about this abuse of a political prisoner."[40]

Miloševic's Timely Death

Slobodan Miloševic died on the same day that his arch-enemy, Agim Ceku, former commander of the KLA was elected Prime Minister of Kosovo. Miloševic death certainly came as a relief to the Hague Tribunal who, for the preceding four years, had been trying unsuccessfully to convict a man who stood his ground before the entire world.

Miloševic was found dead in his prison cell on March 11, 2006, apparently the victim of a heart attack, less than three days after writing a letter addressed to the Russian Foreign Ministry, asking them to intercede to win him permission from his jailers, the Balkan War Crimes Tribunal, to go to Russia for medical care. Miloševic's death was the sixth such incident of an accused Serb in custody of the Hague Tribunal.

In a press conference on March 13, 2006, Russian Foreign Minister Sergei Lavrov stated that, in his letter, Miloševic expressed concern that some of the treatment methods applied to him by doctors of the International Tribunal for the Former Yugoslavia were having a disastrous effect on his health.

In January 2006, Tribunal officials had refused Miloševic's request to go to Russia for treatment, even though the Russian government offered complete guarantees that the former Serb leader would duly return to The Hague after completing his treatment.

Lev Bokeriya, head of the Bakulev Cardiovascular Surgery Center, told Russia's Itar-Tass news agency, "Miloševic belonged to the category of patients with a light coronary condition. He could have been easily cured. If Miloševic had been taken to any specialized Russian hospital, he would have been subjected to coronographic examination, two stents would have been made, and he would have lived for many years to come." Dr. Bokeriya, who headed the delegation of four Russian physicians to the Hague autopsy, stated on record that the evident cause of death was "the narrowing of the main blood vessel, which brought about a heart attack."

Clearly, Miloševic's death remains suspicious. According to my sources within the Belarusian KGB working for Stepan Sukhorenko, whose account of the events has been categorically confirmed by sources in the Russian Foreign Ministry and by senior US counterintelligence operatives overseeing the Miloševic trial, Miloševic's "timely" death was an outright assassination. The former Serb leader was becoming a major embarrassment to the US-led effort to bring former war criminals to trial, and the call had gone out to get rid of him.

Had Miloševic been in Russia and out of reach of an assassin's bullet, or in this case, venom, he may have become a rallying point for a new Serbia, whose citizens are more than disenchanted with the friendly embrace of the Bilderberg-led alliance. Russia's traditional role as "Protector of the Slavs" may have been reasserted, with who knows what repercussions.

The official, publicly pronounced autopsy was a compete whitewash. A KGB officer, who shall remain anonymous and who at one time worked with Alexander Shelepin of the KGB's International Department, made the following comment to an acquaintance of mine shortly after the official announcement became public knowledge: "Disinformation is not just lying. It is expected to serve as a subtle means of inducing another government to do what one wants it to do, or to frighten or bluff a foreign government into inaction or making concessions. However, two can play this game."

There seems to be no lack of potential suspects. The KGB, along with the Bulgarian and Romanian Secret Service, are reckoned to be among the most skilled poisoners in the world. However, they are not alone. The CIA and the British Chemical, Microbiological and Bacteriological Research Division at Porton Down are constantly engaged in refining killer devices. Today, there are apparently more than 400 substances that can kill without leaving a trace. If you know the autopsy will be rigged, you may even be able to leave a trace.

One such useful medication, and the one that is suspected to have killed Miloševic, is good old-fashioned digitalis. This drug will show up only if a proper autopsy is conducted. Digitalis can only be taken in carefully measured doses. An overdose will bring on a heart attack, and it is impossible to distinguish this death from a heart attack due to natural causes. Even people who have never experienced a heart condition will die immediately if digitalis is "improperly" administered.

Whatever the truth may be, there can be no doubt that the death of Slobodan Miloševic has left the former Yugoslavia even riper for plunder.

Notes

1. John Pilger, "John Pilger reminds us of Kosovo," *New Statesman*, December 13, 2004.

2. Neil Clark, "The Quisling of Belgrade," *Guardian* (UK) March 14, 2003.

3. Sara Flounders, "The Serbian Cash Register: A Real Eye Opener," *Workers World*, July 30, 1998.

4. According to NSA sources, in 1998, the US, which is the major supplier of arms to both Greece and Turkey, was just about to offer Turkey a $43 million deal for 30 Harpoon surface-to-surface missiles even as it offered the Greeks 248 Hellfire anti-tank missiles worth $24 million.

5. Bob Djurdjevic, *Truth in Media Global Watch Bulletin*, March 6, 1998

6. Michel Chossudovsky, "Kosovo 'freedom fighters' financed by organized crime," cyberjournal.org, April 7, 1997.

7. Bob Djurdjevic, "New World Order's Inquisition in Bosnia," *Truth in Media Global Watch Bulletin*, July 1, 1998

8. As a side note, a friend of mine, a disenchanted CIA officer, happened to be in Bosnia in July 1995, near Srebrenica, with Dr. Radovan Karadzic and other Serb leaders. He has sworn to me that he saw no massacres for which Gen. Ratko Mladic and Dr. Karadzic were later indicted. What he relayed, however, was very unnerving and worrisome. According to his eyewitness account, he saw "dozens of buses laid on by Gen. Mladic, which took the Srebrenica Muslim civilians to safety in Tuzla (a Muslim-controlled town in Bosnia)." To avoid another travesty of justice, he offered Judge Goldstone of The Hague's court on two separate occasions to testify in the defense of these men. He was flatly refused an opportunity. (Translation: The pre-arranged and pre-determined end result could only be complicated when an unannounced witness takes front stage.)

9. *CIA Inspector General Report of Investigation: Allegations of Connections between CIA and the Contras in Cocaine Trafficking to the United States. Volume II: The Contra Story*; Report 96-0143-IG.

10. In the early part of 1986, Celerino "Cele" Castillo III, a DEA officer, received a telex/cable from DEA Costa Rica, with an order to investigate hangers 4 and 5 at Ilopango. DEA Costa Rica had received reliable intelligence that the Contras

(supported and financed by the US Government) were flying cocaine into the hangars. Both hangers were owned and operated by the CIA and the National Security Agency. Operators of those two hangars were Lt. Col. Oliver North and the CIA contract agent, Felix Rodriguez, a.k.a. "Max Gomez."

11. John Laughland, "The technique of a Coup d'État," Centre for Research on Globalisation, February 15, 2004, http://www.globalresearch.ca/articles/LAU402A.html.

12. An initial investigation about the CIA/Contras/drugs was written by Gary Webb for the *San Jose Mercury News*. Several years later, he committed suicide due to relentless pressure from the CIA. His investigation ignited a firestorm of controversy and made one stunning allegation: The Contras' drug-smuggling operation bore major responsibility for a public-health epidemic in America. "The cocaine that flooded in helped spark a crack explosion in urban America ..." The report said two Nicaraguans, Danilo Blandon and Norwin Meneses, sold tons of cocaine to Los Angeles drug dealer, Ricky Ross. The articles said Blandon and Meneses funneled millions of dollars in profits to CIA-backed rebels fighting the leftist Sandinista government in Nicaragua.

The *New York Times*, *Los Angeles Times* and *Washington Post* ran lengthy pieces hell-bent on proving Gary Webb wrong, rather than attempting to follow up on his stories. "In doing so, the mainstream press shirked its larger duty; thus it bears the larger burden," reported Eric Umansky for *Mother Jones* magazine on August 25, 1998. We can draw a parallel to another Bilderberg unit, Grupo Prisa of Spain, whose Juan Luis Cebrian is a full-time member of the Bilderberger inner circle and whose flagship periodical, *El País*, knowingly hid the date of the Iraq invasion from 40 million Spaniards for one year before it took place.

13. George Szamuely, "The Yugoslavian Fairy Tale," *Foreign Policy In Focus*, May 28, 2004; http://www.fpif.org/fpiftxt/1127.

14. Ibid.

15. As a historical reference, the Serbs were the victims of history's greatest acts of ethnic cleansing, such as the 200,000 or so Serbs who were ethnically cleansed from the Krajina region of Croatia in the US-backed "Operation Storm" in 1995, or the 100,000 Serbs who were ethnically cleansed from Kosovo by the KLA at the end of the NATO bombing. Needless to say, the Hague Tribunal, the mechanism of "justice" for the up-coming New World Order, has done nothing to bring the authors of the atrocity to justice.

16. "More Bogus 'Justifications' for NATO War," May 12, 1999, http://rrojasdatabank.info/agfrank/nato_kosovo/msg00113.html.

17. Peter Schwarz, "Operation Horseshoe – Propaganda and Reality: How NATO Propaganda Misled the Public," World Socialist Web Site, July 29, 1999.

18. *Sunday Times* (UK), April 2, 2000; "Press Reports on False Claims of Genocide in Kosovo"; http://www.btinternet.com/-nlpWESSEX/Documents/Kosovofalsehoods.htm.

19. Bo Pellnas, *Dagens Nyhete*, February 8, 2004.

20. Michael Parenti, "The Demonization of Slobodan Miloševic," *Michael Parenti Political Archive*, December 2003, http://www.michaelparenti.org/Milosevic.html.

21. John Pilger, op. cit.

21. John Pilger, "How Silent Are the 'Humanitarian' Invaders of Kosovo?" *New Statesman*, December 9, 2004; http://www.lewrockwell.com/pilger/pilger20.html.

23. Michel Chossudovsky, "Kosovo freedom fighters financed by organized crime" World Socialist Web Site, April 10, 1999, http://www.wsws.org/articles/1999/apr1999/kla-a10.shtml.

24. Anthony Wayne, "The Hidden Origins of the KLA," Lawgiver.org, April 11, 1999.

25. How powerful is the Albanian Mafia? In 1985, the Albanian Mafia was able to intimidate the then-New York US attorney Rudy Giulliani, who, according to a *Wall Street Journal* story dated September 9 of that year, "was receiving special personal protection after prosecuting a heroin case in New York City connected to a ring of powerful Albanian traffickers."

26. Chris Stephen, "Bin Laden Opens European Terror Base in Albania," *Sunday Times* (UK), November 29, 1998.

27. Michel Chossudovsky, "Regime Rotation in America : Wesley Clark, Osama bin Laden and the 2004 Presidential Elections," Centre for Research on Globalisation, October 22, 2003, http://www.globalresearch.ca/articles/CHO310B.html.

28. AFP, October 13, 1999.

29. US Congress, Testimony of Ralf Mutschke, Criminal Espionaje Division, Interpol, Comgressional Judicial Committee, December 13, 2000.

30. Michael C. Ruppert, "Don't Blink!" *From the Wilderness*, June 29, 1999, http://www.fromthewilderness.com/free/economy/dontblink.html.

31. "Kosovo War Glittering Prize," *New York Times*, July 8, 1998.

32. Chris Hedges, *New York Times*, July 8, 1998.

33. Sara Flounders, op. cit.

34. The technique Soros uses to take over everything is not terribly original. Once a government is ousted, and a Western-friendly regime is installed, Soros swoops in to buy up state assets at fire-sale prices. For example, the massive Trepca mining complex in Kosovo, worth an estimated $5 billion. The Trepca complex not only includes copper and large reserves of zinc but also cadmium, gold, and silver. It has several smelting plants, 17 metal treatment sites, a power plant and Yugoslavia's largest battery plant. Northern Kosovo also has estimated reserves of 17 billion tons of coal and lignite.

35. Michel Chossudovsky, "Regime Rotation," op. cit.

36. UN Interim Administration in Kosovo (UNMIK), Regulation 1999/1, Section 6, State Property.

37. "World Bank Launches First Kosovo Project," World Bank and Kosovo Foundation for Open Society, November 16, 1999, Press Release No. 2000/097/ECA.68.

38. Michel Chossudovsky, "Dismantling Former Yugoslavia, Recolonizing Bosnisa-Herzegovina," http://www.globalresearch.ca/index.php?context=va&aid=370.

39. Karen Talbot, "George Soros: Prophet of an 'Open Society,'" Centre for Research on Globalisation, July 4, 2003, http://www.globalresearch.ca/articles/TAL307A.html.

40. George Szamuely, "'Western Civilization' at the Hague," *New York Press*, http://www.nypress.com/15/10/taki/2.cfm.

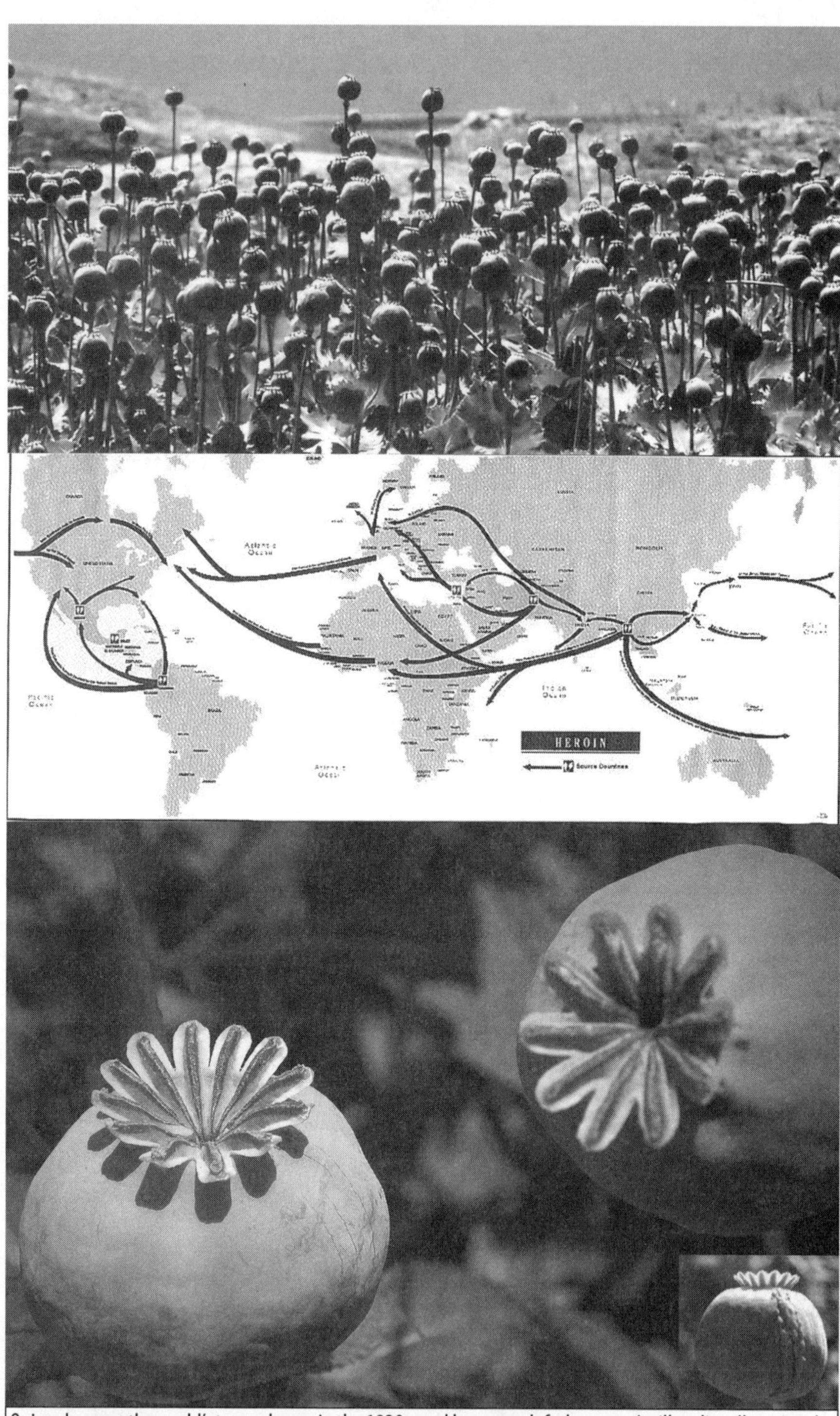

Opium became the world's top cash crop in the 1830s, and has never left that spot. Its illegality allows it to be sold for 8-10 times more than it would be worth otherwise.

Chapter Four

THE UNDERBELLY OF BUSINESS-AS-USUAL

[Professor Alfred] McCoy suggested there was a "natural affinity" between criminals and spies because of their interest in the "clandestine arts." Criminals gave spies a covert network for political assassinations, smuggling, and intimidation while the criminals gained protection for their rackets from these powerful allies, enabling them to openly flaunt the laws.

— John Jiggens, *The Sydney Connection*

THE SECRET WORLD

As noted, the war in Kosovo was intimately linked with the drug trade, especially the trade in heroin. Roger Boyes and Eske Wright writing for the *Times* of London, in an article entitled "Drugs Money Linked to the Kosovo Rebels" published on March 24, 1999, stated that "Albania – which plays a key role in channeling money to the Kosovans – is at the hub of Europe's drug trade." In 2004, somewhere between 400 and 500 metric tons of heroin were consumed world-wide. According to the US DEA and Department of Justice Intelligence reports, about 80% of heroin entering Europe does so through Kosovo. Another intelligence report, which was prepared by Germany's Federal Criminal Agency, concluded, "Ethnic Albanians are now the most prominent group in the distribution of heroin in Western consumer countries."

It took *Jane's Intelligence Review*, the undisputed premier intelligence magazine in the world, almost three additional years (In a January 3, 1999 editorial titled, "Unhealthy Climate in Kosovo as Guerrillas Gear Up for a Summer Confrontation") to come to the same conclusion that we first reported after the 1996 Bilderberg meeting: "Western intelligence agencies believe the UCK [the acronym for the KLA in Albanian] has been re-arming with the aid of money from drug-smuggling through Albania, along with 'donations' from the Albanian diaspora in Western Europe and North America.... Albania has become the crime capital of Europe. The most powerful groups in the country are organized criminals who use Albania to grow, process, and store a large percentage of the illegal drugs destined for Western Europe.... Albania's criminal gangs are actively supporting the war in Kosovo. Many of them have family links to Albanian groups in Kosovo and support them with arms and other supplies, either out of family solidarity or solely for profit. These links mean the UCK fighters have a secure base area and reasonably good lines of communication to the outside world. Serb troops have tried to seal the border but with little success."[1]

If the KLA were "allowed" to sell drugs and to profit from the sales, it is reasonable to infer that the entire operation was *approved from the top down*; that is, by the Bilderbergers themselves (through the usual set of intermediaries such as the US Government, the British, German and the US secret service agencies, the UN bureaucracy, pertinent NGOs, European Commissions and NATO, all of which they control). Going back at least to the 1950s and the surrogate wars between East and West in Southeast Asia, involvement of government "spooks" in the drug trade has become notorious, though of course adamantly denied by the governments themselves.

In 1997 Michael Ruppert submitted a lengthy written statement with exhibits to the Select Intelligence Committees of both houses of Congress. It was not placed in the Congressional record, and he was not allowed to testify. It began as follows:

> Mr. Chairman:
>
> On November 15, 1996, I stood at a town hall meeting at Locke High School in Los Angeles and said to Director of Central Intelligence John Deutch, "I am a former Los Angeles Police narcotics detective. I worked South Central Los Angeles and I can tell you, Director Deutch, emphatically and without equivocation, that the Agency has dealt drugs in this country for a long time." I then referred Director Deutch to three specific Agency operations known as Amadeus, Pegasus and Watchtower.
>
> Most Americans have been lead to believe that the purpose of these hearings is to ascertain whether or not there is any evidence that the Central Intelligence Agency dealt drugs during the Iran-

> Contra era. If these hearings were about evidence, then the most patriotic duty I could perform would be to quote Jack Blum who served as chief investigator for the Kerry Subcommittee on narcotics and terrorism ten years ago. He testified before this committee last year and said, "We don't have to investigate. We already know." We could save a lot of taxpayer money by just rereading the records of the Kerry hearings. There is more evidence in there than any court in the world would ever need to hand down indictments.
>
> At best, I could just quote you one entry from Oliver North's diary dated July 5, 1985, which said that $14 million to buy weapons for the Contras, "came from drugs." I wouldn't need to mention the two hundred and fifty other such entries in his diary which refer to narcotics. Or I could quote Dennis Dayle, a senior DEA supervisory agent, who said, "In my thirty year history in DEA, the major targets of my investigations almost invariably turned out to be working for the CIA."
>
> But these hearings are not about evidence. They are about corruption and cover-up. The CIA did not just deal drugs during the Iran-Contra era; it has done so for the full fifty years of its history. Today I will give you evidence which will show that the CIA, and many figures who became known during Iran-Contra such as Richard Secord, Ted Shackley, Tom Clines, Felix Rodriguez and George Herbert Walker Bush, who was DCI [Director of Central Intelligence] when I first became exposed to Agency drug dealing, have been selling drugs to Americans since the Vietnam era. I have been very careful to make sure that what I tell you today is admissible evidence in criminal proceedings.

The use of the drug trade to secure economic advantage goes back to the British East India Company and its first smuggling of opium from India into China in the late 1600s. It did that for 300 years. Why fiddle with something that brought untold billions to the ruling elites? Drugs also became the principal source of income for the wealthiest banking families associated with the Bilderberg Group, which in a variety of ways is a direct descendant of the East India Companies, both Dutch and British.

By the 20th century, the drug trade was illegal. Now, before the money generated could be used for legitimate business, it needed to be hidden, and then to be laundered. Seven hundred billion dollars a year is too much money to hide in a sock. A lot of experience and expertise is needed to move such funds stealthily. Funds transferred electronically, often in confusing arrays, move so quickly that they become traceable only by those controlling the computers and software.

According to the International Monetary Fund's 2001 report, "The production and laundering of drug money is central because it establishes channels for the flow of other criminal profits." The British Foreign Office reported that "money laundering processes $1.5 trillion or 2-5% of global GDP," a figure that exceeded the gross domestic products of all but the world's five largest economies.

A report of the US Senate Republican Policy Committee from March 1999 put the war in context: "The reported link between drug activities and arms purchases for anti-Serb Albanian forces in Kosovo predates the formation of the KLA, and indeed, may be seen as a key resource that allowed the KLA to establish itself as a force in the first place."[2]

An article published in the *San Francisco Chronicle* in 1994 described a broader context: "Narcotics smuggling has become a prime source of financing for civil wars already under way – or rapidly brewing – in southern Europe and the eastern Mediterranean. The report, by the Paris-based *Observatoire Geopolitique des Drogues*, or Geopolitical Observatory of Drugs, identifies belligerents in the former Yugoslav republics and Turkey as key players in the region's accelerating drugs-for-arms traffic. Albanian nationalists in ethnically tense Macedonia and the Serbian province of Kosovo have built a vast heroin network, leading from the opium fields of Pakistan to black-market arms dealers in Switzerland, which transports up to $2 billion worth of the drugs annually into the heart of Europe, the report says. More than 500 Kosovo or Macedonian Albanians are in prison in Switzerland for drug- or arms-trafficking offences, and more than 1,000 others are under indictment. The arms are reportedly stockpiled in Kosovo for eventual use against the Serbian government in Belgrade, which imposed a violent crackdown on Albanian autonomy advocates in the province five years ago."[3]

Making Smack

Opium is grown in several different regions of the world: South America; the Golden Triangle of Laos, Burma, and Thailand; and Afghanistan, Pakistan, and central Asia in an area called the Golden Crescent. The vast majority of opium poppies are grown in a narrow, 4,500-mile stretch of mountains extending across southern Asia from Turkey through Pakistan and Laos. The opium poppy prefers a warm, dry climate at altitudes above 4,000 feet, and is grown by Thai and Burmese hill tribesmen. When it is about to reach maturity, the plant produces a flower. A week or so later the petals fall off, leaving a pod from which the raw opium gum is harvested by slicing with a razor or thin-bladed knife. The raw opium resin leaks through the cut and is rolled into balls, set out to dry for several days, then wrapped in a banana leaf or plastic. "The tribesmen are paid in 1 kilo gold bars, known as 4/10ths, which are minted by Credit Suisse. These small bars are used *only* to pay the tribesman, the normal-weight gold bars are traded on the Hong Kong market by the big buyers of raw opium or partly processed heroin. The same methods are used to pay hill tribesman in India, the Baluchis, who have been in this business since the days of the Moguls. The 'Dope Season,' as it is called, sees a flood of gold traded on the Hong Kong market."[4]

Raw opium is often transported through Turkey and the Levant to Corsica, for further processing in Europe, though the Mideast areas are increasingly themselves home to lucrative heroin refineries. The Mediterranean coastline from Marseilles to Monte Carlo abounds in them, and many have speculated that the ruling Grimaldi family of Monaco have been involved.

Monaco, where gold-trade tycoon Edmond Safra suffered his strange demise, is the world's most important opium-processing center. Some believe the only way this could be accomplished is if the Grimaldi family is actively supporting and protecting it. They theorize Princess Grace was murdered because Prince Rainier was skimming off the top. He refused to heed several warnings, believing himself to be one of the untouchables. He, or rather she, was promptly dealt with by the New World Order. To this day, the Rover car that Princess Grace drove the night of the accident has remained in the custody of French police.

According to Anthony M. DeStefano's front-page article in the *Wall Street Journal* for September 9, 1985, Albanian Mafiosi residing in the United States, were responsible for moving "25% to 40% of the US heroin supply," in the pipeline reaching back through Belgrade to Istanbul.

Once opium gum is transported to a refinery, it is converted into morphine, and then heroin, by chemical processes. The main chemical used is acetic anhydride, along with sodium carbonate, activated charcoal, chloroform, ethyl alcohol, ether and acetone.

Tough-talking public campaigns launched by central governments in Europe and North America that promise "to take the fight to the drug pushers" are pure nonsense. If governments really wanted to eradicate the vile drug trade, they could make laws that would oblige manufacturers of acetic anhydride, the most essential chemical in the manufacture of heroin, to keep meticulous records showing who buys the chemical, for what purpose and where it is going. But such unilateral action on the part of any maverick government would greatly displease the oligarchic families of Europe and the United States Establishment because, as I have indicated, these people are turning hundreds of billions of dollars each year from the drug trade.

Needless to say, the leader who truly dared to really "take the fight to the drug pusher" would become a target for immediate assassination. Why have the names of the "real culprits," the noble families of Britain and America's top people, remained hidden for so long? Because banks have profited from illegal trading through myriad middle men and ghost companies, leaving their criminal participation well hidden from public scrutiny.

So, the "Albanian issue" – money laundering, drugs, gun running, terrorism – centered in Kosovo was a powder keg waiting to explode. And the Bilderbergers were willing to let that the whole region explode with it.

Once again, the context may be broadened: "Taking sides in this conflict with the Kosovars, and the KLA, and therefore Albania, pleased Turkey, Iran, the Muslim world, and even gave Turkey a chance to fight alongside the Europeans, while side-lining their arch-rival Greece somewhat. That pulls Turkey into Europe, rather than leaving it drifting eastward, which favors Western oil interests in the Caucuses and Central Asia, also by offsetting Russia. This seems to be the crucial point as far as Kosovo is concerned, as well as the longer term geostrategic intent."[5]

Now, you can be sure of several things. One, the Bilderbergers are not physically responsible for moving drugs and laundering drug profits. This task is charged to the CIA.[6] CIA actions usually are accompanied by the explosion of heroin in the region. (Iraq, never known to have had a drug problem, today is one of the hotbeds for Afghan heroin, according to the International Narcotics Control Board, an influential drug agency, quoted by the BBC News on May 12, 2005.) Furthermore, the cash flow and the profits from the smuggling will now be directed through US banks and stocks back into Wall Street coffers. "That is what the CIA does," was the succinct conclusion of former narcotics cop Michael C. Ruppert in an article titled "The Lies about Taliban Heroin."[7]

The final objective of diverting huge quantities of cash is twofold: to weaken Russia and to de-stabilize the entire region from the Balkans, passing through Turkey, Eastern Europe and Russia. Destabilization in the region may well Balkanize Russia. Additionally, the increasing US military and Bilderberger-controlled economic presence will consolidate their New World Order's control over the last remaining oil and gas reserves in the region. This will result in a further drain on Russian influence in the region and greatly increase global instability. Global instability offers the Bilderbergers a golden opportunity to sell guns and butter to both sides.

Dope, Inc.

Do the drug barons in outlaw states benefit from the nefarious business of narcotics? The world's largest and most powerful corporations and some of our leading citizens have been benefitting from the business long before the Pablo Escobars and the Manuel Noriegas came along. What do international terrorism, the world's financial markets, empire building and capitalism have in common? Their utter dependence on drug profits for their very existence.

The war on drugs is a sham. It has always been a sham and for as long as there is money to be made, it will continue being a sham, while our political classes pay lip service to the dangers of substance abuse with easy to remember slogans such as "just say no." There are historical reasons for this.

In his well-researched book, *Opium, Empire and the Global Political Economy*, Professor Carl Trocki argues that an organized drug trade can historically be linked with the development of capitalism. One of the key derivatives of drug trade, according to the author, was the creation of a rudimentary form of monopoly. "The existence of monopoly resulted in the concentration of vast pools of wealth in the hands of a relatively small group of people. Wealth led to accumulation of power. The accumulation of wealth and power created by a succession of historic drug trades have been among the primary foundations of global capitalism and a modern nation-state itself."[8]

As a result of this process, Trocki postulates, a number of fundamental transformations in human life have taken place, dramatically altering both social and economic terrain in the process. "Two major effects are the creation of mass markets and the generation of unprecedented cash flow. Over time, drugs came to be an essential element in the finances of every criminal structure from the sixteenth century European empires up until the present. All depended and depend on enormous profits that come from monopolizing the world's most lucrative business."[9]

In fact, the entire rise of the West, from 1500 to 1900, depended on a series of drug trades. In the process, Europeans became the most prominent producers and purveyors. Opium was the first addictive drug imposed by force on a population. It was sold in order to make a profit. Those profits went first to the institutions which promoted and protected the trade. "Foremost among them were the British and Dutch East Indian Companies, its successor the British colonial government of India, and the community of Dutch and later British merchants who laid the economic foundation of the imperial economy. Opium trade was not simply an aberration of the British Empire. It was a crucial component of it. The British Empire, the opium trade and the rise of capitalism all occurred together."[10] When the opium trade was ended early in the twentieth century, the British Empire began to collapse.

Opium was crucial to the expansion of the British Empire during the late eighteenth and early nineteenth century, and without it, there may not have been an empire at all. "Profits from drugs paid the bills and provided a regular source of high-quality revenue that made it possible for the Indian empire to continue. In addition to being a major source of revenue, it was also the largest single item of export for the first seventy years of the nineteenth century."[11] The drug business also created a concentration of capitalists and a global capitalist structure, without which none of what followed would have been possible. These developments took place first in London, and later in Boston and New York.

The great merchant houses, the banks and the insurance companies that had their roots in the Asian trade, all had their start in opium. Mountains of money were created by the opium trade, as well as a mass market, and fed the accumulating institutions in banking, insurance and transportation.

In the end, capitalism has always been intimately tied to drug economies because it needed ready and off-the-books cash to finance exploitation and "defense," and all under the banner of "free trade." "The coalescence of banking, shipping and insurance around the opium trade was one of the most remarkable features of the era. Not only did they service the opium traffic, but they became the foundation of a commercial infrastructure that ultimately supported a wide range of trade."[12]

Over time, drugs became a commodity that created a need for other commodities. From the fifteenth century until well into the twentieth, land, labor, fiscal relations, and even the state itself were underwriten by the opium trade. This was built on a commodity that previously for millennia had been almost exclusively medicinal, and which the British knew was a poison and addictive. Perhaps today when we refer to "narco-states" such as Colombia and Afghanistan, we should remember that the first true "narco-state" was run and operated from London.

How does it all fit into the bigger picture?

Let's start by saying that drug money is an inherent part of the American and world economy. In following global cash flows, it's staggering to find out the amount of profit generated annually by the drug trade is somewhere around $700 billion. This figure includes heroin, opium, morphine, marijuana, cocaine, crack cocaine and hallucinogens. As noted, drug money is now "an essential part of the world banking and financial system because it provides the liquid cash necessary to make the 'minimum monthly payments' on huge stock and derivative and investment bubbles in the US and Britain."[13]

How can $700 billion in illegal profits crisscrossing international borders get through the international banking system and past the eyes and ears of law enforcement authorities? The answer takes us behind the corporate board rooms and precious metal exchanges to the inner sanctum of some of the world's wealthiest people: eight to ten generations of men who built their empires around the opium trade. This may seem more like fiction than fact. But fact it is. Historical fact, etched in stone for posterity, recorded in the available documents at the National Library of Singapore, the National Archives of India, the University of London, the British Library, the Jardine Matheson Archives at the University of Cambridge Library, and the British East Indian Company Archives, as well as government records in Hong Kong and Macao.

It began in the seventeenth century and involved an entire succession of empire builders. This included Robert Clive and Warren Hastings in the eighteenth century, and Alexander Matheson, David

Sasoon, the Perkins and the Codmans, the Russells and the Appletons, the Boylestons and the Cunninghams amongst a plethora of others in the nineteenth. Opium represented money, fantastic gobs of money, money beyond anyone's wildest dreams. Nobody needed to remind the empire builders that money made the world go around. They were empire builders in the corridors of power, and filthy drug runners in the annals of history.

What may be a surprise is how shamelessly and publicly the drug runners operated. "Opium trading for the British was not a sordid backstreet business, but an honored instrument of state policy, the mainstay of the Exchequer, and the subject of praise from Britain's leading supporters of 'free trade,' Adam Smith, Thomas Malthus, James and John Stuart Mill. The poisoning of the world, did not lead to prison but to peerages and government appointments to important positions."[14] It still does, to this day.

We are talking about the most highly organized, top-down political machinery in the world, enjoying the logistical support of a $700-billion-per-annum international cartel, and the protection of every political entity Britain and the US have created through these vast invisible earnings. This protection applies not merely to growing and distribution, but to providing political, intelligence, and ideological support as well. Like international terrorism, wherever it is retreating, it just can't quite be stamped out: indicating that some of the biggest names in royal circles and the international oligarchy/plutocracy are the puppeteers, even if managed through cut outs and intermediaries concealing the identities of those pulling the strings.

Nor should we forget the gigantic supporting facilities of the world's official credit markets, the world's gold and diamond trade, and "hands-on" management of the retail distribution, or organized crime of the operation. They are all derivatives of Drugs Incorporated. One purpose of the drug trade is to create unseen liquid capital, and to make it available to those wishing to gain an unfair advantage in the marketplace. This cash must go through nominally legitimate channels, in such mind-boggling volumes that the nominally legitimate channels, bank and other financial institutions cannot possibly be unaware of the origin of the moneys. The fact that most of this money flow is seasonal, completed during the two months following the March poppy harvest, can only add to our stupor. Banks pleading ignorance – "We didn't know" – is simply not an option.

If 700 billion dollars a year in illegal drug money is moved and laundered through the American and world economy, that money, again, benefits financial markets and especially Wall Street. That's the reason for maintaining the illegal drug trade.

From The Wilderness Contributing Editor Catherine Austin Fitts, George H.W. Bush's Assistant Secretary of Housing, and a former managing director at Dillon Read with ample experience as a Wall Street investment banker, has been a crusader in the effort to expose the underbelly. She and her new investment firm were quickly targeted for investigation by both the Department of Justice and HUD. This experience is described in some detail in her 13-part Internet article "Narco-Dollars For Beginners: How The Money Works In The Illicit Drug Trade." The following excerpts are from that highly recommended piece, which looks at the problem from the bottom up as well as the top down:

> Every day there are two or three teenagers on the corner dealing drugs across from our home in Philadelphia. We figured that if they had a 50% deal with a supplier, did $300 a day of sales each, and worked 250 days a year that their supplier could run his net profits of approximately $100,000 through a local fast food restaurant that was owned by a publicly traded company.
>
> Assuming that company has a stock market value that is a multiple of 20-30 times its profits, a handful of illiterate teenagers could generate approximately $2-3 million in stock market value for a major corporation, not to mention a nice flow of deposits and business for the Philadelphia banks and insurance companies....
>
> So if I have a company that has a $100,000 of income and a stock trading at 20 times earnings, if I can find a way to run $100,000 of narcotics sales by a few teenagers in West Philadelphia through my financial statements, I can get my stock market value to go up from $2 million to $4 million. I can double my "pop." That is a quick $2 million profit from putting a few teenagers to work ...
>
> The total stock market value generated in the Philadelphia area with $20-40 billion in narco retail sales would be about $80-160 billion. If you add all the things you could do with debt or and other ways to increase the multiples, and you could get that even higher, say $100-250 billion....
>
> The problems this presents to people trying to run an honest business are numerous. The problems it creates for our work ethic and culture are numerous too. It increasingly puts the low performance people in charge, and everyone starts to behave like and follow them....

> John Gotti, Jr, not a reliable source, when asked by a reporter whether or not the New York Gotti family was dealing in narcotics, said, "No, who can compete with the government?"
>
> The CIA, also not a reliable source, backs up Mr. Gotti's position. According to the CIA's own Inspector General, the government has been facilitating drug trafficking. Indeed, according to the CIA and DOJ (Dept. of Justice), the CIA and DOJ created a memorandum of understanding that permitted the CIA to help its allies and assets to traffic in drugs and not have to report it.

What does this mean in the world of high finance? If firms like Hong Kong and Shanghai Bank, Bank of Nova Scotia, Royal Bank of Scotland, Chase Manhattan Bank, Citibank, or General Electric were to have an additional $40 million in earnings from the drug trade, with a price-to-earnings multiplier of 20, the net increase in their company's equity would be $800 million.

If you still believe that there can not really be major, hands-on, institutional involvement in the drug trade, you will be surprised to hear that in late June 1999, numerous news services, including the Associated Press, reported that Richard A. Grasso, then Chairman of the New York Stock Exchange, flew down to Colombia for a jungle encounter with a spokesperson for Raul Reyes of the Revolutionary Armed Forces of Columbia (FARC). FARC is Colombia's major narco-terrorist outfit, with which the United States government is unofficially at war.

The purpose of the trip was "to bring a message of cooperation from US financial services" and to discuss foreign investment and the future role of US businesses in Colombia. What does Colombia have that the United States could possibly want? Money – drug money: over a trillion dollars in equity that has been building up in Colombia for over thirty years now. These are practically limitless resources that make Wall Street salivate at the thought of channeling them through its financial markets.

Of course it's not always easy. If an individual American goes to a bank and deposits $10,000 or more in cash, the bank is obligated by law to fill out a currency transaction report. Large corporations, however, can cash a check for 100 million dollars from any drug lord with no disclosure requirement whatsoever. However, before they can channel this money into actual year-end results, something needs to be done to legitimize it.

Unlike one hundred and fifty years ago, today, profits from the lucrative drug trade are illegal. That's another thing often overlooked by people trying to understand how the entire nefarious business of drugs works. Before that money can be used legally, it needs to hide, then be laundered. You can't hide seven hundred billion dollars in a mattress. "The money moves so quickly that, unless one were in control of the computer systems that handle it, or the software that manages it, it would be impossible to trace."[15] Ignorance, therefore, especially when the laundering transactions are gigantic ones, is not a tenable position.

Additionally, corporations can earn a fantastic amount of money from borrowing illegal money from drug dealers and drug dealing nations at a lower interest rate and laundering it into astronomical benefits. When 100 billion dollars of useless illegal money is loaned at five percent to a giant corporation, the money, in turn becomes legal and liquid.

Le Monde Diplomatique, the premier information source for international diplomats, in an in-depth investigative report, found US intelligence services, banks, and other multinational corporations at the top of a huge global network of organized crime and money laundering. It cited "cartels, insider dealing and speculation, fraudulent balance sheets, embezzlement of public funds, spying, blackmail, and betrayal, among a host of other seamy practices. But these cannot succeed without governments willing to keep restrictive regulations to a minimum, to abolish or override such rules as do exist, to paralyse inquiries . . . and to reduce or grant amnesty from any penalties."[17]

The Central Intelligence Agency is very much plugged into this system. The CIA has had its name linked to the drug trade for most of the Company's sixty-plus years of existence. Most key players in the Agency's history have held a special relationship with America's financial system.

> **Clark Clifford:** Wall Street lawyer and banker. Former secretary of defense for Lyndon B. Johnson. Indicted on criminal charges as Chairman of First American Bankshares, a bank secretly controlled by the corrupt CIA drug bank, BCCI, for earning $6 million in profits from bank stock that he bought with an unsecured loan from BCCI.
>
> **Richard Helms:** CIA Director. Indicted and prosecuted for lying to Congress in 1976. His lawyer was Clark Clifford.
>
> **Allen Dulles:** Dulles was America's top Office of Strategic Services [OSS, precursor to the CIA] spy in Switzerland, meeting frequently with Nazi leaders and looking after US [read Rock-

efeller] investments in Germany. Executive with Standard Oil, a Rockefeller corporation. Designer of the CIA. CIA director under Eisenhower. Profession: Partner in the most powerful Wall Street law firm of Sullivan and Cromwell, and the man responsible for flooding the United Status with LSD in the 1960s.

Bill Casey: Reagan's CIA director and OSS veteran. Served under Nixon as a chairman of the Securities and Exchange Commission. Profession: Wall Street lawyer and stock trader. One classified activity related to CIA drug dealing operations was codenamed *Amadeus*, a CIA umbrella, governing laundering of drug money through a host of banks worldwide. Admitted five months before dying from an inoperable brain tumour that the CIA has been involved in the drug trade. Left a signed notarized affidavit attesting to this fact with Richard Nixon signing on as a witness.[18]

From Vietnam to Cambodia, from Laos to Pakistan and Afghanistan, from Iran to the Contras and beyond, the Agency has been the progressive left's favorite whipping boy. However, it isn't only the CIA who are up to their eyeballs in drugs. In the aforementioned article, *Le Monde Diplomatique* explicitly stated that "the secret services of the world's most powerful state apparatus [i.e., the US] ... have moved into economic warfare," becoming "international financial crime's number-one partner."[19] The same charge can be levelled at the British Foreign Intelligence (MI6), the Israeli Mossad, French DGSE, Russian FSB, not to mention intelligence agencies from Morocco, Colombia, Honduras, El Salvador, Venezuela, Panama, Dominican Republic, the Philippines and beyond.

Popular fairy tales aside, the Vietnam War was about drugs. The French were pushed out, and the ensuing vacuum was immediately filled by the Agency, which took over the drug trade, its processing and distribution. From this stark perspective, little room is left to idealists' vision of the Vietnam War as a conflict pitting good versus evil, us versus them, Old Glory versus the Hammer and Sickle, Onward Christian Soldiers versus Godless Commies. No, it was something else. In the symbiotic relationship between economic and military power, money feeds the military, and military force maintains resources and markets. War and drugs: a match made in heaven.

Christian de Brie and Jean de Maillard, in another brilliant article for *Le Monde Diplomatique's* April 2000 issue titled, "Crime, The World's Biggest Free Enterprise," describe a tangible "operating system" of international drug capital flow: "By allowing capital to flow unchecked from one end of the world to the other, globalization and abandon of sovereignty have together fostered the explosive growth of an outlaw financial market. It is a coherent system closely linked to the expansion of modern capitalism and based on an association of three partners: governments, transnational corporations and Mafias. Business is business: financial crime is first and foremost a market, thriving and structured, ruled by supply and demand. Big business complicity and political *laisser faire* is the only way that large-scale organized crime can launder and recycle the fabulous proceeds of its activities. And the transnationals need the support of governments and the neutrality of regulatory authorities in order to consolidate their positions, increase their profits, withstand and crush the competition, pull off the 'deal of the century' and finance their illicit operations. Politicians are directly involved and their ability to intervene depends on the backing and the funding that keep them in power. This collusion of interests is an essential part of the world economy, the oil that keeps the wheels of capitalism turning."

In other words, drugs are big business, run, controlled and protected by very powerful people who work alongside leading banking institutions on both sides of the Atlantic, members of various governments and principal corporations whose stock is traded on the world's leading stock exchanges. One such institution, apparently, is the Hong Kong and Shanghai Corporation (BHSH). Out of the second Opium War (1858-60), the British merchant banks and trading companies established BHSH, "which to this day serves as the central clearinghouse for all Far Eastern financial transactions relating to the black market in opium and its heroin derivatives."[20]

Another suspect is Canada's Bank of Nova Scotia, now headquartered in Toronto. On the one hand, it serves as a major gold dealer and leader of the Toronto gold market, and on the other, it serves as banker for giant Canadian mining companies operating in the third world. According to knowledgeable US intelligence sources, the Bank of Nova Scotia may be a major dirty money operator in the Caribbean, running flight-capital against currency restrictions, a serious violation of local currency laws.

How do banks with their great air of respectability fit into the drug trade with all of its attendant filth? One way is by financing legitimate purchases of companies registered and licensed to do business as importers of chemicals. The Hong Kong and Shanghai Bank is right in the middle of such trade through a company called

Tejapaibul, which banks with BHSH. What does this company do? It imports into Hong Kong most of the chemicals needed to process raw opium into heroin by the diacetylation of morphine with acetic anhydride, the irreplaceable chemical agent in heroin processing. Acetic anhydride is also used in the conversion of cellulose into acetate, a component of photographic film, and in the production of aspirin. It should be surprising, then, that the largest markets for diverted acetic anhydride continue to be in Afghanistan. I know what you are thinking. Afghanis may simply be more susceptible to the common cold than anyone else on the planet.

Tough-talking public campaigns cynically launched with all the bells and whistles during national elections by governments in Europe and the United States promising "to take the fight to the drug lords" are pure nonsense. As noted, if governments, the European Parliament or the United States Congress for example, were serious about eradicating the vile drug trade, they would make laws requiring the meticulous tracking of acetic anhydride and other essential chemicals. Such unilateral and decisive action however, would greatly displease the empire builders.

Our Islamic Ally

We would be wise to understand Turkey's historically vital importance to America's and the West's geopolitical interests. In fact, Turkey's relationship to opium and to the US goes back to the beginning of the nineteenth century. In 1803, William Stewart, the first US Consul at Smyrna, in Turkey, filed a report on the trade in that port. He noted that, "Our trade with the East & West Indies and South America will always afford us the means of supplying Turkey with [opium] the principal articles of its consumption."[21] Stewart reported that Turkey was an important source of drugs and of opium. By the 1820s Americans were shipping hundreds of chests of Turkish opium to Southern Asia and China. Guess who was making the money?

A November 1996 report by the Paris-based *Observatoire Geopolitique des Drogues*, or Geopolitical Observatory of Drugs, first identified Turkey as a key player in the region's accelerating drugs-for-arms traffic. Heroin-dealing Albanian nationalists, both in the ethnically divided nation of Macedonia and the new mini-narco-state of Kosovo, had built a vast network, stretching via Turkey from the Golden Crescent to black-market arms dealers in Switzerland. According to this report, the amount of drugs originating from Afghanistan was worth nearly $40 billion in the final stage. That's 40 billion dollars of heroin on the street! That's more than Afghanistan's Gross Domestic Product ($35 billion). It would be safe to assume that primitive and barely literate Afghan warlords are not the brains behind the transportation, chemical processing, distribution and extremely sophisticated laundering of the proceeds through most of the world's financial markets.

According to the US State Department's most recent annual *International Narcotics Control Strategy Report*, "Turkey's position astride the main overland trade route between Asia and Europe makes it a significant transit point for narcotics." The country serves as the land-bridge for some 60 tons a year, three-quarters of world's heroin transported for use in Western Europe, a primary victim of the drug war, from its origin in Afghanistan.

The key component in Turkey's part in the global drug trade is its geography. Turkey, one of the closest American allies as well as one of the key members of the NATO alliance, occupies a unique place among the modern nation-states. It lies at the crossroads not only between Europe and Asia, but also between the former Soviet Union and the Middle East. It is also the only Middle-Eastern nation that has counted Israel as a close ally and collaborator.

The Balkan Route is divided into three sub-routes with Turkey always playing a key role: the *southern route*, which runs through Turkey, Greece, Albania and Italy; the *central route*, which runs through Turkey, Bulgaria, the Former Yugoslav Republics of (Macedonia, Serbia, Montenegro, Croatia, Slovenia, and Bosnia and Herzegovina), Italy or Austria; and the *northern route*, which runs from Turkey, Bulgaria and Romania to Austria, Hungary, the Czech Republic, Poland or Germany.

According to statistics available for 1998, Turkey's heroin trafficking brought in $37.5 billion.[22] This was equivalent to nearly a quarter of Turkey's Gross Domestic Product.

As one former FBI agent wrote, "Only criminal networks working in close cooperation with the police and the army could possibly organize trafficking on such a mind-boggling scale." Turkish government complicity became more clear as early as January 1997, when Tom Sackville, minister of state at the British Home Office publicly affirmed that "members of the Turkish government were involved in drug trafficking."[23]

Members of the government, yes. But the government itself is generally working hard to eradicate the drug trade. It hasn't been easy for them. Turkey has been stunned by the indictment of a criminal network, the Ergenekon, for planning a military coup against the government. On July 15, 2008 Istanbul Chief Prosecutor submitted the indictment against the Ergenekon to Turkey's high criminal court. The 2,455-page indictment named 86 suspects, 48 of whom are currently in custody, including retired – and possibly current – members of the armed forces, as well as academics, journalists, political activists, and organized crime figures.

Turkey has its work cut out. Back in the 19th century, the Chinese government tried, but failed, to prevent Britain from imposing opium on its population. Turkey is hoping its efforts will prove to be more successful. There is simply too much at stake for the oligarchs who run the world and who earn fabulous wealth from the nefarious drug trade to simply let an upstart Turkey get in the way.

Nonetheless, Turkey is playing a leading role in going after the multi-billion-dollar drug network responsible for trafficking heroin from Afghanistan. In the process, Turkey serves as a key flank against the empire-builders' new opium wars. According to knowledgeable military sources, the Kurdistan Workers Party, financially supported by the European oligarchy, has been linked to a massive conspiracy to overthrow the Erdogan government in Turkey. A nation-state like Turkey, the only constitutionally secular nation in the Islamic world, may prove a bulwark against both radical Islam and global rule by a financier oligarchy.

Moreover, recent breakthroughs in the global war on drugs, beginning with the stunning July 2, 2008 rescue of French-Colombian dual citizen and a former Colombian Presidential candidate, Ingrid Betancourt, and three American hostages, from FARC narcoterrorists in Colombia, suggest that the "invisible hand of the oligarchy may no longer be so invisible."[24] What happened was a very sophisticated operation, dubbed "Operation Checkmate," carried out by elements of the Colombian government in conjunction with the country's Special Forces and high-ranking military command, with intelligence support from France, including the institution of the Presidency, and institutional elements within the United States.

But Turkey occupies a unique position with respect to the designs of the oligarchs. Their purpose is to perpetuate the secret Sykes-Picot Treaty, which was drafted in 1916 by the soon-to-be "victors" of World

War I, France and the British Empire, in which they divided up the Ottoman Empire between them as the spoils of war, with Britain controlling Iraq, Jordan, and Palestine, and France ruling Syria and Lebanon. Their aim has been to prevent at all costs the economic development of a region that is at both the crossroads of Europe and Asia and of Eurasia and Africa. Their intent is to maintain it as trigger for global war by manipulating ethnic, religious, and tribal groups against one another, and against central governments, to create perpetual war. What they are after is a modern form of feudal anarchy.

Perpetual conflict destroys progress and severely limits the rights of the individual. Stability is bad for business, drug business that is. The drug trade thrives on weak central governments and strong sectarian leadership. Afghan warlords provide a good illustration of these vile synergies. As one of the leading drug-traffickers wrote to his superior almost two hundred years ago in reference to China, "As long as this country maintains its drug traffic, there is not the slightest possibility that it will ever become a military threat, since the habit saps the vitality of the nation."[25] Neither the means nor the intent have changed over the two-hundred-year period.

Drugs, however, are only one aspect of the aforementioned top-down system. Turkey also plays a key role in industrial and military espionage. It is common knowledge that the US government subsidizes $8 billion of Turkey's $10 billion in weapons purchases. What's more, "many Turkish companies establish bases of operations in the Muslim states of the former Soviet Union. These corporations, for being Turkish and allies of the US, have received millions of dollars in the form of the US government grants on behalf of the US Congress."[26]

One of the reasons for such a close collaboration between the two countries has involved a mutual interest in containing Soviet/Russian expansion, and this has provided the foundation of United States-Turkish relations over the past sixty years. Another reason for such generous financial help is because Turkey is a key ally of Israel. Yet, most of the corporations involved are fronts for organized crime, which include everything from money laundering to drug trafficking to arms smuggling. Still, the United States transfers its technology to a country that ranks high on global narcotics, terrorism and weapons of mass destruction-related activities, while at the same the US government is hard at work to cover up the terrorists' main financial source: drug trafficking and illegal arms sales.

There is no end in sight to the deceit, greed, corruption and double-crosses practised in the world of cut outs, special operations, phantom corporations, offshore secret accounts, unscrupulous corporate greed and centuries-long conspiracies. The essential feature of any great conspiracy, as someone once said, is not the dark plotting. Rather, superior motivation is what causes the leaders to conspire together. Money is not the essence of any long lasting conspiracy. Neither is the megalomaniacal desire for power. I believe that a smallish group of people sustaining a conspiracy over hundreds of years requires a powerful sort of ideological motive.

In the case of drug-funded oligarchs and their cohorts, beginning with the British East Indian Company, the ideological motive is the hatred of the ideal of sovereign nation-state republics, of individual liberties and the pursuit of happiness, and of technological progress. As we turn the next and the next and the next corner, we find ourselves enveloped in mind boggling corruption, impunity and disregard for international mores, decency and boundaries. "Peace" and "prosperity" have been sold to the highest and most morally corrupt bidder.

Notes

1. "Life in the Balkan Tinderbox Remains as Dangerous as Ever," *Jane's Intelligence Review*, March 1, 1999.

2. US Senate Republican Policy Committee, "The Kosovo Liberation Army: Does Clinton Policy Support Group with Terror, Drug Ties?" March 31, 1999; http://rpc.senate.gov/releases/1999/fr033199.htm.

3. Frank Viviano, "Separatists supporting themselves with traffic in narcotics, *San Francisco Chronicle*, June 10, 1994.

4. John Coleman, *Conspirators' Hierarchy: The Story of the Committee of 300* (America West Publishers, 1992).

5. Grattan Healy, "A Geostrategic view of the Kosovo Crisis," May 4, 1999, http://www.bilderberg.org/g/EUmil.htm.

6. One classified activity related to CIA drug-dealing operations was codenamed *Amadeus*, a CIA umbrella, governing laundering of drug money through a host of banks worldwide. Some bank records and account numbers connected to the Bahamas and the Jersey islands still remain. Michael C. Ruppert, former LAPD cop, in opening remarks to the US Senate Select Committee on Intelligence related to CIA drug trafficking and Contras operations stated, "We have since obtained tape-recorded statements from James Robert Strauss that *Amadeus* was none other than George Herbert Walker Bush. That tape is safely stored, awaiting an opportunity to be presented to the American people directly for their judgment by Albert V. Carone's daughter, Dee Ferdinand." Carone, was a

detective for the New York Police Department and a bagman for the Genovese crime family, protecting shipments of CIA drugs to the various Mafia families. He was also a US Army colonel and a CIA asset. He died in 1990 from chemical toxicity of unknown etiology. (Translation: He was poisoned.)

7. Michael C. Ruppert, "The Lies about Taliban Heroin," *From the Wilderness*, October 10, 2001, http://www.fromthewilderness.com/free/ww3/10_10_01_heroin.html.

8. Carl Trocki, *Opium, Empire and the Global Political Economy* (Routledge, 1999).

9. Ibid.

10. Ibid.

11. Ibid.

12. Ibid.

13. Michael Ruppert, *Crossing the Rubicon* (New Society Publishers, 2004).

14. U.S. Labor Party investigating team, *Dope, Inc., Britain's Opium War against the US*, (New Benjamin Franklin House, 1978).

15. Michael Ruppert, op. cit.

16. Ibid.

17. Christian de Brie, "Thick as Thieves," *Le Monde Diplomatique*, April 5, 2001.

18. Michael Ruppert, op. cit.

19. Christian de Brie, op. cit.

20. U.S. Labor Party Investigating Team, op. cit..

21. W. Stewart to SoS, 25 April, 1803.

22. Kendal Nezan, "Turkey's Pivotal Role In The International Drug Trade," *Le Monde Diplomatique*, http://mondediplo.com/1998/07/05turkey.

23.http://www.publications.parliament.uk/pa/ld199798/ldhansrd/v0970718/text/70718-08.htm.

24.Jeffrey Steinberg, "Combating Britain's New Opium War," *Executive Intelligence Review*, July 18, 2008.

25. As quoted in Jack Beeching, *The Chinese Opium Wars* (Harvest Books, 1975), p. 258.

26. Sibel Edmonds, "The highjacking of a nation," National Security Whistleblowers Coalition, November 29, 2006.

GAME is OVER

He's been finally caught. The world's biggest arms dealer's was arrested at a Bangkok hotel with seven others

By Visith Chuanpiputpong
DAILY XPRESS

Police arrested one of the world's most wanted arms dealers, Viktor Anatoljevitch Bout, at a downtown hotel in Bangkok yesterday

Acting on a request from the US Drug Enforcement Administration (DEA), Bangkok police nabbed the man in a Sofitel Silom Hotel restaurant.

Police also conducted a search of the eight men's rooms, but did not say if anything illegal was found or seized.

No criminal charges were laid against the men at press time yesterday. A press conference will be held at the Royal Thai Police compound at 3pm today.

CSD officers and DEA agents jointly questioned Bout in a closed session.

revolutionary guerrilla organisation in Colombia - to strike an arms deal.

Police also named a man - Andrew Smilian - who they said entered Thailand together with Bout, but did not say if he had a criminal record or whether he was one of the seven other men arrested.

Bout, 41, a former KGB major, is also known as "the Merchant

XTRA

THE MERCHANT OF DEATH

>> **Ex-KGB spy** and international gunrunner Viktor Bout was portrayed as Yuli Orlov in the 2005 Nicolas Cage film 'Lord of War'.

>> **Nicknamed the** Merchant of Death, Bout was the most powerful illegal-arms dealer the world has seen.

>> **After the collapse** of the Soviet Union, Bout cashed in on its stockpile of weapons, arming conflicts across the globe. Business was good and Bout made a killing

Victor Bout in custody. After watching his court travails up-close and personal, I can tell you that the US government is not alone in wanting to see Bout extradited. Many in the Russian government would also like to see Bout sent to the US. Does the US have some kind of leverage with them, or do they have their own reasons? News article is from Thailand's English-language March 7, 2008, *Nation's Daily Express,* the day after Victor Bout's arrest in Bangkok.

Chapter Five

Merchant of Death?

One way to delve into the innermost secrets of the Shadow Masters and the world's interlocked terrorist networks is to look at clandestine arms trafficking. According to the mainstream press, the most infamous gunrunner of them all is Victor Bout.

Corporate media defines Victor Bout as savvy, ambitious, modern-day, multinational entrepreneur. "He's good with numbers and knows how to seize opportunities when they arise. Bout has no known history of violence, and no political agenda. He loves his family. He's fed the poor. And through his hard work, he's become extraordinarily wealthy. Since the early 1990s, Bout's business acumen has earned him hundreds of millions of dollars."[1]

What, exactly, does he do? "Victor Bout is the poster boy for a new generation of post Cold War international arms dealers who play a critical role in areas where the weapons trade has been embargoed by the United Nations. The story spans several continents and involves a large network of shady individuals, front companies and government officials; corrupt African bureaucrats and thieving East European military officials."[2]

We are told that he, more than most, has succeeded in exploiting the anarchy of globalization, making possible massacres on a scale that has stunned the world. Much of his personal history we are led to believe is unknown; much may be a figment of his own fertile imagination. According to a *Men's Journal* article, "Viktor Bout has been so good at concealing his past that American intelligence agents who have tracked him for years joke that his birth was an immaculate conception."[3] On paper, at least, it appears that Bout is one of the most amoral men alive. His colorful story piqued my curiosity and shortly after 9/11, I decided to investigate. My investigation would eventually take me to the four corners of the world and span almost a decade. The last leg of my exhausting journey took me to Bangkok, to KlongPrem prison, and to face-to-face meetings and interviews with the so-called Merchant of Death, Victor Bout. What I found out will forever help separate that which is fact from what is hearsay and fiction.

Victor Anatoliyevich Bout was born in Russia on January 13, 1967, in Dushanbe, now the capital of Tajikistan, in the far reaches of Soviet territory. His mother was a bookkeeper and his father an auto mechanic. He has one older brother, Sergey, who looks very much like him, born in 1961. After graduating from secondary school, Bout applied to the Soviet Foreign Ministry's Moscow State Institute of International Relations. Unable to pass the entry exam, he was drafted into the Soviet Army. Upon completion of obligatory military service, he applied to the Moscow Military Institute of Foreign Languages, a four-year program that would have made him a Lieutenant upon graduation. However, instead of studying its full course, he was offered a shorter option – a year and a half of intense courses in Portuguese and a rank of Junior Lieutenant, followed by two years of obligatory service in Mozambique as a military interpreter.

But chance intervened with a sort of fumbling coherence, and the world and Victor Bout would never be the same again. I have learned that chance plays an important, if not predominant, part in human affairs. The fact that a man like Victor Anatoliyevich Bout should so much as go to Africa and to Mozambique, not to mention find himself in the position he currently finds himself in, locked up and in leg chains at the worst prison in all of Southeast Asia, is alone eerily intriguing. That in time he should ultimately owe his freedom to the very US government that has tried to put him in prison in the first place is breathtaking in its absurdity.

When Bout failed to catch on at Moscow State Institute of International Relations, chance reared its gangly head. There was a dearth of translators in Mozambique, so Bout was offered to do an accelerated, one-and-a-half year program, with an emphasis on one language – Portuguese, instead of a full four-year program in Moscow.

Upon completion of this program, Bout became a Lieutenant Junior Grade, after which he was posted as a military translator in

Mozambique on a two-year stint. At the end of this period, having shown his aptitude for languages and generally being considered a brilliant translator by his superiors, Bout was all set to finish his higher education, per the initial agreement with the government, by completing the remaining two and a half years of studies in Moscow. But the Soviet Union began its implosion, and Bout decided to forego the remaining years of his career. His life, and for that matter ours, was never the same again.

He speaks Russian, French, Spanish, Portuguese, English and Farsi. According to investigator Ruud Leeuw, his IQ is said to be more than 170, putting him in the top .0002% (one in five million) of the world's population. I got in touch with Mr. Leeuw through his website.

After identifying myself, I got straight to the point.

"170 IQ. That's pretty high. How do you know this? Did you measure it yourself, or do you have a psychological-evaluation report on Bout?"

"Well, I don't really know myself. That's what they say. My interest in Victor Bout is limited; I am a photographer ... Contrary to the impression to what my website may give you ... I stumbled upon him while trying to research the history of certain aircraft ... keep track of those same planes ... and things took off. Do you know what I mean?"

"Actually, Ruud, I don't know what you mean," I persisted. "You are building a profile of a man. Your name appears on several official reports. Thus, you are a credible source for many people. Who told you Bout has an IQ of 170?"

"I think it was Richard Chichakli."

"Bout's former associate?"

"Exactly."

"So, you spoke to Chichakli."

"Not personally, but I read it in a newspaper interview."

"If Chichakli said it, why don't you source it? I mean, why didn't you put it in quotes, attributing this information to him?"

"I have no interest in conspiracy theories in any way, nor am I particularly interested in illegal arms trade. It's just a personal web page," he replied apologetically, clearly uncomfortable.

"And Bout is just an arms dealer, according to many." I hung up without saying goodbye. I was once again in the land of the Shadow Masters.

Now I am a Russian by birth, but consider myself a citizen of the world, with respect for sovereignty, self-determination and self-reliance. My life experiences have given me a strong appreciation of what man's freedoms and liberties are worth. Exiled as a child with my family from the USSR – because of my father's political beliefs – then coming of age in the West, becoming a citizen of Canada, marrying a Spanish lady and living in Spain and Italy for years, has given me an appreciation of the freedoms and unlimited opportunities that many take for granted. I understand the value of a free press, and of an educated, civically involved population, to the health of any nation-state.

As I pulled back the curtain during my research, the implausibility of it all amazed me, snapping me out of the thralldom of the official story. For just as "legends" (cover stories/false IDs) are created for our own spooks, it seems that legends may also be conveniently created for our enemies'. Let's see, the good guys wear the white hats and the bad guys the black ones, right? Let's all hiss at the villain on cue ...

The *Guardian* of London, one of the UK's most prestigious newspapers, stated that Bout "holds at least five passports and uses as many as seven aliases. His aliases include Boutov, Butt, But, Budd, Bouta, all with Victor or Viktor as the first name. Two of his passports are issued in the names of Vadim Aminov and Victor Bulakin, according to inside sources in the British Foreign Service and the US State Department."[4] The insinuation is clear. The Merchant of Death, a most-sought-after international criminal, would certainly hide under false identities in order to avoid capture.

Stephan Talty writing for *Men's Journal* described the lead-up to Bout's 2008 arrest in Bangkok. "Snow drifted down from a malevolent black sky as a stocky, mustachioed man arrived at Moscow's airport on the evening of March 5.... He had chosen carefully among his five passports. The names on them varied, but they were all versions of his given one: Viktor Bout. He had spent years carefully blurring almost every trace of his past, but what is known is that he'd served in the Soviet military in the 1980s, working as a navigator, training commandos for its air force, and flying to Angola to act as a translator."[5]

According to his publisher, Stephan Talty "is a widely published journalist who has contributed to the *New York Times Magazine*,

GQ, Men's Journal, and many other publications. Through Random House, I got in touch with him.

"Stephan, in your article for *Men's Journal* you wrote ..." I repeated the snow-drifted arrival described above. "Were you there? Did you see it yourself?"

"No, of course I wasn't there."

"Did you get it from the DEA?"

"It is a lead-in. Do you know what a lead-in is? I am setting the scene," he clarified.

"I know what a lead-in is. Except that when the first sentence is a fabrication, I might suspect that the rest of the article is too. Do you know what I mean?"

"Whom do you work for again?" he asked, his voice more cautious, edgy.

I ignored him. "You also say that Bout had chosen carefully among his five passports." I paused. "Where did you get this from?"

"What?"

"That he had five passports?"

"I got it from the DEA and from the Internet," came the reply.

"You did? And how do you know it's true?"

"Are you a conspiracy theorist?"

"No, I am a *coincidence* theorist. So, how do you know he has five passports?"

Silence.

"All right. One more question. According to your article, in the 1980s, Bout worked as a navigator, training commandos for the Soviet air force."

Silence.

"Let's do the math, shall we? He was born in 1967. If we take the 1980s as 1987 or 1988, Bout would have been nineteen, twenty, at most. Are you suggesting that a twenty-year-old was training elite commandoes of the Soviet armed forces?"

"Look, it's just background. We know what he is."

"Who is *we*, Stephan? The government, the mainstream press, your family, beer-drinking America, or people who work at Random House?"

"Look, if you want to find out more about Bout, talk to the DEA."

"I will, count on it. I wanted to know what you knew about Bout *before* writing an article on him. It is obvious, you don't know much." There was a click. Widely published author Stephan Talty had nothing else to add.

So, what's the real story with Bout's apparent numerous aliases and endless passports and why are the *Guardian* of London, *New York Times*, CNN, BBC and numerous other publications so diligently trying to ram their version down our throats? In fact, as I found out, he only has one passport.

The rest of the mainstream story is setting the scene, background noise made to appeal to the uninitiated and the gullible. A number of the supposed aliases attributed to Bout are variant spellings of his surname when the Cyrillic alphabet of Russian is transliterated into the Roman letters of English and most European languages. According to tradition, the evangelist Cyril, later St. Cyril, devised an alphabet adapted from the Greek in order to bring the Gospels to the mostly pagan and illiterate Slavic tribes. In Russian, the name is Виктор Бут.

Two letters are derived from Greek beta. By chance, the one most resembling English "B" represents the non-Greek sound of "V," while the "B" sound is represented by the letter beginning Bout's surname. "K" is "K" and "T" is "T." "P" represents the English "R" sound. (You are likely to recall the ubiquitous "CCCP" [USSR] on tanks and athletes from the Soviet era.) So much for the consonants. With the knowledge that "O" is "O" and that "И" represents English "I," Bout's given name is discernible: Viktor, or the more familiar Victor, take your pick. Most sources seem to agree on this point.

His surname can be rendered as Bout, Butt or But, depending on the system employed. The spelling we see most often – Bout – results from the older, traditional system based upon French pronunciation. Beginning in 1996, the Russian Ministry of Foreign Affairs changed to an Anglicized system, which, in a typically chaotic post-Soviet manner, lacked a uniform methodology. Thus Виктор Бут became DEA-invented Victor Butt. However, supplying an ordinary English pronunciation under any of the spellings doesn't approximate the Russian name, which has a "U" sound more like "put" than "but."

The fact is that the alleged arms dealer has had three passports: an old Soviet one, his first Russian passport as "Bout" in accordance with the former French transliteration rules, and a more recent Russian passport as "But" according to the newer rules. I think Bout is resigned to hearing his name mispronounced in English: "bout" as rhyming with "out." But I find it remarkable that "Butt" has not become the standard, given the demonization of the man himself and the common meanings of that English word.

The other two names ascribed to him by the intelligence agencies, Western governments and the mainstream press are the names appearing on US extradition request documents in its unsealed indictment of Bout: Vadim Markovich Aminov and Viktor Bulakin. These are the names of real people who lived and worked in Sharjah, United Arab Emirates, at the same time Victor Bout was there. Aminov, the owner of a travel agency in Sharjah catering to Russians, for example, was overheard on a wiretap talking to Victor Bout.

Later on, the same voice was confused for Bout's voice, and Aminov's name was written into Bout's file as another one of his aliases. Aminov and Bout are two different people, the only similarity being that the two men spoke Russian and each wore a bushy moustache. Why was Aminov talking to Bout? Who knows? However, it is only reasonable for Aminov and Bout to have known each other, as most expatriates stay in touch with fellow countrymen in a foreign land, especially in a place as different as Sharjah is from Moscow.

In another interesting revelation, British military intelligence reported that Bout was stationed in Rome with the KGB between 1985 and 1989. I heard this information on CNN and, not too long ago, read it in Canada's flagship publication, the *Toronto Star*.

Now, let's see. Bout was born in 1967. In 1985, he would have been 17 years old. Is it reasonable to believe that a seventeen-year-old would be working for the KGB at its key European station? Hardly. Are we to assume that British military intelligence made a mistake, or, whatever its source, is this disinformation part of a farsighted policy initiative against Bout? And if not against Bout, then against whom and, most importantly, for what purpose?

What is known about Bout from mainstream press reports is that he is six feet tall, "stocky, and usually sporting a baseball cap and a bushy moustache." At least, that's how Interpol had described him in their Most Wanted files. In photographs taken during Peter Landesman's interview of him in Moscow in 2003, he is wearing an expensive olive-colored suit.

Douglas Farah is considered by many to be the foremost expert on Bout's illegal activities. He is co-author of a best-selling exposé on Bout, *Merchant of Death: Money, Guns, Planes, and the Man Who Makes War Possible*, which certainly limits any suspense regarding its protagonist. According to Farah, Bout had been an instructor of elite Soviet commandos while a senior lieutenant in the air force. There is no evidence that he ever rose above junior lieutenant, and as I've noted, twenty-year-olds did not train commandos of the Soviet military. Furthermore, the book is completely lacking in primary sources of information. There are no names provided. References are always made to "European, Pakistani, US investigators ... sources in the State Department ... contacts in the DEA ... government officials ..." Etcetera.

However, I decided to triple check. One can never be too careful. I sent Douglas Farah an email message on September 21, 2009.

> Doug, this is Daniel Estulin, again. I would like to clarify a point in your book. You say, "Until the collapse of the Soviet Union in 1991, Bout was an air force senior lieutenant training recruits for the GRU, the elite commandos of the Russian Air Force, on a military base in Vitebsk, Belarus."
>
> He was born in 1967. A copy of his latest passport is attached. If we do the math, he was barely out of his teens when he was purportedly training these commandoes. How do you explain this?

A few days later, I got a reply from Farah stating that the passport I sent him was "fake" and that Bout was "much older."

Once I got over the initial shock, I quickly sent him another query.

"Please forgive my ignorance. But, what makes you think the passport is a fake? The Russian government in Bangkok has vouched for it. Or are you suggesting they are in on the conspiracy? I am working on a deadest of deadlines for my book and would dearly love to hear back from you at your earliest convenience."

I never heard back from Douglas Farah, Victor Bout-expert.

Historically, Soviet military intelligence oversaw the flow of Russian military hardware and military services to friendly revolutionary movements around the globe, especially in Africa and Central America, in accordance with its foreign policy objectives. According to one western intelligence official, "Bout's military transport aviation regiment was disbanded in 1991, and essentially they went private." Alla Bout, Victor's wife, explained to me that when the two of them came back from Mozambique at the end of 1991, the Soviet Union had imploded. Bout's junior lieutenant salary barely allowed them enough money to buy an extra cup of coffee.

Overnight, thousands of elite pilots and their crews found themselves out of jobs. The Soviet system crumbled into oblivion before their very eyes. But, out of disaster arose opportunity. Dilapidated weapons, rusting spare parts, jeeps, tanks and clunky Soviet airplanes, which in most cases could be had for a price of a Mercedes 600, attracted an instant clientele of former Soviet republics, rebel leaders and guerrilla armies in far-flung nations. Tin-cup dictators with oversized egos and shining medals hiding behind tacky plastic shades were only too happy and eager to acquire Soviet surplus.

And, according to mainstream press accounts, Victor Bout, who for years was just an unknown face on the edge of wartime photos, was only too pleased to serve them. As the *Los Angeles Times* reported, "During the chaotic period after the collapse of the Soviet Union, Bout was among the Russian entrepreneurs who seized opportunities to make a fortune."[7]

He allegedly started running guns to Afghanistan in the mid 1990s, and then discovered Africa. André Velrooy, a Norwegian journalist who investigated Bout's activities for the International Consortium of Investigative Journalists' special issue of November 20, 2002, stated, "He had access to what the African warlords wanted. The end of the Cold War resulted in a massive amount of surplus weaponry being dumped at often very low prices onto the private market."

According to the UN investigators at that time, "Bout traffics exclusively in weapons bought in the former Soviet bloc, mainly Russia, Bulgaria and Romania," using his expertise and connections to expand weapons trade in Angola. "Local carriers had the established routes and well-formed contacts in the area, but lacked capacity. Mr. Bout, through his numerous contacts in the ex-Soviet air force, was immediately able to provide the required capacity and, in return, took advantage of the established routes and contacts in the southern African region."[8]

According to the British secret service, US State Department documents and Belgian police reports, often cited in the mainstream press, what made Bout's network extraordinary was its ability to deliver both small-caliber arms as well as sophisticated weapon systems virtually anywhere in the world. His associates, ranging from former US military personnel and Russian officials to African heads of state and organized crime figures, gave him a lengthy list of buyers and sellers with whom to do business.

United Nations Resolutions 1521 and 1532, as well as the Angola Report of December 21, 2000 and Interpol intelligence documents, show Bout closely linked with several African dictators and rebel leaders, including the late Angolan rebel leader Jonas Savimbi, former Liberian president and accused mass murderer Charles Taylor, former Zairian president Mobutu Sese Seko, Libyan President-for-life Moammar Gadhafi, Jean-Pierre Bemba, leader of the Congo Liberation Front, as well as the former leaders of Congo-Brazzaville and numerous others. It is said that it is next to impossible to pigeonhole his political affiliations, however. That's because he is completely apolitical. I disagree.

He is a Russian and he wears that distinction as a badge of honor. I can't really explain it. You have to be a Russian to understand.

What is undeniable, as Bout himself admits, is that in the 1990s Bout supplied arms to Ahmed Shah Massoud, leader of the Northern Alliance in Afghanistan. Bout described Massoud "as a great friend with whom he had spent countless hours talking about the everyday." He sent an aircraft to rescue Mobutu Sese Seko, the ailing and corrupt ruler of Zaire, even though he had supplied the rebels who were closing in on Mobutu's last stronghold.[9] Bout bought a Gulfstream One used by a Swedish expedition to fly to the North Pole.

It is said that Bout cleverly combined legal and not-so-legal airline activities, often carrying legitimate wares such as fresh-cut flowers and frozen crayfish from South Africa to Europe. According to Bout himself, he flew over 3,500 missions in Africa in one year. His most profitable enterprise was flying gladiolus purchased for $2 in Johannesburg and resold for $100 in Dubai. He transported United Nations peacekeepers from Pakistan to East Timor, and formed part of the logistics effort in Operation Restore Hope, the US-led military famine relief effort in Somalia in 1993. In 1994, his aircraft flew 2,500 French troops into Rwanda. In 1997, he transported ostriches from Johannesburg in South Africa to Saudi Arabia. Later that same year, he moved 50 elephants from South Africa to Angola in specially outfitted cargo planes. In 2000, acting as a broker, he rented out his crew that transported hostage negotiators to the Philippines, where European tourists were being held by the Islamist terrorist group Abu Sayyaf. And then, in typical Bout turnaround style, we are led to believe, Abu Sayyaf became one of his clients shortly thereafter.

I must admit that the notion of an amoral man selling death for profit is extremely unpalatable. The idea of living off someone else's misery, fueling conflicts the world over, makes me cringe. The first draft of this chapter was a scathing indictment of Bout, and of a world system that simply didn't care enough about the weak and the oppressed.

All I needed was one piece of evidence to put my mind at rest. One original source, one smoking gun, one voice recording, one fingerprint, one anything. Again, providence intervened in the most inexcusable way. I couldn't find anything plausible or tangible on Bout. "Where is the proof, damn it, Merchant of Death? Why can't I find it?"

Proof, irrefutable proof of Bout's guilt was nowhere to be found. Impossible! The man is guilty! He is a Merchant of Death. He sells arms. He profits from war. CNN, NBC, ABC, CBS, BBC, *Time* magazine, the *Wall Street Journal*, the *New York Times*, and the *Washington Post* all say so! Initially, I was dumbfounded, then I got angry at my inadequacy, then mystified at what I was seeing, then puzzled, and finally extremely alarmed.

I had piles and piles of documents on top of piles and at the bottom of piles, filled with Bout's alleged crimes. While he apparently crisscrossed the globe igniting war and hatred, I toiled in reference libraries from Toronto to Florence and Madrid, searching in vain for primary sources of Bout's crimes. Government bureaucrats quoted intelligence sources, intelligence sources quoted government bureaucrats, UN officials quote intelligence sources, who in turn quoted UN reports. Where was the evidence? I was going out of my mind. "Intelligence reports show that Bout has ... delivery was made to ... people working for the Merchant of Death ... the first breakthrough came when one of his closest collaborators told the investigators that Bout ..."

Except that we have never found out what one of his closest collaborators told the government investigators, we have never seen his planes, nor him, anywhere near conflict zones, and intelligence agencies have never released their findings to the public. Even with the plethora of available technology, until his arrest in Bangkok in March 2008, few had ever heard his voice or seen him on video.

Where was the proof? I needed to finish my book; my publisher was threatening to cut one finger off for every extra week I took to hand in the manuscript. Once, he called me at 3:00 a.m., telling me I had one week to hand in the (I can't repeat what he said to me) manuscript. Still, I was looking for proof. I changed my phone number, moved houses, changed continents and finally moved to Thailand. I was determined to get the despicable Merchant of Death.

Lying in bed at night, I imagined Bout's fat cheeks laughing at me. "You will not find anything on me! I have it all hidden. I am an invisible man! They can't get me!"

I will get you. I promise you, Bout. Even, if I have to follow you to the ends of the Earth, I will find proof of your transgressions. We will put you in prison. You will not be a menace to society. I searched every sewer and every back alley, called back every favor owed me by people in high and not so high places. "Get me the evidence! Get me something, anything!" I screamed at one informant. But, the harder I searched, the more I was beginning to realize that I might never find one credible shred of evidence tying Victor Bout to even one of the crimes he was being accused of committing. As a last resort, I went back to the mainstream press and re-read everything I had compiled on him. There was a chance that in my haste, I had missed key evidence, overlooked key information. It had to be there!

According to an article in London's *Guardian* newspaper, Bout "conducts his illicit deals from the privacy of a walled compound in the Gulf state of Sharjah,"[10] the third largest emirate in the United Arab Emirates. "Walled compound." Is it walled because Bout is a bad man and he needs to protect himself from people trying to catch him? Is that why he "managed his legal activities and clandestine deals" from a walled compound? What were they insinuating? Is it another case of numerous passports and aliases, of a bad man trying to avoid detection? A real life Jason Bourne?

In my efforts to get Bout, I travelled to Sharjah. Does the editor of the *Guardian* newspaper realize that every compound in Sharjah, and for that matter in the entire United Arab Emirates, is walled? It's simply part of their culture and aesthetics. Are we to assume they are all criminals? Supporters of terrorists? Al-Qaeda lovers? Bin Laden followers?

Summarizing mainstream accounts of Bout, we receive the following picture. His private fleet of old Soviet Antonov cargo aircraft, employing over 1,000 air and land personnel, has been based in Central African countries, South Africa and the UAE of Sharjah, and his operations have prompted investigations in at least four countries – the United States, Belgium, Great Britain and South Africa.

"What do you know about Bout?" asked the man from BBC-4 *World Report*. Whitney Schneidman of the United States State Department, quoting National Security Agency signal intelligence and intercepts, replied, "They told me that Victor had a very efficient operation. They told me he had a great ability to move arms at will. It indicated that he had an ability to move money very quickly. He was operating on a scale much larger than anybody could imagine. He has a fleet of forty, fifty, sixty aircraft."

I did a double take. Wouldn't a man from the State Department, armed with NSA intelligence reports and working on capturing Victor Bout know the exact number of planes the Merchant of Death had at his disposal? Then, came the icing on the cake. I eagerly listened.

Schneidman: "He delivered vast amounts of weapons, he was very agile in his movements. He worked with a fax machine, a cell phone and pretty much that's it." I was about to scream, but then, something occurred to me. What if *I* called the State Department and told them that my publisher had two cell phones, a fax machine and a Xerox machine in his garage. Would they be willing to put him away for a few months, at least, until I finished my book?

A man who is familiar with Bout's operation better than most is Lee Scott Wolosky, former National Security Adviser and White House counterterrorism official under Presidents Clinton and George W. Bush. He is a partner at Boies, Schiller & Flexner LLP in New York, not to mention a life member of the Council on Foreign Relations, an American arm of the all-powerful Bilderberg Group.

"How many planes did Bout have in his heyday, Lee?"

"I'd say close to two hundred."

"How many?" I thought I misunderstood.

"He was all over the place. Most of Africa, Middle East, South-East Asia."

"Whitney Schneidman, in a BBC-4 interview said sixty, at most. What gives?"

"He scaled back, you know, after we really went after him."

"But you didn't really go after him, according to the US government, until after 9/11, Lee. That's end 2001, beginning 2002," I clarified. "When did he scale back?"

"Beginning 2002."

"You mean, after moving back to Russia."

"Russia was his headquarters, but he was all over the place."

"Lee, according to a letter from the Russian government addressed to the Thai court in relation to his extradition hearing, Victor Bout travelled twice abroad since he relocated to Moscow. One trip to Montenegro and the other to China." What did Lee Wolosky have to say to that?

"I can't comment on that."

Okey dokey.

Each time he was subjected to scrutiny, we are led to believe by the press accounts, he moved his airfreight operations elsewhere. Andre Velrooy, expert on Victor Bout matters with the International Consortium of Investigative Journalists, claims that Richard Chichakli, one of Bout's many associates, said that he never saw him put his signature on a document. It makes one wonder which of the many aliases he would use if he did.

I called Chichakli in Moscow, where he has been residing in exile from the US since his escape from Syria.

"This is absolutely absurd," he replied in a thick accent. "I have seen him sign many documents."

"What name did he use?" I asked him, trying to catch Chichakli in a lie.

"His name, of course. Victor Bout."

In fact, I have personally seen Bout sign over a dozen court documents right in front of me, and seen his personal petitions to Russian Foreign Minister Lavrov. Of course, I might have just lucked out. In case you are wondering, his signature is small and scratchy looking. I would hate to have to read anything of his written out in longhand.

Of course, journalists representing the corporate press wouldn't know this, as I am the only Western media representative to attend all of Bout's court hearings. As is the case with the super secret Bilderberg Group meetings, I am the only Western face to report on the comings and goings of the Shadow Masters. Why is that?

Still holding the phone in my right hand, I pulled out one of my manila envelopes; it had "Belgium" written across the top in bold, blue letters. Putting the phone down, I checked the case file and went on-line to read the final report. "I finally got you, Bout. You are mine!" I thought to myself. I sent my publisher an email.

"I am on the home stretch. One more day!" I wrote triumphantly. Then, I read the report, and my blood went cold. Bout's involvement in the trade of war weapons was an illusion according to what I was reading, found groundless in the final summation of the Court, to be mere politics, after being investigated, tested, and then discredited by the Royal Court in Belgium in case number BR27.97.2780/97. What was truly painful to come to terms with for me was the fact that when the Belgian court asked for evidence, the US administration failed to produce any. Case closed. Bout is found not guilty.

But CNN, the *New York Times*, the BBC? I was speechless and utterly confused. The mainstream media, they said Bout was a criminal, a monster. I want to believe them! I must believe them! My book, I mean, I have to publish it! Give me my proof, I deserve my proof. I have worked very hard at this!

Still, I wasn't going to give up this easily. Something stirred inside of me. I recognized it right away. It was hope, the last thing to die. A man possessed, I went back to mainstream media reports.

A confidant of dictators, warlords and guerrilla leaders, Bout juggled a murky group of companies for much of the 1990s,[11] proclaimed the *Los Angeles Times* in 2004. Having a toehold in South Africa gave him access to Swaziland, a tiny landlocked country in Southern Africa where he registered a total of 43 aircraft, opening offices on August 20, 1997 of Air Cess Swaziland, an airfreight company that would later play an important role in the war in Iraq, proclaimed Ruud Leeuw who quoted the Center for Public Integrity, who in turn referenced Douglas Farah and the *Los Angeles Times*.

According to Bout himself, though, this is wrong. During his heyday in the mid 1990s, the maximum number of aircraft he had was 29, including three Mi-8 helicopters. The rest were old Antonov-8, Antonov-12, Antonov-72, Antonov-24, Antonov-32 and Il-76. In vain, I searched for the phantom 43, 60, 200 aircraft. They seemingly dropped off the face of the Earth.

The complexity of Bout's arms-trafficking networks and financial transactions, through myriad cut-out and shell companies, brokers, transportation companies, corporations, financiers and transshipment points, was intended to make transactions untraceable, proclaimed Douglas Farah on CNN. "In the murky world of arms trafficking, a Russian national has established himself as a premier player in Africa," Farah further asserted in the *Washington Post* in February 2002.[12]

Bout used the balmy Persian Gulf state of the United Arab Emirates as his primary location for several reasons. For one thing, utter lack of regulations related to weapons trafficking and aircraft registration put information about his clandestine operations on a purely need-to-know basis: No one asked and no one cared. For another, the Emirates are ideally situated for flight routes to Afghanistan and Africa, where Bout's business was growing exponentially.

Yet another attraction: The disintegration of the Soviet Union and opening up of borders turned the duty-free Emirates into the vacationland of choice for marauding hordes of *nouveau riche* Russians. Seventy years of Communist austerity overnight had been turned on its head. For decades of the Soviet Union's inexorable march under Communism, "the Russians," as they became known in the Emirates and beyond, had been weaned on a daily diet of potato and beet salads. Now, they were being treated to mouth-watering delicacies from the farthest reaches of the globe. The Russians responded in kind, helping to quench seventy years of hunger with mind-boggling consumption. Gluttony, in the early 1990s, becoming the primary cause of their hospitalization in Dubai. Bout saw the opportunity to multiply his wealth by catering to his countrymen's increasingly obscene and banal whims, selling them everything from Czar Nicholas II-shaped duty-free cellular phones to African-made gold plated statuettes of Lenin in a G-string.

Bout's Enterprises Impact a Wider Circle

Initially, I thought that Western intelligence agencies were very slow to comprehend important connections between weapons trafficking, diamond smuggling and links to the financial apparatus of terrorist groups such as al-Qaeda, which were covertly interlocked with clandestine groups in Europe and in Israel. Following Victor Bout's associations led me to a network of Texas oil interests, Russian-Israeli mobsters, Muslim fundamentalists and off-the-book government black operations. After tirelessly investigating these links and trying to make sense of their interlocked relationships, I understood that Bout was only an example, a case study if you wish, of this underworld of the Shadow Masters. Something else has nagged at me, especially in the face of ever-mounting inconclusive evidence against the Russian arms dealer himself. Were Western intelligence agencies "very slow" to comprehend links between weapons trafficking, diamond smuggling and terrorism, or were these links and criminal synergies allowed to take place and flourish? Why is it being insinuated by Western governments and the official press that the Victor Bouts and his supporting cast of characters are so much smarter than the United States government, the FBI, the CIA, Interpol and the United Nations investigators? And to what end? Could the demonization of the Bouts and the bin Ladens and the Saddam Husseins of the world simply serve as an extension of someone else's foreign policy?

One discovery of note came about as a result of an arrest in New York City in August 2003 of a diamond dealer, accused as part of a weapons smuggling ring. This Israeli-American and Afghanistan-born diamond dealer, Orthodox Jew Yehuda Abraham, had business ties to the Saudi government and to the Saudi Royal family, as a provider of gems to many of its members.[13] Abraham worked alongside Hemant Lakhani, an Indian-born Hindu clothing merchant from Mumbai's prosperous cloth-trading Kutchi Lohana community.[14] Lakhani, as it turned out, was an arms dealer with links to al-Qaeda and the ruling elites of the United Arab Emirates.

During one of Lakhani's many trips to East Africa, he met a key international arms dealer, Sanjivan Ruprah, an ethnic Indian and a politically well-connected Kenyan businessman.[15] Ruprah, in turn, was associated in the press with Victor Bout. I sent an email to Anil Padmanabhan, the journalist from *India Today* who had made this startling revelation, asking for confirmation.

In case you are wondering, I am still waiting. This doesn't mean that Ruprah is not connected to Bout. Simply, I couldn't find any credible proof of it. Bout categorically denies any dealings with him. In fact, he called Ruprah a "small time hoodlum." This doesn't mean I believe Bout either. The burden of proof is on me, and, to my chagrin, at this time I can't find any. Not black and white, anyway, just shadows.

For a long time, though, I was wondering where was the connection? The smoking gun? The fingerprint? Modus Operandi? How do we know these two are pals? I wonder if when he approached the FBI, Ruprah brought a letter of introduction from Victor Bout. And Bout claims not to have any business dealings with Ruprah. Farrah and co-author Stephen Braun, in turn, claim they are pals and co-conspirators.

Now I thought of the disastrous US proceedings against Bout in Thailand. In the multiple testimonies heard during the extradition hearing meant to back up the allegations, the agents of the United States government failed to deliver any evidentiary matter in support of the allegations upon which their request for extradition was based. Exhibits the American legal team produced included pictures of two cargo planes and Bout's alleged notes during the supposed meeting (more correctly, scribbled numbers and doodles on a 3x5 inch post-it).

The decision of the Thai court explicitly stated, on page 49, "Although the prosecutor's witness, Mr. Robert Sahari Vazevit, the head of investigation and inquiry who collected evidence connected with the accused's trade of war weapons, came to testify for confirmation, it is found that the witness is the officer of the United States who testified without any documentary evidence containing photographs or materials."

Surely, the US government had more evidence than that? According to the DEA, Bout's capture had cost the agency over $30 million. Where was the proof of his guilt? If the DEA went into this operation without adequate proof, heads would roll, I thought. If Bout is guilty, the Drug Enforcement Administration had this one chance of nabbing him before he would disappear into the bowels of his Motherland. No proof. What's going on?

My phone rang. I looked at the number flashing impatiently on the screen. 1-541- ... I didn't need to see the rest. My publisher, surely, was ruing the day he met me. Please, I thought to myself, just a little more time.

Numerous open sources stated that Bout's connections to arms deals were often obfuscated by a number of cut outs and middlemen, such as the aforementioned Sanjivan Ruprah. Ruprah was being called, by some, "window dressing" to disguise Bout's association with the notorious Ukrainian-Israeli citizen, Leonid Minin, leader of the ruthless Odessa Mafia.

"Do you know him?" I asked Bout, sitting beside in court next to him. He, in four-pound leg irons over heavy wool grey socks, I in my multi-colored florescent socks and Pikolino runners.

"Know who?"

"Minin. Leonid Minin," I repeated.

"This is an invention of people who want to see me behind bars. I don't know the man."

Bout, Minin, Ruprah, Lakhani, Abraham. Who next? On paper, they were all connected to Bout. What if they too were *permitted* to be connected to Bout and his empire as a result of someone's farsighted policy decision? Still too soon to tell, I thought to myself.

But these seemingly interlocked relationships amongst allegedly some of the world's most unsavory characters made me wonder: Was Abraham a cut out for the Saudi Royal family? If he was, then did the Saudis act independently or as a secondary cut out for someone else? Was *the* supposed someone else a nation or an independent operator? After all, Saudi Arabia, Pakistan and the United Arab Emirates are the only three nations in the world to have officially recognized the Taliban. Pakistan's links to the Taliban and terrorism are well documented. I had been informed that the Emirates were being used as a money-laundering center by bin Laden, al-Qaeda and the Taliban. It was quite a stretch to imagine the Saudis acting independently. But who were they covering for?

Ken Silverstein, writing for the mainstream *Washington Monthly*, stated in the magazine's January/February 2002 issue that Bout and Minin were longtime arms suppliers to former Liberian dictator Charles Taylor, and responsible for transforming his allies, the Revolutionary United Front (RUF) rebels in Sierra Leone, from a rural army of 400 men in 1997 into a conventional army of 20,000 by 1999. As "Bout's man in Liberia," Ruprah aided Bout in his frequent dealings with Taylor. In return for his assistance, the RUF supplied Taylor with looted diamonds from areas it controlled. Bout and his associates were given Liberian diplomatic passports and, with Taylor's blessing and protection, they registered a number of their front companies in Monrovia, the Liberian capital.[16]

"How well do you know Taylor?" I screamed at Bout. He was in the visitor's area of prison, leaning against the glass, trying to make out what I was saying over the cacophony of other prisoners, who were also straining to hear what was being said to them.

"Have never met him. Wouldn't be caught in the same room with him!" he shouted back in Russian, pressing his face against the small opening.

He looked taller and thinner than his six feet, with a full head of short, brown hair parted strategically from left to right across his high forehead, dressed in a worn out, wrinkled, ill-fitted orange prison jump suit, brand new leg irons, and wearing a smile of apologetic self-protection. His gaunt, still youthful face was betrayed by several deeply imbedded lines around the eyes, eyes that didn't easily give away its secrets.

"Do you have a Liberian diplomatic passport as the mainstream media alleges?"

"How would I have a Liberian diplomatic passport if I have never dealt with Taylor?"

In 2005, the UN Security Council Committee on Liberia identified Leonid Minin as one of Victor Bout's closest associates and provided further personal details of the Odessa Mafia crime lord:

> Minin, Leonid Efimovich
> Nationality: Israel
> Bolivian Passport: 65118
> Forged German Passports: 5280007248D, 18106739D
> Greek Passport: no details
> Israeli Passports: 6019832, 9001689, 90109052
> Russian Passport: KI0861177
> Arms dealer in contravention of UNSC resolution 1343 – supported former President Taylor's regime in effort to destabilize Sierra Leone and gain illicit access to diamonds
>
> UN Security Council SC/8570, "Security Council Committee on Liberia Updates Freeze List"
> November 30, 2005

Born in Odessa in 1947, Minin immigrated to Israel in the 1970s and established a global web of companies, many of them discreetly incorporated offshore. Minin's primary business vehicle is Monaco-based Limad AG, which also has offices in Switzerland, China, and Russia.

Acting on a tip in Cinisello Balsamo, on the outskirts of Milan, Italian police arrested Minin in August 2000, writes investigative journalist Wayne Madsen, citing a PBS *Frontline World Report*. In his room, police found $500,000 worth of uncut diamonds, a duffel bag filled with more than $35,000 in American, Italian, Hungarian and Mauritian currency, and over 1,500 documents, in Russian, Ukrainian, French, German, Dutch, English and Italian, relating to Minin's wide variety of business operations. Specific findings included a record of a $10,263.02 payment to Marc Rich, an international financier and reputed Russian-Israeli-American Mafia don, soon to be known for his 11th-hour pardon from President Clinton on charges of fraud and extortion.

According to Wayne Madsen's sources, "The pardon of Rich was urged in a phone call to Clinton by then-Israeli Prime Minister Ehud Barak, as well as Shimon Peres and Ehud Olmert."[17] Why, I thought to myself, was Rich, a reputed Russian-Israeli-American Mafia don, attracting so much interest from the Israeli government and the

President of the United States? Was he, too, a player, or was he being used as an extension of America's or Israeli's foreign policy? In what capacity did he serve the governments of Israel and/or the United States to warrant a Presidential pardon? Why would the President of the United States risk a historical rebuke to pardon someone with such a dubious reputation? Was the Israeli government a cut out or were they using Rich as a cut out for some unsavory black op?

As Madsen notes, "In 1983, a little known US Attorney for the Southern District of New York had urged jail time for Rich for racketeering. The name of that US Attorney was Rudolph Giuliani. Marc Rich's onetime lawyer was Vice President Dick Cheney's former chief of staff, Scooter Libby."[18] Furthermore, *Forbes* magazine puts out a Russian edition; its Moscow editor, Paul Klebnikov, wrote about Rich's connections to Boris Berezovsky, a business partner of Neil Bush, and also discussed this in his book, *Godfather of the Kremlin*. On July 9, 2004, Klebnikov was shot and killed gangland style on a Moscow street. Marc Rich's oil company, Glencore, once shared a London phone number with one of Leonid Minin's companies, Galaxy Management.[19] A world of Shadow Masters. A small world, indeed.

After an exhaustive investigation, the Italian police concluded, "Minin was the head of a Ukrainian criminal network associated with international drug and weapons trafficking, money laundering and extortion."[20] But, this was only the beginning of the story.

In February 2002, Belgian police arrested diamond- and arms-smuggler Sanjivan Ruprah for using a false passport. *Frontline*, in a special report on illegal arms and diamond trafficking in Africa, reported that Ruprah "was directly involved in the operations of Leonid Minin's arms sales to Liberia, and owns diamond mines in Liberia."[21] A Bout-Minin link was confirmed by Bout himself, according to a *New York Times Magazine* article.[22]

Bout claims his relationship with Minin is a fabrication, and that he never said he had any. Bout's wife Alla showed me an email from Peter Landesman, the author of the famed Bout exposé in the *New York Times Magazine*. It was sent before the article came out. Landesman apologizes ahead of time for the article's final version, pleading clemency and claiming that even though he wanted to write a true report on Victor Bout, his big, bad editor had other ideas.

His article was a hit piece, forever cementing Bout's reputation as a Merchant of Death. Incidentally, both Peter Landesman and Douglas Farah have landed juicy Hollywood option deals as a result of their relentless Bout coverage. Landesman has produced a screenplay titled *Arms and the Man*. This work has been picked up by Universal studios, part of the Vivendi SA empire, one of the world's top media groups, and will be directed by Michael Mann, who has done such films as *The Last of the Mohicans* and *Collateral*. In Landsman's screenplay, Bout the bad guy is involved in a plot to steal plutonium from the Ukraine, but later turns into a good guy after his brother, Sergei, is killed. There is also talk of a video game based on the film.

Vivendi Universal was formed in 2000, "through the merger of Vivendi, a French multimedia group, and Edgar Bronfman's Seagram Co. Ltd. Seagram had, in 1995, bought MCA, including MCA's Universal movies division, with its 14.7% share of the US box-office market. Universal Music bought up PolyGram, and now owns the copyrights works by to Jimi Hendrix, Bob Marley, the Jackson Five, U2, Elton John and, among others, 50% of the "Gangsta Rap" label Interscope. In 2006, General Electric acquired an 80% stake, thus creating the current NBC Universal through a merging of GE's NBC unit and Vivendi's Vivendi Universal Entertainment group.

"Vivendi's boss Jean-Claude Messier himself was, from 1986-88, responsible for the French government's privatization program. Then, he joined the influential US-French investment bank Lazard Frères [a key bank in the Bilderberg Group power structure] before he took over the Lyon-based water utility Générale des Eaux, which he transformed into the Vivendi media group.

"The big media conglomerates share part of the business with the biggest military producers. Many of the games are based on Hollywood film scripts, like *Terminator* or *Mission: Impossible*, and rely on intellectual property rights sold or leased by the original film producers, who share part of the royalties income and have a lot of political clout."[23]

Fact and fiction, real life and Hollywood, shadows and the Shadow Masters. The lines, at least in this tale are blurred on more than one occasion. Considering that Landesman and Farah are two of the more visible anti-Bout crusaders, could their Hollywood good fortune simply be a payoff for creating an erroneous illusion of Bout for public consumption?

Another project is an outgrowth of Douglas Farah's work *Blood from Stones*. The film will have a fictitious plotline sprinkled with factual information. Bout's character will take a back seat to former Liberian strongman Charles Taylor and his merry band of thugs.

"Why did you agree to the [Landesman] interview?" I asked Bout.

"It was Chichakli. For over six months he tried to convince me. I didn't have a good feeling about it, but he insisted."

"Did Landesman record the interview?"

He shook his head. "He took down notes."

Good idea, I thought to myself. If you were going to write a hit piece on someone, don't leave evidence behind. "Why didn't *you* record it yourself?" I asked him incredulously.

"I trusted him."

Can it really be that simple? I thought to myself.

"The exploits of Bout and Ruprah in [Africa's] worst killing fields are the subject of numerous United Nations reports on mercenary activity, diamond smuggling and arms trafficking in Angola, Sierra Leone, the Democratic Republic of the Congo, Liberia, Uganda and Rwanda."[24] According to UN investigators, "Ruprah was tied to the illicit diamond trade in West Africa and arranged for Bout to be paid for his weapons deliveries with diamonds from Sierra Leone."

Even if we are to take this piece of evidence at face value without checking for primary sources, I thought to myself, we would have to assume that if the United Nations investigators knew, then, so did the US government. Yet, again, nothing of substance was being done. Bout was still active; the weapons were getting through, feeding some of the worst atrocities and abuses in human history. Why? Initially, none of it made sense, at least not until I understood the Shadow World of the Men behind the Curtain. You see, if what we are being told is true, that is, in a *real world*, a Victor Bout would not have existed, because governments have the diplomatic, financial and intelligence clout to eliminate the elements that threaten their sovereignty and the rule of law.

Unless, of course, "arms-for-diamonds" and other scenarios were being used as an extension of a farsighted agenda, designed from the behind the scenes at some of the most prestigious think tanks and foundations. Vivendi and General Electric, Lazard Frères and the Bilderberg Group. As I later discovered, this is exactly what was happening.

Diamond Trading

Diamonds can be sold easily on the international black market, but the financial trails of the transactions are virtually non-existent, and undetected by international law enforcement.[25] Shockingly little is known about the political and criminal twilight world that conceals the commerce of international diamond trading. Diamond dealers the world over are known by the Hebrew term *yahalom manin*. Jewish diamond dealers strike deals based on a handshake and the Hebrew words *mazal ubracha*, or "luck and be blessed." As with Islamic *hawalahs*, payments for diamonds are wired around the world through a variety of pass-through companies and middlemen.[26] Gems can be brought or sent halfway around the world for inspection without any guarantee of purchase. In this environment, your good name is worth everything. "Disputes are settled internally at peer-review courts. Wrongdoers face a penalty more serious than jail – expulsion from the diamond community."[27]

The Hasidic community in London's Hatton Garden is considered one of the leading centers for diamond smuggling and money laundering. "The gem trade appeals to money launderers because, following the introduction of new banking regulations, it is one of the few remaining industries where large cash transactions can be carried out with complete anonymity. There is an environment of almost complete secrecy and it is a very cash-intensive marketplace. These are all things that money launderers find very attractive."[28] One of Osama bin Laden's top lieutenants, Wadih el Hage, now serving a life sentence for his role in the 1998 US Embassy bombing in Kenya and Tanzania, visited Hatton Garden to raise funds for al-Qaeda by smuggling tanzanite gems from Tanzania.[29]

Such a means of raising funds points to another benefit of dealing in diamonds. They are very easy to transport, much more so than gold or even paper money. Gold, for example, has lately been selling for over one thousand dollars per troy ounce. Depending upon quality, a diamond may be worth several thousand dollars *per carat*. As one carat is one fifth of a gram, there are over 155 carats in a troy ounce. The value to any high-priced illicit trade of both diamonds and diamond experts is thus apparent.

Over the past decade, Israel's intelligence agency responsible for counterterrorism and covert operations, the Mossad, has become aware that terrorist groups such as al-Qaeda, Hamas and Hezbollah launder money through diamonds in places like West Africa without detection by international financial surveillance authorities. These findings reveal additional background on terrorist links to diamond smuggling.

Lebanese Shiite immigrants, fleeing economic depravation, first arrived in West Africa at the beginning of the 20th century.[30] They were welcomed by the British colonial authorities, who saw in their arrival an opportunity to displace local merchants in commodity trade with the African interior. After diamonds were discovered in eastern Sierra Leone in 1930, Lebanese traders quickly gained control of this lucrative market.[31] More recently, as the *Middle East Intelligence Bulletin* of June/July 2004 reported, "The most lucrative source of funds [for terrorists] was the Lebanese diamond traders of Sierra Leone … a number of powerful Lebanese gem merchants … helped the brutal Liberian-backed Revolutionary United Front (RUF) sell diamonds from mines under its control."

The United Nations Angola Report issued December 21, 2000 had first brought the issue of the "conflict diamonds" trade to the world's attention. It detailed how, in many regions in Africa, civil strife has turned into all-out war over diamond-mining territory, gems that end up paying for African wars at the cost of millions of lives. "The proceeds from the diamonds are then used to buy illicit weapons and deepen the conflicts."[32] These arms, sold by shadowy merchants, have often ended up in the hands of child soldiers, as was the case in Sierra Leone and Angola, two of the leading employers of child soldiers in combat operations. To get these child soldiers to fight, the rebel forces fed them cocaine and amphetamines, thus negating whatever compassion the children might have felt for their victims; they played real soldiers "rampaging through the countryside, killing, mutilating, raping, and pillaging until they collapsed from fatigue and hunger."[33]

In the Congo, Hezbollah simply "muscled their way into the business and began purchasing diamonds directly from miners and local middlemen at a fraction of their market value."[34] A glimpse into the scale of Hezbollah profits from the diamond trade came in December 2003, "when a Union des Transports Africains airliner loaded with Lebanese passengers crashed off the coast of Benin – on board, according to news reports and Western diplomats in Sierra Leone, was a Hezbollah courier carrying $2 million."[35]

It's important to understand that, although most experts mention al-Qaeda and Hezbollah in the same breath when terrorist links to the diamond trade are discussed, the *modi operandi* of the two organizations are quite different. Al-Qaeda, with its global reach, buys diamonds as a way of *hiding* money, whereas Hezbollah, a regional player in the Middle

East, is involved to *make* money. Terrorism truly has become a global enterprise, not only in matters of warfare but in the way these organizations tap into existing distribution routes and delivery systems.

Hezbollah is a Shi'a Islamic militia and political and paramilitary organization based in Lebanon, whose name is translated as "The Party of God." It grew out of a collapse of the Lebanese political system in the 1970s under the impact of the Palestinian guerrilla movement. A 1978 Israeli invasion was followed in 1982 by a full-scale Israeli assault aimed at driving out the Palestine Liberation Organization (PLO). This resulted in more than 30,000 people losing their lives. In one of the most documented massacres of late 20th century, the Israeli army stood by as hundreds were massacred by Lebanese Christians in the Sabra and Shatila refugee camps, where many Lebanese Shi'a had sought refuge. In this environment, Hezbollah emerged and grew.

Diamonds and bin Laden

And that brings us to Osama bin Laden's connections to the Israeli diamond trade. Here is some information I received from one of my most trusted sources, showing some correspondence between him and one of *his* sources, referred to as ABC.

> ABC: "On the last day of October 2001, Osama bin Laden finally realized that he was trapped between the Northern Front and the US forces. Traditional escape routes were all cut off. He called an old business partner, who whisked Osama and his party of 26 people to Africa on a private jet on November 4 [2001]. You may find it rather surprising, but you must understand that in the ancient middle eastern world of tradition and rituals, which may seem utterly absurd to a Western person, a business partnership is based on years of trust, and it is totally separate from political or national loyalties. This trusted ally was an Israeli.
>
> "During Osama's exile in Sudan in the 1990s, he was clandestinely approached by Israelis who wanted him to take over the African diamond business from the Lebanese. Traditionally, Muslims were the guardians of the raw diamond trade in West Africa. They provided the logistics and the muscle. The Israelis' proposition to Osama was quite simple. They wanted for the wily Saudi to take the trade away from the Shiites. You see, the idea of suicide bombers from southern Lebanon being financed by the Israeli-run diamond trade out of Antwerp, Belgium, turned their stomach.

Osama was feared and respected by the terrorists. It would take a battle hardened bin Laden to get the job done."

"Why would a Saudi terrorist want to deal with the Israelis."

ABC: "You see, neither Osama bin Laden nor the Taliban were anti-Jewish. In the case of the Taliban [mostly Pashtuns], the Pashtun tribe of Afghanistan is one of the 'lost tribes of Israel.' Their customs and names are identical to those of the Jews. As for the bin Ladens, the family is of Yemeni-origin and the man who started the dynasty, Mohamed Bin Awad bin Laden, was a contractor who became one of the wealthiest men in the world. Mohamed bin Laden had numerous wives, too many to count, as he always married into the people who lived in the places where he was working in order to become one of them and not be looked at as a stranger. As a result, the family construction empire routinely dealt with Jewish businessmen through Yemen for building materials and equipment. That's how Osama's father got rich. Since Saudis could have no direct dealings with the Jews, the bin Ladens used Yemenis, who lived alongside Jews in their Yemeni homeland.

"Once bin Laden wrestled control of the raw diamond trade away from the Shiites, he became an instant billionaire. The diamonds were sent from West Africa to the Russian Mafia through Osama's trusted diamond courier, who used a very non-Muslim name of Cyril Jacob. The Mafia then sold them to the Jews in Antwerp."

This information comes from a former US Naval Intelligence officer who has also worked for the National Security Agency, and maintains a network of contacts in the intelligence communities. In one of our conversations, he dropped this bombshell, citing one of his intelligence sources in Peshawar, Pakistan. This source was a "high value target," someone recruited from a foreign intelligence agency. This source has not "come in from the cold," meaning has not physically defected to the recruiting country; thus, if found out, the source will be assassinated.

This information from the source dovetailed very nicely with the activities of the Afghani Jew, Yehuda Abraham, president of Ambuy Gem Corp., his diamond business with the Saudi Royal family, his arrest for involvement in a Russian shoulder-mounted-missile-launcher smuggling ring including Hemant Lakhani, who in turn was linked to various client terrorist organizations. The multiple unrelated dots proverbially came together.

As you now may begin to realize, seemingly extraneous information acquires a degree of importance in our story: Abraham's primary clientele was the Saudi royal family. It was also discovered that Abraham was operating a *hawalah* – an Islamic money transfer network based on trust and a handshake – from his diamond business. It was that *hawalah* that was used to transfer money from weapons sales out of the United States without leaving a trace. Was Abraham being used as an extension of bin Laden's "foreign policy"? If yes, by whom, bin Laden himself or by the United States government? And to what end? Were the United States government and the intelligence agencies on purpose "very slow" to comprehend the links between weapons trafficking, diamond smuggling and terrorism?

In light of this speculation, is it possible that Osama bin Laden was referring to al-Qaeda's diamond-smuggling network during his interview with the Pakistani newspaper, *Ummat*? In it, on September 28, 2001, he noted that al-Qaeda uses "three alternative financial systems that are separate and independent," adding that any attempt to remove them would not succeed.

In this context, it is surely no surprise that in the mid 1990s, the city of Dubai, al-Qaeda's premier money laundering center in the Middle East, became a major rival to Antwerp, Tel Aviv and London as a leading diamond processing center, a business in which bin Laden later became heavily invested.

Going Global

Al-Qaeda's financial network was not limited to the Islamic world. The August 25, 2002 *Sunday Express* reported that al-Qaeda financial front men associated with the Islamic charity, Mercy International Relief Agency, had used Irish bank accounts to transfer money to Warsaw, Poland.[36] According to the official version of events, Tim Shipman, writing for the *Sunday Express*, stated, "Some of the fund transfers, picked up by National Security Agency and British Government Communications Headquarters (GCHQ) intercepts, were likely used to fund part of the 9/11 attacks."[37]

An article in the *Moscow Times* on September 4, 2002, not only confirmed these findings, but also added a few precious nuggets of its own. "Victor Bout's planes have been used to fly al-Qaeda and Taliban gold to Sudan in recent weeks. Several shipments of gold were delivered by boat from Karachi, Pakistan, to either Iran or the United Arab Emirates," said the newspaper citing unidentified European intelligence officials. The report continued: "From there, the gold was flown on charted planes to the Sudanese capital of Khartoum, where al-Qaeda has broad business contacts." Air Bas, one of Victor Bout's flagship airlines, supposedly transported the gold.

"Not true," said Bout. "I have never had business dealings with the Taliban or al-Qaeda." I checked the primary source. As I suspected, it wasn't the *Moscow Times*. The information came via Douglas Farah in the *Washington Post*.[38] I scanned the article for precise information. "Financial officers of al-Qaeda and the Taliban have quietly shipped large quantities of gold out of Pakistan to Sudan in recent weeks, transiting through the United Arab Emirates and Iran, according to European, Pakistani and US investigators." Once again, those ever-handy "European, Pakistani, and US investigators."

I skipped a paragraph. "Although it is not clear how much gold has been moved, US and European officials said the quantity was significant." Are these the same officials who claim to have irrefutable evidence against Bout's transgressions only to show up in Belgian and Thai courts empty handed, claiming the irrefutable evidence to be locked up in the DEA secure facility in New York? Thai courts didn't buy it, neither did the Belgian justice system. Why should we?

Michael Chandler, a retired British colonel who led a UN panel on the Taliban and al-Qaeda, is quoted in Moisés Naím's book, *Illicit: How Smugglers, Traffickers and Copycats are Hijacking the Global Economy*: "If you look at all the escapades of Bout and his associates, how easy it was for them to move weapons, get end-user certificates, and change aircraft registration, you get an amazing picture of how corrupt many parts of the world are."

In their book, Farah and Braun excused US lack of early action against Bout: "The notion [in the 1990s] that transnational threats – the Clinton administration's phrasing for terrorists, narcotics cartels, global organized crime, and other dangerous 'non-state actors' – might prove as dangerous as hostile nations was an idea still in its infancy."[39] That much I could buy.

However, what I was unwilling to buy was the notion that for over a decade, a Victor Bout remained a step ahead of the supposedly helpless United States government, the FBI, the CIA, the NSA, Interpol and their hundred-billion-dollar budgets, with Total Information Awareness and Echelon's global spy system. One man against the world.

"Why are we subtly being led down this path?" I kept asking myself. "Could the Bouts and the bin Ladens simply serve as extensions of someone else's hidden agenda, were they part of the Shadow World where the Men behind the Curtain operate?" The question made sense. If the answer to the question is a "yes," as it surely is in CIA-trained Osama bin Laden's case, then the world we live in is indeed a cesspool of duplicity and lies and double-speak and secret government agendas, of changing loyalties, brainwashed black-ops agents, rogue dictators and telegenic villains who act as extensions of someone's foreign policy.

When the UN made its April 2001 report on the Democratic Republic of the Congo,[40] it cited how easy it was for Bout to run his operation from Burundi. Sounds great, except Bout's business was never registered in Burundi, according to the Ministry of Transportation's Database Records located in Bujumbura. Furthermore, I went online and with the help of GP Fleet's tracking and tracing fleet management technology, I double-checked Bout's business practices in Burundi. Nothing. Either Burundi and/or Bout deliberately erased all traces of his unwholesome business practices in the country or ... the UN was outright lying.

According to a January 2005 report of the UN Security Council, "Burundi has in the past served as a 'flag of convenience' for operators in the Democratic Republic of the Congo by issuing aircraft registrations for their planes and licenses for foreign pilots."

The term "flag of convenience" refers to aircraft registration in less scrupulous countries that allow circumvention of international regulations on air cargo. Many fly from airports like Burgas in Bulgaria, Ostend in Belgium and Sharjah in the UAE. These airports are known for their "lax oversight of airfreight operations." Additionally, airfreight documents do not require cross-referencing of the goods described in the arms export and import licenses. Arms shipments are often described as engineering, mining, agricultural or hospital equipment.[41] One of the oddities of the freight business is that you are not required to specify the travel route, nor any possible subcontractors, nor the ultimate customer. In fact, it is not even necessary for an airplane to be physically present in a country in order for it to be registered there. No wonder outlaw Liberia is one of the behemoths of the business.

Once again, the message coming from the United Nations was crystal clear. It was not too difficult for someone like Victor Bout, with his shadowy connections, who excelled at getting around international rules and regulations, to go unnoticed and be one step ahead of the UN investigators and governments alike in changing aircraft registration from one country to another, and then another.

I checked the April 2001 report on the Democratic Republic of the Congo. The individual I was most interested in was Johan Peleman, listed as a technical adviser in Point 3. In fact, every damning UN report on Bout had Peleman as one of the authors. And only UN reports that involved Peleman incriminated Bout as a slippery, notorious arms-runner.

I called him, after an initial exchange of pleasantries and emails.

"Johan, this is Daniel Estulin. We spoke several days ago. You must feel good about Bout being finally in prison."

He sighed. It was a prolonged sigh of a man who carried the weight of the godless world on his wide shoulders.

"Johan, I know you are busy, so I will get right to the point. How much money did you personally make from being Bout's leading antagonist?"

There was a pause. It sounded like Peleman held his breath, and then he said, "I worked for the United Nations."

"Are you saying you worked for free? If yes, what did you live on? I mean, what is the source of your income?"

Another pause. "I was getting a salary for my work."

"Johan, in a *Groot Bijgaarden De Standaard* newspaper interview, you said that the operational budget of the UN panel on Liberia amounted to 1 million Euros and that you would never be given the same freedom of movement as you were enjoying whilst working on the report. You also said you went to Africa thirty times that year."

"It proves that illegal arms trafficking was not a top priority for the Belgian Government," he interrupted me.

"It also proves you had access to a fabulous trough of cash. You have done numerous reports for the UN and have been working with them for years. How much money did you make in the name of putting the bad guys behind bars?"

"You are dealing with—"

"Two million dollars," I interrupted him. "Three, four, five?"

"This guy is the worst offender—"

"Six? Seven, Ten? Eleven million dollars? Ten years of going after Bout, Johan. How much money?

"Bout deserves to be where he—"

"Thirteen? Fifteen? Twenty?"

"I wasn't alone. We had staff, people working for us, researchers, investigators, secretaries."

I was madly scribbling it all down. "Twenty million dollars, Johan! That's a lot of money for staff and expenses. What kind of an operation did you people run at the United Nations?"

"You have any idea what it takes to track down someone like Bout?"

"I am beginning to," I shot back. "By the way, do *you* have Bout's story optioned to Hollywood as well?" No response.

"One last question, Johan. In your April 2001 Congo report you mention Bout doing business out of Burundi. I checked every available registry and guess what? Nothing. Can you —"

"I don't have time for this," he cut me off. "If you want to see the real story, go to BBC and watch their report." He hung up.

I turned to the BBC page, found their *BBC World Report* on Victor Bout and pressed play.

Some three minutes into it, Peleman's name came up along with the UN report on Angola dated December 18, 2000. According to the BBC report, "the name Bout became known to the general public in late January 2001." Then, Peleman's face appeared, cigarette in hand. "It was the first time Bout was mentioned in an official report as being a sanctions buster. What was different was that this report was sexy enough to be picked up by the media." I bolted up in my chair. Come again? I was sure I misunderstood. I rewound the video and listened again. Yes, Peleman said "it was sexy enough." How do you *sex up* a report? Well, actually, we know how. The Bush administration and the British did it as part of the campaign to scare the public into rubberstamping their illegal war in Iraq. Published by the British government on September 24, 2002, the September Dossier was part of a campaign by the Blair administration to bolster support for the 2003 Iraq invasion. It contained a number of later-proven-baseless allegations, according to which Iraq possessed WMDs, including chemical and biological weapons. A sexed up report, which lead to a human carnage in Iraq.

HUNTING VICTOR BOUT

According to the August 17, 2003 issue of the *New York Times Magazine*, during the final year of the Clinton administration, US intelligence began tracking Bout's activities and his network, which included the likes of Ruprah and Lakhani. In the summer of 1999, faced with multiple conflicts in West and Central Africa, the National Security Council authorized electronic surveillance of government and militia leaders in war zones like northeast Congo, Liberia and Sierra Leone. Every morning, NSC officials cross-referenced transcripts of overheard telephone conversations with American satellite imagery and with field reports by British spies on the ground. The documentation was massive, without obvious patterns, until, finally, astute analysts noticed that every conflict had something in common: Victor Bout. Belgium already had an international arrest warrant out for Bout for money laundering and diamond smuggling. Clinton's National Security Council believed Bout was aiding terrorism. Landesman writes in the *New York Times Magazine*:

> Gayle Smith, the National Security Council's (NSC) top Africanist, whose staff uncovered the Bout connection, sent an e-mail message to her fellow NSC members: "Who is this guy? Pay close attention to this. He's all over the place."
>
> An answer was provided by a CIA aviation expert from Langley, who showed up at the White House with covert photographs shot at various African jungle airstrips between 1996 and 1999. The photos, according to a former White House official who studied them, show different Antonovs and Ilyushins, Russian cargo planes built to land on (and escape from) almost any surface. In the pictures, the planes' bellies are open. African militiamen in fatigues are offloading crates of weapons. One photo shows a younger Bout standing before one of the planes. The White House official said the planes were traced to Bout.[42]

At least on paper, it looked as if America was prepared to act. Smith and others took their information to Richard C. Clarke, then the chief of counterterrorism for the NSC. "Get me a warrant," Clarke responded, but US laws could not extend to Bout's foreign arms deliveries.[43]

Clarke, of course, would have known this; then why the charade? Was this another case of powerful people playing games with us, dancing between raindrops perfectly content to hold our lives in the balance? What further complicated the issue was that the United Nations has no law enforcement powers: its investigators cannot subpoena, detain or arrest suspects. "Big arms are the province of individual countries, but no country is configured to deal with it because its jurisdiction stops at the border," said Jonathan M. Winer, deputy assistant secretary of state for international law enforcement in the Clinton administration.

In addition to efforts of American intelligence, we were led to believe, "Bout's clandestine activities in Africa were shadowed by the British MI6 on the ground,"[44] Interpol and United Nations inspectors. US and British intelligence had eavesdropped on his telephone conversations. Interpol had issued a "red notice," requesting his arrest on Belgian weapons-trafficking and money-laundering charges.

Arms dealer Victor Bout, the Merchant of Death, allegedly the largest known illicit trafficker, sought by the International Community for feeding conflicts throughout much of the Eastern Hemisphere – was being squeezed, methodically ... until George W. Bush came into office and Iraq "happened."

Then Bout was supposedly working for the Pentagon, and apparently had permission to fly into Iraq. I needed definitive proof, but at this point in my investigation, I was overwhelmed with research and underwhelmed with help. What's more, I wasn't about to take the media reports at face value. But the proof would have to wait. For now, I used open sources and mainstream press reports.

The storyline out of the corporate media camp was clean and simple to follow. Bout's Texas-based Air Bas had rights to refuel at US bases in Iraq. One of Bout's other airfreight companies, Airbus, was subcontracted through another firm called Falcon Express of Dubai, by Kellogg Brown and Root, then a subsidiary of Halliburton.[45] Before acquiring his fiefdom at the US Naval Observatory, former Vice President Dick Cheney was CEO of Halliburton.

I checked my Iraq timeline. Spring 2004 "roughly coincided with the early and still-disorganized stages of the Iraqi resistance. Utterly unprepared, coalition forces found themselves in a massive logistics crunch."[46] Bush, Cheney, Donald Rumsfeld and Richard Perle had promised a cakewalk, and told the world that grateful Iraqi people would greet American soldiers "with flowers and music." They had lied.

Road transit became a living nightmare. American SUVs were picked off like flies by the insurgency. Someone thought of a Plan B to get supplies and ammunition to the troops. According to one contractor in Iraq working for Dyncorp, the Pentagon began leasing aircraft from just about anyone who had them, while simultaneously outsourcing convoy duty to private security firms in order to limit the exposure of American troops.

At least one company tied to Bout's network was hired by the Bush administration for the war effort in Iraq, reported Michael Scherer on September 20, 2004. "Records obtained by *Mother Jones* show that, as recently as August, Air Bas, a company tied to Bout and his associates, was flying charter missions under contract with the US military in Iraq. Air Bas is overseen by Victor Bout's brother, Serguei, and his business manager, Richard Chichakli, an accountant living in Texas; in the past, payments for Air Bas have gone to a Kazakh company that the United Nations identifies as 'a front for the leasing operations of Victor Bout's aircraft.'"[47]

Mother Jones was being rather sparing with its information.[48] Chichakli, in fact, was more than a mere accountant. According to some sources he was an ex-CIA operative and a relative of the former president of Syria, Adib Shishakli, who after resigning the office of president in February 1954 lived in exile in Brazil, where he was assassinated in the town of Ceres on September 27, 1964.

Richard Chichakli became close to the bin Laden family while studying in Saudi Arabia between 1977 and 1986. Mohamed bin Laden, the patriarch of the family, had 52 children by a number of wives, and two of his wives were Syrian. The mother of Osama bin Laden is a Syrian, and the mother of Saad bin Laden, a half-brother to Osama whom Chichakli had met in Riyadh University, was also Syrian.

Saad bin Laden introduced Chichakli to the rest of the bin Laden family after the two of them became close friends, a relationship which was enhanced by their Syrian family background. All of that led to Chichakli getting liked and trusted by the mother, and subsequently by the other members of the family, including Salem bin Laden.

Chichakli alleges that Salem bin Laden was ordered killed by George H.W. Bush in 1988 in order to protect his son George W. Bush, who had been stealing money from bin Laden funds in the United States. At the timc, the fund was under the management of "Major" James Bath, a former National Guard major who had served with Dubbya and was the financier of the latter's oil-drilling ventures. Contrary to what has been written on the subject, Chichakli maintains, Salem was not killed in an ultra-light airplane that hit power lines in Texas; he was assassinated over the Mediterranean while headed to the US to revoke Bath's power as trustee over the bin Laden monies, when his BAC 1-11 aircraft was shot down over international waters by the Israeli air force at the order of Yitzhak

Rabin, then Minister of Defense. But, I am getting away from my story.

Douglas Farah has claimed that Chichakli used to sit around and eat sandwiches and sing songs with bin Laden and his siblings, back when Osama was OK.

I sent Chichakli an email.

> I have some points that I need to clarify. Unfortunately, certain parts of your audio recording weren't very good.
>
> 1. Your relationship to the former president of Syria, Adib Shishakli.
>
> 2. Your relationship to the bin Ladens. There are several references in mainstream sources essentially stating the following: you "hung out with a youthful Osama and ran a free-trade zone in the United Arab Emirates."
>
> 3. Your relationship to Miles Copeland.
>
> 4. Were you working for the US intelligence, as has been suggested?

"I do not know Osama bin Ladin nor I have met him, he lived in Jeddah and went to School in King Abdul Aziz University there, while I was in Riyadh and went to university in Riyadh, emailed Chichakli. "The 'hang out story' is a made up tale." He did acknowledged that *Saad* bin Laden had been present at his wedding on July 14, 1983.

I checked the original source for Osama bin Laden and Chichakli hanging out together. Douglas Farah, *Merchant of Death*, pages 53-56. Someone was obviously "wrong." But who?

Why would Chichakli make up a story of hanging out with the terrorist wanted for masterminding 9/11? Not a good way to make friends and influence people. On the other hand, if you are Farah and you are creating a background, "setting the scene" so to speak, linking Chichakli and Osama bin Laden and later Chichakli and Victor Bout would be ideal for negatively influencing people's opinions. Is this another case of multiple passports, walled compounds and phantom fleets all made to serve someone's far-reaching policy objectives?

Chichakli refused to comment on his relationship with US intelligence officer Miles Copeland, a key player in US intelligence operations in the Middle East, a veteran of Wild Bill Donovan's wartime

OSS, and a founding father of the CIA. I have been told by reliable sources that Chichakli was a close confidant of Miles Copeland.

On point one, he *is* related, though not immediate family, to former Syrian president Shishakli. Thus, a Victor Bout "accountant" was closely linked to the CIA, to the bin Ladens and to a former president of Syria. Of course, *Mother Jones* would have known at least some of it, had they dug a little deeper. It took me less than one hour to cross reference some of this information through several popular search engines, and a couple of emails to Richard Chichakli himself. Why, then, didn't they?

Was Chichakli being protected as someone's foreign policy asset through a publication that claims to be a non-profit "Foundation for National Progress"? In 1997, *Mother Jones* was given a $3 million grant by the Alfred P. Sloan Foundation "to establish a Center for Working Families" at the University of Berkeley. The Sloan Foundation's board of trustees includes former chairmen of the General Motors, J.P. Morgan and Morgan Stanley corporate boards.

If Chichakli was being protected or being used as someone's foreign policy asset, I thought, the corollary was clear: so was Victor Bout. Taking it one step further, if Bout's actions were part of the plan, then the entire elaborate construct of smoke and mirrors could become visible as we followed its implications into a parallel world beyond logic.

"Why are you doing this?" asked my aunt, shortly before she died, the aunt who had clucked over the "terrible things" done to our family.

Because universal corruption and abuse of power and privileges at the deepest level of society must be exposed, even at the risk of one's life. And because the notion of the Shadow Masters acting as our puppeteers is too unpalatable, too intolerable.

Perhaps the best response to my aunt's question is another. What are the moral consequences of freedom?

Bout-Taliban Link

By Douglas Farah's account, Victor Bout's alleged dealings with the Taliban and al-Qaeda "were the subject of an ongoing, classified US operation that began in early 2000." Aware of the lack of international instruments to prosecute Bout, the United States embarked on a campaign against him. "There was a concerted effort at the tail end of the Clinton administration, continued into the Bush administration, to put him out of business," Farah reported, citing another phantom former US government official "working out of the State Department."[49] Hoping against hope for something concrete, I checked the article for names of real people. Nothing. It was the familiar Farah sleight of hand.

Of course, any investigator might check for himself. How many such officials could there be in the given time frame, you might ask? Try thousands.

The intelligence community claims to have known for a long time of Bout's extensive ties to Afghanistan. For example, according to a 1998 Belgian intelligence report, one of Bout's Boeing 707s with a crew from Switzerland and registered in the Democratic Republic of the Congo was "partially financed by Afghan generals."[50] Unlike his relationships with other Afghan forces, Bout's supposed links to the Taliban have been mostly unknown, even within the rank-and-file of international intelligence communities. According to Douglas Farah, they go back to August 1995, when the Taliban was in opposition to President Burhanuddin Rabbani's government in Kabul.[51]

In reference to Bout's supposed link to the Taliban, a PBS documentary on gunrunners stated that Taliban officials impounded "30-odd tons of AK-47 small arms ammunition" meant for government forces in Kabul. At the time, the Taliban had captured ten provincial capitals, but had not yet taken Kabul, and little more was heard about the event until after 9/11.[52]

On January 1, 2002, the *Washington Monthly* shed additional light on supposed Bout-Taliban connections, saying that an apolitical Bout started selling to the Taliban while negotiating for the release of his plane and Russian crew in 1995. "When his plane was detained, he used the opportunity as a business introduction to the Taliban."[53] The Center for Public Integrity website also reported, "Bout, together with Russian diplomats, met Mullah Omar and other Taliban leaders to negotiate the release of the detained crew in Kandahar, but they were not successful."[54]

Bout doesn't deny meeting Omar, quite the opposite. "Of course I met with him. This was my crew. I was responsible for them. But selling arms to the Taliban? Never." According to Bout, Mullah Omar was simply awful. A leader without ideas.

Do I simply take Bout at his word? Of course not. But he may well have been telling the simple truth. I noted a grumble of resentment in Bout's voice, and nary a trace of dissembling or guile. It sounded like the truth to me.

"What side are you on?" I have been asked repeatedly throughout my investigation.

I am on my side, gentlemen, and I represent those who have no voice. If anyone is apolitical, I am. Not amoral, but apolitical.

Bout's denials of his Taliban dealings are all lies, if we are to believe the "UN and US government officials." They apparently said Bout made a deal with the Taliban in 1996 in the UAE, one of only three countries in the world, along with Pakistan and Saudi Arabia, which recognized the regime. "Starting in 1998, according to aircraft registration documents found in Kabul by Afghan officials, Bout's operation based in Sharjah sold the Taliban military a fleet of cargo planes that was used to haul tons of arms and materiel into Afghanistan."[55] Who made this statement? Douglas Farah.

Off went another email to Douglas Farah:

> How many planes did Bout sell to the Taliban? The reason I ask is that the operation doesn't make sense. If Bout is a transporter, then his business is buying, not selling, planes to maximize profit through operations, unless the planes he sold were clunkers. In which case, why would the Taliban buy them in the first place? Also, I am somewhat uncomfortable with the following phrase: "Starting in 1998, according to aircraft registration documents found in Kabul by Afghan officials." It sounds too convenient. So, would it be too much to ask for you to explain, who were these officials, or in the absence of this information whom did they work for and how is it that a man of Bout's supposed talents for invisibility would leave incriminating documents to be found by Afghani officials who luckily for you, told you about them?"

In an email of September 29, 2009, Farah simply replied that it was "all in the book." No, I was asking precisely because it is *not* in the book.

Of course, really replying to nosy independent investigators may not be in the interests of someone's farsighted agenda.

But, there was more to the campaign against Bout.

On January 7, 2002, the German weekly, *Der Spiegel,* claimed that Bout helped arrange the sale of up to 200 Russian T-55 and T-62 tanks to the Taliban. The tanks were alleged to have been transported by one of Bout's airfreight companies. Reportedly, undercover Russian SVR (intelligence) agents in Kabul discovered that Pakistan's Inter Service Intelligence (ISI) agency was also in on the arms-smuggling deal, a violation of UN sanctions against the Taliban.[56] The primary source on this information apparently was Stephen Braun, Douglas Farah's co-author on *Merchant of Death*.

As of this writing, NATO forces arguably control much of Afghanistan, and what isn't directly controlled is subject to constant surveillance by the most sophisticated detection systems known. Yet the tanks are nowhere to be found. Are they all in some Taliban caves? Or is this another case of missing WMDs? Have anyone tried calling Afghanistan's lost and found department? The serious accusations against Bout and his 200 tanks have lost all credibility, but this fact has been quietly swept under the rug.

According to intelligence sources in Ministry of Foreign Affairs Russian President Putin, in late February or early March 2002, reported to the White House that ISI agents known to Russian intelligence were connected to arms rings supplying not only the Taliban but also an offshoot of both the Chechen and al-Qaeda cells. President Bush promised to send an FBI team to St. Petersburg to further investigate, but that turned out to be an empty promise. The Russian intelligence was buttressed independently in August 2000, when a purchase order found during Leonid Minin's arrest in Italy showed that ISI ran guns for the Taliban, without any apparent help from Bout.

Just Another V.P.

On December 14, 2004, the *Los Angeles Times* opened its morning edition with a startling story: "Air cargo companies allegedly tied to reputed Russian arms trafficker Victor Bout have received millions of dollars in federal funds from US contractors in Iraq, even though the Bush administration has worked for three years to rein in his enterprise."[57]

The story continued with the *Times* reporters throwing one firebomb after another. "Planes linked to Victor Bout's shadowy network continued to fly into Iraq, according to government records and interviews with officials, even though the Treasury Department froze his assets in July [2004] and placed him on a blacklist for allegedly violating international arms sanctions. Largely under the auspices of the Pentagon, US agencies including the Army Corps of Engineers and the Air Force, and the US-led Coalition Provisional Authority, which governed Iraq until last summer, have *allowed their private contractors* to do business with the Bout network [emphasis added]. Four firms linked to the network by the CIA and international investigators have flown into Iraq approximately 195 times on US business, government flight and fuel documents show. One such flight landed in Baghdad last week. The list of the Bout network's suspected clients over the years includes the Taliban, which bought airplanes for a secret airlift of arms to Afghanistan. The Taliban was known to have shared weapons with al-Qaeda."[58]

Initially, no other US mainstream corporate media came within shouting distance of this story with the exception of a veteran journalist, Mike Isikoff, of *Newsweek*. And he added one additional item: "The exact number of flights Bout-connected firms made into Iraq, 142 ... were contracted by Halliburton's subsidiary Kellogg Brown & Root (KBR)."[59] As reviewers of the war-zone contracting have noted, Halliburton was then an oil-services company "that also provides construction and military support services – a triple-header of wartime spoils."[60] "Wartime spoils" have immensely profited the corporation that Vice President Cheney had headed.

According to the Center for Public Integrity, the Cheney-Halliburton story is the classic military-industrial revolving door tale. As Secretary of Defense under Bush's father, Dick Cheney paid Brown & Root services (later Kellogg Brown & Root, now KBR, Inc.) $3.9 million to report on how private companies could help the US Army, as Cheney cut hundreds of thousands of Army jobs. Then Brown & Root won a five-year contract to provide logistics for the US Army Corp of Engineers all over the globe. In 1995 Cheney became CEO, and Halliburton jumped from 73rd to 18th on the Pentagon's list of top contractors, benefiting from at least $3.8 billion in federal contracts and taxpayer-insured loans.[61]

According to the aforementioned *Los Angeles Times* article, "UN investigations and American officials have linked Air Bas, incorporated in Texas but based in the United Arab Emirates, and Irbis, a company registered in Kazakhstan, to Bout's aviation empire." Before 2001, Air Bas was called Air Cess.[62]

When I was digging for evidence, I came across several pages of documents from intelligence files that indicated one of the Bout-linked firms was drawing fuel from the Army as of March 10, 2004, and another as of April 5, 2004. Bout, again, I thought to myself, refueling at American bases? Through a captain in the US Army's special security unit stationed in Iraq who has followed my investigations for years, I was finally able to secure a copy of the fuel purchasing agreements with Air Bas, one of ... Richard Chichakli's companies!

What the Hell is going on? I thought. Chichakli? Air Bas is Bout's company. It is Bout, not Chichakli. Everyone from the United Nations to *Newsweek*, the *New York Times*, *Washington Times* to *Le Monde*[63] insisted on linking Bout's Air Bas activity in Iraq to US government lack of oversight regarding contracts after the Merchant of Death's assets had been frozen.

Douglas Farah made the Bout-Air Bas connection very clear in his *Washington Post*, September 23, 2007 article.[64] *Merchant of Death* co-author, Stephen Braun's August 13, 2007 *Washington Post* article clearly stated that "Bout's planes were used as what former Deputy Defense Secretary Paul D. Wolfowitz described as second-tier contractors. The Army or the Army Corps of Engineers would hire KBR or other prime contractors to fly in supplies, and the firms would then hire Bout planes, either directly or through air charter services."

This too, was apparently a lie. Bout didn't fly anything for the United States government! Chichakli did. I held the agreement in my hand, signed on March 9, 2004. There was no doubt about it, Air Bas belonged to Chichakli. Then why, did the United Nations insist on freezing Air Bas assets as belonging to Bout? To muddy the waters further, several weeks later, I acquired Air Bas Jet Fuel identification card issued to the company by the Department of Defense of the United States.

The Center for Public Integrity, part of the International Consortium of Investigative Journalists, is a non-profit organization based in Washington, DC. Its work is generally considered authoritative, and I have cited their reporting on the meeting between Bout and Taliban leaders regarding his downed aircraft and crew. They stated categorically that "Air Cess, just like Air Bas, exists mostly on paper, but it has given Victor Bout the right to use the "N" number given to planes *registered in North America*, a vital advantage, especially when you fly illegal cargo and contraband" [emphasis added].[65]

I Googled for their website, quickly found what I was looking for, clicked on the *supporting documents* section and waited. I became particularly interested in the extensive Leonid Minin documentation they claimed to have accessed, since multiple corporate media reports claimed that Minin and Bout were partners in their arms-for-drugs-for-diamonds trade. To my chagrin, all Minin documents had been taken offline. I picked up the phone.

"What happened to the Minin archive in the documents section of your webpage?" I asked.

"Well, you see, we ... we had to take it down."

"Why?"

"Ah, we didn't have permission from the authorities."

"Which authorities?" I insisted.

"I don't know. You should speak to Alain Lallemand."

"OK. Can I speak to him?"

"Well, he is not here. But I can give you a number to call."

"I wanted to ask you about Victor Bout. I am working on a deadline, and unless I hand in my manuscript in the next few weeks, my publisher may do unseemly bodily harm to me."

She laughed.

So did I. The mood had been set. It was time to sink the line.

"What's so special about Bout's passports?" I asked.

"He has two of them," came the reply.

"Yes?" I asked expectantly.

There was a pause. Then I continued. "If you look closely, one was issued in 1998 and the other in the year 2000," I said.

"Why would he change his passports so often?"

"Perhaps because he travels a lot," I quipped, "and ran out of blank pages for stamps."

"Or perhaps, he doesn't want to be caught," she replied significantly.

"With what?"

"You know what I mean," she answered.

"No, actually, I don't. Let me ask you another question. Under the subheading Bout Arms Transactions 1996-1998, there is a flow chart."

"That's Bout's operation," she clarified.

"How do you know this," I asked somewhat puzzled.

"It's from the UN report."

"Do you know who wrote the report?" I inquired.

"Johan Peleman," she said triumphantly.

"And the flow chart of Bout's operating network is from the same report?"

"Exactly."

Before saying goodbye, I had to know one more thing. "Have you actually seen the evidence purported to show the extent of Bout's arms smuggling network?"

"No," she said. "Just the flow chart."

A few minutes later, I called and left a message for Alain Lallemand. That was many weeks before press time, and I doubt the man intends to get back to me. You see, the Belgian courts found a great part of Minin's documents to be fakes. I am sure that's why they were taken down. It had made someone important look bad and exposed their lies, and perhaps their true intentions. Someone was lining ducks up for a kill. I could smell it. In this business, one's nostrils never quite adjust. Instead, they develop a kind of hypersensitivity – to the innumerable variations of the basic rotten smell.

It was the *sequence* of events that concerned me.

Zero, one, one, two, three, five, eight, thirteen, twenty-one, thirty-four, and so on. That is the Fibonacci sequence. Anyone might look and not see a pattern, but it is right there and staring one in the face (every third numeral is the sum of the previous two). I needed to see how each event was connected to the one before it. I pulled up everything I could on Bout, including the timelines of the corporate news stories on him, UN reports, government actions and announcements, not to mention an extensive file I had compiled on Internet traffic regarding Bout and the sites that most covered him. Who said what about him and when? What did a major announcement on Bout coincide with? That will give me the sequence, the pattern, that makes order out of chaos, I thought to myself.

"Fibonacci sequence?" asked a friend, dumbfounded. "Have you been reading Dan Brown?"

"True sequences don't change. Neither do the patterns of human thought. I just need to find it," I replied, absolutely sure I had walked through looking glass into a parallel universe of smoke and mirrors, but one where the actual outlines were still discernible.

Aside from his numerous qualifications for phantom journalism, Douglas Farah is a very intelligent man. He is closely associated with the Council on Foreign Relations, the US arm of the powerful and secretive Bilderberg Group, and the Hudson Institute, a neocon hotbed. The CFR boasts a membership of about 4,000. But its roster includes literally hundreds of powerful figures occupying key positions in the media – not merely writers, reporters, and news anchors who deliver the news, but also editors, publishers, and executives who define *what* news is and *how* it is covered. Just as significantly, the tiny CFR clique has for decades had a virtual stranglehold on the executive branch of the US government, as well as much of academia.

In his October 30, 1993 "Ruling Class Journalists" essay, *Washington Post* ombudsman Richard Harwood candidly discussed how the CFR dominates our news media. Harwood described the Council on Foreign Relations as "the closest thing we have to a ruling Establishment in the United States ... Its members are the people who, for more than half a century, have managed our international affairs and our military-industrial complex." After listing the executive-branch positions then occupied by CFR members, Harwood continued: "What is distinctively modern about the council these days is the considerable involvement of journalists and other media figures, who account for more than 10 percent of the membership.

"The editorial page editor, deputy editorial page editor, executive editor, managing editor, foreign editor, national affairs editor, business and financial editor and various writers as well as [the now deceased] Katherine Graham, the paper's principal owner, represent the *Washington Post* in the council's membership," observed Harwood. He went on to describe CFR representation among the owners, management, and editorial personnel for the other media giants – the *New York Times*, *Wall Street Journal*, *Los Angeles Times*, NBC, CBS, ABC, and so on. These media heavyweights "do not merely analyze and interpret foreign policy for the United States; they help make it," he concluded. Rather than offering an independent perspective on our rulers' actions, the Establishment media act as the ruling elite's voice – conditioning the public to accept, and even embrace "insider" designs that otherwise might not be politically attainable.

Back in 2003, when Douglas Farah was coming into his own, the Hudson Institute was heavily financed by Lord Conrad Black, the now disgraced former owner of the Hollinger Corporation. The Hudson Institute "has done more to shape the way Americans react to political and social events, think, vote and generally conduct themselves than perhaps any except the kingpin of the brainwashing establishment – Tavistock Institute of Human Relations itself."[66] Hudson primarily specializes in defense policy research and relations with Russia. Might Victor Bout fall under this specialized category? Of course.

Furthermore, "most of Hudson's military work is classified as secret. One of its largest clients is the US Department of Defense which includes matters of civil defense, national security, military policy and arms control."[67] In the mainstream media, Hudson and the CFR are usually portrayed as having opposite viewpoints. However, they serve the same interests, and Farah's job seems to be to lecture, travel, and issue reports on Victor Bout, Islam, Islamic terrorism, aviation, arms trafficking, diamonds, African politics, and whatever is hot in the media in such a way as to manipulate public opinion favorably to cartel interests.

But another apparent piece of the puzzle fell into place when I found a 2003 UN Security Council report on several violations of the arms embargo, first in Somalia implicating Air Bas in Bout's aviation empire, and then in Rwanda where Air Bas was accused of supplying Hutu extremists with arms for carrying out the Rwanda genocide.

Just when I thought I had stumbled onto one of Bout's transgressions, I drew another blank. The UN Security Council report was referring to Air Bass FZE of Sharjah, an entity utterly unrelated to Bout's empire. How do I know this? The two companies incorporation documents. That didn't stop Office of Foreign Assets Control to add Victor Bout and his onetime accountant Richard Chichakli to its Specially Designated Nationals and Blocked Persons (SDN) list,[68] citing the aforementioned UN report as evidence. In the BBC-4 *World Report* special on Victor Bout, the host interviewed Adam Szubin, the head of the US Treasury's Office of Foreign Assets Control (OFAC).

Voice over: "Finally, OFAC decided to put a bullet straight through Bout's wallet. In 2005, his company assets were frozen and put off limit to others."

Szubin: "If Mr. Bout had assets in the United States, they would have been immediately frozen."

Did I hear right, did the OFAC man just contradict the BBC? Did Bout have assets in the United States or didn't he?

"I never did any business in the United States," Bout told me. "I have principles." OFAC agrees, at least on the first point. Bout, to their chagrin, never did business in America. Here was a real *but* (not as in Victor But, but as in a simple, to the contrary, English "but").

BBC program host: "How much money did you find, roughly?"

Szubin: "A close conspirator of his assesses that he lost in the region of six billion dollars in profit due to pressure that was put on him thanks to sanctions."

Six billion dollars? In profit?

A good story. Yes, definitely a good story. True? No, most definitely not true, although it makes for compelling television. There is no arms surplus available for illegal trading in the entire world that comes close to even 10% of this number. How can my assertions be verified? A Thai court identified a US claim about the hundreds of surface-to-air missiles that Bout supposedly agreed to sell to the FARC (Revolutionary Armed Forces of Colombia) as "lacking foundation and credibility." The excerpt from the Thai Court of First Instance verdict (page 48), as somehow translated from Thai into Russian and then back into English, is as follows: "...the accused was charged with selling the large quantity of war weapons and fighter aircrafts which have the large quantity and the price is too high to believe that it can be illegally traded. *It [the Court] is in doubt where to find the illegal source of large quantity of war weapons* ... [emphasis added]."

For example, it took nine years to officially deliver $20 billion worth of arms in the Al-Yamamah deal between the UK's BAE systems and the Saudi Arabian government, the largest arms deal ever contracted. If Szubin's assertion is to be taken at face value and the US indeed denied Bout $6 billion in profit, how much should he have sold in arms to make such a profit, and how on earth can such a quantity of arms be moved without anyone taking notice?

Furthermore, UN investigators examining bank records in the United Arab Emirates in 2001, a known terrorist money-laundering center, claimed they "found frequent money transfers between British Gulf and another Bout-linked company, San Air General Trading."[69] This article appeared in the *Los Angeles Times* in late December 2004. Among its authors is Stephen Braun, Douglas Farah's co-author on the *Merchant of Death*.

It took a little digging, but in the end, this too proved to be utterly baseless. Off went an email to Stephen Braun.

> Hey Stephen.
> My name is Daniel Estulin. I am working on a very tight deadline re. Victor Bout. I would like to clarify a point and would love to have your cooperation. In your *LAT* article you write that investigators found frequent money transfers between various Bout companies. Specifically, "payments for many of the weapons that went to Liberia through Victor Bout's network in 2000 and 2001 were

> directed to San Air's bank accounts." That's not what I found. Can you get back to me ASAP?

Did he? Of course not.

San Air USA was created in 2000 for Victor Bout in the US by Richard Chichakli. Apparently the plan was to manufacture panels for Russian aircraft, which business would provide a basis for Bout and family to establish a residence in the US. After Bout's application in Dubai for a US visa was rejected, the project died, and Chichakli dissolved the firm after a couple of years. Only Chichakli's name appears on the company documents, and it never did any business beyond maintaining a small banking account in Richardson, Texas.

San Air UAE, a completely different company, to which account an alleged payment from the Liberian Maritime located in the US was made, was founded by Andrei Semenchenko who has been locked up in a United Arab Emirates jail for the past eight years.[70] In fact, UAE-based San Air would have been "Sun Air" except for a typo in the incorporation documents, which turned it into San Air. The name remained unaltered on the books because Semenchenko did not have the money to correct the incorporation document.

Did Stephen Braun know this? If I found out, working on a limited budget, so could he. Furthermore, The US treasury's OFAC used the exact language stated in a UN resolution about Liberia to credit their action against Bout's 30 companies, as per UN reports S/2006/976 and S/2007/340. Is it the case of one hand washing the other? Another example of converging interests of the Men behind the Curtain?

In fact, as I discovered, none of the assets frozen by OFAC belonged to Victor Bout, but rather to Richard Chichakli. I have in my possession every financial transaction that took place through the 30 "Victor Bout" entities OFAC brags about freezing.

Furthermore, the 30 big financial entities, as described by OFAC, weren't big at all. In addition to Chichakli's aircraft brokerage business, there were six dormant corporations with no activities, one tax preparation office, one payroll and accounting practice, one used motorcycles dealership, two continued professional education providers with no activities, a home renovation venture, and a swimming pool cleaning service. The other named entities were either closed or dissolved, such as "Airbas Transportation," Chichakli's airline the US government contracted to service American forces in Iraq.

What I found telling, and at the same time disturbing, is that with all the extraordinary media hype that accompanied OFAC action against Bout, and to a lesser degree Chichakli, the latter was not, and still is not, listed as having any frozen assets in the United States. How do I know this? The US State Department is under obligation to report to the United Nations' Security Council the names of people who are sanctioned, and whose assets are frozen. Chichakli's name is not listed as a person sanctioned by the US government, yet his assets were reported as if they belonged to Victor Bout.

I asked Richard Roper, United States attorney in charge of the Chichakli case, why the government had taken over seven years as of this writing (9/15/2002 - late 2009) to investigate Chichakli without any charges or indictment brought against him. In context, the Enron investigation lasted slightly over one year.

"I can't comment on that," replied the US attorney, Richard Roper. Where have I heard that before?

The US Treasury ordered the freezing of Chichakli's assets and virtual termination of his right to work, live, or exist in the United States. The Treasury acted at the recommendation of the State Department, and in cooperation with the DOJ, the CIA, Homeland Security, and other departments in the executive branch according to the official statement released later by the US government. The cause of the action remains "SECRET" and the justification of the search warrant is forever "SEALED."

When I was searching for evidence against Chichakli, I came across an April 7, 2006 UN Security Council report pursuant to resolution 1521 concerning Liberia. The report started with a note from the Syrian Arab Republic: "We have the honor to inform the Committee that the Syrian authorities found, on 13 June 2005, the name of Mamdouh Chichakli, which appears in the above mentioned list [the assets freeze list], on the account of Amal Amin Sabagh, as guardian of the account. Accordingly, the Syrian authorities have frozen the assets of Mr. Chichakli and have blacklisted him.

I did a double-take. This didn't make any sense. The official United Nations report was stating in black and white that they had frozen the account of Chichakli's seventy-year-old mother, Dr. Amal A. Sabagh. What's more, the name blacklisted on the report, Mamdouh Chichakli, belongs to Richard Chichakli's dead father.

No, I thought to myself. This was no mere mistake. This was done on purpose.

If the United States government didn't have Chichakli on their list, why would Syria go out of their way and put him on theirs? Furthermore, whose assets did they freeze? What's going on? Chichakli left Syria almost 45 years ago; because of his past family history in Syria he surely wouldn't leave assets in a Syrian bank. If he had no assets in the country, then, what did the Syrian authorities find?

They found, according to the report, an "amount of monies not available." Why not available? Because Chichakli's assets in Syria amounted to *zero*. Therefore, Syria froze nonexistent Chichakli assets in the country he hadn't set foot in almost half a century. Interesting. Something else drew my attention to the UN report – the unsolicited, voluntary report by the Syrian government.

Syria and the United States government working together? What's the world coming to, I thought to myself. Paragraph 116 at the bottom of page 34 of the UN report clearly shows that Syria was not among the countries contacted by the UN panel on Liberia. Then, why are sticking their nose into someone else's business? What's it to them?

Onward Christian Soldiers

Chichakli might not have known anything about non-existing assets in a Syrian bank, but he knew plenty about Operation Blessing, televangelist Pat Robertson's "charity" in Africa, organized with the very same characters who were allegedly working hand-in-glove with Victor Bout.

To prevent him from talking, Chichakli maintains, the US government offered him a deal – his life back and witness protection in exchange for saying that he knew Victor Bout to be an arms dealer. Chichakli refused, offering to testify, without immunity, to what he knew, not what the government wanted him to say. He was refused. Then, on April 26, 2005 the government counterattacked, seizing all of his records and assets.

What did a God-fearing, Christian missionary like Pat Robertson do in Africa? Robertson's African Development Company apparently used the cover of Robertson's tax-exempt "Operation Blessing" to smuggle conflict diamonds out of civil war-ravaged Zaire, later renamed the Democratic Republic of Congo.[71] Bout would have surely known this. So would have Chichakli. Africa was Bout's stomping ground for almost a decade.

Who was Robertson's partner? Mass murderer Charles Taylor, former Liberian strongman. The Robertson-Taylor Cayman Islands-based front company was called Freedom Gold, whose operations were overseen from Robertson's offices in Virginia Beach, USA. What's more, the US Special prosecutor for war crimes in Sierra Leone, David Crane, charged in May 2005 that Taylor was harboring al-Qaeda members and training rebels throughout West Africa in exchange for blood diamonds.[72] Now, if you are the US government, having a Richard Chichakli shine the light of truth on the transgressions of the Bush government's favorite Bible thumper simply wouldn't do.

Chichakli was evidently ready to go public to show that Robertson was using his Operation Blessing, a supposed non-profit Christian-aid organization, not to provide aid to African victims of famine and war, but to transport equipment and supplies for his various diamond-mining ventures on that continent, and at US taxpayers' expense. This was later confirmed by Max Blumenthal, a highly respected journalist writing for *The Nation* magazine on September 19, 2005: "Far from the media's gaze, Robertson has used the tax-exempt, non-profit Operation Blessing as a front for his shadowy financial schemes, while exerting his influence within the Republican Party to cover his tracks." And all, of course, in the name of Jesus.

Chichakli needed to disappear. He was dangerous. Guantanamo was out of the question. He was too old to have been suddenly discovered as an al-Qaeda fighter. What did the United States government do? In July 2006, they renditioned him to Syria, where he ended up in the hands of Syrian intelligence agents. Impossible? Precedent setting case? Hardly. Ask Syrian-born Canadian Maher Arar, a telecommunications engineer, who was deported by the US government to Syria in 2002, where he was detained and tortured for almost a year. Despite a Canadian court ruling exonerating Arar of all charges and links to terrorism, the United States government to this day publicly insists that Arar is affiliated with members of organizations they describe as terrorist.

Intelligence sources have confirmed to me that the US government paid $4 million to the ex-leader of the Syrian Republican Guard, General Adnan Makhlouf, to have Chichakli liquidated in Syria. The US government representative who made the payment was a CIA operative working in Syria with diplomat status. But Chichakli, a former US Army intelligence officer, escaped. For the United States' plans, that was a serious bummer. In fact, Chichakli's liquidation was taken for granted to such an extent that some of his confiscated assets began disappearing, even before he was renditioned to Syria. All in all, Chichakli states the FBI removed nearly $500,000 in diamonds, jewelry, cash and collectible US notes of $500 and $1000 denominations. When Chichakli demanded to know their whereabouts, the FBI claimed that the assets in questions were delivered to OFAC. OFAC, in turn, claim not to know anything about them.

If I ever had any faith in the mechanics of the United Nations and their inner workings, after my Bout investigation that faith has been shattered forever.

Back in 2002, a 59-page UN Security Council report confirmed British Gulf International formed part of the Bout empire. The same UN investigators have also scrutinized British Gulf International's link with another airline that flew into Iraq, Jetline, and found them to be tied to Bout. The *Los Angeles Times* obtained Baghdad flight records, which clearly demonstrated that British Gulf also flew for KBR, Halliburton's subsidiary.

With the UN Security Council conclusions in hand, and the true ownership of Air Bas safely buried by the mainstream press, that made it a stunning four Bout air cargo firms working as subcontractors for the US government in Iraq at a time when Bout was apparently wanted for money laundering and arms smuggling by Interpol and the Belgian authorities, not to mention by the US government for his ties to the Taliban and al-Qaeda! How can any of this be possible, I thought to myself. Then, I remembered. I had stepped through the looking glass into a parallel universe were everything was in reverse. The universe of changing loyalties and black ops in the name of someone's far-reaching and farsighted foreign policy. For whom did all of these people work?

The mainstream press' timeline on the next series of events wasn't difficult to put together. "Soon after the *Los Angeles Times* story appeared, Senate Democrats asked the State Department's Richard Armitage and then Defense Department's Paul Wolfowitz to comment on the allegations. Neither knew anything, or so they claimed. Both, however, promised to look into the allegations."[73] Ironically, the final call on the contractors belongs to the Pentagon, and it was quite obvious that the State Department's inquiries, if they were ever made, were rejected.

Wolfowitz finally responded when the pressure from Democrats in Congress became unbearable. In a January 31, 2005 letter to Wisconsin Democratic Senator Russell Feingold, Wolfowitz acknowledged that "both the US Army and the CPA in Iraq did conduct business with companies that, in turn, subcontracted work to second-tier suppliers, who leased aircraft owned by companies associated with Mr. Bout. However, spokesmen for the US Central Command and the Pentagon brushed off inquiries on the subject saying they knew of no contracts with Bout-related companies. At the same time, they stressed the need to understand how complex contracting arrangements were in Iraq. The Pentagon, a military official said, could not check out the subcontractors who actually flew the flights into Iraq and Afghanistan."[74]

If we are to believe the aforementioned reports from America's leading corporate media publications, the consequences of Bout's "far-flung operations" have been devastating both in human cost and for long-term US geopolitical interests. Yet, the Pentagon, the paragon of American military might, would not give the subject matter the time of day. Perhaps, I thought to myself, there are too many people who feel they need to keep Bout around to fly into the next Iraq or Afghanistan.

There was something else that caught my attention in Michael Isikoff's *Newsweek* article. He stated that "it took the Bush administration until July 2004 *to issue* an Executive Order # 3348 directing the Office of Foreign Assets Control (OFAC) to finally freeze Bout's assets in the United States and forbid American firms from doing business with him [emphasis added]." Furthermore, it took the US government *an additional nine months,* until April 26, 2005, to freeze US assets of the 30 Bout-related companies. There was only one way to interpret that – the Bush administration was stalling for time. There is only one way to interpret the media's assertions regarding Bout's assets. They lied, brazenly and blatantly. OFAC only has the power to go after Bout's assets in the United States. Bout never had any assets in the United States, at least none that Farah, Braun or the United States government has been able to show belonged to Bout. The media knew that, of course, because we know. Someone was lining a duck up for a kill.

Indeed, "the move against Bout proved largely symbolic. During the time between the US designation and the UN listing, according to US and European intelligence sources, Bout revamped his operations, moving aircraft registrations and incorporating new companies. As a result, most of the designated companies no longer have any assets to be frozen, and it will take months to identify the new companies and begin sanctioning them."[75] Who says so? You guessed it. Douglas Farah.

As I continued to uncover one startling fact after another, I asked myself the same, nagging question. If Bout was indeed a Merchant of Death, why was the United States government being "very slow" to act on comprehensive links between weapons trafficking and terrorism? Were these links and criminal synergies allowed to take place and flourish? With irrefutable evidence mounting in front of me, was it just possible that Victor Bout simply served as an extension of America's foreign policy in Iraq, Afghanistan or Africa? How else could we interpret the stonewalling and the lies?

Needless to say, if we take this information at face value and try to rationalize it, none of it makes any sense, at least not in any world we know. Again, in the *real world*, a Victor Bout operation would not have succeeded because governments have the diplomatic, financial and intelligence clout to destroy the elements that threaten their sovereignty and the rule of law. And a Bout-Taliban link would certainly qualify as such a destructive element.

STILL HUNTING

The US government's punitive actions "were based on Bout's relationship with [then-Liberian president] Taylor, but, in announcing the OFAC action, the Treasury Department stressed another facet of Bout's activities, noting that he made $50 million in profits from arms transfers to the Taliban when the regime was hosting Osama bin Laden and al-Qaeda."[76]

Still, if we were to take the aforementioned US Treasury Department statement at face value, Bout was delivering weapons to the Taliban and al-Qaeda at the same time as the US government clandestinely contracted with him to work with American forces in Afghanistan and Iraq. How surreal is that? The Office of Foreign Asset Control, however, is based out of the Treasury Department, and Bout was being contracted by the Pentagon. Could this be a case of some remarkable incompetence in one department being utterly oblivious to what was going on in another department of the government?

This possibility loses credence with the addition of another strange coincidence. How could both the US State Department and the British Foreign Office allow such a high-profile case to slip through their nets? Perhaps the real reason Victor Bout continued to enjoy relative immunity was his usefulness in Iraq. What else could explain the undeniable fact that the coalition partners, the United States and Great Britain showed him exceptional favors while he did some of the dirtiest jobs for them? One French diplomat complained that "the American defense forces are using Victor's planes for their logistics." Would that make Bout an extension of someone else's foreign policy? You bet, it would. "Is that why the condemnation of his role in the diamond wars and other conflicts in sub-Saharan Africa over the past decade is being silently repudiated?" poignantly asked the PBS documentary *Gunrunners*.

The period of supposed "action" against Victor Bout coincided with the first Sadr uprising. In April 2004, Shiite firebrand cleric Muqtada al-Sadr and his Jaysh al-Mahdi militia rose in revolt against the US-led coalition in Iraq. The US forces quickly lost control of the roads and faced a serious problem. Neither supplies nor ammunition were getting through. Even the heavily fortified Green Zone was suffering from a food shortage.

According to *Mother Jones* in 2004, "Air Bas has continued to fly US military missions into Baghdad as well as the northern Iraqi air base of Balad, according to refueling records kept by the Defense Energy Support Center (DESC). DESC notes that Air Bas flights have been approved by military commanders for official government purposes."[77]

Still, in the wider scheme of things, there was something missing. I scanned through Isikoff's *Newsweek* article again and zeroed in on a paragraph I had previously underlined. "The firms were contracted by Halliburton's subsidiary Kellogg Brown & Root (KBR)." Then, I re-read the *Los Angeles Times* story. One of the paragraphs jumped out at me. "Among the firms holding US government contracts that officials said were using the network's services: Federal Express."

Federal Express, I must admit, clearly took me by surprise. Could the reference to FedEx be a mistake? Then, I found a reference to it in an Argentine publication, *Edicioni*, through the LexisNexis search engine: "A Federal Express official in the United Arab Emirates said Irbis was paid $22,000 for each of its round-trip flights." So, then, Bout was apparently cashing in through FedEx as well by flying shipments for the US Air Force.

I went back to the *Times* story. "KBR, formerly known as Kellogg Brown & Root, is a subsidiary of Halliburton, the Houston conglomerate formerly headed by Vice President Dick Cheney and holder of a massive no-bid contract for reconstruction projects in Iraq. Under pressure to move quickly on the crisis in Iraq, officials have paid little attention to the welter of subcontractors and sub-subcontractors involved in the massive reconstruction effort."

Back in May 2003, the CIA discreetly let it be known to the Pentagon that Bout's firms were cashing in on US-funded reconstruction efforts, but, "the warning did not reach the Coalition Provisional Authority (CPA) until May 2004."[78] Another coincidence, perhaps? No, simply a well juxtaposed lie, as we now know that Air Bas was a Chichakli company and not a Bout company. After conducting its own inquiry, the CPA allowed the companies to keep flying, "saying that only military officials could terminate their contracts."[79] The CPA was washing its hands of the entire matter.

Going over the Bout-Bush-Halliburton-KBR-Cheney-private contractor story made me wonder. When did anyone in charge become aware that supposedly one branch of the US government was offloading millions of dollars to an individual whom the United Nations, Belgium, France and another branch of the US government was trying to put in prison? "After all, it takes an internationally organized network of individuals," according to the United Nations December 21, 2000, report, "well-funded, well-connected and well-versed in brokering and logistics, to move illicit cargo around the world without raising the suspicion of law enforcement."

The report was insinuating that Bout is larger than life, more powerful than any nation on Earth, destined to control the world, unless he is permanently stopped. The worse it looks (meaning the "sexier" the report), the better it sells. The more attention being paid to it by the mainstream press, the greater the media frenzy and the higher the ratings. Higher ratings attract advertisers willing to spend lavishly, knowing that the American people need a daily diet of ever-present images of suffering, malnourished and dead bodies as part of a glossy propaganda campaign beamed into every living room in America.

What was never explained in any of the hundreds of articles on Bout was the sources of the sophisticated weaponry that he sold. As a retired CIA whistleblower (who had run an illicit gun trade through members of the Pakistani intelligence in the Waziristan tribal autonomous area situated between Pakistan and Afghanistan) once told me, "You don't just walk into a weapons factory and order 15 million rounds of ammunition." We can surmise that much of this materiel came from the old Soviet bloc, but at least its distribution has required the connivance of Western factions.

"When the Bush administration took over," reported Peter Landesman in the *New York Times Magazine*, "National Security Adviser Condoleezza Rice told US intelligence, as far as Victor Bout was concerned, to look but not to touch."[80] According to former intelligence officer for the NSA, Wayne Madsen, "US intelligence agencies considered Rice's move to call off all operations, aimed at Bout to be inexplicable, given Bout's direct links to arms smuggling to the Taliban and al-Qaeda, as well as to other areas rife with Islamic terrorist groups."

But, the Bush administration was not the only Western government covering up for Bout. In May 2004, the French government complained, according to a *Financial Times* article, that Washington and London were not supporting a move by the UN to freeze Bout's assets for his role in supporting Liberia's dictator Charles Taylor. Paris also alleged that the US and Britain were permitting Bout's firms to operate freely in occupied Iraq, including his air cargo companies being involved in supplying coalition forces.[81] When Britain appeared ready to agree to put the squeeze on Bout's operations, the Bush administration pressured London to relent.[82]

This was sheer madness. As I examined Bout's supposed network of international criminals, I realized that Bout had merely become the fall guy for a criminalized political structure much larger, far more hidden and more dangerous, than Bout himself. Something else dawned on me about Victor Bout. He was nothing but a creature of the post-Cold War era, the personification of disorganized crime, the exploiter of chaos – he was well funded, well connected, well versed in brokering and logistics, a highly mobile global enabler, apparently loyal to no country and with only the unadulterated motive of pure profit in mind.

But just when I thought I had reached the end, the world was treated to spectacular scenes of Bout-inspired pandemonium during his high profile arrest in Bangkok in March 2008. No, I thought to myself as I boarded a Thai Airlines Bangkok-bound flight, the world had not heard the last of Victor Bout, nor of his ragtag partners in crime.

Bout's Arrest

Victor Bout, an alleged international arms trafficker was arrested at the Sofitel Hotel on Silom Road in Bangkok on March 6,

2008 along with his associate, Mr. Andrew Smulian, by six officers of the US government and three Thai officers following a long-term international sting operation involving dozens of US undercover drug agents and agencies, the Royal Thai Police, the Romanian Border Police, the Romanian Prosecutor's Office Attached to the High Court of Cassation and Justice, the Korps Politie Curacao of the Netherlands Antilles, and the Danish National Police Security Services. The operation included over 200 Thai special forces operatives who immediately locked down the hotel. Bout was the man the United States government wanted most after Osama bin Laden.

Jewel in the crown. Man behind the terror. Merchant of Death. The most unsavory character alive. High priest and the foremost representative of a global potpourri of scum. After years of retracing Bout's steps, one would assume the US government would have hit the ground running in their extradition request, in what many experts felt at the time was a mere formality.

According to the official March 6, 2008, court documents, the United States Drug Enforcement Administration (DEA), announced the unsealing of charges against Viktor Bout, a/k/a "Boris," a/k/a "Victor Anatoliyevich Bout," a/k/a "Victor But," a/k/a "Viktor Budd," a/k/a "Viktor Butt," a/k/a "Viktor Bulakin," a/k/a "Vadim Markovich Aminov," an international arms dealer, and his associate Andrew Smulian, for conspiring to sell millions of dollars worth of weapons to the Fuerzas Armadas Revolucionarias de Colombia (FARC) – a designated foreign terrorist organization.

I'm not sure of the basis of much of this information, but I do know that during Bout's extradition hearing in a Bangkok courtroom, the judge asked the DEA officers if they knew who Bout was. "Of course we do," one man replied. "I have seen the film." He was referring to a Hollywood movie, *Lord of War*, a political crime thriller starring Nicholas Cage in the role of Victor Bout, Merchant of Death.

I carefully re-read the full complaint and over 800 pages of pertinent documents. According to the Complaint unsealed in Manhattan federal court:

Between November 2007 and February 2008, Bout and Smulian agreed to sell to the FARC millions of dollars worth of weapons — including surface-to-air missile systems (SAMs) and armor-piercing rocket launchers. During a series of recorded telephone calls and emails, Bout and Smulian agreed to sell the weapons to two confidential sources working with the DEA (the "CSs"), who held themselves out as FARC representatives acquiring these weapons for the FARC's use in Colombia.

In addition, during a series of consensually recorded meetings in Romania, Smulian advised the CSs, among other things, that: (1) Bout had 100 SAMs available immediately; (2) Bout could also provide helicopters and armor piercing rocket launchers; (3) Bout could arrange to have a flight crew airdrop the weapons into Colombian territory using combat parachutes; and (4) Bout and Smulian would charge the CSs $5 million to transport the weapons. During one of the meetings with the CSs, Smulian provided one of them with a digital memory stick that contained an article about Bout, and documents containing photographs and specifications for the SAMs and armor-piercing rocket launchers that Smulian had previously said Bout could provide.

In between his meetings with the CSs, Smulian spoke to Bout over a cell phone provided to him by one of the CSs at the direction of the DEA. These conversations between Smulian and Bout were legally intercepted by foreign authorities. During one of these conversations, Bout and Smulian discussed the $5 million delivery fee for the weapons. Bout also told Smulian, in coded language, that the weapons requested by the CSs were ready to be delivered. Subsequent to these phone calls with Smulian, Bout engaged in multiple recorded phone calls with one of the CSs, during which they arranged the March 6, 2008 meeting in Bangkok. According to the court documents, Bout and Smulian were charged with conspiracy to provide material support or resources to a designated foreign terrorist organization.

The following day, I watched a live press conference starring the lead prosecuting US Attorney, Michael J. Garcia, who said, "Viktor Bout and Andrew Smulian agreed to arm terrorists with high-powered weapons that have fueled some of the most violent conflicts in recent memory. Today, they face charges in the United States for agreeing to provide weapons to a terrorist organization that has threatened, and continues to threaten, American interests."

"This arms trafficker was poised to arm a narco-terrorist organization, but he now faces justice in the United States," said DEA Acting Administrator Michele M. Leonhart. It looked like Bout's extradition was a foregone conclusion.

Remarkably, after 533 days, on August 11, 2009, Mr. Jittakorn Wattanasin, Chief Justice of the Thai court, rejected the United States plea to extradite him.

I called James Entwistle, deputy chief of mission at the US embassy in Thailand.

"Are you familiar with the full set of documents presented in the case, signed by the Secretary of State Condoleezza Rice?"

"Of course, I am."

"Point "gg" on page 10 states that 'On or about March 6, 2008, during a meeting in Thailand, after CS-3 explained that the FARC wanted to kill American forces in Colombia, Bout indicated that the fight against the United States was also his fight and that he intended to supply the FARC with arms.' Do you have it on tape and if you do, can I hear it?" I asked him.

"I can't comment on that," he shot back.

Of course.

I called Michael A. Braun (no relation to author Steven Braun), a 34-year DEA veteran who had spearheaded the Bout hunt from the beginning. Since retiring from the force, he had joined Spectre Group International as its Managing Partner. Michael Braun appears to be a poster boy of 21st century law enforcement, a gun-wielding goon with a my-way-or-the-highway, end-justifies-means attitude. It seemed to me that nothing was out of bounds for this fellow, from lying to cheating to kidnapping witnesses to forging official government documents to bribing key witnesses, all in the name of law and order, or should I say, One-World law and order.

I introduced myself and asked him about Bout's arrest.

"Do you know if the meeting was recorded?"

"I can't comment on that," he said decisively.

"What happened in court?" I asked him.

"We are mystified by the ruling, to be honest with you, Daniel."

"Why is that?"

Michael Braun explained to me the dangers of international terrorism, and the FARC in particular, to world stability.

"But the people who were allegedly buying weapons from an alleged arms dealer were not FARC, but rather US government agents."

"In the United States, you need to show the intent of sale to *alleged* terrorists. That's enough."

"Except, you were not in the United States, but in Thailand," I shot back. "And in Thailand, according to the law, you have to actually *be* FARC to show intent, not someone masquerading as FARC."

"There is no doubt FARC are terrorists," he replied. Michael Braun clearly "missed" my point.

"When the DEA were planning this operation, why didn't it occur to anyone to check the local laws? I mean it looks like someone wanted this man to get off."

"I can't answer that, Daniel."

Then I asked a key question.

"Michael, why didn't the US government agree to pay Bout the $2 million advance he asked for? I mean it would be stupid for not to pay the money when you have the once-in-a-lifetime opportunity to seize both 100 anti-aircraft missiles as well as Victor Bout. Don't you agree?"

"Hello, hello? I can't hear you."

All right, I thought to myself, I will pretend you can't hear me, and you can pretend that you would really love to help, except for the bad connection.

On September 29, 2009, I emailed Braun a list of 10 questions dealing with specifics of the case, explaining the urgency of the request due to a pending deadline.

> Michael
>
> I am sorry for the bad reception. I wanted to ask you a few questions and it would be great if you find a few moments to answer them. Thank you in advance. Hope you are well.

Most of my questions involved the obvious discrepancies discussed here. One was obvious, but not yet mentioned: *Why is the DEA involved in this case?* Another was so far from obvious that it may startle you: *How did Andrew Smulian end up in the United States?*

Failing to hear from Michael Braun, special agent in charge of the Victor Bout investigation, I sent him another email one week later.

> Hi Michael
>
> This is Daniel Estulin, again. I have a feeling you might not have received my email....
>
> As you can see my questions are very case-specific. Again, I am working on the deadest of deadlines and need to hear back from you by Wednesday of this week, meaning tomorrow. My publisher has very magnanimously extended my deadline.
>
> I would like to add another matter to this list.
>
> About eight months ago, one of your men by the name of Derek Odney, an assistant US District Attorney, met with a former Russian officer, a specialist in nuclear technology who was working on

Bout's defense. The meeting took place in front of the US Embassy. This two-hour meeting was photographed by your people.

How do I know? Because several of your Embassy staff are my readers.

What I imagine you don't know is that the meeting was also audio- and video-recorded by the Russians. As it turns out, the Russian officer was a lot smarter than Odney because after two hours of beating around the bush, he was able to get Odney to say on tape that you (i.e., the US) will pay him (a Russian officer) any amount of money he wants if he just gets out of the way and lets you extradite Bout. If you have the proof that Bout is the Merchant of Death, why would you compromise the entire operation in this way?

Michael, my books are read by millions around the world and my interviews are heard by tens of millions. I would very much like to get your side of it correctly. If I can't, I will just have to work with the assumptions I have, based on available information or lack of it.

Hoping to hear from you.
Daniel Estulin
Author of *The True Story of the Bilderberg Group*

After more queries, I finally received a reply from Michael Braun, on October 16, 2009, tartly claiming that he dealt only with "professional journalists," not "conspiracy buffs." Ouch! He then wished me a "wonderful weekend," with "regards." Aaah, that felt so much better!

Having failed to get anywhere with former special agent Michael Braun, I contacted Andrew Smulian's lawyer, Mary Elizabeth Mulligan. She is a partner at the New York law firm Friedman Kaplan Seiler & Adelman LLP. The company's client-list reads like who's who of the rich and famous. Certainly, some of the most powerful of the Bilderberg Group heavyweights and Wall Street were at one time or another represented by Friedman Kaplan Seiler & Adelman: Bertelsmann, Lazard Frères, and MasterCard.

As Bout's and Smulian's cases are intimately linked, I sent Ms. Mulligan an email on October 12, 2009.

Hi Mary
My name is Daniel Estulin. I understand you represent Andrew Smulian.

I am an investigative journalist working against the deadest of deadlines on a book. One of the chapters deals with Victor Bout. I am in Bangkok, so I am very familiar with the case....

> Amongst other things, I would love to find out how did Andrew make it to the United States?
>
> Again, Mary, I am working on a deadline. My books on the Bilderberg Group have sold millions of copies around the world. My work is followed by tens of millions.
>
> Let me know when it might be convenient to speak to you. If there is anything I can do to help you in your case from here, please let me know.
>
> Daniel Estulin

In less than twenty-four hours, I received Ms. Mulligan's reply: "No comment." Hoping against hope, a couple of days later I tried another tack.

> Mary
>
> In the real world we would be playing on the same team. Your client and Bout are in the same boat, sort of. The difference is that Bout is going to go free and your client will be imprisoned, unless, of course he is a government agent.
>
> Michael Braun, former DEA agent in charge of Bout's investigation and currently employed as a senior partner with Spectre told me he had nothing to say when I asked him how Smulian got to New York....
>
> I have a lot of very valuable information to offer your client in his defense. Information, that will most surely get him off.
>
> Needless to say, in the real world, a lawyer looking after the client's best interests would jump at a chance to talk to me.
>
> Do you?
>
> Hope you are well.
> Daniel

I have not heard back from Mary Mulligan.

Andrew Smulian's first court appearance took place on March 10, 2008. Since then, there has been a virtual lockdown on any information about him. Bout has been in court over a dozen times in the same span of time, every one of his appearances followed by a media frenzy. Yet, the mainstream press has been suspiciously silent on Andrew Smulian. Why?

There was something else that bothered me about Smulian's camp. Why would a powerful Wall Street law firm defend the interests of someone who is by most reports a penniless, low-life gunrunner, one of the "potpourri of scum" as Michael Braun called them. Compassion? Gosh, can you imagine! Were they actually planning on beating the United States government in court? Smulian was being accused of *conspiracy to provide material support to a foreign terrorist organization*. That's at least a decade in the slammer, by my calculations. What if Mary Mulligan and her people were making sure he was safely delivered into the waiting arms of Uncle Sam? After all, if the entire Bout case is a farce, as has been shown thus far in Thai court and in my book, you wouldn't want Smulian represented by an honest lawyer, truly working on Smulian's defense. The fact that the United States government always knew that Bout, the so-called Merchant of Death, had no rockets to deliver to anyone, be it the FARC or Santa Claus, must forever remain hidden from the susceptible masses. Otherwise ... No, there won't be an otherwise. That's why one of Wall Street's most prestigious firms is there, marking territory.

I gave it one last shot. On October 20, 2009 I emailed Brendon Robert McGuire, who has represented the US government in its proceeding against Smulian.

> Hi Brendan
> My name is Daniel Estulin. I am an investigative journalist working against the deadest of deadlines on my new book. One third of the book deals with Victor Bout and Andrew Smulian.
>
> Since we haven't heard anything about Mr. Smulian lately, I wanted to ask you if the US government and Smulian are negotiating a plea bargain?
>
> Also, can you tell me when is Mr. Smulian's next court appearance?
>
> Finally, I would love to know how Mr.Smulian made his way to New York. If you have the time, I would love to interview you for my book.
>
> Thank you ahead of time
> Daniel Estulin

I wasn't holding out much hope, but Mr. McGuire surprised me and responded the following day. He stated that Yusill Scribner, of the Southern District of New York US Attorney's press office, was being assigned to assist me "to the extent possible." Less than three hours later, I received a follow-up email from Mr. Scribner, supplying the docket sheet and "waiver of indictment" in the case of US v. Smulian. He also asked for my phone number and a "convenient time" when we might be able to chat.

I replied immediately, hoping that my very relevant questions would for once, be answered.

> Yusill
> Thank you very much for your reply. Probably the easiest thing to do is for me to send you a list of case-specific questions re Smulian/Bout. Once I have your answers I will most definitely call you.
>
> 1. How did Andrew Smulian make it to New York?
>
> 2. How much of your success in Smulian's prosecution depends on whether Victor Bout is acquitted or convicted?
>
> 3. Where are the weapons Bout and Smulian were allegedly willing to sell to the undercover DEA agents posing as the FARC?
>
> 4. Why didn't the US agree to pay Bout the $2 million he allegedly demanded as an advanced payment? Wouldn't it make it easier to prosecute them both if you actually had something concrete to show as evidence? The reason I ask is that in a Thai court the US had no evidence of Bout's transgressions. Doodles and a map do not count.
>
> 5. Why is the DEA involved in the case?
>
> 6. What is Derek Odney's role in the case? The reason I ask is the following:
>
> About eight months ago, Derek Odney had met in Bangkok with a former Russian officer, specialist in nuclear technology who was working on Bout's defense. The meeting took place in front of the US Embassy. This two-hour meeting was photographed by the US people. What I imagine Derek doesn't know is that the meeting was also audio- and video-recorded by the Russians. As it turns out, the Russian officer was a lot smarter than Odney because after two hours of beating around the bush, he was able to get Odney to say on tape that the US government will pay him (a Russian officer) any amount of money he wants if he just gets out of the way and let's the USG extradite Bout. If the government's case against Bout and Smulian is airtight, why would Derek compromise the entire operation in this way?
>
> Furthermore, how can I arrange to see Mr. Smulian in prison for an interview? I emailed Mary Mulligan, but she is away on business until October 26.
>
> Hope you are well.
> Daniel

Six days later, I received the all-to-familiar reply: "No comment." Also included was an invitation to "feel free to email or call" regarding any "follow-up." How can I "follow up" on no information? That was the end of that.

All the detours had only led to one more "Dead end.... Road out.... Proceed at own risk."

Thai Food for Thought

The Court's decision was called "a bitter blow" by the US government, but seeing what transpired throughout the case, it could only have been expected. Most significantly, the Public Prosecutor states that the Defendant was allegedly "involved in conspiracy to commit crime with 'FuerZas Armadas Revolucionarias de Colombia Ejercito del Pueblo' (FARC)." Unfortunately for the prosecution, this is a non-starter, because, as appears from the materials of the actual case-file, Victor Bout was not dealing with any real person from FARC, but rather with a group of agent-provocateurs (all of them American nationals, none of them Colombian).

Of course, as one would expect in a sting, it was not Bout who approached the phony FARC operatives in the first instance. The DEA ops masquerading as FARC first approached him, with offers to buy *a plane*. This was later presented as soliciting "portable anti-aircraft missiles and other war weapons." And over the course of the Thai proceedings these morphed into "guided ballistic missiles," as the latter description appears in the Public Prosecutor's appeal.

What is absolutely clear is that Bout was not involved in a conspiracy to commit a crime with FARC in Thailand, as claimed by the Public Prosecutor, because *under Thai law* one can not enter a conspiracy with someone who is only *impersonating* a conspirator. Phantom FARC was joining phantom evidence, phantom journalism, phantom sources and not-so-phantom-but-equally-absurd walled compounds and multiple passports.

The Thai police from the Crime Suppression Division, acting on an explicit request of Mr. Derek Odney, one of the American DEA agents in Bangkok, have investigated Bout in connection with the Penal Code of Thailand, Section 135. They spent 33 days on their inquiry into the events, but were unable to discover sufficient evidence to prosecute Bout in a Thai court.

The actual points the Public Prosecutor appeals against the judgment of the Court of First Instance are haphazardly concocted of half-truths. The Public Prosecutor has claimed that all four counts of the offences alleged against the Defendant in the United States are also considered crimes in accordance with the law of the Kingdom of Thailand. Bout's defense team rather easily dismissed these claims.

Consider counts 1 and 2: "Conspiracy to kill US nationals" and "Conspiracy to kill officers and employees of he US." How was this to be done? Why, through the acquisition and use of the alleged missiles by FARC of course. But these counts fail for the reason discussed above: the alleged FARC conspirators were imposters.

Count 3, "Conspiracy to acquire and use anti-aircraft missiles," fails for the same reason, but also has an even more glaring defect. Though an offence under US law, which prescribes a sentence of at least 25 years up to life imprisonment, *no such or similar crime is defined in Thai law*. Can this really have been simply a bonehead move on the part of US authorities? The acts were committed in Thailand, Thai law does not prohibit the acts, case closed.

Count number 4, "Conspiracy to provide material support to a foreign terrorist organization," provides another interesting window on the case. This is indeed a crime under the penal code of both countries – the United States of America and the Kingdom of Thailand (Section 135 of its Penal Code). In fact, as noted, Thai authorities investigated the charges leveled against Bout there. Their investigation has led to no charges against him, but the extradition proceedings, now under appeal by the US, have made clear that the Thai judicial system stands ready to prosecute him under its own laws should appropriate evidence be found. Again, why would US officials not anticipate this?

The American agents were unable either to catch Victor Bout, the alleged Merchant of Death, red-handed with missiles destined for the FARC or to seize any single missile that could be traced back to him. When the US government went to court, not even one anti-aircraft missile was produced as evidence. Thai courts recognized the obvious: It is not possible to conspire to kill anyone with a missile if you do not have a missile.

The court proceedings in Thailand have been a disgrace. If only the American people knew what was being done in their name. The

Three Stooges could have done better on their worst day. Unless, of course, we are playing with a marked deck of cards, and the Victor Bout diversion is just another stop in the endless parallel universe of lies and deception.

There are too many unanswered questions in the whole scenario. Where are the missiles? Why did the US government go into court empty handed, asking the Thai court to take them at their word? Why didn't the DEA pay the $2 million as Bout had allegedly asked when they had already spent in excess of $30 million trying to capture him? The acceptance of the payment would seal his fate. Why didn't they trace the origin of the missiles? Why didn't anyone double-check the Thai laws for compatibility?

In the light of the above considerations, it is absolutely irrelevant if the FARC were indeed a truly political organization, or a truly terrorist organization, just as it doesn't matter if the Thai government recognizes the FARC as a terrorist organization or not. The logic of the case under Thai law, bound with total absence of physical anti-aircraft missiles, exonerates Bout and precludes his extradition to the United States. This is something that former DEA agent-in-charge, Michael Braun, apparently refuses to acknowledge.

How can the US government not have foreseen this? Another coincidence, perhaps? The mere fact that alleged FARC terrorists were proven to be true-blue American DEA agents and the mere fact that these American agent-provocateurs were not able to seize a single anti-aircraft missile alleged to belong to Bout are enough reason to dismiss the accusations against him and for the Thais to refuse the extradition request.

But, there is more. Just when it appeared the Thai courts might acquiesce and extradite Bout to the United States, the Colombian government, following the United States' official request, sent the Thai court a 607-point brochure on the dangers of the FARC. The Colombian Foreign Minister lecturing the Thai judiciary on the possible inadequacy of Thai laws? If you wanted to antagonize someone, can you think of a more ingenious way of doing it? I can't.

Then, there is the overriding question of morality. Does the United States, today, have the international moral authority to be taken at its word? Perhaps not.

Consider Dutch timber merchant, Gus Kouwenhoven, charged, at the request of the United States, with arms smuggling and war crimes in Liberia in the 1990s. The UN's Expert Panel Report on Sierra Leone alleged Gus Kouwenhoven to be "part of [former Liberian president Charles] Taylor's inner circle, responsible for the logistical aspects of many of the arms deals." On June 7, 2006, Kouwenhoven was sentenced in the Netherlands to 8 years in jail for arms smuggling. The allegations were later found to be groundless, when the UN Court of Appeal in The Hague acquitted Kouwenhoven of all charges on March 10, 2008, and sharply criticized the work of the prosecution. The Dutch government had already acknowledged that the Kouwenhoven trial was ridden with false accusations, bribing of witnesses, and gross mismanagement of justice by the Dutch courts.

Then, there is the case of United States vs. Cassin Abdullah Kati and Al Baraka International Foundation, who were sanctioned, persecuted, and prosecuted because the US government alleged to have evidence that these entities were spearheading terrorism and terror groups around the world. On September 3, 2008, the European Court of Justice ruled that the allegations presented as evidence by the US government were false. The European Court of Justice ordered the members of the EU to disregard the UN sanctions placed upon these entities.

And conversely, on October 27, 2009, the French courts convicted a power-elite-connected group that had flaunted a UN embargo, selling $790 million dollars worth of arms into the Angola civil war arena between 1983 and 1998. The group included a son of the late French president Francois Mitterrand, Jean-Christophe Mitterrand; a "Russian-Israeli businessman," Arkady Gaydamak; a French arms dealer, Pierre Falcone; and scandal-plagued right-wing politician and former French Interior Minister, Charles Pasqua. This was at the time and in the arena focused upon by UN investigator Johann Peleman. Yet with all the resources at his disposal, not one word appeared about these power-elite arms smugglers. Instead those resources focused strictly upon Bout, beginning his demonization.

At one point during Bout's last court appearance in September 2009, against the guard's objections, I moved to the front row and sat next to him, to his left. He acknowledged my presence with a nod. For several seconds neither one of us said anything.

"Victor," I whispered, leaning my head in his direction, "if there is one thing you could wish for now, what would it be?"

There was a very long pause. "Home." All traces of a smile left his lips.

The images were there, the indescribable moments remembered, but until this very moment, they had been pushed out of his life only to rise up and attack him whenever the memories refused to stay buried. He closed his eyes. How he wished for oblivion, for temporary reprieve, if only long enough to drown his sorrow and have the nightmare recede. A veiled, vacuous look passed his face and Victor Bout turned around and looked at me. Then, he smiled.

"Do you know that joke about the Moon and the Russian President?" he asked in Russian.

To his right, the Russian consul moved his large body sideways to hear it. Two Russian journalists walked in and sat in the last row, talking quietly.

Time is a true narcotic for pain. Either the pain disappears when it runs its course, or the person learns to live with it. The pain had not disappeared, but I could tell Victor Bout sensed that there was going to be an end to his confinement.

*****

What a world we live in. Competing nation-state propaganda and psychological warfare operations tell us black is white and white is black, these lies and misdirections create gray areas, the operative realm of the Shadow Masters. For when governments operate in extreme secrecy, allowing their intelligence agencies to operate with impunity and beyond oversight, then the noble ideals of statecraft may be hijacked by the Men behind the Curtain, playing nation-states against each other in a Hegelian dance of conflict and resolution.

The terrorist attacks on American soil in 2001 were nurtured by a far greater menace than simple blind hatred acted out by Islamist insurgents from their Afghani and Pakistani hideouts. These acts come from beyond the two-dimensional landscape of opposing sides presented daily by the pundits and talking heads. These shadow plays disrupt our lives with blatant corruption, loaded agendas, and continually spin us from one "crisis" to another. This aberration, like a hidden monster, drives many acts, whether ushered from right-wing Christian fundamentalist groups, oil company board rooms, Wahhabi mosques, lobbying firms and think tanks in Washington and New York, private banks in the emirates of the Persian Gulf, Hasidic-run "blood diamond" centers in Europe and New York, or arms depots of the former Warsaw Pact.

This sinister influence is confirmed by an epic number of "coincidences," and documented connections, among the CIA, the United Nations, the DEA, the FBI, Interpol, Belgian and British authorities, the United Nations, Christian fundamentalists and Russian-Israeli mob interests. The engine driving many world-changing events is not ideology, not religion, not politics and certainly not patriotism. And money does seem to motivate many players – willing pawns of those who lust for control of humanity's future.

Once any large-scale military venture, be it "legitimate" or terrorist, acquires significant *funding*, greed will compete to supply its needs.

Notes

1. Douglas Farah and Stephen Braun, "The Merchant of Death," *Foreign Policy*, November/December 2006.

2. Matthew Brunwasser, "Victor Anatoliyevich Bout – The Embargo Buster: Fueling Bloody Civil War," *Frontline World* (PBS), May 2002, http://www.pbs.org/frontlineworld/stories/sierraleone/bout.html.

3. Stephan Talty, "Taking Down Arms Dealer Victor Bout," *Men's Journal*, January 2009.

4. Owen Bowcott and Richard Norton-Taylor, "Africa's Merchant of Death: UN Names Former KGB Officer as Millionaire Gun-Runner," *Guardian* (UK), December 23, 2000; http://www.globalpolicy.org/component/content/article/168/29546.html.

5. Stephan Talty, op. cit.

6. Douglas Farah and Stephen Braun, op. cit.

7. Stephen Braun, Judy Pasternak and T. Christian Miller, "Blacklisted Russian Tied to Iraq Deals," *Los Angeles Times*, December 14, 2004.

8. Final report of the Monitoring Mechanism on Angola Sanctions, paragraphs 111-144, December 21, 2000.

9. Douglas Farah and Stephen Braun, op. cit.

10. Owen Bowcott and Richard Norton-Taylor, op. cit.

11. Stephen Braun, Judy Pasternak and T. Christian Miller, op. cit.

12. Douglas Farah, "Top Associate of V. Bout arrested and reveals ...", *Washington Post*, February 26, 2002.

13. Wayne Madsen, *Jaded Tasks Brass Plates, Black Ops & Big Oil: The Blood Politics of George Bush & Co.* (TrineDay, 2006), p. 140.

14. Ibid., p.142.

15. Anil Padmanabhan and Sandeep Unnithan, "Hemant Lakhani: Trading in Terror," *India Today*, September 1, 2003, p. 34.

16. Ibid.

17. Wayne Madsen, *Wayne Madsen Report*, July 5, 2007.

18. Ibid.

19. Matthew Brunwasser, "Leonid Efimovich Minin: From Ukraine, a New Kind of Arms Trafficker," *Frontline World* (PBS), May 2002, http://www.pbs.org/frontlineworld/stories/sierraleone/minin.html.

20. Gail Wannenburg, *ISSA Special Africa Report*, 2004.

21. Ibid.

22. Peter Landesman, "Arms and the Man," *New York Times Magazine*, August 17,

2003, p. 28.

23. Alexander Hartmann, "Media, Arms Producers Make Killer Video Games," *EIR*, May 17,

2002.

24. Wayne Madsen, *Jaded Tasks*, p. 145.

25. Ibid., p. 146.

26. Ibid., p. 147.

27. "Inside Israel's Diamond Trade: A Family Affair," *Christian Science Monitor*, February 22, 2002.

28. Tony Thompson, "Criminals are laundering their profits in new ways and Hatton Garden is braced for a flood of stolen gems," *Observer* (UK), March 9, 2003.

29. Maxim Kniazkov, "Regulations For African Gems Trade Approved After Report Of Terror Links," *AFP*, February 10, 2002.

30. Ivory Coast is home to over 100,000 Lebanese; Senegal to roughly 20,000; Sierra Leone to roughly 6,000 today, about 30,000 prior to the outbreak of civil war in 1991.

31. "Hezbollah and the West African Diamond Trade," *Middle East Intelligence Bulletin*, June/July 2004.

32. Matthew Brunwasser, "Victor Anatoliyevich Bout – The Embargo Buster: Fueling Bloody Civil War," *Frontline World* (PBS), May 2002, http://www.pbs.org/frontlineworld/stories/sierraleone/bout.html.

33. Douglas Farah and Stephen Braun, *The Merchant of Death: Money, Guns, Planes and the Man Who Makes War Possible* (Wiley & Sons,2007), p. 73.

34. Douglas Farah, "Digging Up Congo's Dirty Gems; Officials Say Diamond Trade Funds Radical Islamic Groups," *Washington Post*, December 30, 2001.

35. "Hezbollah Profiting from African Diamonds," Associated Press, June 29, 2004.

36. Wayne Madsen, *Jaded Tasks*, p. 167.

37. Tim Shipman, "Face up to terror threat at home, Security Chiefs tell Blair; 1000 of bin Laden's men active in UK," *Sunday Express* (UK), August 25, 2002, p. 2.

38. Douglas Farah, "Al-Qaeda Gold Moves to Sudan," *Washington Post*, September 3, 2002.

39. Douglas Farah and Stephen Braun, *The Merchant of Death*.

40. Report of the Panel of Experts on the illegal exploitation of natural resources and other forms of wealth of the Democratic Republic of Congo, S/2001/357, April 12, 2001: § 91.

41. André Verlöy, "Making a Killing – The Merchant of Death," Center for Public Integrity, November 20, 2002, http://projects.publicintegrity.org/bow/report.aspx?aid=157.

42. Peter Landesman, op. cit.

43. Ibid.

44. "Revealed: Al-Qaeda Arms Dealer," *Sunday Times* (UK), February 17, 2002

45. Michael Isikoff, "Government Deal with a Merchant of Death," *Newsweek*, December 20, 2004, p. 8.

46. Douglas Farah and Stephen Braun, *The Merchant of Death*, p. 221.

47. Michael Scherer, "Dealing with the Merchant of Death," *Mother Jones*, September 20, 2004.

48. A brief note about this publication. *Mother Jones* magazine claims to be a nonprofit "Foundation for National Progress." Yet, *Mother Jones* magazine took in nearly $6 million in annual revenues last year. Not bad for a non-profit. I wonder how much money they would rake in if they went capitalist.

49. Douglas Farah, "Top Associate Of Bout Arrested," Washington Post Foreign Service, February 26, 2002.

50. Belgian intelligence report, 1998, Victor Bout - ECR 449; 1 CMLR 515.

51. Douglas Farah, "Top Associate Of Bout Arrested," op. cit.

52. Matthew Brunwasser, "Victor Anatoliyevich Bout," op. cit.

53. Ibid.

54. André Verlöy, op. cit.

55. Douglas Farah and Stephen Braun, "Merchant of Death," op. cit.

56. John C.K. Daly, "Victor Bout," Global Policy Forum, October 21, 2004, http://www.globalpolicy.org/component/content/article/165/29535.html.

57. Stephen Braun, Judy Pasternak and T. Christian Miller, op. cit.

58. Ibid.

59. Michael Isikoff, op. cit.

60. Lee Drutman and Charlie Cray, "Halliburton, Dick Cheney, and Wartime Spoils," CommonDreams.org, April 3, 2003, http://www.commondreams.org/views03/0403-10.htm.

61. Knut Royce and Nathaniel Heller, "Cheney Led Halliburton to Feast at Federal Trough," Center for Public Integrity, August 20, 2000. The original article was taken off the Internet when reported Russian mobsters sued in Federal court for

libel; the case was dismissed, and the article has been available at http://www.apfn.org/enron/halliburton.htm.

62. According to September 2002 Florida state records, incorporation papers were filed in September 1997 and the company was dissolved on September 13, 2001. However, Air Bas titles never appeared on any aircraft, according to a December 14, 2004, *Los Angeles Times* story, and just like Irbis, Air Cess aircraft have been reregistered into the Kazakhstan register.

63. Jean-Philippe Remy, "Trafficker Victor Bout Lands," Le Monde, May 18, 2004.

64. Douglas Farah, "War and Terror," *Washington Post*, September 23, 2007.

65. "Making a Killing – Victor Bout's American Connection," Center for Public Integrity, http://projects.publicintegrity.org/bow/report.aspx?aid=159.

66. John Coleman, *Conspirators' Hierarchy: The Story of the Committee of 300* (America's West Publishers, 1992).

67. Ibid.

68. US Department of the Treasury, Office of Foreign Assets Control, Recent OFAC Actions, April 26, 2005, http://www.treas.gov/offices/enforcement/ofac/actions/20050426.shtml.

69. Stephen Braun, Judy Pasternak and T. Christian Miller, op. cit.

70. Marten Youssef, "Chained Together by a Dark History," National (UAE), August 11, 2009, http://www.thenational.ae/apps/pbcs.dll/article?AID=/20090811/NATIONAL/708109858/1001.

71. Wayne Madsen, "Additional Ties Discovered Between Christian Right And Diamond Smuggling," *Wayne Madsen Report*, December 11, 2005.

72. "Al-Qaeda Working With Taylor," News24, South Africa, May 25, 2005.

73. Ibid.

74. Douglas Farah and Kathi Austin, "Victor Bout and the Pentagon," *New Republic*, January 12, 2006.

75. Ibid.

76. Ibid.

77. Michael Scherer, op. cit.

78. Stephen Braun, Judy Pasternak and T. Christian Miller, op. cit.

79. Ibid.

80. Peter Landesman, op. cit.

81. Mark Huband, "UK Snubs France Over Arms Trafficker: Bid To Help Dealer Linked To Coalition Sanctions," *Financial Times* (UK), May 17, 2004, p. 1.

82. Wayne Madsen, *Jaded Tasks*, p.174-175.

Chapter Six

Nuclear Gamesmanship

A few days before I was supposed to go to print, I received a call from one of my sources. "Call me back from a pay phone. I will send you the number with the usual encryption." He hung up.

It might sound like an easy task, but pay phones are hard to come by in Thailand. I was imagining Jason Bourne or James Bond running around Bangkok, trying to find a payphone? Did I say running around? I meant sitting around in a taxi, stuck in a monstrous traffic jam.

"I need to use your phone," I told a taxi driver. He shook his head, pretending not to understand. I pulled out 500 Bahts, an equivalent of $15, a twentieth of the local average monthly salary. "Now!" I said. The man grabbed the money and handed me his beat-up cell phone.

"Where are you calling me from?" my source asked inquisitively.

"A taxi. Did you know there are only six payphones for fifteen million Bangkok residents?" I added.

"Let me talk to the driver," my source requested coldly, maybe concerned I was kidnapped and held at gunpoint.

I passed a puzzled driver his phone. After several quick questions the taxi driver bobbed his head affirmatively up and down and gave me back his phone.

"I didn't know you spoke Thai?" I told my source half mockingly.

"There are lots of things you still don't know about me, sweetheart."

"So ..." My question hung in the air for a split second before dissolving into the muggy Bangkok early-morning air.

"You know what was the first question DEA agents asked Victor Bout?"

"No," I replied. "Do you?" A fire truck went by, the wail of its sirens drowning out every other noise around us.

He paused. "They asked him the name of the cruise missiles he had sold to Iran."

I bolted forward, in the process bumping my head against the windshield.

"Why would they ask him that? What's their game?" I asked, my mind working at a thousand revolutions per second.

"This is a big-boys game."

Bout was being set up, the ground cleared, the markers fixed.

"X-55!" I blurted out, realizing instantaneously the monstrosity of the gambit being run from behind the scenes.

"That's right. Cruise missiles, nuclear warheads," came a low-pitched voice from the other end of the line. A moment later the line went dead.

I needed time to figure this out. Then I winced, suddenly remembering last night's short message from my publisher: "We are supposed to be going to print in three days. What's up?"

There was no going back. Publishing a book is like assembling a car. The book itself is not the car, but a small piece of the car, say an engine. Once the date is set, the ghost in the machine responsible for the entire operation becomes insatiable. Distributors prepare the delivery trucks, stores prepare book-shelf space, radio stations book interviews and build their programs around your title, graphic designers at local and national newspapers work diligently at making your advertising campaign look the best possible, online stores such as amazon.com sell pre-ordered copies at discount, hoping to cash in on loyal readers' excitement. Therefore, when the book is delayed, sometimes even by a day, it can cause considerable damage not only to the author's reputation, but also to everyone's bottom line.

Three days. I had three days. There is an old saying in Russian that once a fight is over, waving your fists around is a royal waste of time. If I had missed something, I had three days to figure it out. After that ...

I reeled myself in, shut down that line of thought. Thinking tangentially, at this point, was the enemy, as was time.

Cruise missiles, nuclear warheads, Iran, big-boys game, X-55?

Iran was knee-deep into their nuclear program. But, what did it have to do with Bout?

What was the game? What were they after? The DEA wouldn't have asked Bout about cruise missiles unless they had a very good reason. This wasn't a knee-jerk reaction from an inexperienced agent, questioning a presumed weapons merchant. This was well thought out, a lever pulled at the right moment, approved at the highest levels of the US government, part of the United States government's unspoken policy initiative. I knew that nobody would make a move without the directive itself being signed and countersigned by everyone from the Secretary of State and the Director of the CIA through their various underlings and beyond. The DEA's involvement implied the consent of the US Attorney General.

But why? And for what purpose? I leaned against the wall, staring at a wall-to-wall collection of boxes related to the Shadow Masters investigation, filled with documents and other papers, labeled according to subject matters and months.

Wait a moment! That report!

I pulled off three heavy yellow boxes atop an even larger red box, ripping with my fingers at the thick tape. "It better be here," I thought to myself, rummaging through a box full of papers separated by markers and plastic.

"Here it is," I exclaimed aloud, feeling a charge going through me. Could I really have missed something this significant and not realized it until now?

The report in question was the March 2008 (volume 6, number 3) issue of *Transnational Threats Update*, put out by the Washington, DC, Center for Strategic and International Studies.

The very first section dealt with Victor Bout's arrest. I had read it back in March 2008, then again several months later. It was from "combined dispatches," a term referring to material rehashed from the international media. It contained the usual disinformation, with Bout possessing "more aliases and identification papers than a sports team," and described his arrest in a sting operation along with his associate Robert [*sic*] Smulian. Now, a couple of pages further on, something else jumped out at me.

"FARC seeking uranium for a dirty bomb" read the subhead under "Nuclear Threats." It reported reports of "a Ukrainian organized crime group" selling enriched uranium stolen from Russia, and that they had negotiated with the FARC in Bucharest, Romania regarding the sale of "uranium and other arms." But the last paragraph underscored what I had missed, linking Bout to the FARC dirty-bomb plot through noting that *Andrew* Smulian (yes, this time they got the name right) had been "captured on the strength of a Romanian intelligence tip."

Until my source gave me the heads-up, I must admit, I didn't put the two elements together into one sentence. Now, there was a clever wickedness to the entire episode, which smelled of someone else's farsighted foreign policy agenda. Bout was being aligned with the other little ducks for a major kill.

To be triple sure, I went back and re-read the entire case history of Victor Bout's arrest. If the DEA had set "markers," something in the US Public Prosecutor's documents would have to back it up. It had to be there. A ticking time bomb primed to go off, exposed at a pre-determined time – a public record buried among a myriad of accusations and boring drivel.

I rolled the dice and they came out snake eyes, twice. First, the original set of documents consisting of 50 pages and signed by Secretary Rice had no ticking bomb. Neither did the second set of documents consisting of 45 pages and technical information of alleged manuals confiscated from Bout. Then I rolled the third time and hit the jackpot.

Deeply buried within sheet 2 from the Public Prosecutor's August 26, 2009 appeal, point 3 clearly stated, "In/about November 2007 to March 2008, the accused and his conspirator(s) conspired to provide, supply and train the use of war weapons such as surface-to-air missiles, *guided ballistic missiles*, including devices and components for assembly, installation and modification to FARC group ..." [emphasis added].

Christ Almighty! How skillful and how deceptive. It was unfathomable, yet it was there, in front of me, in black and white.

The FARC equals Bout equals ballistic missiles equals nuclear terrorism. This wasn't Mickey Mouse stuff. This was serious shit.

Three days. Three days to figure it out, write it down, and send it off.

The FARC: the nuclear "taint" all started with them. Here's what I have found.

On Saturday, March 1, 2008, Colombian commandoes carried out a combined ground and air cross-border assault on the encampment of unsuspecting FARC guerillas; the FARC had been fighting the Colombian government for over four decades. The assault took place in the jungles of Ecuador, about 1.2 miles south of the Ecuadoran border city of Lago Agrios. Raul Reyes, the FARC's second-in-command, along with twenty-four other guerillas, was killed.

I again re-read several hundred articles I had amassed on the subject. Most appeared in mainstream publications between March 2 and March 20, 2008. The party line as well as the narrative was clear and easy to discern. The Colombian government claimed that they recovered, at the scene of the carnage, three laptop commuters belonging to Raul Reyes, which showed:

- FARC connections with Ecuadoran president Rafael Correa.
- Records of $300 million offerings from Hugo Chavez.
- Uranium purchasing records.
- An admission to planting a 2003 car bomb that killed 36 at a Bogota upper-crust club.
- Directions on how to make a dirty bomb.
- A letter to Libya's Moammar Gadhafi asking for cash to buy surface-to-air missiles.
- Information on Russian illegal arms dealer Victor Bout.
- FARC funding of Correa's campaign.
- Cuban links to the FARC.

The allegations were made without a shred of documentary evidence to back up the Colombian government's assertions. None of it was new. All the usual potpourri of individuals who collectively represented anti-American interests, from Chavez to Castro's Cuba to Chavez's ally, Ecuadoran president Rafael Correa, to Moammar Gadhafi and even the "Merchant of Death" Victor Bout were present and accounted for. Most of the information apparently gleaned from the FARC computers has by now been exposed as fraudulent, even though none of the US mainstream media bothered to report this trifling fact.

For example, on March 17, 2008 the Bogotá daily *El Tiempo* published a photograph, reportedly from Reyes' laptop computer, which it said showed Reyes together with Ecuadoran security minister Gustavo Larrea. The story was widely reported in the mainstream US press, with the influential *Miami Herald* leading the way. However, several days later, *El Tiempo* had to retract the story, as the image said to be Gustavo Larrea turned out to be none other than Patricio

Etchegaray, general secretary of the Communist Party of Argentina, who said he had had a long interview with Reyes three years earlier at a rebel camp.

Furthermore, the mainstream media apparently had no issue with the fact that three laptop computers, along with key flash drives and external storage disks, miraculously survived *unscathed* a scorched-earth overkill of multiple US smart bombs dropped on less than half an acre of Ecuadoran jungle. This reminded me of accused 9/11 hijacker Sattam al Suqami's passport, found intact by a fortunate passerby in the dusty rubble of what remained of the World Trade Center, if we are to believe the 9/11 Commission.

It also reminded me of the George W. Bush administration using, as irrefutable evidence, 1,000 pages of technical documents supposedly found in a stolen Iranian laptop – evidence of Iranian intentions to build a nuclear weapon. Yes, I know, another lucky coincidence. Go figure. I guess the good guys are luckier than the bad guys, whoever they are. Of course, one can think up another version to this story, the one that has the good guys planting pre-loaded laptops with incriminating intelligence for all to see. Or am I being paranoid?

But, this was different and new. I was exploring a nuclear angle, seeing the same things from a different perspective. I knew the case information by heart, but there was something I had missed, something important that would make a difference in the way Bout's history will be written. The more I focused, the more individual components were beginning to take on a life of their own. And a very, very scary life of their own it was, at that.

On March 3, 2008, Bloomberg News, citing Colombia's National Police Commander Oscar Naranjo, reported that "FARC was seeking to buy 50 kilos of uranium for bomb making with the aim of getting involved in international terrorism." Could this have been a trial balloon for a potential *casus belli* that the US government was hoping to use later on, in a very complicated geopolitical chess game against Russia, China and other players? Back in March 2008, scrambling to follow the real story and keep my eyes on the proverbial ball, I had dismissed the uranium angle as incredible and idiotic.

A March 4, 2008, *Miami Herald* article was headlined, "Rebel Documents Talk of Uranium Offer." It described the FARC rebels supposed attempt to purchase uranium that could be used for a dirty bomb. About halfway through, James Lewis, a former State Department expert on arms smuggling now with the aforementioned Center for Strategic and International Studies in Washington, stated, "In a lot of cases involving uranium deals, somebody usually gets snookered."

Without a doubt, I was seeing a discernible pattern of news management being accomplished through a disingenuously thought-out and nuanced media operation using overt and covert psychological subversion complementary to the Shadow Masters' long-ranged agenda. Please understand, this is war, not a typical, traditional guns blazing war, but a 21st century, asymmetric war – the war of the Shadow Masters.

Citing James Lewis, a former State Department official currently employed by the people who penned a report about Bout, the FARC and nuclear terrorism, and in a mainstream publication like the *Miami Herald*, legitimizes the accusation and silences the naysayers. Who wants to be made to look bad when your opponent in debate has the State Department and mainstream press as sources?

On March 19, 2008, the *Washington Times* reported, "Scientists studying a purported proposal by Colombian rebels to sell uranium for about $2.5 million per kilo say the plan sounds like a scam ... Matthew Bunn, a nuclear specialist at Harvard's Kennedy School of Government, and other scientists expressed skepticism about the proposal. Mr. Bunn said the e-mail [recovered on the FARC computer] contains 'considerable indications that a scam of some kind was involved, since the *quoted price of $2.5 million per kilogram is roughly 10,000 times more than natural uranium is worth,*'"[emphasis added].

The pattern was becoming clearer. The seed of concern is planted in the minds of the people by a skillfully written *Washington Times* article. On one level the article is made to put people's minds at ease, painting the FARC as easily fooled patsies. On a deeper level, written for the more discerning reader, the message is quite the opposite: be afraid, be very afraid. $2.5 million per kilo is the going rate for enriched, nuclear-weapons-ready, and very difficult to obtain "weapons-grade" uranium. To muddy the water even more, an additional level of disinformation is created when the newspaper quotes *unnamed* Colombian officials who "speculated that the uranium offered by the FARC could be used to make a so-called dirty bomb, in which conventional explosives are used to spread radioactive debris."

On March 28, 2008, *Los Angeles Times* reported that although "US officials expressed concern over charges that the Colombian rebel group the FARC was seeking ingredients for a radioactive dirty bomb, the material discovered this week poses little danger." But two paragraphs later we read, "I think you have to take at face value what the Colombians are saying," quoting a senior US intelligence official who, like others, only spoke anonymously, then underlined the point: "There's no reason at this point to think they're [the Colombians] making this up."

Very subtle and very clever. *Unease. Danger. We had better watch ourselves. If the US government is concerned about the bad guys acquiring radioactive dirty-bomb material, we, the people, should be too. And what if the threat is greater than we are being told? What if the bad guys already have the material to nuke New York? After all, wasn't it Osama bin Laden who flew those airplanes into the Twin Towers from his five-star luxury cave in Afghanistan?*

Several paragraphs later, the *Los Angles Times* quoted Charles Ferguson, a nuclear affairs specialist at the Council on Foreign Relations: "Depleted uranium is not sufficiently radioactive to be suitable for a device that could be used as a dirty bomb. A bomb made with depleted uranium might have panicked people for a little while, but the alarm wouldn't have lasted." Then, came his counterpoint. "If it were weapons-grade, highly enriched uranium, I'd be freaking out because you can make a low-yield improvised nuclear device from that." This was accompanied by a proviso: "I'm not aware of any highly enriched uranium of appreciable quantities in the region of Colombia, Venezuela or anywhere else near there."

On one level, our simple minds are put at ease, but the germ of doubt and worry for the welfare of our loved ones remains.

A March 19, *Washington Times* article warns us that the FARC have access to enriched uranium. A March 28, *Los Angeles Times* article confirms our worst fears. If uranium is indeed enriched, weapons-grade, you might as well kiss this world goodbye. A lever is pulled. A button is pressed. *A paradigm is being implanted, subtly and stealthily.*

The Council on Foreign Relations is a cousin to the powerful Bilderberg Group. Their shared ideology is control. Not a One-World-Government type of control, but rather as a One-World-Company-Ltd. control. Who stands in the way of this monstrous, One World Company Ltd. conglomerate? Aside from some patriots in the West and perhaps some stubborn tribal folk still living in the remote mountains and jungles of the world, only Russia and China. And Victor Bout is a pawn in the play of a Russian endgame.

The ubiquitous Charles Ferguson then appeared again in the *WMD Insights* April 2008 issue restating the "company line": "At high enrichment levels, uranium can be used as the core of a nuclear weapon. 50 kilograms of weapons-grade uranium, which has been enriched to 80 percent or more in the fissile isotope uranium-235, would provide enough fissile material to make an improvised nuclear explosive, which could release as much explosive energy as the Hiroshima bomb." Wow! Scary.

Speaking at a news conference one week later, on March 10, 2008, the aforementioned Colombian National Police Commander Oscar Naranjo repeated his part in the story, quietly informing us that additional evidence in the FARC's computers suggests they purchased 50 kilograms of uranium that month.

The game of smoke and mirrors went on. Frank Bajan, in an article of March 5, 2008 for AP, "Colombia Worried Rebels Seek Uranium," stated cunningly, "The Vice President of the Republic of Colombia, Francisco Santos Calderón told the Associated Press that despite fears he expressed at the world disarmament agency in Geneva, his government doesn't have any indication that the FARC are seeking to build a radioactive dirty bomb." This is a typical technique used in psychology and intelligence operations: confirm something by outright denying its existence.

Furthermore, he reported, Santos told the 65-member United Nations Conference on Disarmament in Geneva on March 4, 2008, "To put the FARC and the word uranium in the same sentence is to make anyone's hair stand up." Then more panic was introduced through the FBI's two-cent's worth of reassurance. "The FBI, which has an office in Bogota, also has no information or intelligence regarding the FARC attempting to use WMD, spokesman Richard Kolko said in Washington."

On March 12, 2008, an *Investor's Business Daily* (*IBD*) editorial, "Colombia Has Earned Its Trade Pact," stated, "FARC might have obtained enriched uranium, either to sell to other terrorists or to make a dirty bomb of its own. Computer correspondence shows that FARC offered millions for 50 kilograms of enriched uranium to one shady figure in Bogota."

Remember the figure: *50 kilograms*. It will turn out to be critical to our understanding of the deception.

Several paragraphs later, *IBD* cites Colombia's *El Espectador*, stating, "Reyes made a secret trip to Romania to scope out sellers." Then comes the slight of hand: "Colombia's swift use of intelligence also may have contributed to the fall of Victor Bout, a Russian weapons trafficker whose arms sales to savage regimes made him known as the Lord of War. He was not only a FARC quartermaster. He also supplied guns to Afghanistan's Taliban, al-Qaida in Iraq and the monstrous warlords who scourged western Africa in the 1990s."

What has just happened? An explicit connection was established between FARC, uranium, terrorism, WMDs and Victor Bout.

The FARC's second-in-command, Raul Reyes, allegedly made a secret trip to Romania to scope out sellers. Allegedly, because no proof of this trip has ever been shown to the public. No proof of Reyes' trip to Romania. No proof of Bout's transgressions. Proofs of Bout's transgressions are to be apparently revealed in a secret tribunal, which the general public will not be allowed to attend. This is what 21st century Empire-administered justice looks like from the outside in. We are supposed to take their word for it, just like the Thai judiciary was asked to do with the Victor Bout extradition request.

From Bout's indictment we now know that Andrew Smulian, allegedly representing Victor Bout, tried to arrange a meeting in Romania between Bout and undercover DEA agents posing as FARC. Do you see any relevance in the supposed "Romanian Connection"? No? Neither do I. But, the power of suggestion is such that it doesn't matter if Bout had nothing to do with al-Qaeda, nor does it matter that the supposed 200 tanks Bout apparently had delivered to the Taliban turned out to be a chimera of the mainstream press. The insinuation, the insistence, the suggestion, the wink, the nod, the meaningful silence, the whisper, the four-star generals and their cronies parading in front of TV cameras, like circus performers, for the mainstream press giving us all the details of the news they consider fit to print. Disinformation – or is it art? – taken to the nth degree.

Propaganda as War, War as Propaganda

Newsflash: *The British Government has learned that Saddam Hussein recently sought significant quantities of uranium from Africa.*

Does this ring a bell? How about George W. Bush's Niger yellowcake that wound up as pie in Collin Powell's face? This sort of campaign has by now become rather commonplace. In the lead-up to the first Gulf War, the "babies from incubators" stories were a hot item in newspapers across the entire planet. During their invasion of Kuwait, Iraqi soldiers were said to be plundering hospitals of their incubators and viciously killing any tiny inhabitants thereof. *Outrageous! Retribution!* screamed the editorials. Of course, the story turned out to be a complete fabrication, but the damage had been done. In the meantime, the tail and the dog just kept on wagging each other.

How is it all done? The same way we sell soap or beer: through repetition, *ad nauseam*. Multiple sources inject the same falsehood into the media cycle, each phrasing it in its own manner. But the message itself, the gist never changes. Richard Dearlove, head of British MI6, in a "secret" document released by a whistleblower in the UK, described the process: "the intelligence and facts being fixed around the policy."

The FARC are terrorists. They kill people with guns. Who supplies the guns? Victor Bout, the bad Russkie. Now, the FARC want to kill even more people. How? By acquiring WMDs. Is that why the DEA's first question to Bout focused on the particular kind of cruise missiles he had allegedly sold to Iran? That's called setting the markers. Once set, they are almost impossible to move. It's like moving a goal line in the middle of the game. The missiles in question are X-55, the Russian version of the US Tomahawk, but far more deadly, powerful and accurate, according to a May 2009 television program about Bout on *TB Centre*, a Russian documentary channel.

In the early twentieth century, thanks to the efforts of two men, the words "propaganda" and "war" became synonymous with one another. This was no accident. One was Walter Lippmann, the most influential political commentator of his time. The other was Edward Bernays, Sigmund Freud's nephew and one of the founders of the field of public relations, i.e., opinion-manipulation techniques. In 1928, Bernays wrote in Propaganda, "It was, of course, the astounding success of propaganda during the [First World] War that opened the eyes of the intelligent few in all departments of life to the possibilities of regimenting the public mind [emphasis added].... We are governed, our minds are molded, our tastes formed, our ideas suggested, largely by men we have never heard of. Whatever attitude one chooses to take toward this condition, it remains a fact that in almost every act of our daily lives, whether in the sphere of politics or business, our social conduct or our ethical thinking, we are dominated by a relatively small number of persons, a trifling fraction of our hundred and twenty million [US citizens at the time], who understand the mental processes and social patterns of the masses. It is they who pull the wires, which control the public mind, and who harness old social forces and contrive new ways to bind and guide the world."

Walter Lippmann and Edward Bernays participated in a secret study on the effects of manipulating war information for the purposes of mobilizing mass support for the war. The study was sponsored by the Royal Institute for International Affairs, an organization interlocked with Council on Foreign Relations in the United States.

Researchers discovered that less than 10% of people understand that the process of reasoning requires the ability to observe a problem without immediately passing judgment on it. Since then, the brainwashers have used this fact to control war and every important issue in society in general. In 1991, over 87% of Americans wanted Saddam Hussein's head on a platter, throwing their support behind the first Gulf War. That was a remarkable turn-around, considering that in 1990, less than 10% of Americans were able to pinpoint Iraq on a map and less than 20% knew who Saddam was. A similarly high percentage of Spanish citizens voted for the European Constitution, even though polls have clearly shown that only a tiny number of these people had actually read the document.

"In this manner," writes John Coleman in *Conspirators' Hierarchy: The Story of the Committee of 300*, "irrationality is elevated to a high level of public consciousness. The manipulators then play upon this to undermine and distract the grasp of reality governing any given situation and, the more complex the problems of a modern industrial society became, the easier it became to bring greater and greater distractions to bear so that what we ended up with was that the absolutely inconsequential opinions of masses of people, created by skilled manipulators, assumed the position of scientific fact."

At the Tavistock Institute, Coleman says, Eric Trist and Frederick Emery developed a theory of "social turbulence," a so-called "softening up effect of future shocks" – wherein a population could be softened up through mass phenomena such as energy shortages, economic and financial collapse, or terrorist attack. "If the 'shocks' were to come close enough to each other and if they were delivered with increasing intensity, then it was possible to drive the entire society into a state of mass psychosis," claimed Trist and Emery. They also stated that "individuals would become disassociated, as they tried to flee from the terror of the shocking, emerging reality; people would withdraw into a state of denial, retreating into popular entertainments and diversions, while being prone to outbursts of rage."

In fact, we are talking about two sides of the same coin here. On one side, guiding the covert, subtle manipulation and control of thought and human consciousness through the power of media. "On the other side," wrote the pseudonymous "John Quinn" for *News-Hawk* online on October, 10 1999, "directly and overtly shifting the paradigm, changing the basic concepts, widening the parameters, and changing the playing field and all the rules of play by which society defines itself within an exceptionally short period of time."

Into this fray of a "changing paradigm" in modern-day thought entered the newly-minted FARC, uranium, dirty bombs, nuclear suitcases, WMDs, unscathed laptop computers, Russian pickle-eating arms merchants, South American and African dictators and all the other potpourri of ready-made scum.

Uranium. I thought back to the first months of my investigation. As it turned out, I was dead wrong on this count. Uranium *was* the message. A lever pulled, a message sent, fear level raised. These, in the end, are *the* most explosive charges, allegations that the FARC intended to purchase enriched uranium for the construction of "dirty bombs."

Back in March 2008, I had dismissed all this as fear-mongering tactics on the part of the US government and its Colombian surrogate, thinking that uranium was the slight-of-hand trick, and the real message was somewhere else. It was too silly an angle to pursue, given that the FARC's sophisticated arsenal consisted of highly inaccurate gas-canister bombs, mortars, heavy machine guns and rocket-propelled grenades ... That is until the DEA had ensnared Bout and asked him a very pointed first question – about the cruise missiles he had allegedly sold to Iran.

Now, let's get back to the 50 kilograms of uranium. Recall that Charles Ferguson said, "At high enrichment levels, uranium can be used as the core of a nuclear weapon. 50 kilograms of weapons-grade uranium, which has been enriched to 80 percent or more in the fissile isotope uranium-235, would provide enough fissile material to make an improvised nuclear explosive, which could release as much explosive energy as the Hiroshima bomb." Sounds convincing, but what does it really mean, and more importantly can the primitive FARC, who technologically speaking are still fighting almost with sticks and stones, have access to their own makeshift version of a nuclear weapon? Do we have reasons enough to fear their nuclear prowess? After all, we are being subliminally beaten into submission by the mainstream press on this point. Dirty bomb, nuclear suitcase, weapons-grade uranium, depleted uranium, FARC, terrorism.

"What does it mean?" I asked a fifty-something Spaniard in a bar in Madrid. He was holding court on how third-world dictators hate us for our freedom and wouldn't hesitate to use nukes unless we do something about them.

"What?" he replied.

"A dirty bomb," I said. "Is it dirty because it hasn't been washed, or because the guy who uses it is dirty, or what?"

"Because they fill it with other stuff," he answered without batting an eyelash.

"Like, what stuff, for example?"

"Nuts and bolts. You know, like the Palestinians when they make their bombs." He looked around the bar for moral support. People shifted uneasily.

"And a nuclear suitcase?"

"It's like in the movies. The President has a suitcase strapped to his wrist."

"How many nuclear suitcases are there?" I asked.

"Two," he said confidently. "The Americans and the Russians."

"What about the terrorists?"

"That's what I mean," he said, raising his voice and hitting the bar top with his hand. "Don't give them a chance, or they will nuke us."

Do you understand? No? Neither do I. But then again, it's not about understanding, but rather about feeling. Emotionally charged language projected through TV images by telegenic teleprompter readers, four-star generals, unnamed government officials, alphabet-soup agencies. Welcome to the circus.

How many people really understand the terminology being bandied around? In the case of this sort of nuclear propaganda, I'd say, surely no more than ten percent have a rudimentary understanding, while real understanding is not possessed by even a fraction of one percent of the populace.

Dimitri Khalezov is a former Soviet nuclear intelligence officer and the author of a soon-to-be published book on covert operations, nuclear terrorism and 9/11. He is also the specialist working for Victor Bout's defense team who met with Derek Odney outside the US Embassy in Bangkok. He provided most of the detail in the following over the course of a lengthy interview. My goal was to try to separate the nuclear wheat from the chaff regarding the charges against Bout re dirty bombs, nuclear terrorism, etc. At the outset I had no inkling of the bombshell Khalezov would be dropping.

We began with a general discussion, distinguishing nuclear weapons from conventional explosives and further identifying the type of nuclear weapons under our consideration: employing nuclear *fission*, rather than *fusion*, "atomic" bombs rather than the far-more-powerful "hydrogen" bombs, which use atomic bombs for ignition. The power of atomic bombs is rated in kilotons, each equivalent to 1000 metric tons of TNT; hydrogen bombs are rated in megatons, each equivalent to *one million* metric tons of TNT. The largest hydrogen bomb ever tested is said to have gone off at 50 megatons. Fusion weaponry is simply too sophisticated, expensive, cumbersome, and perhaps even too deadly, to be useful to terrorists.

Fission weapons, like atomic reactors, exploit the physical properties of certain isotopes of radioactive elements, such as uranium-235, which can produce a cascading "chain reaction," leading in a bomb to an enormously powerful blast with attendant radiation, fallout, etc. Only rare and highly radioactive isotopes of elements like uranium and plutonium will work. The prodigious energy released from "splitting" atoms comes from the enormous bonding force required to hold protons and neutrons together in their nuclei.

Khalezov, adding to what Charles Ferguson had stated, quickly dismissed the notion that the FARC or anyone else would be seeking uranium for the purpose of building a "dirty bomb": "It is not possible to make a so-called 'dirty bomb' from uranium, either depleted or enriched, because uranium is not a highly radioactive material. Scary 'dirty bombs' are made from other, highly radioactive isotopes – such as radioactive cobalt or radioactive cesium – both of which are quite readily available. No one should be duped by these ravings about a 'dirty bomb' made from $2.5-million-per-kilo uranium. A discerning reader should know how to read between the lines – the FARC sought to build an *atomic bomb*. That is what they meant to imply."

Ferguson was correct in asserting a threshold enrichment level of 80 percent uranium-235 to make a weapon, but countries producing nuclear weapons from U-235 will enrich it to 90, 95, or even 100 percent. Furthermore, the term "enrichment" is a bit misleading, as the process is one of refinement by removal of the other unwanted isotopes. This, not surprisingly, requires an extremely sophisticated industrial capacity. Then you need not only some of this enriched uranium to make a weapon, you need *enough*: the so-called "critical mass."

"Without critical mass," Khalezov told me, "no nuclear explosion is possible. To avoid a premature nuclear explosion, a critical mass of nuclear material is separated into sub-critical masses that are kept apart. When a nuclear explosion is desired, these sub-critical masses are joined together, and the explosion follows immediately." On this point, he again confirmed Ferguson, specifying the amount of enriched U-235 needed to make a functional weapon as "50 to 52 kilograms. In fact, the exact amount would depend on its exact level of enrichment as well as on its exact geometrical form."

I asked Khalezov why such precise technology is required to make an atomic bomb, adding, "Why can't a wealthy billionaire with bad intentions working out of his five-star Afghani cave make it?"

"On paper, at least, to make such a crude charge seems easy, but it only seems so. The problem arises when you try to join two pieces of uranium. Once you get them close to each other, and their corresponding neutron fields overlap, a *slow* nuclear reaction will start, instantly heating up these pieces of uranium. So when you try to get them closer, they will overheat, melt, and evaporate. You won't be able to actually join these two pieces together, because they will always evaporate before you could get them to physically touch each other. Therefore, to join the two sub-critical masses of uranium into one over-critical mass required for the nuclear explosion, they need to converge at very high speed – 2.5 km/sec [2.5 kilometers per second, over 1.5 miles per second]. Only then, will you have a chance for these two pieces to join before the slow nuclear reaction evaporates them."

"Can you put the 2.5 km/sec into perspective?"

"Considering that the most advanced modern long-barreled anti-tank or anti-aircraft cannon could speed up its shell to slightly over 1.2 km/sec [slightly over .75 miles/sec], to reach speeds of 2.5 km/sec in a short barrel is quite a difficult task. Still, it is possible to achieve it, if you use, instead of ordinary gunpowder, a well-calculated combination of slow and fast explosives. Therefore, it is possible to imagine Osama bin Laden in his famous cave in Afghanistan producing such a crude nuke – if only someone would supply him with over 50 kilograms of enriched uranium-235. But, by no means would such an imaginary nuke be 'mini.' Osama bin Laden would need to use something like a piece of an anti-aircraft cannon's barrel, as the Americans themselves used in their first Hiroshima bomb. However, such a primitive nuclear charge would never ever fit into a small suitcase. In a best-case scenario, it would fit into a middle-sized truck."

Khalezov described the effects of such a bomb: "While primitive nuclear weapons designs can not achieve high yields, they could likely produce a nuclear blast of some 10-12 kilotons [of TNT], which is more than enough to level a middle-sized town, killing nearly all its inhabitants. Just for your reference, while the officially claimed yield of the [uranium-based] Hiroshima bomb was 20 kilotons, all specialists agree that it went off at only a 12- to 13-kiloton yield due to flaws in its design."

Newer nukes have used plutonium-239, with a critical mass only one-fifth that of uranium-235. But acquiring even a small amount is quite difficult, even in a developed nuclear-weapons program: "Plutonium-239 can only be obtained in small quantities from working nuclear reactors, because it is a by-product of the uranium-based nuclear reaction in such reactors. Plutonium-239 is about ten times more expensive than uranium-235, and working reactors accumulate its quantities very slowly – mere hundreds of grams per year. Use of plutonium-239 allows manufacturing nuclear weapons that are much smaller in size than uranium-based ones."

This naturally led to a question about a weapon we have come to hear about with greater and greater frequency in the mainstream press, the "nuclear suitcase," or "mini-nuke: "How difficult is it to produce a 'mini-nuke' of a fraction of a kiloton yield?"

"The term 'mini-nuke' is obviously an unofficial term, and probably it is not correct from a point of logic. It generally refers to a portable nuclear charge designed to explode at variable yields, as small as .01 kilotons [10 tons of TNT] up to 1 kiloton and sometimes up to several kilotons. An actual yield is set by its end-user.

"There is, however, another term – 'micro-nuke' – which purports to refer to even smaller nuclear charges – topping out at around .01 kiloton. There is also another term – 'suitcase-nuke' – which simply refers to the overall size of the fissionable material along with its ignition apparatus.

"You have to understand that you have to be able to control, and not just control, but *precisely control* the exact amount of fissionable material that would be involved in a chain nuclear reaction. Making a workable nuclear bomb is quite difficult, but it is *much more* difficult to be able to control such a small amount of nuclear material into an actual explosion."

The critical-mass requirement dictates that mini-nukes be plutonium-based, but this presents another hurdle in the ignition process: "The problem of plutonium-239 is that it has a much higher reactivity than uranium-235, and you would need speeds of about 12 km/sec [7.5 miles/sec] to actually join two sub-critical pieces of plutonium into one over-critical piece before the two pieces would be overheated and evaporated."

"What countries," I asked, "have the level of sophistication needed to manufacture such a weapon?"

"Old nuclear players, such as the United States, France, Russia, and Israel, have the technology to manufacture a precisely wrought mini-nuclear device that could cause a precisely calculated mini-nuclear explosion equivalent to 0.3 to 0.1 kilotons [300-100 metric tons of TNT] or even 0.01 kiloton. On the other hand even if al-Qaeda, the Taliban, bin Laden, the FARC or some other rogue organization were theoretically able to assemble the crudest of atomic bombs, they would never be able to achieve any level of control whatsoever over how much of its fissile material would really be involved in a chain nuclear reaction.

"With such rudimentary conditions, the most Osama bin Laden & Company could hope for is a nuclear explosion itself. If they get 'lucky,' the charge might reach 12 kilotons; in case of bad luck, perhaps, 7 or 8 kilotons. They could not even dream of achieving a precisely calculated yield, such as only 1 kiloton, not to mention a fraction of it. The technology is too sophisticated, even for most developed nations in the world."

Khalezov provided additional evidence that rogue operations like al-Qaeda and the FARC "would never be able to reach the speed of 12 km/sec required to join two pieces of plutonium-239."

"Plutonium-based charges," he explained, "do not use the primitive canon-design, but use, instead, the so-called implosion scheme, where a slightly sub-critical mass of plutonium-239 is compressed into a critical mass by well-calculated simultaneous explosions of conventional explosive materials, charges of which are positioned equally around the plutonium nucleus. The plutonium nucleus is being compressed not from only two directions, but from every direction – where charges of conventional materials are positioned in a sphere around the plutonium like sections of a soccer ball. The problem of the implosion scheme is that the implosion charges must be precisely calculated and precisely wrought – and *this* you can achieve in neither your kitchen, nor inside a cave in Afghanistan.

"Moreover, the detonators have to be precisely synchronized, practically on a microsecond level. Even a millisecond level synchronization is not enough, because if these implosion charges detonate even slightly asynchronously, the detonation waves would destroy the plutonium nucleus, and the nuclear charge would be rendered useless.

"Only a few developed countries possess such precise technology, which may enable them to produce plutonium-based nuclear weapons. And only a couple of countries are capable of miniaturizing these nuclear weapons to a size suitable to fit into a suitcase. To illustrate how difficult is to miniaturize such a plutonium-based charge, here is one good example. India, which embarked on development of plutonium nuclear weapons [India does not have any uranium] as early as the beginning of the 1950s, despite its considerable financial and intellectual resources, allocated within frames of an extensive national program, was not able to come up with any really workable plutonium-based nuclear charge before the mid-'70s. And even then, their nuclear charge was far from being 'mini.' Though the actual plutonium nucleus weighed less than 10 kilograms, the entire construction built around it weighed slightly over *one-and-a-half tons*. Even today, thirty-five years after their first successful nuclear test, the Indians are not capable of producing a 'mini-nuke' – they can only master warheads [sized] for ballistic missiles."

"If someone sincerely believes that the late Saddam Hussein and Osama bin Laden could produce such a mini-nuke, that person might as well believe that Osama bin Laden together with [Taliban leader] Mullah Omar could land on the Moon in a makeshift spaceship."

Much of this confirmed what I either knew or suspected, but I admit to being stunned by Khalezov's reply to what I had thought was a routine question.

"In your opinion," I asked, "has anyone ever detonated a nuclear charge other than the two cases of Hiroshima and Nagasaki?"

"You must mean apart from nuclear testing and nuclear explosions for civil purposes.

"There are more than fifty episodes of low-yield nuclear weapons being used. The most famous of them are, of course, the 1983 Beirut barracks bombing of US Marines – which set the gold standard for future nuclear terrorism – the 1996 Khobar Towers bombing in Saudi Arabia, the two nuclear bombings in Buenos Aires in 1992 and 1994, the 1992 Tarata, or 'Miraflores,' bombing in Lima, Peru. Not to mention the 2002 micro-nuclear blast in a Bali nightclub that was used to justify the Iraqi adventure in search of alleged weapons of mass-destruction.

"And of course, the most remarkable of all of them was the double nuclear bombing of the US Embassies in Kenya and Tanzania in 1998, which 'strangely' occurred on an anniversary of the Hiroshima bombing. If you follow the news you probably know that the Hiroshima atomic bombing was used by Osama bin Laden in one of his sermons to justify using nuclear weapons against the US' own civilians – so it's unlikely anyone could find a better way of implicating al-Qaeda than nuking the US Embassy right on such an anniversary.

"And, of course, the very El Nogal bombing in Colombia in 2003 mentioned in the supposed Reyes laptop computer was also a nuclear bombing. Which was not the first nuclear bombing in Colombia, in any case – for example, there was another nuclear bombing in November 1999 in Bogota, and it too was blamed on the FARC – with the same result as the 1992 Tarata bombing in Lima, Peru, which was blamed on the *Sendero Luminoso* [Shining Path] that led to the quick and imminent demise of that formidable political movement, which after the supposed use of a nuclear weapon immediately lost support from the lower classes and was relegated to the status of a 'terrorist organization.'"

"Wait a moment," I said, shaking my head. "According to the information allegedly found on Reyes' computer, the FARC admit to planting the 2003 car bomb that killed thirty-six at a Bogota club. Are you saying they were *not* behind it?"

"How could they be? It was your casebook mini-nuke explosion where a typical plutonium-based high-precision mini-nuke went off at about 0.1 kiloton [100 metric tons] in TNT yield. Look at the evidence. The explosion caused a large crater, which tells me that the nuclear charge was buried in the ground; car bombs do not dig craters, because the power of explosion goes by the way of least resistance – i.e. upwards and to the sides, but never downwards to dig a crater. It also caused burns along with radiation injuries to people, and fried all [nearby] electronic equipment with its electro-magnetic pulse [EMP]. For any forensic nuclear expert, this is an unmistakable signature of a nuclear explosion. A regular bomb, and I don't care what you mix into it, does not burn people. Neither does it produce an EMP or radiation. You would be surprised if you reviewed contemporary newspapers where you can see such 'nuclear' terms as 'ground zero' and 'millisecond' used in connection with the El Nogal bombing.

"Besides, security specialists immediately established that the device used was of the type used in another well-known, to specialists, nuclear bombing – that in Oklahoma City in 1995. Don't forget that the spot of the Oklahoma bombing was also immediately dubbed 'ground zero' – and such a nuclear term was used long before the 9/11, so it had nothing to do with its newer reference. It was used in its pure former sense: 'a hypocenter of a nuclear explosion.'

"Besides, look at the damage produced by the explosion in Oklahoma, and look at the actual properties of the explosion, which are publicly available. To begin with, the Oklahoma bombing managed to produce a seismic signal of 3.0 on the Richter scale. This is the official number. How would a truck loaded with two tons of cheap explosives produce such a seismic signal? Do you know that the seismic signal of 3.0 corresponds to 29 tons of TNT buried deep under ground? Meaning, buried deep enough to communicate its entire explosive energy to the Earth, and nothing at all to the atmosphere. You have to understand that a truck loaded with explosives would not produce any seismic signal whatsoever, because its entire explosive energy would go by the way of least resistance, that is to the atmosphere with nothing going to the Earth.

"In Oklahoma, a standard mini-nuke was set to explode at 0.1 kiloton, but it was not buried sufficiently deep under ground. It was placed into a sewage tube in front of the building. Therefore the actual explosion was able to communicate to the Earth approximately 30% of its entire energy – which produced the above mentioned seismic signal of 3.0, which was recorded by seismic observatories. The rest of its energy was used to dig a crater and was communicated to the targeted building and to its surroundings, causing typical atomic damages. If you look at the official description of the Oklahoma bombing and check how many ordinary structures were demolished or damaged by that explosion you would be surprised indeed. The explosion managed to collapse or damage not more and not less than 324 buildings in a sixteen-block radius. Does that look like an explosion of two tons of fertilizer? You can't argue against rules of elementary mathematics. The officially recorded seismic signal of 3.0 on the Richter scale is proof that the device buried into sewage in front of the Oklahoma building was not less [in explosive force] than 100 tons of TNT.

"Do you think Timothy McVeigh would be able to fit 100 tons of TNT into his Ryder truck? Of course, it was a mini-nuke used in the Oklahoma bombing. Otherwise why would they call that place 'ground zero'? And why would they officially indict Timothy McVeigh of using WMD against US citizens? Count one of the grand jury's charges against Timothy McVeigh was "Conspiracy to use a weapon of mass destruction." Count two: "Use of a weapon of mass destruction." All of this is available in official court documents. Along with the seismic signal of 3.0 as officially recorded. Don't forget also that all electronic equipment was fried in a certain radius around the targeted building by the electromagnetic pulse of a nuclear explosion. Have you ever heard that explosions of fertilizer can fry electronics nearby? So, as long as the security officials admitted that at El Nogal the same kind a device was used as in Oklahoma, you can draw your own conclusions ...

"While early generation mini-nukes employed some uranium-238 in their design, smaller modern mini-nukes do not use any uranium at all, so nothing like that could be found in their residue after the explosion, but only plutonium alone. So, if you are told that a mini-nuclear explosion has been executed using the latest generation mini-nuke, and the attack is blamed on al-Qaeda, bin Laden or Hezbollah, a reasonable person should immediately understand that his perceptions and reality are being manipulated. The same thing could be said regarding the alleged 'enriched uranium' of the FARC – if there was a mini-nuclear explosion and then someone tries to draw a connection between such a plutonium-based nuclear explosion and weapons-grade uranium allegedly found around the FARC camp, you have to understand that someone is trying hard to insult your intelligence.

"And where on Earth would Timothy McVeigh or the FARC obtain such a mini-nuke? And even if we imagine that the FARC could somehow obtain such an unusual thing, would it be reasonable to presume that the FARC, which is a military organization after all, would use it against a night club instead of annihilating a building of the Ministry of Interior or Ministry of Defense?"

I walked out of our interview deep in thought. Khalezov's logic seemed unassailable. Few would want to argue with him, I thought.

And few ever successfully had, as far as I was able to ascertain. It was clear to me from his explanations and analysis that the FARC were not behind the El Nogal bombing which took the lives of thirty-six innocent people. By extension, if they were not responsible, then the information allegedly found on Raul Reyes' computer was a giant hoax, contrary to what the mainstream press wanted us to believe.

El Nogal was most definitely a mini-nuke explosion. At least four nations, according to Dimitri Khalezov, had the technical know-how of pulling it off – the United States, Russia, France and Israel. Who did it? I don't know. I wish I did. But I do know who *didn't* do it.

Interestingly, one month after the El Nogal bombing, the Colombian Secretary of Defense flew to Washington in search of political support and lucrative arms contracts. From Victor Bout? No, from the US government.

Don't get me wrong. The FARC are cold-blooded killers. I would love to see most of them hang, maybe all of them. But in this case, they were being used as an extension of someone else's agenda. Caught in the middle were the innocent people whose lives are so often and so easily snuffed out.

Tangentially to the FARC and El Nogal, my thoughts returned to Victor Bout, X-55 missiles and Iran. If we are to take the DEA at face value, Bout stands accused of supplying strategic-weapons systems to Iran. At this point, I must conclude that God only knows how they got there and who delivered them.

Bout is a pawn. The US and Russia are the big players. If Bout were somehow involved, it would have been on a very low level. Why? Because, it is unfathomable to imagine one individual dealing as an equal with the Iranian government (or the Ukrainian government) without the full support of a large and powerful nation in the shadows.

And the Shadow Masters? Could Bout's arrest be part of a much deeper political blackmail against a global power? Is that the game? If the charges of nuclear terrorism can be pinned on the FARC, and by extension on Bout, then the fallout would severely undermine Russia's standing in the world community, the "global village." When I asked myself shortly after his arrest whether Bout was being used as an extension of someone else's foreign-policy agenda, I had no idea of the repercussions of that question.

As we go to print, Victor Bout is still awaiting the outcome of the Thai proceedings in his prison cell. Extradition to the US, or a home-bound flight to Mother Russia. Much is riding on the court's decision. The Shadow Masters have a high-stakes interest in Bout's future. He is a stepping-stone. A pawn. The game itself is about Russia's total destruction. The Shadow Masters feel they own Bout. They surely paid enough for propaganda to make him into a "Merchant of Death." The script has been set. The play rehearsed. The leading characters have gone through their lines.

Now, if only the Thai court will follow the prompter ...

EPILOGUE

Walking out of KlongPrem prison after my umpteenth visit with Victor Bout, my view was a stark contrast with the island over 500 miles to the south where I resided with my family. Phuket looks like paradise today, but a few years ago it was devastated by the Boxing Day tsunami of 2004, a memory still fresh among the locals.

I jumped into a waiting taxi and before long found myself between Silom and Sathorn Road, in Bangkok's commercial business district and surrounded by the cacophony of Asia's most vibrant city. Twenty million Bangkok natives went about their lives in cars and tuk-tuks, those strange three-wheeled auto rickshaws, and on bikes, scooters and motorbikes, all with the obstinate and infuriating repetitiveness of peoples whose routines haven't changed in a thousand years. Against these backdrops, I thought, what's the life of a single man or, for that matter, the pretensions of the Shadow Masters.

Significant numbers of Chinese have been present in Thailand for centuries. Both cultures are history-minded, but the Chinese are the only people with a continuous recorded chronicle of their own for twenty-five hundred years. No people escape history – the Chinese are simply more aware of it than most other nations.

Like most big cities, Bangkok has its ethnic enclaves. Sampeng Lane is the heart of the Chinese section of Bangkok, an old densely-populated neighborhood, where the dilapidated buildings, the carton-and-plywood houses are Bangkok, but the sounds and the smells are Chinese and the store signs come in two languages and two alphabets. The store windows seem never to lose that musty look, with last season's holiday lights surrounded by Chinese dragons against red awnings and the occasional plastic plant. The women of high-strung temperament and colorful aprons and loud voices are talking a peculiar local dialect to their companions, a blend of Mandarin and Thai.

This is another type of paradise, insofar as humanity is able to reproduce it in crowded cities. It never feels claustrophobic, despite the fact that people are all over the place, not only Chinese, but also Thais of course, and Laotians and the poorest of the poor from Burma and Nepal, and in fact from all over Southeast Asia. All are drawn to Bangkok by the allure of a big city, re-creating in different ways and in different places what they used to do back home, wherever that home might have been at one time.

A sharp sound to my right brought me back to Bangkok's smoggy reality. Turning the corner, I focused on a small cross-section of houses in front of me. From my vantage point, they appeared as a horizontal brown box contained within a floating shell. There was a continuing conversation between different materials and different textures ... smooth and rough, hard and soft. I again turned the corner and found myself in front of a brand-new house with its fully glazed stairwell above a garden court at basement-level, where two small children passed the time against the backdrop of a Chinese cemetary sitting four meters above the rear of the house. That's the thing about Bangkok – one moment you are standing in front of an aluminum shack, the next in front of a $300-million skyscraper.

"Buddha is strong," the Thais say. Their King, eternal. Their belief in both of them – unshakeable. The Mafias and the assassins and the ambitions of the elite, at least to the Thais, pale in comparison. Good karma is the best antidote to an assassin's bullet. That, and the love of their King, Bhumibol Adulyadej. The man with an unpronounceble name. How different we are as cultures. East and West. The quiet wisdom of one, the impetuousness and irrational zeal of the other, convinced that for history to favor us, we have to write the record ourselves.

At Chakkrawat Street, I passed near the Grand China Princess Hotel, a favorite hangout of the Chinese triads in Bangkok. Overtaking some sausage vendors, I cut across an alley that took me from the dilapidated shanty-town within Chinatown to the shore of Bangkok's Chao Phraya river. The air was hot and heavy, making movement difficult. Thoughts clung to my forehead like beads of sweat.

In a kind of drooping reverie, my mind returned to the theme of my book and to the different characters forever locked into its two-dimensionality. Alexander Litvinenko and Victor Bout. Boris Yeltsin and gangster oligarchs with blond-haired mistresses and Hugo Boss suits. Russian Mafia linked to enriched uranium-seeking FARC terrorists linked to the world's biggest bogeyman, Osama bin Laden. Or has Victor Bout came along and taken bin Laden's crown? The world of shadows and shadow dancers, shadow players and Shadow Masters. The world of One World Company Limited. The world of globalization with a happy face. The world of an Empire. A parallel world of smoke and mirrors where reality has been sugar-coated and sold to the highest bidder.

How deftly the Victor Bout story was spun into our brains. Spun, as in spin – the native language of politics. It is inherently disingenuous: based on the premise that words are moves in a game of strategy. The Shadow Masters, with deep pockets and aggressive agendas, have reshaped the debate on the fundamental issues that affect all of us, and in the process they have made the mainstream media compliant partners in their mission.

The rise of powerful organizations such as the Heritage Foundation, Hudson Institute, Alfred P. Sloan Foundation, Sage Foundation, Cato Institute and Manhattan Institute into the role of savvy idea peddlers with millions to spend on marketing has profound implications for the future of the world. In key policy debates, these organizations have discredited their opponents, dominated the media, and engineered sweeping changes in public opinion and public policy. But none of this is being mentioned in the mainstream media, which is under the tight control of political operatives and policy launderers.

For Freud's nephew Edward Bernays, the father of the field of "public relations," news was made "when reality is distilled down to the most simplified and dramatized form and it appeals to the instincts of the public mind. The public relations counsel must create news around his ideas, isolate ideas and develop them into events so they can be more readily understood and so they may claim attention as news."

Victor Bout, a KGB-trained, amoral, gun-selling Russkie. He is a bad man. The DEA, who are trying to apprehend this man, are good men. Never mind that both the DEA and the CIA are eyeball-deep into the drug trade. Reality must be distilled down to the most simplified and dramatized form for public consumption. Us and them. The shadows and the Shadow Masters.

Never mind that in all these years of search-and-destroy against Bout, not one shread of real evidence has been presented to the public. Never mind that. "Take our word for it," they say. I did, initially. And why not? How was I supposed to imagine that the entire operation against Bout was a brilliant slight of hand, a gigantic conspiracy among unprincipled DEA agents, US senators, UN investigators, highly paid Washington spin-doctors and their mass-media mouthpieces. If they had *me* convinced initially, imagine John Q. Public.

The news agenda has been driven by their own pre-fabricated messages, issues and concerns. Yes, it is elitist. And yes, it is anti-everything we should believe in. How is it done? By insinuating messages into the public consciousness, into the minds of people – especially into their subconscious minds – by adopting a disinformation policy dedicated to changing people's perceptions of reality.

With the mainstream US and UK press led by the *Washington Post* and the BBC, and their sordid commentators spouting forth the most jingoistic propaganda billed as news, the publics are not being told the truth about Iraq, Afghanistan, Kosovo, Russia, the nefarious drug trade or Victor Bout.

The Shadow Masters regime does not want bad news, only good news. The Soviet Union was known for a similar policy -- there was no bad news in the old Empire. Airplane crashes, earthquakes, dissidents and epidemics were never covered by the Soviet media. The Shadow Masters-controlled media is gradually adopting the same policy – the war in Afghanistan is not about protecting the drug trade, but is rather about bringing democracy to a God-forsaken land; the war in Kosovo had nothing to do with taking control of the country's most treasured natural resources, but rather with freeing an oppressed and long-suffering people who sought self-determination and who were punished for it by the big, bad Serbs; the all-out assault on Russia must be seen in context of international community and nation building rather than wiping out the only nation capable of destroying the NATO alliance ten times over; Victor Bout must be locked away forever, for he is the worst gunrunner in the world, who managed to outwit every intelligence agency on the planet, their spy satellites, their armies, their electronic equipment, and, without detection, single-handedly made deals on a scale unseen in the annals of history. Propaganda. Deception. Lies. Control.

Back in the dark days of World War II, Nazi propaganda minister Josef Goebbels understood this well: "Voice or no voice, the people can always be brought to the bidding of the leaders. That is easy. All you have to do is tell them they are being attacked, and denounce the pacifists for lack of patriotism, and exposing the country to greater danger." It works this way in any country and at any time.

In the immediate aftermath of that war, a fellow Russian émigré, Vladimir Nabokov, wrote one of the great dystopian novels of the twentieth century, *Bend Sinister*. In an imaginary country ruled by the Party of the Average Man, its philosopher protagonist is systematically destroyed by a tyrannical state "at war with its own subjects." *Bend Sinister* defends the freedom of the individual mind not only from dictatorships abroad, but from the coercion of mass culture, mass propaganda and mass mobilization at home.

Yet even in his most political novel, conceived in the heat of war, Nabokov turns from the problem of the moment to the strength and mystery of consciousness: the power of one's mind and heart and soul in resisting the political pressure brought to bear. The novel's own resistance, in the name of consciousness, is against the group thought that levels the individual human mind.

He was all too aware of the dangers inherent in group-think, like the "utopia" longed for by an obscure Soviet beaurocrat in the 1930s: "If the state is to be saved, if the nation desires to be worthy of a new robust government that can protect its people, then everything must be changed; popular commonsense must prevail, and simple words, intelligible to man and beast alike, and accompanied by fit action, must be restored to power."

If we are to replace "state" with "Shadow Masters," "nation" with "One World Company Ltd," and "people" with "interests," a new, twenty-first century version emerges, with its grisly echo of the torturous past. The alternative advanced by the Shadow Masters today requires that things should be kept simple ... brought down to the lowest common denominator. Bout is a modern day Satan, Russians are ex-KGB assassins, Kosovo drug pushers and terrorists are good people who have been misunderstood, Litvinenko was a loyal servant of the state who became disillusioned with the corruption of the ex-KGB assassins, Bilderberg is an informal meeting of private citizens concerned for the welfare of the world. And Daniel Estulin is a conspiracy theorist, because if what he claims to be facts, *were* facts, they most certainly would be reported in the *New York Times*.

Consciousness and unconsciousness. The Shadow Masters accept consciousness as something to be handed out in small doses, to the select few willing to play along.

The credo of the Pan-World Empire zealously promoted by the Shadow Masters, that individual differences should be limited for the sake of some abstract "common good" – whether it be defeating terrorism or putting up a united front against a phantom menace – is a *reductio ad absurdum*, and far too like Stalin's terror, Hitler's lunacy and any number of other smaller, more insignificant and less lethal varieties of tyranny.

Some believe that the third millennium must be the age of religion. I would say rather that it must be the age in which we finally grow out of our need for religion. But to cease to believe in gods is not the same thing as commencing to believe in nothing. To believe, we must take on the richness of man, his existential destiny, and not some sectarian, simplistic, visceral millenarianism.

Of all worldly powers, the only eternal power is that of thought. The Shadow Masters are more than aware of this. Take my word for it. They know that ideas are more powerful weapons than guns, fleets and bombs. In order to secure acceptance for their imperial ideas, they seek to control the way we think. To control our language and, through the language, to control us.

We use words to label and help us comprehend the world around us. "At the same time, many of the words we use are like distorting lenses," said nineteenth-century English jurist Sir James Fitzjames Stephen, "they make us misperceive and hence misjudge the object we look at because of our incurable propensity to prejudge all the great questions by stamping our prejudices upon the language." Bout – Merchant of Death. Litvinenko – loyal servant of the state who became disilusioned with the corruption of the system. Osama bin Laden – terrorist who hates us for our freedom. Russia – a mafiocracy led by unscrupulous ex-KGB assassins. The *New York Times* – all the news that's fit to print. Empty slogans. Distorted meanings. Suggestion by stealth. Memory, or a lack of it.

Memory saves people from oblivion. The inherent danger for today's society, however, is that its prerequisite is lacking: curiosity deriving from respect for deeply alien cultures. As one character in *Bend Sinister* declares, "Curiosity ... is insubordination in its purest form." We need a healthy curiosity about Russia, Afghanistan, China, India, Syria, Iraq, Iran. The Shadow Masters and their enemies-on-demand.

The first decade of the new millenium rushes to a close as I sit on my terrace overlooking the Indian Ocean. I am asking myself something over and over again, making an attempt to understand what is happening to us: Where are we going as nations? As a world? What will happen to us if the Shadow Masters finally win? What is the destiny of the human race?

I am convinced that truth and destiny can be fused into one. The need is for the younger generation to step forward and take responsibility for the future of the planet. It is not my fight. Nor is it a crusade. But the people of my generation – not all people, but many people – we instinctively knew that our parents' generation had been living a no-future fantasy. And we knew that we had to find our way out of this no-future endgame.

Us and them. The rainmakers and the Shadow Masters. Either we start re-writing history through a great blinding light of truth – from which people stumble only gradually, their eyes dazzled, toward more coherent attempts to understand what happened to them – or we plunge into a new Dark Age and madness. Call it a fairy tale with a twist, or a horror tale with a happy ending.

Or perhaps call it a story of corrupted idealism – a pursuit of a Platonic reflection of "perfection": an exalted dream. And since so much of what corrupts mankind is connected to the temptations that surround wealth and power, call it a very human story.

History, someone said, teaches by analogy, not identity. The historical experience is not one of staying in the present and looking back. Rather it is one of going back into the past and returning to the present with a wider and more intense consciousness of the restrictions of our former outlook.

Documents & Photographs

Above: Queen Beatrix of the Netherlands (daughter of Bilderberg founder and former Nazi, Prince Bernhard) at Bilderberg 2004 in Stresa, Italy. Beatrix is one of the most powerful women in the world, along with the British Queen Elizabeth II.

Below, at Stresa: What do Indra Nooyi (PepsiCo CEO), Henry Kissinger and *Washington Post* chairman Donald Graham have in common? Their annual participation in the Bilderberg conferences. The goal of this gang has always been to establish an empire. Globalization is nothing but an empire, and a new form of empire. It is elimination of nation-states, elimination of liberties, elimination of the rights of individuals, and the creation of a One World Company Ltd. Russia, to Bilderberg's chagrin, is why the globalists are so far behind in their plans. It is they who unleashed the alcoholic Boris Yeltsin on the world and almost succeeded in destroying Russia back in the 1990s. Now they are back at it with their attempts to smear Victor Bout, laying nuclear terrorism at Bout's, and by implication Russia's, feet.

Above: David Rockefeller "up-close and personal" during Bilderberg 2005. Visibly frail, David is unlikely to see his New-World-Order plans realized.
Below, at Rottach Egern, Germany, 2005: Bilderberg president, Count Etienne Davignon of Belgium. Behind him, marathon-man Mike Pritchard of Star Media Group, Canada's largest media enterprise, publishers of the flagship *Toronto Star* and many other papers. Needless to say, no coverage of the 2005 Bilderberg conference appeared in his newspapers.

Above, at Rottach Egern: At right, Jako Elkann, vice president of Fiat and a member of one of Bilderberg's most powerful families, the Agnellis, a family of the old Venetian Black Nobility. He is with Heather Reisman, owner of Indigo Books and Chapters, Canada's largest and most influential bookstore chains, with hundreds of outlets throughout the country. Her uncle was the key negotiator for Canada of the North American Free Trade Agreement, a prelude to a North American Union.

Below: former Swiss president Pascal Couchepin, escorted by Italian police to the 2004 Bilderberg meeting.

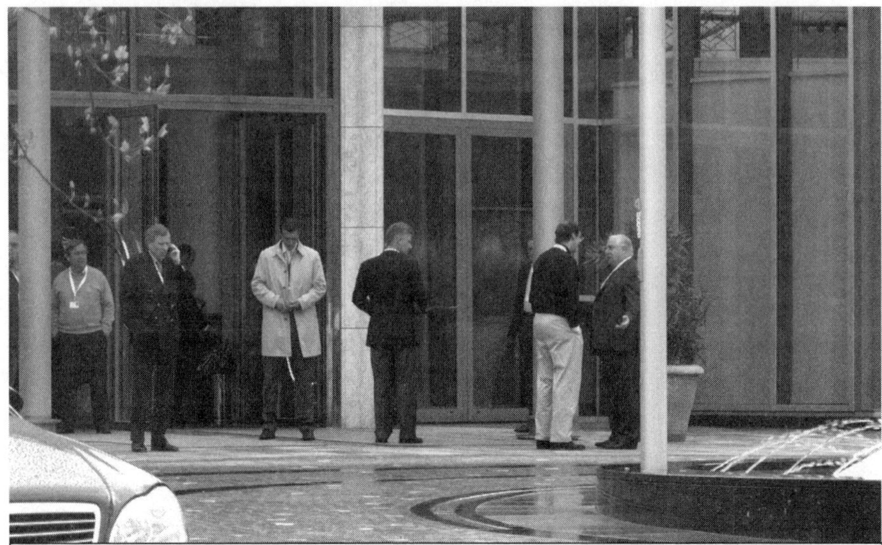

Above: Bilderberg does not shy from inviting representatives from both left and right, here in 2005. What all Bilderberg attendees share is their vision of the world under the control of One World Company Ltd. At left, Antonio Gutierrez, president of the Socialist International; on cell phone, Jaap de Hoop Scheffer, former Secretary General of NATO; with back turned, Prince Phillipe, heir to the Belgian throne; with hand in pocket, Royal Dutch Shell CEO, Jeroen van der Veer, who is speaking to Goldman Sachs/British Petroleum chairman, Peter Sutherland.

Below: Hotel in Rottach Egern, Germany, the site of the 2005 Bilderberg conference, where an oil price-hike to $150/barrel by summer's end 2008 was planned. Their plan succeeded, with its primary victim being China, whose ever-increasing demand can only be met by importing oil from the Middle East.

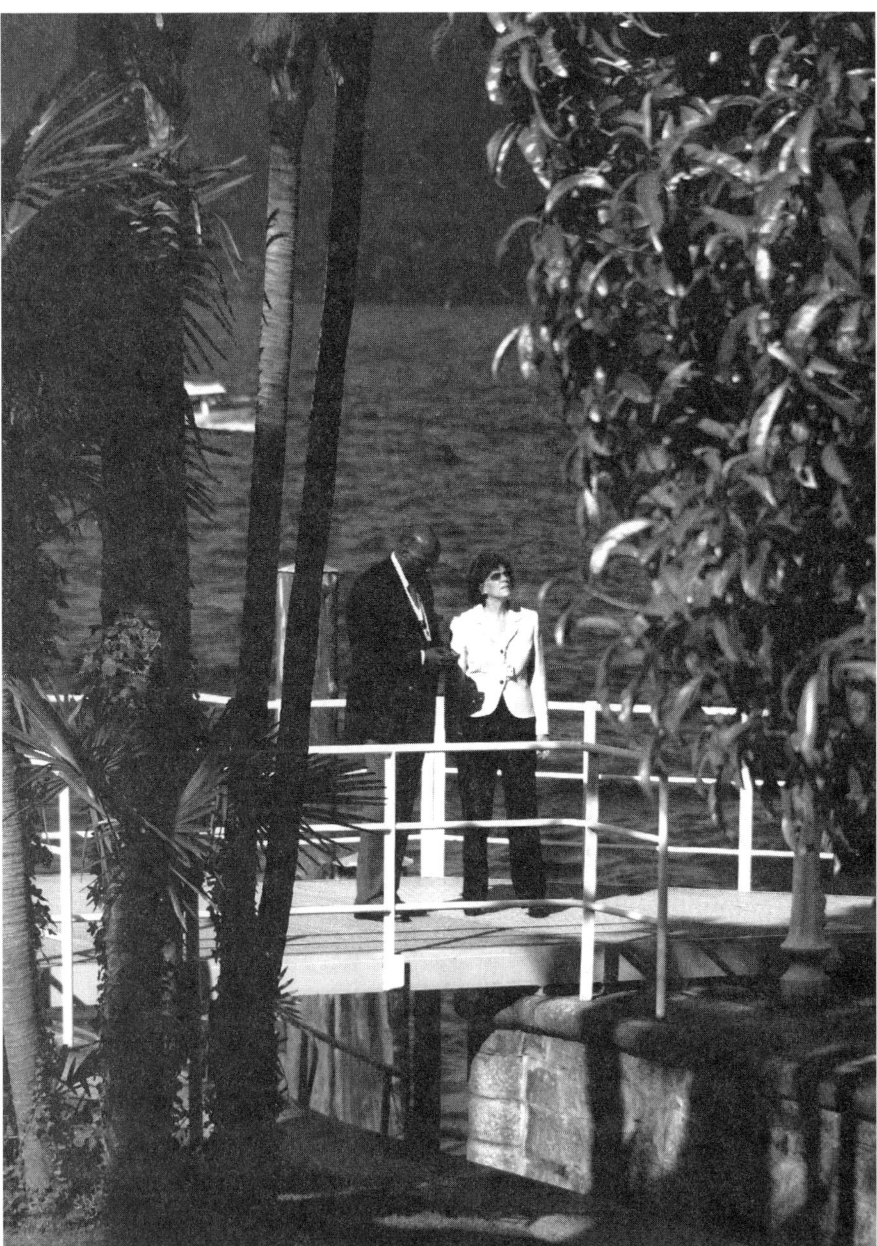

Vernon Jordan, a life member of the Council on Foreign Relations, with Jessica Matthews of the Carnegie Endowment, at Stresa 2004. It was Jordan who first suggested that the little-known governor of the backward state of Arkansas should be invited to the 1991 Bilderberg conference. The rest is history. Jordan is senior managing director of Lazard Frères, once the leading Synarchist bankers behind Hitler and Mussolini. Many of the economic policies of the international financial oligarchy led by Lazard are disseminated at the private Bilderberg conferences to the bankers and government bureaucrats who will implement them.

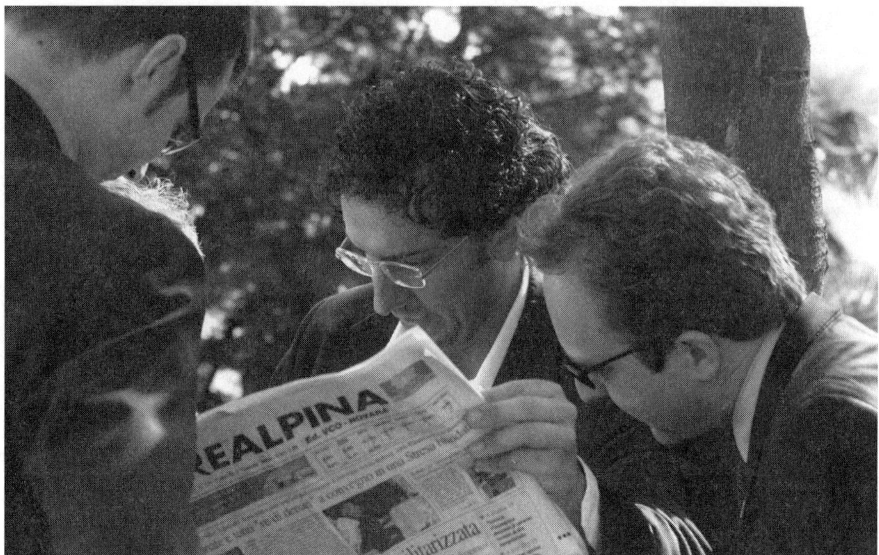

Above: Italian police in Stresa, 2004, reading the Bilderberg coverage in the local paper, *Prealpina*. The front page showed David Rockefeller dining. Several of the security police would become our friends and confidants over the years.

Below: Here I am appreciating some benign neglect. Italians have always shown themselves to be good sports when dealing with Bilderberg journalists like me, far from the more "robust" approach of Canadian and British security forces. Stresa, on the banks of Lake Maggiori, is some 25 miles from Milan.

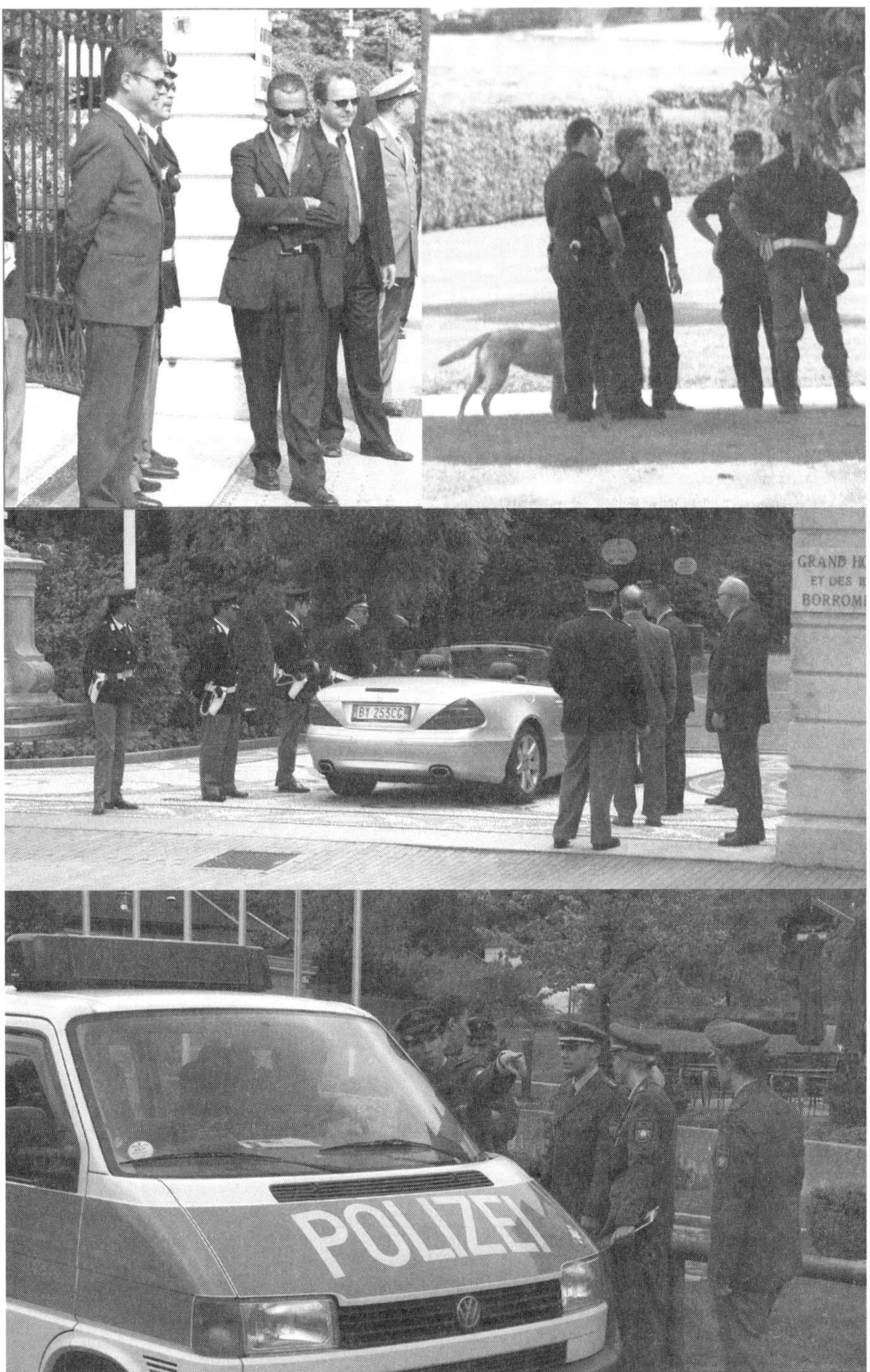

One would have to be a virtual James Bond or Jason Bourne to penetrate the fortress-like security of Bilderberg conferences. Fortunately, there have been leaks.

BILDERBERG GROUP

GARMISCH-PARTENKIRCHEN CONFERENCE

23-25 September 1955

INTRODUCTION

The third Bilderberg Conference was held at Garmisch-Partenkirchen in Germany from 23 to 25 September, 1955, under the chairmanship of H.R.H. The Prince of the Netherlands.

It will be recalled that previous conferences of the same kind were held at Bilderberg in Holland in May, 1954, and at Barbizon in France in March, 1955. The purpose of this series of conferences is to reach the highest possible denominator of mutual understanding between the countries of Western Europe and North America and so to work for the removal of causes of friction, to study those fields where action may be necessary to prevent friction from arising in the future and to examine the general areas in which agreement may be sought. To this end it was thought desirable to bring together a group of men of ex-perience, outstanding qualities and influence from different countries of the Western world in an atmosphere of mutual confidence and personal friendship which would admit of free and frank discussion. It is not the purpose of the Bilderberg series of conferences to construct policy. Participants include statesmen and diplomatists; trades unionists, intellectuals, business and professional men. They speak as individuals and not as representatives of their respective countries or the political parties, associations, or organizations to which they may belong. All, however, share a high purpose and a clear recognition of the urgency of the situation.

It was a conclusion of the first Bilderberg Conference that for historical reasons, together with many factors which were the ingredients of the present political, economic, and social situation, there would always be differences of opinion between the countries of Western Europe and those of North America, and in fact between any two countries in the world. Divergencies of view are not in themselves deplorable, and indeed, they are the quintessence of democratic life. Nevertheless, it is a matter of the utmost urgency that the will and the means should exist for finding a common basis on which to build our future.

At the second conference, held in Barbizon this year, subjects were chosen for the agenda which were bound to be controversial

to a certain extent, but the discussion of which could clarify the situation, and in some cases could be followed up in the future.

The problem of the uncommitted peoples was discussed and the general question of communist infiltration and propaganda, together with the approach of the Western European and North American countries to this question. It was felt that there must grow up not only a better understanding between the countries of the Western alliance but a closer contact and better understanding with the Asian and African countries, to many of which belong the so-called uncommitted peoples of the world.

There was a strong current of opinion also that there might be great value in arranging a subsequent meeting between leaders of

the mind and spirit of the East and West in an atmosphere similar to that of the Bilderberg series of conferences.

It was also generally agreed that too little was being done to counteract the unceasing and insidious encroachment of communist propaganda. The participants agreed that whenever they had the opportunity they would try to further those ideas and suggestions which had found general agreement at the two previous meetings, by making whatever use might be possible of the press and other contacts with public opinion. It is believed also that in the wide and important field presented by the European-American Associations much could be done towards creating the friendly atmosphere needed for the growth of the highest degree of co-operation.

It will be seen from the list of participants that the Garmisch Conference was attended by men from thirteen different countries. The subjects discussed were:

I. Review of events since the Barbizon Conference.

II. Article 2 of the North Atlantic Treaty Organization.

Report of the third Bilderberg conference, September 1955, which first discussed the integration of Europe; the Common Market was established in 1958. At the 1968 conference at Mont Tremblant, Canada, George Ball, senior Lehman Brothers banker and top Establishment figure, using the term "world company," called for further integration, which took a bit longer; the European Union formed in 1993. Today, most of Ball's wishes have come true. A final step would be the merger of different economic unions around the world. Russia and China stand in the way of the Bilderberg grand plan.

E. *European Unity*

The discussion on this subject revealed general support for the idea of European integration and unification among the participants from the six countries of the European Coal and Steel Community, and a recognition of the urgency of the problem.

While members of the group held different views as to the method by which a common market could be set up, there was a general recognition of the dangers inherent in the present divided markets of Europe and the pressing need to bring the German people, together with the other peoples of Europe, into a common market. That the six countries of the Coal and Steel Community had definitely decided to establish a common market and that experts were now working this out was felt to be a most encouraging step forward and it was hoped that other countries would subsequently join it. The need was generally accepted to press forward with functional integration in the economic domain particularly with regard to the industrial utilization of atomic energy.

It was generally recognized that it is our common responsibility to arrive in the shortest possible time at the highest degree of integration, beginning with a common European market. It was also generally agreed that the tariff walls surrounding this common market should certainly not be higher and should possibly be lower than the average of the existing tariffs now applied by the individual countries concerned.

F. *The Industrial Aspects of Atomic Energy* During this discussion a consensus of opinion manifested itself in certain points.

1 The future of the human race is bound up with the development of nuclear energy.

2 The cost of research, development, installation, and the training of large numbers of specialists is very high. Thus the developmental expense which must be put into what might be called the first and second generations of reactors meant that economic justification would come after this. Nevertheless in the next few years this problem can be expected to be solved.

3 As a result of the high cost it is of vital importance that Europe should combine her resources, since the cost *per capita* in any single country would be far greater than that in the United States with its larger population and resources.

4 The opportunity to initiate joint action in Europe should be seized before atomic development has been crystallized along national lines and at a time when vested interests have not yet established the obstacles which may make co-operative action more difficult, if not impossible, in a few years' time.

5 The opportunity to develop this new source of energy is an opportunity to increase productive output and is directly connected with the establishment of a common European market. Around it can be built, if the opportunity is not lost, a new aspect and a new hope for the unification of Europe.

6 The quickest possible steps should be taken towards the integration of Europe in respect to the industrial use of atomic energy, and joint planning, training and research should be started as soon as possible. The possibility of extending this particular form of integration to other than European countries was also emphasized.

I. REVIEW OF EVENTS SINCE THE BARBIZON CONFERENCE

A European rapporteur surveyed the international events of the past six months. There had been a political evolution which might be called sensational; the conclusion of the Austrian Treaty, the visit of Bulganin and Khrushchev to Yugoslavia, the Summit Conference in Geneva, and lastly, the Atomic Conference in Geneva. The question was whether this was illusion or reality.

There seemed to be no serious reason to believe that the communist leaders had become less communist and therefore the changes in Soviet foreign policy were only tactical changes. Perhaps we were entering into a new "Litvinov" period. There seemed to be a parallel in the situation today according to what the Soviet leaders had themselves told us. Their statements indicated that there was a serious crisis in Soviet agriculture and in the productivity of Soviet industry, and there was an undoubted political crisis as a result of the adjustments made after Stalin's death. There was a tendency in the West to say "In spite of threats and Soviet actions we have set up the Western European Union and this has brought the Russians to the negotiating table." Was this really true? Or was it that Russia, having been unable to prevent the ratification of the Western European Union, was trying to prevent its implementation and aiming at neutralizing NATO? Russia could be likened to malaria. It was wrong to believe oneself dead when the fever was high and even more wrong to believe oneself cured when the attack was over. It was necessary to use the period when the fever subsided to take a cure and build up resistance against the next attack and this should indicate the action which we should take to meet the new turn in Soviet policy.

The cold war, as we had known it, had been a trench war, whereas the new conflict, called co-existence, was a war of movement. The change over from a trench war to a war of movement had often resulted in serious military disasters and we should be very careful lest this transition also caused disasters in the political field. There were serious dangers in the new diplomacy by television rather than by negotiation and it was of great importance that we should not lower our guard. While we all sincerely hoped that the Russians really wanted peace, we must never forget that they may only wish to disrupt the military and political organization of the Western world and that they will try to exploit all the difficulties which may arise between Europe and America.

It was significant that Khruschev himself, speaking recently in Moscow, had said that the Russians always spoke the truth to their friends as well as to their adversaries. They were in favour of the relaxation of tension but if anyone thought that, to achieve

BILDERBERG MEETINGS
P.O.Box 3017 Fax +31 71 5280 522
2301 DA LEIDEN
The Netherlands

FAX

Date	19 May 2009
To	Mr. Wesznewsky
Fax #	+49 89 4115 5467
Subject	**Press release**
From	Maja Banck

PRESS RELEASE

BILDERBERG MEETINGS
17 May 2009

The 57th Bilderberg Meeting will be held in Vouliagmeni, Greece 14 – 17 May 2009. The Conference will deal mainly with the financial crisis, governments and markets, role of institutions, market economies and democracies, Iraq, Pakistan and Afghanistan, US and the World, cyberterrorism, new imperialisms, protectionism, post-Kyoto challenges. Approximately 130 participants will attend of whom about two-thirds come from Europe and the balance from North America. About one-third is from government and politics, and two-thirds are from finance, industry, labor, education, and communications. The meeting is private in order to encourage frank and open discussion.

Bilderberg takes its name from the hotel in Holland, where the first meeting took place in May 1954. That pioneering meeting grew out of the concern expressed by leading citizens on both sides of the Atlantic that Western Europe and North America were not working together as closely as they should on common problems of critical importance. It was felt that regular, off-the-record discussions would help create a better understanding of the complex forces and major trends affecting Western nations in the difficult post-war period.
The Cold War has now ended. But in practically all respects there are more, not fewer, common problems - from trade to jobs, from monetary policy to investment, from ecological challenges to the task of promoting international security. It is hard to think of any major issue in either Europe or North America whose unilateral solution would not have
What is unique about Bilderberg as a forum is the broad cross-section of leading citizens that are assembled for nearly three days of informal and off-the-record discussion about topics of current concern especially in the fields of foreign affairs and the international economy; the strong feeling among participants that in view of the differing attitudes and experiences of the Western nations, there remains a clear need to further develop an understanding in which these concerns can be accommodated; the privacy of the meetings, which has no purpose other than to allow participants to speak their minds openly and freely.
In short, Bilderberg is a small, flexible, informal and off-the-record international forum in which different viewpoints can be expressed and mutual understanding enhanced.

Bilderberg's only activity is its annual Conference. At the meetings, no conclusions are reached, no recommendations are made and no policy statements issued. Since 1954, fifty-six conferences have been held. The names of the participants are made available to the press. Participants are chosen for their experience, their knowledge, and their standing; all participants attend Bilderberg in a private and not an official capacity.

There will be no press conference. A list of participants is appended.

Official notice of the 2009 Bilderberg conference of "leading citizens," held in Greece.

17-5-2009

BILDERBERG MEETINGS
Vouliagmeni, Greece
14-17 May 2009
FINAL LIST OF PARTICIPANTS

	Honorary Chairman	
BEL	Davignon, Etienne	Honorary Chairman, Bilderberg Meetings; Vice Chairman, Suez-Tractebel
DEU	Ackermann, Josef	Chairman of the Management Board and the Group Executive Committee, Deutsche Bank AG
USA	Alexander, Keith B.	Director, National Security Agency
GRC	Alogoskoufis, George	Member of Parliament
USA	Altman, Roger C.	Chairman, Evercore Partners Inc.
GRC	Arapoglou, Takis	Chairman and CEO, National Bank of Greece
TUR	Babacan, Ali	Minister of State and Deputy Prime Minister
GRC	Bakoyannis, Dora	Minister of Foreign Affairs
NOR	Baksaas, Jon Fredrik	President and CEO, Telenor Group
PRT	Balsemão, Francisco Pinto	Chairman and CEO, IMPRESA, S.G.P.S.; Former Prime Minister
FRA	Baverez, Nicolas	Partner, Gibson, Dunn & Crutcher LLP
ITA	Bernabè, Franco	CEO, Telecom Italia S.p.A.
SWE	Bildt, Carl	Minister of Foreign Affairs
SWE	Björklund, Jan	Minister for Education; Leader of the Liberal Party
CHE	Blocher, Christoph	Former Swiss Counselor; Former Chairman and CEO, EMS-Group
FRA	Bompard, Alexandre	CEO, Europe 1
USA	Boot, Max	Jeane J. Kirkpatrick Senior Fellow for National Security Studies, Council on Foreign Relations
AUT	Bronner, Oscar	Publisher and Editor, Der Standard
FRA	Castries, Henri de	Chairman of the Management Board and CEO, AXA
ESP	Cebrián, Juan Luis	CEO, PRISA
BEL	Coene, Luc	Vice Governor, National Bank of Belgium
USA	Collins, Timothy C.	Senior Managing Director and CEO, Ripplewood Holdings, LLC
GRC	David, George A.	Chairman, Coca-Cola H.B.C. S.A.
GBR	Dearlove, Richard	Master, Pembroke College, Cambridge
GRC	Diamantopoulou, Anna	Member of Parliament
ITA	Draghi, Mario	Governor, Banca d'Italia
USA	Eberstadt, Nicholas N.	Henry Wendt Scholar in Political Economy, American Enterprise Institute for Public Policy Research
DNK	Eldrup, Anders	President, DONG A/S
ITA	Elkann, John	Chairman, EXOR S.p.A.; Vice Chairman, Fiat S.p.A.
DEU	Enders, Thomas	CEO, Airbus SAS
ESP	Entrecanales, José Manuel	Chairman, Acciona
AUT	Faymann, Werner	Federal Chancellor
USA	Ferguson, Niall	Laurence A. Tisch Professor of History, Harvard University
IRL	Gleeson, Dermot	Chairman, AIB Group
USA	Graham, Donald E.	Chairman and CEO, The Washington Post Company

CONFIDENTIALITY NOTE: This fax and/or document is legally privileged and confidential information intended only for the use of the individual or entity named above. If the reader of this message is not the intended recipient, you are hereby notified that any dissemination, distribution or copy of this telecopy is strictly prohibited.

Here and following pages: list of said "leading citizens." Note legal notice, in the event that the document may have fallen into the "wrong" hands.

17-5-2009

NLD	Halberstadt, Victor	Professor of Economics, Leiden University; Former Honorary Secretary General of Bilderberg Meetings
NLD	Hirsch Ballin, Ernst M.H.	Minister of Justice
USA	Holbrooke, Richard C.	US Special Representative for Afghanistan and Pakistan
NLD	Hommen, Jan H.M.	Chairman, ING N.V.
INT	Hoop Scheffer, Jaap G. de	Secretary General, NATO
USA	Johnson, James A.	Vice Chairman, Perseus, LLC
USA	Jordan, Jr., Vernon E.	Senior Managing Director, Lazard Frères & Co. LLC
FIN	Katainen, Jyrki	Minister of Finance
USA	Keane, John M.	Senior Partner, SCP Partners; General, US Army, Retired
USA	Kent, Muhtar	President and CEO, The Coca-Cola Company
GBR	Kerr, John	Member, House of Lords; Deputy Chairman, Royal Dutch Shell plc
DEU	Klaeden, Eckart von	Foreign Policy Spokesman, CDU/CSU
USA	Kleinfeld, Klaus	President and CEO, Alcoa Inc.
TUR	Koç, Mustafa V.	Chairman, Koç Holding A.Ş.
DEU	Koch, Roland	Prime Minister of Hessen
TUR	Kohen, Sami	Senior Foreign Affairs Columnist, Milliyet
USA	Kravis, Henry R.	Founding Partner, Kohlberg Kravis Roberts & Co.
USA	Kravis, Marie-Josée	Senior Fellow, Hudson Institute, Inc.
INT	Kroes, Neelie	Commissioner, European Commission
GRC	Kyriacopoulos, Ulysses	Chairman and Board member of subsidiary companies of the S&B Group
FRA	Lagarde, Christine	Minister for the Economy, Industry and Employment
INT	Lamy, Pascal	Director General, World Trade Organization
PRT	Leite, Manuela Ferreira	Leader, PSD
ESP	León Gross, Bernardino	General Director of the Presidency of the Spanish Government
DEU	Löscher, Peter	CEO, Siemens AG
GBR	Mandelson, Peter	Secretary of State for Business, Enterprise & Regulatory Reform
INT	Maystadt, Philippe	President, European Investment Bank
CAN	McKenna, Frank	Former Ambassador to the US
GBR	Micklethwait, John	Editor-in-Chief, The Economist
FRA	Montbrial, Thierry de	President, French Institute for International Relations
ITA	Monti, Mario	President, Universita Commerciale Luigi Bocconi
ESP	Moratinos Cuyaubé, Miguel A.	Minister of Foreign Affairs
USA	Mundie, Craig J.	Chief Research and Strategy Officer, Microsoft Corporation
CAN	Munroe-Blum, Heather	Principal and Vice Chancellor, McGill University
NOR	Myklebust, Egil	Former Chairman of the Board of Directors SAS, Norsk Hydro ASA
DEU	Nass, Matthias	Deputy Editor, Die Zeit
NLD	Netherlands, H.M. the Queen of the	
ESP	Nin Génova, Juan María	President and CEO, La Caixa
FRA	Olivennes, Denis	CEO and Editor in Chief, Le Nouvel Observateur
FIN	Ollila, Jorma	Chairman, Royal Dutch Shell plc
GBR	Osborne, George	Shadow Chancellor of the Exchequer
FRA	Oudéa, Frédéric	CEO, Société Générale
ITA	Padoa-Schioppa, Tommaso	Former Minister of Finance; President of Notre Europe
GRC	Papahelas, Alexis	Journalist, Kathimerini

2

GRC	Papalexopoulos, Dimitris	Managing Director, Titan Cement Co. S.A.
GRC	Papathanasiou, Yannis	Minister of Economy and Finance
USA	Perle, Richard N.	Resident Fellow, American Enterprise Institute for Public Policy Research
BEL	Philippe, H.R.H. Prince	
PRT	Pinho, Manuel	Minister of Economy and Innovation
INT	Pisani-Ferry, Jean	Director, Bruegel
CAN	Prichard, J. Robert S.	President and CEO, Metrolinx
ITA	Prodi, Romano	Chairman, Foundation for Worldwide Cooperation
FIN	Rajalahti, Hanna	Managing Editor, Talouselämä
CAN	Reisman, Heather M.	Chair and CEO, Indigo Books & Music Inc.
NOR	Reiten, Eivind	President and CEO, Norsk Hydro ASA
CHE	Ringier, Michael	Chairman, Ringier AG
USA	Rockefeller, David	Former Chairman, Chase Manhattan Bank
USA	Rubin, Barnett R.	Director of Studies and Senior Fellow, Center for International Cooperation, New York University
TUR	Sabanci Dinçer, Suzan	Chairman, Akbank
CAN	Samarasekera, Indira V.	President and Vice-Chancellor, University of Alberta
AUT	Scholten, Rudolf	Member of the Board of Executive Directors, Oesterreichische Kontrollbank AG
USA	Sheeran, Josette	Executive Director, UN World Food Programme
ITA	Siniscalco, Domenico	Vice Chairman, Morgan Stanley International
ESP	Solbes, Pedro	Vice-President of Spanish Government; Minister of Economy and Finance
ESP	Spain, H.M. the Queen of	
USA	Steinberg, James B.	Deputy Secretary of State
INT	Stigson, Björn	President, World Business Council for Sustainable Development
GRC	Stournaras, Yannis	Research Director, Foundation for Economic and Industrial Research (IOBE).
IRL	Sutherland, Peter D.	Chairman, BP plc and Chairman, Goldman Sachs International
INT	Tanaka, Nobuo	Executive Director, IEA
GBR	Taylor, J. Martin	Chairman, Syngenta International AG
USA	Thiel, Peter A.	President, Clarium Capital Management, LLC
DNK	Thorning-Schmidt, Helle	Leader of The Social Democratic Party
DNK	Thune Andersen, Thomas	Partner and CEO, Maersk Oil
AUT	Treichl, Andreas	Chairman and CEO, Erste Group Bank AG
INT	Trichet, Jean-Claude	President, European Central Bank
GRC	Tsoukalis, Loukas	President of the Hellenic Foundation for European and Foreign Policy (ELIAMEP)
TUR	Uğur, Agah	CEO, Borusan Holding
FIN	Vanhanen, Matti	Prime Minister
CHE	Vasella, Daniel L.	Chairman and CEO, Novartis AG
NLD	Veer, Jeroen van der	Chief Executive, Royal Dutch Shell plc
USA	Volcker, Paul A.	Chairman, Economic Recovery Advisory Board
SWE	Wallenberg, Jacob	Chairman, Investor AB
SWE	Wallenberg, Marcus	Chairman, SEB
NLD	Wellink, Nout	President, De Nederlandsche Bank

3

NLD	Wijers, Hans	Chairman, AkzoNobel NV
GBR	Wolf, Martin H.	Associate Editor & Chief Economics Commentator, The Financial Times
USA	Wolfensohn, James D.	Chairman, Wolfensohn & Company, LLC
USA	Wolfowitz, Paul	Visiting Scholar, American Enterprise Institute for Public Policy Research
INT	Zoellick, Robert B.	President, The World Bank Group
	Rapporteurs	
GBR	Bredow, Vendeline von	Business Correspondent, The Economist
GBR	McBride, Edward	Business Editor, The Economist

AUT	Austria	GRC	Greece
BEL	Belgium	INT	International
CHE	Switzerland	IRL	Ireland
CAN	Canada	ITA	Italy
DEU	Germany	NOR	Norway
DNK	Denmark	NLD	Netherlands
ESP	Spain	PRT	Portugal
FRA	France	SWE	Sweden
FIN	Finland	TUR	Turkey
GBR	Great Britain	USA	United States of America

Former Attorney General of Ireland, steering committee member Peter Sutherland is one of Bilderberg's most important insiders, and also a chairman of the Trilateral Commission. He is chairman of Goldman Sachs, chairman of British Petroleum and chairman of the London School of Economics: a perfect example of interlocked financial, business, academic and political interests. He is considered by many to have been the driving force behind the World Trade Organization.

By comparison, Flemish former Belgian Prime Minister and member of the European Parliament, Jean-Luc Dehaene, is a virtual nonentity: an uninspiring grey technocrat, but useful. In Belgian political circles he is known as "the plumber," the man who is called upon in a pinch to fix a problem.

02/09/1996 16:28 2026878312 ISD PAGE 02
VERL. UR. ; 1- 2-96 ; 10:01 ; 0206244289→ 2026878312;# 8

CONFIDENTIAL
NOT FOR CIRCULATION

BILDERBERG MEETINGS

Toronto, Canada
May 30-June 2, 1996

LIST OF INVITEES

STATUS 31 January 1996

Chairman

**	Carrington, Peter	Former Chairman of the Board, Christie's International plc; Former Secretary General, NATO

Honorary Secretary General for Europe and Canada

**	Halberstadt, Victor	Professor of Public Economics, Leiden University

Honorary Secretary General for U.S.A.

**	Yost, Casimir A.	Director, Institute for the Study of Diplomacy, School of Foreign Service, Georgetown University, Washington

AUSTRIA

**	Kothbauer, Max	Deputy Chairman, Creditanstalt-Bankverein
*	Vranitzky, Franz	Federal Chancellor
	+1	

BELGIUM

**	Davignon, Etienne	Executive Chairman, Société Générale de Belgique; Former Vice Chairman of the Commission of the European Communities
	Dehaene, Jean Luc	Prime Minister
	Huyghebaert, Jan	Chairman, Almanij-Kredietbank Group
	Philippe, H.R.H. Prince	

CANADA

**	Black, Conrad M.	Chairman, The Telegraph plc
**	Desmarais, Paul	Chairman, Power Corporation of Canada
**	Drouin, Marie-Josée	Executive Director, Hudson Institute of Canada
**	Flood, A.L.	Chairman, Canadian Imperial Bank of Commerce
**	Gotlieb, Allan E.	Former Ambassador to the United States of America
**	Griffin, Anthony G.S.	Honorary Chairman and Director, Guardian Group
**	Harris, Michael	Prime Minister of Ontario
	+4	

CZECH REPUBLIC
+1

* = invited but not yet accepted

Beginning of country-by-country list of candidates for participation at 1996 conference, sent out to the steering committee members. No one can buy his or her way into Bilderberg. Participants are invited on the strength of their knowledge of the subjects Bilderberg finds of value to its future world plans. There would be at least another two rounds of cuts before the final list was sent out and approved by all involved. Once accepted into Bilderberg, participants never leave. They are always "welcome" and urged to network with current and past members. This is one way to encourage former participants to keep their mouths shut about what went on at a meeting.

01/09/1996 16:28 2026878312 PAGE 01

OFFICE OF THE

SECISD

1996 JUN -4 AM 10: 40

American Friends of Bilderberg, Inc.

477 Madison Avenue, New York, N.Y. 10022 • (212) 752-6515 • Fax (212) 752-6518

Officers and Directors
John C. Whitehead, *President*
Casimir A. Yost, *Secretary*
James D. Wolfensohn, *Treasurer*
Henry A. Kissinger
David Rockefeller

MAY 3 0 1996

February 9, 1996

The Honorable William J. Perry
Secretary of Defense
The Pentagon, Room 3E944
Washington, D.C. 20301-1000
FAX: (703) 697-7381

Dear Mr. Secretary:

I am delighted to hear from Vernon Jordan that you may be able to join us at the next Bilderberg Meeting to be held outside of Toronto, Canada on the evening of May 30 through lunch on Sunday, June 2, 1996. Melba Boling, in your office, indicated that you might be available for dinner on the 30th and the morning of the 31st.

May I suggest that you join us for dinner and then address the conference participants first thing on the 31st. I would be glad to work with your staff in identifying a topic for your remarks which fits comfortably into the agenda of the conference which will be focused on the political, economic, and security issues confronting the Atlantic community.

I am attaching a provisional list of attendees for your information. I would be pleased to respond to any questions you or your staff might have. I can be reached at Georgetown University at (202) 687-6279.

It will, of course, be a personal pleasure for me to see your again and to welcome you to Bilderberg.

Sincerely,

Casimir A. Yost
Honorary Secretary General
for the United States

Attachment

BILDERBERG MEETINGS International Steering Committee: Lord Carrington, Chairman
Victor Halberstadt, Honorary Secretary General for Europe and Canada; Casimir A. Yost, Honorary Secretary General for U.S.

AUSTRIA: Max Kothbauer; BELGIUM: Etienne Davignon; CANADA: Conrad M.Black, Marie-Josée Drouin; DENMARK: Tøger Seidenfaden; GERMANY: Christoph Bertram, Hilmar Kopper; FINLAND: Jaakko Iloniemi; FRANCE: André Lévy-Lang, Thierry de Montbrial; GREECE: Costa Carras; IRELAND: Peter D. Sutherland; ITALY: Umberto Agnelli, Renato Ruggiero; NETHERLANDS: Victor Halberstadt, Pieter Korteweg; NORWAY: Westye Høegh; PORTUGAL: Francisco Pinto Balsemão; SPAIN: Jaime Carvajal Urquijo; SWEDEN: Percy Barnevik; SWITZERLAND: David de Pury; TURKEY: Selahattin Beyazit; UNITED KINGDOM: Andrew Knight; J. Martin Taylor; UNITED STATES: Paul A. Allaire, Vernon E. Jordan, Jr., Louis V. Gerstner, Jr., Henry A. Kissinger, Jack Sheinkman, John C. Whitehead, James D. Wolfensohn, Paul Wolfowitz, Casimir A. Yost. THE ADVISORY GROUP: Giovanni Agnelli, Ernst H. van der Beugel, William P. Bundy, Anthony G.S. Griffin, Max Kohnstamm, David Rockefeller, Lord Roll of Ipsden, Otto Wolff von Amerongen

U08137 /96

American Friends of Bilderberg have emerged as go-betweens for the US invitees selected by the Bilderberg steering committee.

2.

BILDERBERG MEETINGS

Amstel 216 Phone +31 20 625 0252
1017 AJ Amsterdam Fax +31 20 624 4299
The Netherlands

1996 APR -2 PM 4: 31

The Hon. William J. Perry
Secretary of Defense
U.S. Department of Defense
The Pentagon
WASHINGTON, D.C. 20301-1000
U.S.A.

18 March 1996

Subject: Bilderberg Meeting near Toronto, Canada from the evening of Thursday, May 30 through lunch on Sunday, June 2, 1996

Dear Mr. Perry,

Thank you for confirming your participation in the forthcoming conference. I am pleased to enclose:

1. The current list of participants. If you wish to have changes made in the way your affiliation is mentioned, please let me know before May 15; the suggested corrections will then be made in the next version.

2. The preliminary agenda.

3. The notice to participants, detailing various arrangements.

4. A travel advisory form. **Please do follow the instructions about completing this form and return it as soon as possible by fax to the Bilderberg office in Amsterdam (fax nr. +31 20 624 4299)**. This will assure prompt reception at points of arrival, timely transportation and smooth departure.

U0 4668 /96

Nothing is left to chance: Bilderberg is the paragon of professionalism and efficiency, as the cover letter (here and next page), the four-page conference brochure (p. 257) and the travel advisory form (p. 258) clearly demonstrate.

2

5. Special Bilderberg labels for rapid identification at the reception points; please attach these to all your luggage.

6. A copy of your biography which we have on file. Please return it to me with any changes you may wish to make, or advise me that it may be used as it is for the 1996 Profiles of Participants which, as you know, will be distributed to all participants at the conference.

I would like to take this opportunity to ask you to send me

- a copy of a **recent passport photograph, marking your name on the back**. The photograph will appear on your security badge.

Please note that all participants are expected to stay through the entire conference and to join in all of the conference programme, which begins Thursday before dinner.

Participants are strongly urged **not to bring personal staff** unless prior agreed with the Honorary Secretary General.

Please do not hesitate to contact me if you have any questions about the conference.

Yours sincerely,

Maja Banck (mrs.)
Executive Secretary

Enclosures

CHARACTER OF MEETING

- Participants are expected to stay through the entire conference and to join in all of the conference programme (which begins Thursday before dinner), unless otherwise agreed with the Chairman.

- The meetings do not formulate policies or reach conclusions, and no resolutions are submitted for discussion or vote.
  The sole purpose of the debate is to have an exchange of views about the issues on the agenda, from which participants are free to draw their own conclusions.

- Participants attend in a private capacity, irrespective of their official position.
  Fruitful discussions are enhanced by an atmosphere of mutual trust in which participants can express themselves freely. **All discussions are therefore private and off-the-record**; the press is excluded from the meetings.

- A list of participants and the agenda will be made available to the press the day the conference starts.
  Participants are expected not to give interviews to the press during the meeting. A point which should be strictly adhered to in contacts with the news media, is that no attribution should be made to individual participants of what was discussed during the meeting.

- The summary report of the conference includes the names of all participants and opinions are summarized; speakers are not referred to by name. This report is circulated only to participants, former participants of the Bilderberg Meetings and sponsors.

-1-

CONFERENCE PROGRAMME 1996

- Participants should plan to arrive at the CIBC Centre on Thursday, May 30. Drinks will be served from 19.00; buffet dinner will be served from 20.00. Working sessions start daily at 08.30 and end before dinner, with a recreation break on Saturday from lunch till 17.00.
- The closing session on Sunday will take place from 8.30 until 11.00. Buffet lunch will be served at 12.00 noon.

PLACE OF THE MEETING

The meeting will be held at the CIBC Centre, King City, near Toronto, Canada. The full address is:

CIBC Centre
12750 Jane Street
R.R. # 1
King City, Ontario LOG 1KO
Canada
Phone +1.905.833 3086
Fax +1.905.833 3075

The CIBC Centre has been reserved exclusively for the meeting and all activities will take place there.
Weather in June is usually pleasant, but the evenings tend to be chilly. Guests should bring a sweater and/or a raincoat.

ACCOMPANYING AND SECURITY STAFF

Participants are strongly urged not to bring personal staff. However, participants who must be accompanied by personal staff should be aware that staff cannot attend sessions nor share meals at participants' tables: a separate dining room will be provided.

-2-

☞ **Accompanying personal and security staff will be accommodated at their own expense.**

SPOUSES

It is emphasized that participants may not bring spouses to Bilderberg Meetings. Our staff is prepared to assist spouses travelling with participants in finding suitable accommodation elsewhere.

EXPENSES

- Rooms, meals, wines, and pre-dinner cocktails will be provided free of charge to participants from dinner on Thursday, May 30 through lunch on Sunday, June 2.

- Personal charges, such as telecommunication, laundry, room service, bar bills etc. will be at participants' own expense.

CONFERENCE PORTFOLIOS

On arrival participants will receive detailed information on the schedule and procedures of the conference, lay-out of the site, seating arrangements in the conference room, the final list of participants, and other supporting information.

CONFERENCE LANGUAGE

The official language of the conference is English.

-3-

RECREATION

The CIBC Centre offers an indoor and outdoor swimming pool, a tennis, squash and racketball court, a jogging track and fitness rooms.

TRANSPORTATION AND RECEPTION

- The CIBC Centre is at about 20 minutes drive by car from Toronto Airport. Participants are expected to make their own travel arrangements to the reception point in Toronto and from this point to their next destinations. Transport will be provided by the host country between the reception/departure point and the CIBC Centre.

- Participants arriving by commercial and private planes will be met at Toronto Airport by hostesses who will show the Bilderberg symbol (similar to the Bilderberg luggage labels enclosed). A participant who fails to make contact with a hostess should telephone the Bilderberg Transportation Desk at the CIBC Centre:

  Phone +1.905.833 3086
  Fax +1.905.833 3075

☞ **Security requires that all participants attach the enclosed Bilderberg labels to all their luggage, including their hand luggage**

-4-

BILDERBERG MEETINGS

CIBC Centre, King City, near Toronto, Canada
May 30-June 2, 1996

TRAVEL ADVISORY FORM

NAME and initials ______________________________

ADDRESS ______________________________

____

____

TELEPHONE ______________________ TELEFAX ______________________

ARRIVAL INFORMATION

☐ **AIR**
Date of arrival ______________ Time of arrival ______________

From ______________ Airline and flight number ______________ Private aircraft ______________

Place of arrival

☐ TORONTO ☐ OTHER ______________

☐ **ROAD**
Date of arrival ______________ Expected time of arrival at CIBC Centre ______________

Car ______________ Registration number ______________ Name of driver ______________

DEPARTURE INFORMATION

☐ **AIR**
Date of departure ______________ Time of departure ______________

Airport ______________ Destination ______________

Airline and flight number ______________ Private aircraft ______________

☐ **ROAD**
Date of departure ______________ Time of departure from CIBC Centre ______________

INSTRUCTIONS

- All participants are requested to complete this form and return it by fax to: Bilderberg Meetings, Amsterdam, The Netherlands **Fax nr.: +31 20 624 4299**
- Advise promptly any change in previously reported travel information to ensure being met on arrival at the reception points in Toronto.
- Attach Bilderberg travel labels to **ALL** your luggage including your hand luggage, to facilitate reception arrangements at points of arrival

SIGNATURE ______________________ DATE ______________________

VERZ. DR: ; 9- 5-96 ; 12:15 ; 0206244299→ 0017036979080;# 1

CONFIDENTIAL

BILDERBERG MEETINGS

PHONE +31 20 625 0252
FAX +31 20 624 4299

1996 MAY -9 AM 11: 11
OFFICE OF THE SECRETARY OF DEFENSE

DATE	:	**9 May 1996**
TO	:	**The Hon. William J. Perry**
FAX NUMBER	:	**1.703.697 9080**
FROM	:	**Maja Banck, Executive Secretary**
REF. #	:	**1375**
SUBJECT	:	**Agenda Toronto Conference**
PAGES TO FOLLOW	:	**1**

Annexed is the preliminary agenda for the forthcoming Bilderberg Meeting, near Toronto, May 30-June 2, 1996.

Early next week the current list of participants and four background papers will be mailed to you.

DECLASSIFIED BY AUTHORITY OF
Principal Deputy - EUR/NATO
960701 96-F-1203
DATE CASE #

CONFIDENTIAL

X01010 /96
Sec Def Cont Nr.

Cover letter to invitees to 1996 Bilderberg conference, with preliminary agenda on next page. The agenda would have been debated, and finalized by late January, by the Bilderberg steering committee.

NOT FOR CIRCULATION

DECLASSIFIED BY AUTHORITY OF

DATE — CASE #

0017036979080:# 2 0208244299→ : 9- 5-98 : 12:18 : VERZ. DR:

9 May 1996

BILLDERBERG MEETINGS
CIBC Centre, King City, near Toronto, Canada
May 30-June 2, 1996
PRELIMINARY AGENDA

	SPEAKERS	MODERATORS
STATUS REPORT ON THE ALLIANCE	William J. Perry [US]	Peter Carrington
FORMER YUGOSLAVIA	Carl Bildt [S] Richard C. Holbrooke [US]	Peter Carrington
RUSSIA: POLITICAL FORCES AND ECONOMIC PROSPECTS	Anders Åslund [S], background paper Franz Vranitzky [A]	Christoph Bertram
EUROPE: THE POLITICS OF EU ENLARGEMENT	Timothy Garton Ash [GB], background paper Pierre Lellouche [F] György Surányi [H]	Peter D. Sutherland
HAS EUROPE'S ECONOMY RUN OUT OF STEAM?	Percy Barnevik [S] Ulrich Cartellieri [D]	....
THE US AGENDA	Paul A. Gigot [US] George Stephanopoulos [US]	Conrad M. Black
ARE THERE LIMITS TO GLOBALIZATION?	Martin S. Feldstein [US] John Monks [GB] Sylvia Ostry [CDN], background paper	Umberto Agnelli
WHERE IS CHINA GOING?	Chas. W. Freeman, Jr. [US], background paper Henry A. Kissinger [US] Winston Lord [US]	Henry A. Kissinger
WTO AND WORLD BANK: BRIEFING	Renato Ruggiero [INT] James D. Wolfensohn [INT]	Vernon E. Jordan, Jr.
CURRENT EVENTS		

PLEASE NOTE: • the program may undergo changes • the order of sessions will only be decided on the eve of the conference

13-MAY-1996 14:58 LORD CARRINGTON 01 823 9051 P.

:13- 5-96 : 13:27 : 0206244299→ 01 823 9051;

BILDERBERG MEETINGS

Amstel 216
1017 AJ Amsterdam
The Netherlands

Phone +31 20 625 0252
Fax +31 20 624 4299

BY FAX

Date : 10 May 1996
To : Peter Carrington, moderator
William J. Perry
From : Victor Halberstadt
About : Your session about The Alliance at the Toronto Conference

It is much appreciated that you have agreed to moderate or be panelist in the session on **Status Report on The Alliance** at the upcoming conference.

Though you all know Bilderberg well, I need to ask your attention for the following:

1. It is a tradition of Bilderberg that there are no formal speeches and no read texts; experience shows that spontaneous presentations are most successful. Most of the session is to be devoted to an active discussion among panelists and participants.
2. Moderators are strongly encouraged to really lead the debate from a substance point of view; the discussion should be kept within the framework of key questions outlined briefly at the start of your session.
3. The moderator is asked to summarize the rules for interventions at the opening of the session to make sure that all attendees understand the strict application of the 1, 3 and 5 minute system. Moderators should only permit "1-minute interventions" which are really addressed to the points then being discussed.
4. Introductory statements by the panelists cannot exceed 10 minutes as you already know from the letters confirming your participation. Please keep in mind that all sessions are relatively short. Your session is 80 minutes.
5. The moderator should make sure that sessions begin and end exactly on schedule; this also applies to the breaks for coffee and tea. Ms. Marlieke de Vogel of the Secretariat is responsible for your session; she will contact you upon your arrival at the conference and assist you with any arrangement before the session.
6. We expect that the moderator, in this case Peter Carrington, will want to coordinate with each of the panelists well in advance of the conference in order to ensure a successful session; phone and fax numbers are annexed.

With characteristic Dutch efficiency, Victor Halberstadt lays down the law for a former NATO Secretary General, Peter Carrington, and the US Secretary of Defense William Perry. Halberstadt is a professor of public economics at the University of Leiden. Note the lack of titles for the addressees compared to the following letter from Carrington to Perry. Bilderberg insiders outrank functionaries.

13-MAY-1996 14:58 — — LORD CARRINGTON 01 823 9051 P.01

32a Ovington Square
London SW3 1LR
Tel. 0171-5841-4243
Fax. 0171-823-9051

OFFICE OF THE
SECRETARY OF DEFENSE
1996 MAY 13 PM 1:49

13 May 1996

Fax to The Hon William J Perry
Secretary of Defence
001 703 697 9080

From Lord Carrington

Pages 2

Dear Mr Perry

I am so glad that you can come to Toronto. This is very good news for all of us, and you will get a very warm welcome.

I don't know whether you have been to Bilderberg before, but I enclose the house rules which may be of some use to you.

With best wishes.

Yours
Peter Carrington

Lord Carrington

Then-Bilderberg president, Lord Peter Carrington, sends warm greetings to the Honorable William Perry, thanking him for his upcoming participation in Bilderberg 1996. Carrington has long been associated with Barclays Bank and the Rio Tinto Group minerals conglomerate, which dominate southern Africa. As Margaret Thatcher's Foreign Secretary, Carrington played a dirty part in Britain's incitement and orchestration of Serbian military aggression and crimes against humanity during the 1990s Balkan crises. The same "bait and switch" had been practiced upon Argentina in negotiations over the Malvinas (Falkland Islands), which incited Argentina in 1982 to a futile preemptive invasion in an attempt to enforce its claim.

VERZ. DR: ;23- 5-96 ; 18:00 ; 0206244299→ 0017036979080;# 2

5 0011126

BILDERBERG MEETINGS

Amstel 216
1017 AJ Amsterdam Phone +31 20 625 0252
The Netherlands Fax +31 20 624 4299

OFFICE OF THE SECRETARY OF DEFENSE
1996 MAY 23 PM 3:49

Date : 23 May 1996
To : The Hon. William J. Perry ✓
The Hon. Malcolm L. Rifkind
Mr. Carl Bildt
Mr. Richard C. Holbrooke
From : Maja Banck, Executive Secretary
About : Bilderberg conference:
Your sessions on Friday May 31 1996

Lord Carrington would like to discuss the procedure at your sessions with you and invite you to a breakfast meeting on Friday, May 31, at 7:30 a.m.

A table will be reserved for you in The Music Room at the CIBC Centre.

96-7-1203

U07568 /96 #824

Without the authorization of President Clinton, Secretary of Defense William Perry would have almost certainly violated the Logan Act, passed in 1799 and last amended in 1994, which forbids American citizens to communicate with officials of foreign governments or their agents "without authority of the United States" about "any disputes or controversies with the United States." He would surely not have participated without proper authority, but why then is the citizenry, which after all is supposedly the sovereign power, kept in the dark about American officials' participation in this ongoing *private* international institution?

·CONFIDENTIAL
NOT FOR CIRCULATION

BILDERBERG MEETINGS

CIBC Centre, King City, near Toronto, Canada
May 30-June 2, 1996

CURRENT LIST OF PARTICIPANTS

STATUS 14 May 1996

Chairman

GB	Carrington, Peter	Former Chairman of the Board, Christie's International plc; Former Secretary General, NATO

Honorary Secretary General for Europe and Canada

NL	Halberstadt, Victor	Professor of Public Economics, Leiden University

Honorary Secretary General for U.S.A.

USA	Yost, Casimir A.	Director, Institute for the Study of Diplomacy, School of Foreign Service, Georgetown University, Washington

I	Agnelli, Giovanni	Honorary Chairman, Fiat S.p.A.
I	Agnelli, Umberto	Chairman IFIL
FIN	Ahtisaari, Martti	President of the Republic of Finland
USA	Allaire, Paul A.	Chairman, Xerox Corporation
USA	Andreas, Dwayne	Chairman, Archer-Daniels-Midland Company
S	Åslund, Anders	Senior Associate, Carnegie Endowment for International Peace
CDN	Axworhty, Lloyd	Minister for Foreign Affairs
P	Balsemão, Francisco Pinto	Professor of Communication Science, New University, Lisbon; Chairman, IMPRESA, S.G.P.S.; Former Prime Minister
S	Barnevik, Percy	President and Chief Executive Officer, ABB Asea Brown Boveri Ltd.
USA	Bentsen, Lloyd M.	Former Secretary of the Treasury; Partner, Verner Lüpfert Bernhard McPherson and Hand, Chartered
I	Bernabè, Franco	Managing Director and CEO, Ente Nazionale Idrocarburi
D	Bertram, Christoph	Diplomatic Correspondent, Die Zeit; Former Director International Institute for Strategic Studies
NL	Beugel, Ernst H. van der	Emeritus Professor of International Relations, Leiden University; Former Honorary Secretary General of Bilderberg Meetings for Europe and Canada
TR	Beyazit, Selahattin	Director of Companies
INT	Bildt, Carl	EC Mediator, International Conference on Former Yugoslavia
CDN	Black, Conrad M.	Chairman, The Telegraph plc
NL	Bolkestein, Frits	Parliamentary Leader VVD
USA	Bryan, John H.	Chairman and CEO, Sara Lee Corporation
USA	Buckley, Jr., William F.	National Review
GR	Carras, Costa	Director of Companies
D	Cartellieri, Ulrich	Member of the Board, Deutsche Bank A.G.
E	Carvajal Urquijo, Jaime	Chairman and General Manager, Iberfomento
CDN	Chretién, Jean	Prime Minister
F	Collomb, Bertrand	Chairman and CEO, Lafarge
USA	Corzine, Jon S.	Senior Partner and Chairman, Goldman Sachs & Co.
CH	Cotti, Flavio	Minister for Foreign Affairs

Here and following pages, the final list of Bilderberg attendees for the 1996 conference in Canada. At that conference, the dissolution of Canada was again on the table, along with the future war in Kosovo and the destruction of Russia.

STATUS 14 May 1996

USA	Dam, Kenneth W.	Max Pam Professor of American and Foreign Law, The University of Chicago Law School
GR	David, George	Chairman, Hellenic Bottling Company S.A.
B	Davignon, Etienne	Executive Chairman, Société Générale de Belgique: Former Vice Chairman of the Commission of the European Communities
CDN	Drouin, Marie-Josée	Executive Director, Hudson Institute of Canada
CDN	Eaton, Fredrik S.	Chairman Executive Committee, Eaton's of Canada
DK	Ellemann-Jensen, Uffe	Member of Parliament
TR	Erçel, Gazi	Governor, Central Bank of Turkey
USA	Feldstein, Martin S.	President, National Bureau of Economic Research
INT	Fischer, Stanley	First Deputy Managing Director, International Monetary Fund
USA	Fites, Donald	Chairman and CEO, Caterpillar, Inc.
CDN	Flood, A.L.	Chairman, Canadian Imperial Bank of Commerce
USA	Freeman, Jr., Chas. W.	Former Assistant Secretary of Defense for International Security; Chairman of the Board, Projects International Associates, Inc.
GB	Garton Ash, Timothy	Fellow of St. Antony's College, Oxford
USA	Gerstner, Jr., Louis V.	Chairman, IBM Corporation
USA	Gigot, Paul	Columnist, The Wall Street Journal
TR	Gönensay, Emre	Minister for Foreign Affairs
CDN	Gotlieb, Allan E.	Former Ambassador to the United States of America
CDN	Griffin, Anthony G.S.	Honorary Chairman and Director, Guardian Group
CDN	Harris, Michael	Premier of Ontario
D	Haussmann, Helmut	Member of Parliament
N	Höegh, Westye	Chairman of the Board, Leif Höegh & Co. ASA: Former President, Norwegian Shipowners' Association
USA	Holbrooke, Richard	Former Assistant Secretary for European Affairs
B	Huyghebaert, Jan	Chairman, Almanij-Kredietbank Group
FIN	Iloniemi, Jaakko	Managing Director, Centre for Finnish Business and Policy Studies; Former Ambassador to the United States of America
N	Jagland, Torbjorn	Chairman, Labour Party
GB	Job, Peter	Chief Executive, Reuters Holding PLC
USA	Jordan, Jr., Vernon E.	Senior Partner, Akin, Gump, Strauss, Hauer & Feld, LLP (Attorneys-at-Law)
F	Jospin, Lionel	First Secretary of the Socialist Party; Former Ministre d'Etat
A	Karner, Dietrich	Chairman of the Managing Board, Erste Allgemeine-Generali Aktiengesellschaft
USA	Kissinger, Henry A.	Former Secretary of State; Chairman, Kissinger Associates, Inc.
GB	Knight, Andrew	Non Executive Director, News Corporation
INT	Kohnstamm, Max	Senior Fellow, European Policy Centre, Brussels; Former Secretary General, Action Committee for Europe; Former President, European University Institute
NL	Korteweg, Pieter	President and CEO, Robeco Group; Honorary Treasurer Bilderberg Meetings
A	Kothbauer, Max	Deputy Chairman, Creditanstalt-Bankverein
USA	Kravis, Henry R.	Founding Partner, Kohlberg Kravis Roberts & Co.
DK	Lavesen, Holger	Chairman of the Board of Directors, The Danish Oil & Gas Consortium
F	Lellouche, Pierre	Member of the National Assembly
F	Lévy-Lang, André	Chairman of the Board of Management, Banque Paribas
USA	Lord, Winston	Assistant Secretary for East Asian and Pacific Affairs
P	Marante, Margarida	TV Journalist
CDN	Martin, Paul	Minister of Finance
B	Maystadt, Philippe	Vice-Prime Minister, Minister of Finance and Foreign Trade
USA	McHenry, Donald F.	Research Professor of Diplomacy and International Affairs, Georgetown University

2

STATUS 14 May 1996

F	Messier. Jean-Marie	CEO and Chairman of the Executive Committee, Compagnie Generale des Eaux
GB	Monks. John	General Secretary, Trades Union Congress (TUC)
F	Montbrial, Thierry de	Director, French Institute of International Relations; Professor of Economics, Ecole Polytechnique
INT	Monti, Mario	Commissioner, European Communities
NL	Netherlands, Her Majesty the Queen of the	
ICE	Oddsson, David	Prime Minister
PL	Olechowski, Andrzej	Chairman of the Supervisory Board, Bank Handlowy W Warszawie S.A.; Former Minister for Foreign Affairs
CDN	Ostry, Sylvia	Chairman, Centre for International Studies, University of Toronto
GR	Pangalos, Theodore G.	Minister for Foreign Affairs
USA	Perry, William J.	Secretary of Defense
N	Petersen, Jan	Parliamentary Leader, Conservative Party
CH	Pury, David de	Director of Companies; Former Co-Chairman of the ABB Group and former Ambassador for Trade Agreements
GB	Rifkind, Malcolm L.	Foreign Secretary
GB	Robertson, Simon	Chairman, Kleinwort Benson Group plc
USA	Rockefeller, David	Chairman, Chase Manhattan Bank International Advisory Committee
CDN	Rogers, Edward S.	President and CEO, Rogers Communications Inc.
GB	Roll, Eric	Senior Adviser, SBC Warburg
INT	Ruggiero, Renato	Director General, World Trade Organization; Former Minister of Trade
S	Sahlin, Mona	Member of Parliament
D	Schrempp, Jürgen E.	Chairman of the Board of Management, Daimler-Benz AG
INT	Schwab, Klaus	President, World Economic Forum
DK	Seidenfaden, Toger	Editor in Chief, Politiken A/S
USA	Sheinkman, Jack	Chairman of the Board, Amalgamated Bank
CH	Sommaruga, Cornelio	President, International Committee of the Red Cross
USA	Soros, George	President, Soros Fund Management
E	Spain, H.M. the Queen of	
USA	Stephanopoulos, George	Senior Advisor to the President
D	Strube, Jürgen	CEO, BASF Aktiengesellschaft
H	Surányi, György	President, National Bank of Hungary
IRL	Sutherland, Peter D.	Chairman and Managing Director, Goldman Sachs International; Former Director General, GATT and WTO
NL	Tabaksblat, Morris	Chairman of the Board, Unilever N.V.
GB	Taylor, J. Martin	Chief Executive, Barclays Bank plc
LUX	Thorn, Gaston E.	Président Directeur Général, CLT
D	Töpfer, Klaus	Federal Minister for Regional Planning, Building and Urban Development
USA	Trotman, Alexander J.	Chairman, Ford Motor Company
I	Veltroni, Valter	Editor, L'Unità
P	Vitorino, António	Deputy Prime Minister and Minister of Defence
D	Voscherau, Henning	Mayor of Hamburg
A	Vranitzky, Franz	Federal Chancellor
S	Wallenberg, Marcus	Executive Vice President, Investor AB
USA	Weiss, Stanley A.	Chairman, Business Executives for National Security, Inc
USA	Whitehead, John C.	Former Deputy Secretary of State
CDN	Wilson, L.R.	Chairman, President and CEO, BCE Inc.
INT	Wolfensohn, James D.	President, The World Bank; Former President and CEO, James D. Wolfensohn, Inc.
D	Wolff von Amerongen, Otto	Chairman and CEO of Otto Wolff GmbH
USA	Wolfowitz, Paul	Dean, Nitze School of Advanced International Studies; Former Under Secretary of Defense for Policy

3

Observers

NL	Orange, H.R.H. the Prince of
B	Philippe, H.R.H. Prince

Rapporteurs

GB	Micklethwait, John	Business Editor, The Economist
USA	Victor, Alice	Executive Assistant, Rockefeller Financial Services, Inc.

In Attendance

NL	Maja Banck	Executive Secretary, Bilderberg Meetings
CDN	Mary Alice Carroll	Local Organizer 1996
USA	Charles W. Muller	President, Murden and Company; Adviser, American Friends of Bilderberg, Inc.

List of Abbreviations

A	Austria	I	Italy
B	Belgium	ICE	Iceland
CDN	Canada	INT	International
CH	Switzerland	IRL	Ireland
D	Germany	L	Luxemburg
DK	Denmark	N	Norway
E	Spain	NL	Netherlands
F	France	P	Portugal
FIN	Finland	PL	Poland
GB	Great Britain	S	Sweden
GR	Greece	TR	Turkey
H	Hungary	USA	United States of America

WORLD ECONOMIC FORUM

COMMITTED TO IMPROVING THE STATE OF THE WORLD

OFFICE OF THE SECRETARY OF DEFENSE

1996 JUN 12 PM 2:38

Professor Klaus Schwab
President

The Honourable William Perry
Secretary of Defence
Department of Defence
The Pentagon, Room 3 E 944
USA WASHINGTON, DC 20301-6352

6 June 1996 / sh

Dear Mr. Secretary,

Your presentation at the recent Bilderberg Meeting was very convincing and impressive.

It is now my great pleasure and honour to invite you to join the 1997 Annual Meeting of our members and constituents, which will take place in Davos, Switzerland, from 30 January to 4 February.

The issues of creating a comprehensive security architecture for Europe will be certainly at the forefront of our discussions at our Annual Meeting in Davos next year. In particular, we are planning a session to which we would like to invite the Russian Minister of Defence at the time of the Annual Meeting and Minister Rühe to discuss together with you in detail such issues as preventive defence and in general the role of the military at the beginning of the 21st century.

Your presence in Davos would provide you with a unique opportunity to deliver a strong message on these or other issues of most concern to you and the United States. Your views and expertise would be greatly valued by the 1000 chief executives of the world's largest companies and the foremost leaders from government, academia and the media who participate in our Annual Meeting each year.

We would be pleased to discuss the details of your specific role at Davos with your office in coming months, but I hope you will reserve for us in your agenda the prolonged weekend of 31 January to 2 February 1997.

I look forward to the possibility of welcoming you in Davos at the beginning of next year.

Yours sincerely,

Klaus Schwab

53 chemin des Hauts-Crêts. CH-1223 Cologny/Geneva. Switzerland
Tel (41 22) 869 1212 Fax (41 22) 786 2744 E-mail: contact@weforum...

After Perry's great impact on Bilderberg attendees during the 1996 meeting in Canada, World Economic Forum president Klaus Schwab invited him to participate in its Davos meeting in late January 1997. As you can see (facing page), Perry turned him down. Compared to the importance of actions initiated at Bilderberg conferences, discussions at the annual World Economic Forums are nothing more than ritualized debates.

6/12 8

OFFICE OF THE ASSISTANT SECRETARY OF DEFENSE

2400 DEFENSE PENTAGON
WASHINGTON, D.C. 20301-2400

INTERNATIONAL
SECURITY AFFAIRS

17 JUN 1996

OS 1100

Professor Klaus Schwab
President, World Economic Forum
53 chemin des Hauts-Crets
CH-123 Cologny/Geneva
Switzerland

Dear Professor Schwab:

Thank you for your kind invitation to Secretary of Defense Perry to participate in your next World Economic Forum, scheduled for 30 January - 4 February 1997. Unfortunately, Secretary Perry cannot make a commitment to join you for your forum. We are well aware of the outstanding reputation of the World Economic Forum and regret that we will be unable to join you. If new developments arise, we will initiate contact. In the meantime, we wish you all the best for a successful conference.

Sincerely,

Robert T. Osterthaler, BG, USAF
Acting Deputy Assistant Secretary of Defense
for European and NATO Affairs

(16 Jun 96)

U05633-96

Anders Åslund
Carnegie Endowment for International Peace
2400 N Street, NW
Washington, DC 20037

Moscow
April 30, 1996

Russia: Political Forces and Economic Prospects in the Face of Presidential Elections

On June 16, Russia is to hold its second democratic presidential elections, after having held two democratic parliamentary elections. Even so, this date signifies a milestone in the Russian post-communist development. Either it means the consolidation of democracy and market economy in Russia or a nasty turn to a dismal society. These presidential elections are likely to determine Russia's future for years to come and are the natural focus of this note.

Contrary Perceptions of the Situation

Today, Russia is characterized by a deep polarization between supporters of democracy and market economy, on the one hand, and an alliance of communists and "national-patriots", on the other. This polarization is based on contrary perceptions of the current situation.

From a reformist point of view, a great deal has been accomplished. Russia is a democracy which has held two democratic parliamentary elections in a row. Media are free and highly pluralistic. Legislation and the legal system are developing swiftly, and the crime rate peaked three years ago. More than two thirds of the labor force works in the private sector. The Russian economy is a market economy, though somewhat messy. The inflation rate has at long last

A 13-page 1996 pre-meeting report on Russia by the assigned speaker, Anders Aslund from the Carnegie Endowment for Peace. Aslund and Carnegie did their mighty best to send Russia tumbling back to the Stone Age. It makes interesting reading, if only for the obvious distortions. His evident bias toward Boris Yeltsin showed him for what he was – an apparatchik of agendas of the Men behind the Curtain. (Continued on next page.)

fallen below 40 percent a year, and the IMF agreement helps it to stay there. You get more rubles for a dollar today than a year ago. A great deal of economic restructuring has taken place. Russia is ready for growth of possibly a couple of percent this year to rise to 6 percent in 1998 according to IMF forecasts. Last years exports rose by no less than one quarter.

However, a communist looking upon the Russian situation sees something completely different. The Soviet Union has fallen apart, inter-republican economic links have collapsed, a war persists in Chechnya, and nobody respects Russian any longer. The official GDP has fallen officially by 50 percent (perhaps by one quarter in reality); the military industry has declined even more and Russia's science is in tatters; the standard of living has fallen catastrophically (probably by some 20 percent in real terms), and Russia has become one of the most unequal countries in the world (not quite true - it is still less unequal than the US, and the income distribution became more equal in 1995). Law and order have broken down and organized crime prevails. In short, an imperial nostalgia prevails, many old communists have lost out, the social costs have been high, and the communists do not approve of anything that has been accomplished.

Regional disparities are great, which makes it particularly difficult to get a proper over-all view. The reformers are strong where there has been a great deal of reform, most of all in Moscow and St. Petersburg, while the communists prevail where little reform is to be noticed - in the Russian southern agricultural belt and the stagnant north.

<u>The Presidential Candidates</u>

Russian opinion polls have proven highly unreliable. There are great regional disparities, communications are poor, voting patterns and participation vary

He was of course spot-on about Yeltsin winning reelection (p. 278) despite his great unpopularity (p. 275). Note the approving reference (p. 275) to the assassination of ex-Soviet air force major-general Dudaev, president of the breakaway republic of Chehnya, who was killed by two Russian laser-guided missiles after being located speaking on a cell phone. There have been claims that US National Security Agency eavesdropping operations also participated, a violation of US law.

greatly, so it has proven difficult to establish representative samples. Therefore, we must be more sceptical than elsewhere of all opinion polls. Even so, the polls have helped clarifying who the front-runners are: communist leader Gennady Zyuganov with up to 27% of the vote, and President Yeltsin who has risen from a low of 3% in January to up to 27% in recent polls. They are followed by four candidates with usually 8-10% each: General Alexander Lebed, Grigory Yavlinsky, Svyatoslav Fedorov, and Vladimir Zhirinovsky.

The present expectation is that there will be a run-off on July 7 or 14 - depending on how fast the votes will be counted - between President Yeltsin and communist leader Zyuganov.

Lebed, Yavlinsky and Fedorov have formed a vague alliance called the "third force", occupying the center. Together they have about 27% in the polls, so they have a considerable vote potential. They all appear both anti-communist and anti-Yeltsin. Yavlinsky could possibly be considered social democrats, while Fedorov is further to the left, and Lebed a milder nationalist. It would make sense if these three centrists united and won.

However, these are three big personalities, their programs are not very similar, and their electorates are pretty incompatible. Most importantly, they have proven no organizational skills, which appear vital in a Russian election campaign. Only Yavlinsky leads a party that entered the Duma, while Lebed and Fedorov are one-man shows without organization or programs. They have little money and minimal media support. For good or bad, they have the common innocence of not having been in power. So far, neither of them is perceived as a credible candidate. This large uncertain center appears the big prize to win in the election rather than an independent option. In the end, their anti-communism is likely to be more important than their anti-Yeltsinism, but their eventual inclination appears open to negotiation.

3

Zhirinovsky will certainly stand on his own, and after having been underestimated in the last three elections, caution is in place. He has a strong organization and a committed electorate. Zhirinovsky's voters are both against communism and the reforms, but his electorate appears more anti-communist than anti-Yeltsin, and Zhirinovsky frequently makes deals with the government and supports it in crucial moments. If Zhirinovsky does not go to the second round, he is likely to support Yeltsin.

The whole campaign focuses on the two lead candidates Yeltsin and Zyuganov, and we shall leave the others aside. Since the polls have such a poor record, it appears more relevant to analyze the election strategies of these leading candidates.

Yeltsin's Electoral Strategy

During the first two months of 1996, Zyuganov looked very impressive, but Yeltsin has gradually picked up. It is frequently argued that it does not really matter who wins because Yeltsin has embraced so much of the communist program. To some extent that was true in January 1996, but important and positive changes have occurred in the Yeltsin camp, particularly in March.

First, Yeltsin is evidently in better physical shape than he has been for very long. Rumours that he has stopped drinking are substantiated by his daily public appearances. Yet, his collaborators are afraid that his health will collapse and he is clearly over-strained.

Second, Yeltsin has broadened his circle. In January, Yeltsin appeared to have given up the balancing of different groups around him and given in to the group led by his chief body guard Alexander Korzhakov, assisted by the FSB (formerly KGB) Chairman Mikhail Barsukov, and First Deputy Prime Minister Oleg Soskovets, but this group has suffered serious set-backs. In January,

4

Barsukov led a strikingly incompetent attack on Chechens, who held hostages in Pervomayskoe in Dagestan. Soskovets was the official chairman of Yeltsin's election campaign but failed completely. In January and February he was more or less Yeltsin's prime ministerial candidate, but that is no longer the case. When Yeltsin is well and sober, his reliance on this "sauna" gang diminishes.

Instead, other people in the Yeltsin circle have gained more influence. Yeltsin's first personal assistant Viktor Ilyushin is now a major counterweight to Korzhakov. Moscow Mayor Yuri Luzhkov has used is considerable powers. Prime Minister Chernomyrdin is not out yet and fights back. Yeltsin's daughter Tatyana has started playing an important liberalizing role. Hence, while nobody has been sacked, the power distribution within the Yeltsin camp has improved, but a vicious power struggle continuous within the Yeltsin camp.

Third, the Yeltsin campaign has assumed democratic features. Originally, the official Yeltsin campaign was merged with the state apparatus, but it failed to collect the necessary one million signatures for Yeltsin's presidential candidacy. Instead, a group of unknown democrats did so on their own initiative, and Yeltsin realized that he had to abandon his reliance on the FSB for information and the state apparatus for campaigning and turned to various democratic groups prepared to work for him. Notably, liberal Anatoly Chubais plays a discrete but important role in the campaign.

Fourth, Yeltsin is pursuing a popular election campaign. He is going out in his old style and talks to people, listens to their concerns and responds. He displays his humble qualities and confesses that he is not satisfied with his achievements as President. He appears to listen to people and care about people again, which few Russian politicians do.

Fifth, Yeltsin's program has changed in a democratic and popular direction. Although he has no formal program yet (it is supposed to be announced on May 15), his many election speeches make clear his economic priorities and they are sound.

The main task is to beat inflation, and inflation has been below 3 percent a month during the last two months. When inflation is beaten, growth is bound to re-emerge. Task number two is to make sure that pensions and wages are being paid on time. This is less a budgetary issue than a matter of fighting fraud. Typically, officials and managers use such money to their own benefit before they pay the legal claimants. A third task is land reform. Yeltsin has issued a good decree, and the communists and agrarians oppose it because it threatens the vested interests of their local elites. A fourth issue is to fight crime and corruption, but that is done more in declarations than in reality, but at least it is done, and a few former senior officials are being prosecuted.

Yeltsin's big political handicap is the war in Chechnya. While he hardly can solve anything before the elections, he is at least doing a lot about it. The killing of General Dudaev was certainly to Yeltsin's benefit, as he showed that he could do something.

To a considerable extent, Yeltsin has disarmed the nostalgia for empire by dealing energetically with the practical issues of realistic economic integration with the most positively inclined neighboring countries - Belarus, Kazakhstan and Kyrgyzstan. In the case of Belarus, the cooperation might go further but that appears not all too likely.

President Yeltsin's great problem remains that he is very unpopular with a large share of the population. His negative rating i still close to 60 percent. The communist dislike is inevitable, but many people in the center dislike him for the war in Chechnya, the proliferation of crime even in high government circles, and flaws in reforms. There might be a ceiling for Yeltsin's vote that cannot yet be established, and this is a major worry in the Yeltsin camp.

6

The Communist Electoral Strategy

Unlike the Yeltsin campaign, the communist campaign has started with organization. Gennady Zyuganov proudly proclaims that he has been endorsed by 200 organizations representing 22 million people. Virtually all communist and "national-patriot" groups have signed up. Zyuganov's main plank is nationalistic and he explains his chief mission to be to unite the red and the white. He has all extreme communists and nationalists in his camp.

However, as a consequence of this organizational approach, Zyuganov's electoral strategy has become to consolidate of communists and national patriots rather than reaching out to the center. The decisive event was than the Duma in early March voted to abrogate the Belovezhsky agreement of December 1991 on the dissolution of the Soviet Union. This was an absolute condition for the support of Viktor Anpilov and his extreme communist party Working Russia (4.6% of the vote in December 1995) and Alexander Rutskoi and his nationalist party Great Power (2.6% of the vote in December 1995). In effect, that appears to have been the turning point in Zyuganov's campaign, and the party is now stuck in imperial nostalgia and moralization. Moreover, Anpilov's storm troops are sharply anti-democratic and truly frightening even to ordinary communists. Zyuganov has become a prisoner of the communist and nationalistic extremists.

Economic policy was supposed to be a major plank in the communist platform, as falling production, poverty and rising income differentials are obvious problems. The leading economic politician is Yuri Maslyukov, former Chairman of the State Planning Committee under Gorbachev. Maslyukov used his chairmanship of the Duma Committee on Economic Policy to call for hearings in mid-April designed to help the communists to elaborate their economic policy. The slogan was that all the best economists and ideas should be mobilized.

7

Curiously, this was the same approach that Mikhail Gorbachev used. The communists clearly wants to avoid the hard choices between socialism and capitalism.

However, those who responded to the calls for economic programs were communists who wanted to re-establish the Soviet economic system, either in a soft Ryzhkov-Gorbachev form (that broke down) or in a hard Stalinist form. Standard demands that emerged were: the re-establishment of Gosplan and central planning with state orders, far-reaching controls over prices, foreign trade and currency operations, massive re-nationalizations and confiscations of privatized property. The published communist platform, which is pretty vague, does not even mention private property and certainly does not endorse it.

The comparatively moderate communist leaders were left in an awkward position with a choice of either a Soviet economic system, that most people know broke down, or no economic policy. For the time being, it appears as if Zyuganov has chosen the latter option, which means that he leaves the economic stage completely to Yeltsin and fails to exploit one of the top issues. Yet, also the communist intent to present their election program on May 15, giving them some time to change, but the underlying forces will hardly allow Zyuganov to opt for a winnable position.

As time proceeds, it becomes ever more clear how extreme the communists really are. There are many reasons. Zyuganov's strategy of gathering all extremists within his camp is one explanation. Another reason is that the communists won too many seats for their own good in the Duma last December, and the candidates lower down on the lists tended to be more extreme than the leaders. Hence, extreme communists appear to constitute a majority of the communist deputies. A third reason is that the communists have become

8

convinced that they will win, and they have shown the arrogance of power before getting it. Finally, their urge for revenge is strong and frightening.

By any ordinary standard, the Russian Communist Party is simply not electable. Zyuganov's strategic ambition is to win extreme nationalists rather than the center, and it no longer appears plausible - though not altogether excluded - that Zyuganov can move to the center. Still, Yeltsin is the all dominant alternative, and many would not consider him electable.

Reasons for a Yeltsin Victory

Much will change during the remaining one and a half months before the elections. The behavior of the four second-level candidates will be very important, and they are all likely to be open to deals that are difficult to predict. Yet, for many reasons, President Yeltsin appears most likely to win the elections.

First of all, Yeltsin remains the most skilful popular politician in Russia and he is an unstoppable locomotive when he gets going and he appears in splendid shape right now. He has a wonderful popular touch. Note that Yeltsin did not run himself in the unsuccessful elections in December 1993 and 1995.

Second, at long last the reforms are producing visible positive results. Today, Yeltsin can say that he has carried out financial stabilization and made the ruble a stable currency. While economic growth initially is likely to be sluggish, it should make itself felt throughout a large part of the country this year. There is a widespread popular sense that the crisis is behind us.

Third, the communists have frightened much of Russian society with their abrasive old communism. Participation is likely to be high, and the polls already indicate 68 percent participation, and such indicators usually rise over time. Especially, the Russian business community is dead frightened by the communists and has woken up to an extraordinary political activity, and the businessmen have both money and authority. The open letter from 13 top businessmen issued on April 26 swiftly changed the political debate.

Fourth, Yeltsin has adjusted his program and his policies to satisfy legitimate popular demands and he is reaching out outside of his government base, while the communists try to consolidate their base.

Fifth, all the four intermediary candidates now appear more likely to support Yeltsin than Zyuganov in a second round, but Zyuganov could play a trick and make a broader alliance to get out of the extremist corner where he is currently caught.

Sixth, almost all other countries favor Yeltsin. It is most notable in the other former Soviet republics, where the fear of Russian communists is striking. The domestic communists are seen as a fifth column, collaborating with the Russian communists against national independence. The western preference for Yeltsin is obvious and self-evident. However, also the Chinese communists much prefer Yeltsin, as they showed during his recent visit to China.

Seventh, Russia looks very different in the summer and in the winter. Therefore, people are likely to be much happier and satisfied in June than in December and that should have an effect on the vote. (Sweden and Norway do not hold parliamentary elections in the winter.)

Finally, the communist alternative appears a bit too old-fashioned and absurd at present to be really credible. It appears more like the last cheer of the middle-level communist apparatchiki who have lost out than a plausible vision of Russia's future.

Yeltsin has almost total media support, which might be a mixed blessing, because Russians are suspicious and they might vote for the communists because they are continuously attacked on TV and much of the government propaganda is pretty crude. In July 1994, the establishment communist candidate Kebich lost

10

unexpectedly to populist Alexander Lukashenko in Belarus, and Lukashenko got no less than 80% of the votes, although Belarusian media overwhelmingly praised Kebich.

A worrisome feature is the widespread assumption that the President "will not allow himself to lose". One statement runs: "Either the President wins the elections or he just wins." The assumption is that the President can and will rig the elections. It is dubious that he can do so, because much of the regional and local administration is pro-communist, and the communists are strongest in faraway places, were rigging is comparatively easy. Apparent fraud will seriously undermine the legitimacy of the regime, and the belief that Yeltsin will win in any case undermines the willingness of his potential supporters to vote.

Although Yeltsin's negative vote is falling now, the question remains whether he is simply to unpopular to be able to win. A curiosity in the Russian election system is that in the second round is that people can vote against both the candidates in the run-off, while a winning candidate must get more than 50 percent of the votes cast. Thus, Russia might be left without an elected President after two rounds of elections.

Speculation continues on some kind of compromise deal between the communists and Yeltsin, possible after the first round of the elections, as the stakes are so high, and the losing side would lose all. There are many options and speculations, and all sides keep talking to all sides.

<u>After the Elections</u>

If Yeltsin wins the elections fairly, Russia has essentially succeeded in its arduous transition to a democracy and a market economy based on the rule of law. Most of the essential economic reforms have already been undertaken. The medium-term IMF agreement constitutes a good base for future structural reforms. A large number of foreign investors are no looking at the Russian market and a rise of the stock prices by 40 percent in April indicates the potential of the Russian market. A major remaining problem is the law and order situation. The bank crisis is bound to get aggravated with lower inflation, but these are normal problems that Russia now can deal with. However, it is completely unclear what government Yeltsin would choose after the elections, and considering his mental state, the general expectation is that Yeltsin will fade in a depression for months, if he wins the elections. Questions about his health remains. Yet, however unclear the Yeltsin alternative is, it does mean that Russia has made the transition. Russia will be more assertive in its international relations, but it will not be an enemy of the West.

In accordance with the argument above, Zyuganov is not likely to win if the communists do not change their policy through an alliance with centrists, which remains an option. If Zyuganov would win with his current policies, it would be a serious set-back not only for Russia and its neighbors, but for the whole world. There are some levers restricting the sway of the communists. Some are economic. The three-year agreement with the IMF will undoubtedly be broken, if Zyuganov implements communist economic policy. It is reinforced with bilateral credits conditioned on the IMF agreement. The Russian debt burden of some $130 billion needs rescheduling and servicing, but such a huge debt is more of a threat to the outside world than to the Russian government. The Russian business community can do a great deal - either buy suitable communists, pressure the government, or emigrate with their capital. After all Russia has a democratic system with a constitution, an elected parliament, many elected regional and local officials, and free pluralistic media. A communist victory would be a serious test of the strength of these institutions.

12

An intermediary solution would be some kind of compromise between Yeltsin and the communists, but it is difficult to discuss such an option since it can take many forms. It could be democratic or anti-democratic.

The outcome of these vital elections is by no means a given, and it will be of extraordinary importance.

FINAL

BILDERBERG MEETINGS

Baden-Baden, Germany
June 6-9, 1991

AGENDA

FRI JUNE 7	08.30-08.40	Opening remarks by Lord Carrington, Chairman of Bilderberg Meetings
	08.40-10.15	**EASTERN EUROPE: ECONOMIC PROSPECTS**
		Moderator : Hilmar Kopper [FRG] Panel : Jean-Louis Cadieux [EUR.COMM] Thomas W. Simons, Jr. [US]
		Discussion
	10.15-10.45	Coffee-break
	10.45-12.30	**DEVELOPMENTS IN THE SOVIET UNION: POLITICAL AND ECONOMIC IMPACT ON THE ALLIANCE**
		Moderator : Rozanne L. Ridgway [US] Panel : Klaus Blech [FRG] Jack F. Matlock [US] Volker Rühe [FRG]
		Discussion
	12.30-14.15	Buffet Luncheon
	14.15-16.15	**THE MIDDLE EAST: POLITICAL FALLOUT AND FUTURE PROSPECTS**
		Moderator : Lord Carrington [UK] Panel : Richard N. Haass [US] Tugay Özçeri [TURK] William B. Quandt [US] Patrick Wright [UK] Lawrence D. Freedman, author background paper [UK]
		Discussion
	16.15-16.45	Tea-break
	16.45-18.00	**CURRENT EVENTS: GERMAN ECONOMIC RECONCILIATION: THE TREUHAND EXPERIENCE**
		Moderator : Franz Vranitzky [AUS] Panel : Birgit Breuel (FRG)
		Discussion
	19.00	Cocktails
	20.00	Dinner
SAT JUNE 8	08.30-10.15	**THE PRACTICAL AGENDA FOR THE ALLIANCE**
		Moderator : John Whitehead [USA] Panel : Henning Wegener [NATO] Henry A. Kissinger [US]
		Discussion
	10.15-10.45	Coffee-break
	10.45-12.30	**DO WE HAVE THE INSTITUTIONS TO DEAL WITH THE AGENDA?**
		Moderator : Etienne Davignon [BEL] Panel : Robert D. Blackwill [US] Ruud F.M. Lubbers [NETH] Manfred Wörner [NATO]
		Discussion
	12.30-14.15	Buffet Luncheon
	AFTERNOON FREE	
	17.00-19.00	**ECONOMIC AND FINANCIAL THREATS TO THE ALLIANCE**
		Moderator : John Smith [UK] Panel : Michael J. Boskin [US] Karl Otto Pöhl [FRG]
		Discussion
	19.30	Cocktails
	20.00	Dinner
SUN JUNE 9	08.30-09.30	**CURRENT EVENTS: SOUTH AFRICA**
		Moderator : Thierry de Montbrial [FRA] Panel : Conrad Black [CAN] Vernon E. Jordan, Jr. [US]
		Discussion
	09.35-10.50	**CURRENT EVENTS: YUGOSLAVIA**
		Moderator : Peter D. Sutherland [IRE] Panel : Gianni De Michelis [ITA] * Franz Vranitzky [AUS]
		Discussion
	10.50-11.00	Closing remarks by Lord Carrington
	12.00	Luncheon
		Departures

* to be confirmed

Agenda for 1991's three-day Bilderberg conference at Baden-Baden, Germany. Of session topics, only South Africa has receded as a global "hot spot." The "Alliance" is of course NATO, with the omnipresent Henry Kissinger in a leading role in the discussion.

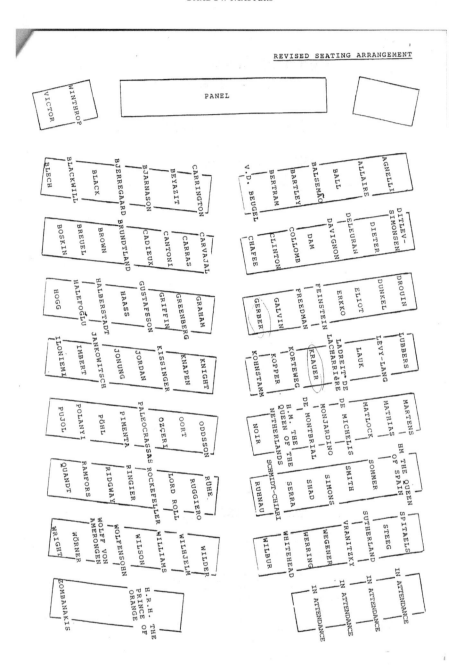

REVISED SEATING ARRANGEMENT

WINTHROP
VICTOR

PANEL

CARRINGTON
BEYAZIT
BJARNASON
BJERREGAARD
BLACK
BLACKWILL
BLECH

AGNELLI
ALLAIRE
BALL
BALSEMÃO
BARTLEY
BERTRAM
V.D. BEUGEL

CARVAJAL
CARRAS
CANTONI
CADIEUX
BRUNDTLAND
BROWN
BREUEL
BOSKIN

DITLEV-SIMONSEN
DIETER
DELEURAN
DAVIGNON
DAM
COLLOMB
CLINTON
CHAFEE

GRAHAM
GREENBERG
GRIFFIN
GUSTAFSSON
HAASS
HALBERSTADT
HALEFOĞLU
HOGG

DROUIN
DUNKEL
ELIOT
ERKKO
FEINSTEIN
FREEDMAN
GALVIN
GERBER

KNIGHT
KNAPEN
KISSINGER
JORDAN
JONUNG
JANKOWITSCH
IMBERT
ILONIEMI

LUBBERS
LEVY-LANG
LAUK
LADREIT DE LACHARRIÈRE
KRAUER
KORTEWEG
KOPPER
KOHNSTAMM

ODDSSON
OORT
ÖZÇERI
PALEOCRASSAS
PIMENTA
PÖHL
POLANYI
PUJOL

MARTENS
MATHIAS
MATLOCK
DE MICHELIS
MONJARDINO
DE MONTBRIAL
H.M. THE QUEEN OF THE NETHERLANDS
NOIR

RÜHE
RUGGIERO
LORD ROLL
ROCKEFELLER
RINGIER
RIDGWAY
RAMFORS
QUANDT

HM THE QUEEN OF SPAIN
SOMMER
SMITH
SIMONS
SHAD
SERRA
SCHMIDT-CHIARI
RUHNAU

WILDER
WILHJELM
WILLIAMS
WILSON
WOLFENSOHN
WOLFF VON AMERONGEN
WÖRNER
WRIGHT

SPITAELS
STEEG
SUTHERLAND
VRANITZKY
WEGENER
WERRING
WHITEHEAD
WILBUR

H.R.H. THE PRINCE OF ORANGE
ZOMBANAKIS

IN ATTENDANCE
IN ATTENDANCE
IN ATTENDANCE
IN ATTENDANCE

Bilderberg 1991 seating arrangement, which is always strictly alphabetical, with the order reversing each year: Aa-Zz alternates with Zz-Aa. Oh those wild and crazy Bilderbergers!

BILDERBERG MEETINGS

Baden-Baden, Germany
June 6-9, 1991

GENERAL INFORMATION

1. To ensure proper security control during the conference all persons authorized to enter the hotel have a special ID-card incorporating their photograph and with borders in various colours to designate their function. Please wear your ID-card at all times during the conference; security officers will be on duty in the hotel and will challenge anyone not wearing a badge. Please also take your badge with you if you leave the grounds: when you return you will be asked to show your badge.

   Only cars showing an authorized parking permit behind the windscreen are allowed to enter the hotel garage. Parking permits are available at the Bilderberg courtesy desk.

2. In the portfolio you will also find:

   a. Agenda

   b. List of participants

   c. List with profiles of participants

   d. General procedure for participating in plenary discussions

   e. Seating arrangement: conference room

   f. Ground floor plan of the Steigenberger Hotel Badischer Hof

   g. Alphabetical list of participants with addresses

   h. Telephone instructions

3. Press contacts

   Participants are requested not to give interviews during the meeting, nor should any reference be made, in post-conference interviews, to what an individual participant has said during the meeting.

4. The Steigenberger Hotel Badischer Hof has been reserved exclusively for this conference.

5. Signs guiding you to the Conference rooms will be clearly posted in the corridors.

Here and following four pages, general information for participants at the 1991 conference. The primary emphasis on wearing the official photo ID "at all times," and the role of "security officers" in enforcement of the rule, underlines the by-invitation-only nature of Bilderberg. Amenities of course are first-rate, and meals are provided, but note (p. 287) that free drinks are limited, presumably making for more coherent discussions.

2

6. **Secretariat**

- Members of the Bilderberg Secretariat (Salon 5, ext. 144)

Mrs. Maja Banck, Executive Secretary
Mrs. Eskelien Braggaar
Mrs. Ronnie Glattauer
Miss Felicity Saunders
Miss Pauline Zonneveld

- German Organization (Salon 4, ext. 143)

Mr. Günther F.W. Dicke
Ms Antje Humml
Ms Rita Rittershaus

7. **Telephone calls**

You will find instructions for making in-house, local, domestic long-distance and international calls in your portfolio.

8. **Fax messages**

Fax messages to be sent can be handed in at the Bilderberg Secretariat, Salon 5.

For incoming messages, please check the message board outside the Conference Room.

The fax number of the Steigenberger Hotel Badischer Hof is (7221) 28729.

9. **Mail**

Incoming mail will be delivered to you personally through the Secretariat.

10. **Newspapers**

A supply of local and foreign newspapers can be found in the corridor outside the Conference Room.

11. A TV monitor room, (shown on the ground floor plan), will be at the disposal of personal staff.

12. For **medical emergencies** please dial "143".

13. **Currency**

The Steigenberger Hotel Badischer Hof accepts travellers cheques and the following credit cards: Access, American Express, Diners'Club, Eurocard, Mastercard and Visa. Personal cheques are not accepted.

14. **Meals**

All meals will be served in the Parkrestaurant. Breakfast will be served each day from 7:00 a.m. to 8:30 a.m. There are no fixed seating arrangements.

3

15. **Bar**

Bar service is available in the Jockey Bar.
Pre-dinner drinks will be provided by the host in the Saulenhalle.

16. **Personal expenses**

Personal charges, such as telephone calls, faxes, all drinks (except those served with meals during the conference and before dinner), recreation, laundry, and expenses incurred prior to the dinner on Thursday, June 6 and after luncheon on Sunday, June 9, will be on the participant's own account.

17. **Transportation**

Cars will be available to take you to the airport of your departure or Baden-Baden Station. You will be notified well in advance of the time you should be in the lobby for departure.

Participants who have not yet informed Ms. Rittershaus, (Transportation Office, Salon 4, Ext. 143), of their departure time on Sunday are urgently requested to do so, preferably by 5:00 p.m. on Friday.

Please note: Before leaving the Hotel, please identify your luggage so that it may be transported with you in the same car. Unidentified luggage could be left behind or mis-directed.

Confirmation of or changes to your return flights should be made with the Transportation Office (Salon 4, ext. 143).

18. **Check-out time** is 1:00 p.m. on Sunday, June 9. Please notify the Front Desk if you wish to depart later.

19. **Recreation**

Recreational activities for Saturday afternoon include:

- Golf
- Tennis
- Conducted visit to the Casino of Baden-Baden, departing at 2.00 p.m.
- Conducted visit to Strasbourg Cathedral, departing at 1.30 p.m.

Please notify the Transportation Office, (Salon 4, Ext. 143), if you wish to book any of the above activities.

20. Names and affiliations of participants will appear in the final conference report. Please advise the Executive Secretary, prior to your departure, of any changes or corrections to your personal listing.

The Steigenberger Hotel Badischer Hof
Baden-Baden, Germany

June 6-9, 1991

GENERAL PROCEDURE FOR PARTICIPATING IN PLENARY DISCUSSIONS

1. Participants are encouraged to speak freely and without reservation. All discussions are private and off-the-record. The conference report will not identify the names of the discussants but will only summarize the debates.

2. Conferees may participate in the discussions by contributing either three or five minute commentaries, or interventions of one minute, all within the framework set by the moderator of the session.
   One minute interventions are designed to expedite, responses to a particular point straightaway, even though the order of speakers has been established.

   Please note that brief interventions are preferable to lengthy ones, as they are likely to make for more lively discussions.

3. A participant wishing to speak may so indicate by raising his hand or sending a note to the moderator. The participant may indicate how much time he would like by showing one, three or five fingers when he raises his hand. The moderator will call on the individual in due course.

4. A timing device on the dais will alert the individual as he approaches his allowed limit of one, three or five minutes by an orange warning light which turns red when the time is up.

5. When called on by the moderator, the participant should press the button on the microphone base and identify himself.

2

UK	Gordon Brown	Member of Parliament (Labour Party) Shadow Secretary of State for Trade and Industry
NOR	Arne Olav Brundtland	Senior Research Fellow, Norwegian Institute of International Affairs
BEL	Jean-Louis Cadieux	Deputy Director-General for Foreign Affairs, European Community
ITA	Giampiero Cantoni	Chairman, Banca Nazionale del Lavoro
GRE	Costa Carras *	Director of Companies
SPA	Jaime Carvajal Urquijo *	Chairman and General Manager, Iberfomento
USA	John H. Chafee	Senator (Republican, Rhode Island)
USA	Bill D. Clinton	Governor of Arkansas
FRA	Bertrand Collomb	Chairman and Chief Executive Officer, Lafarge Coppée
USA	Kenneth W. Dam *	Vice President, Law and External Relations, IBM Corporation; Former Deputy Secretary of State
BEL	Etienne Davignon *	Chairman, Société Générale de Belgique; Former Vice Chairman of the Commission of the European Communities
DEN	Aage Deleuran *	Editor-in-Chief, "Berlingske Tidende"
GER	Werner H. Dieter	Chairman of the Board, Mannesmann A.G.
NOR	Per Ditlev-Simonsen	Managing Director, Sverre Ditlev-Simonsen & Co.
CAN	Marie-Josée Drouin *	Executive Director, Hudson Institute of Canada
INT	Arthur Dunkel	Director General G.A.T.T.
FIN	Aatos Erkko	Publisher, "Helsingin Sanomat"
USA	Dianne Feinstein	Former Mayor of San Francisco
UK	Lawrence D. Freedman	Head of Department of War Studies, King's College
CAN	Lysiane Gagnon	Journalist, La Presse
INT	John R. Galvin	Supreme Allied Commander Europe, SHAPE
SWI	Fritz Gerber	Chairman of the Board, F. Hoffmann-La Roche AG
USA	Katharine Graham	Chairman, The Washington Post Company
USA	Maurice R. Greenberg	Chairman, American International Group, Inc.
CAN	Anthony G.S. Griffin **	Director of Companies
SWE	Sten Gustafsson *	Chairman of the Board of Directors, AB Astra
USA	Richard N. Haass	Special Assistant to the President and Senior Director Near East and South Asian Affairs, National Security Council
TUR	Vahit M. Halefoğlu	Former Minister of Foreign Affairs
UK	Christopher Hogg	Chairman, Courtaulds plc
FIN	Jaakko Iloniemi *	Managing Director, Council of Economic Organizations in Finland; Former Ambassador to the United States of America
FRA	Claude Imbert	Chief Editor, "Le Point"
AUS	Peter Jankowitsch *	Minister of State in charge of European Integration and Development Cooperation

Note (top) that current British Prime Minister Gordon Brown was among those "encouraged to speak freely and without reservation" at Bilderberg 1991. The procedures (facing page) are intended to insure that the moderators are able to control discussions considerably through their power to recognize speakers "in due course."

WORLD
ECONOMIC
FORUM
COMMITTED TO
IMPROVING THE STATE
OF THE WORLD

Guidelines:
essential reading for participants

1997 Annual Meeting
Davos 30 January-4 February

The spirit of Davos

The Annual Meeting is known for its direct, personal, highest-level interaction among participants.

Participants are encouraged to initiate as many individual contacts and discussions as possible, taking full advantage of the meeting's networking and information system (electronic, printed and personal contact services).

Through this system, participants should feel they belong to the same club and should respect each other's time and integrity. There must be no unsolicited selling of products or services at the Annual Meeting, nor to its participants at a later date. No promotional or advertising material is distributed through our official channels. Any participant disturbed by inappropriate approaches should bring the matter to our attention.

U0 8633 /96

1997

As you can see, the procedures at the Davos conferences are much less detailed than Bilderberg's. Note also (p. 292) the provision for private meetings of selected participants that may conflict with conference sessions. At Bilderberg, scheduled sessions trump all other activities.

Concept of the 1997 Annual Meeting

1997 Annual Meeting
Davos 30 January-4 February

Purpose

The Annual Meeting is the world's foremost gathering of leaders from business, government, science, academia, culture and the media, with a considerable impact on world affairs.

The Annual Meeting helps leaders to develop long-term perspectives in a world of accelerating political, economic, social, technological and cultural change. It is global in terms of its scope and contents.

The Annual Meeting allows participants, at the beginning of the year, to determine their own priorities and to clarify the action agenda.

Participation

Participation in the 1997 Annual Meeting is reserved for chief executives of member companies, and is strictly limited in number so as to maintain a club-like atmosphere and foster true interaction.

Spouses are considered full partners and have access to the majority of sessions, as well as to a programme of additional activities.

Programme

The programme is designed to permit participants to take the "global pulse" of key issues shaping the corporate environment, as well as to explore the latest approaches to management leadership and to share ideas with the world's eminent thinkers.

Interactive and small-scale activities dominate the programme, to allow participants individualized contact and conversation with colleagues and leaders from politics and academia.

To this end, the World Economic Forum has reinforced its partnership with leading universities and institutes.

Participants will be kept up to date on the programme as it develops, as well as on other participants. Final documentation, including the detailed chronological programme, information on other participants and on the meeting's many services and activities, is distributed in Davos.

(Please turn over ⇨)

1997

U08633 /96

The Davos club: rules of the game

The Annual Meeting bring together chief executives of the world's foremost companies with leaders from government, academia, science, culture and the media.

accompanying staff
Since the meeting's purpose is to facilitate and foster personal contacts at the highest level, we strongly advise that participants should not come to Davos accompanied by members of their staff.
Accompanying staff is in principle not admitted to the Congress Centre.

Global Event Management (GEM), our operations partner, cannot make available accommodation for staff in the same hotel as the person they accompany since all available rooms are strictly reserved for participants. They will however provide information on accommodation in exceptional cases where a participant is obliged to have accompanying staff in the Davos vicinity.

electronic message service
Networking among club members will only be successful if the rules of the game are respected: the electronic message service of the Annual Meeting is restricted to registered participants only and in no circumstances can be accessed by third parties.

Private events

You may receive invitations to private events taking place in Davos on the margins of the Annual Meeting; these clearly reinforce the networking character of such a gathering. As such events sometimes conflict with a session or dinner of the Annual Meeting you may wish to check the official programme before accepting private invitations.

Member companies of the World Economic Forum who wish to take advantage of the presence in Davos of their chief executive and that of many of their clients, suppliers and other partners (actual or potential) to host an event or meeting of their own at the very end of the Annual Meeting should contact us.

Should **individual participants** wish to organize a lunch, dinner or reception, please note that:

- only events in the official programme can take place in the Congress Centre
- your office should inform us on which day the event is planned, in which hotel and the number of participants invited
- the printed list of participants and their organizations is sent to participants in advance of the meeting
- replies to your invitations should be addressed directly to your office
- invitations should be personally addressed, in the spirit of Davos
- participants' pigeonholes in the Congress Centre cannot be used for large-scale disctribution of material.

With regularity, the annual general meeting of the Council on Foreign Relations takes place in March, the annual Bilderberg conference and G8 meeting are in April and May, the IMF/World Bank conference gathers in September. A kind of international consensus emerges and is carried over from one meeting to the next, but no one is really leading. This consensus becomes the background for G8 economic communiqués, it becomes what informs the IMF when, for example, it imposes an adjustment program on Argentina, and it becomes what the US president proposes to Congress.

At the World Economic Forums in Davos, Switzerland at the end of each January, by contrast, a plethora of who's who debate, and are there for all to see. None of the discussion carries any real weight, but it does make for good publicity and provides world political and economic leaders a great photo-op. Below we see Henry Kissinger sharing a laugh with Tony Blair. Both are war criminals. What might they be laughing about? Perhaps how they conned the world and got away with it. These and the following photos are from Davos 2008.

Shown lower left is embattled British Prime Minister, Gordon Brown. Before succeeding Blair as Prime Minister, Brown was the longest-serving Chancellor of the Exchequer in modern history, from 1997 to 2007. His term is noted for the loosening of British governmental control of the Bank of England. Despite this boon, Bilderberg has been profoundly disappointed in Brown's performance as PM, where he has not managed the unruly Labour Party like his predecessor. It appears that they have decided he should be replaced, and it is unclear how long Brown will remain in office, even if Labour maintains its majority in Parliament.

At lower right is Jeroen van der Veer, former CEO of Royal Dutch Shell. As a vertically integrated "supermajor" oil company, its operations include exploration and production, refining and marketing, and trading and shipping, along with other energy-related projects. Shell operates in over 140 countries. *Fortune* magazine listed Shell as the world's largest corporation in 2009; *Forbes* had it at number two. Its 2008 revenues were slightly less than one-half trillion dollars, dwarfing the operating budgets of most countries in which it does business, where Shell usually gets its way. In 1996 a number of human rights groups sued Royal Dutch Shell over abuses, including summary execution, in Nigeria. In 2009, Shell agreed to a legal settlement of $15.5 million, without, of course, admitting any actual culpability.

Above: Jean Claude Trichet, European Central Bank chief. Trichet has been a member of the influential Group of Thirty, a Washington-based international advisory group of bankers and academics, since 1987. In 1993 he was appointed governor of the Banque de France, and became president of the European Central Bank in 2003. As the European Parliament is a little more than a toothless debating society, the real power rests with the money people: the European Central Bank, the World Bank and the IMF, as well as the British Treasury, Bank of England and even the US Federal Reserve. Not one of these organizations in any way represents the interests of the people of the world. They stand with the Shadow Masters and are a key part of the drive towards the creation of George Ball's World Company.

Below: PepsiCo's pride and joy, Indra Nooyi, a key player in the Bilderberg inner circle, seen here during her Davos presentation. Not one of the more than one hundred media representatives dared to ask her about her role in Bilderberg conferences. And if one did, what would she say?

Above: Swedish bilionaire, Jacob Wallenberg, chairman of the Swedish financial powerhouse, Investor AB. Wallenberg is a member of the Blackstone Group, whose board of directors includes Lord Jacob Rothschild and Niall FitzGerald, a Knight Commander of the British Empire and a former chairman of the Bilderberg-controlled Anglo-Dutch firm, Unilever. In October 2004, FitzGerald became the chairman of Reuters. Can we expect this venerable mainstream organ to report objectively on the news? Decide for yourself: Using Reuters' search engine, I found exactly one article on Bilderberg. When I clicked to read it, the Reuters caption read, "Our apologies, the requested page was not found." Imagine that.

Below: US billionaire and KKR founding partner, Henry Kravis. A major speculator, Kravis was financial manager of George H.W. Bush's New York State campaign committee in 1988. KKR engineered some of the biggest leveraged buyouts of the 1980s, among them the record-setting buyout of R.J. Reynolds-Nabisco. The company also played a key role in building the speculative bubble which paved the way for the derivatives fiasco of the late 1990s.

Above: The Turkish Minister of Foreign Affairs, Ali Babacan, during his Davos presentation. His publicly distributed curriculum vita strangely omitted his role as the key Turkish Bilderberg attendee. Modesty perhaps, or is it deception?

Below: Bernard Kouchner, former head of the United Nation's Mission in Kosovo and founder of Doctors Without Borders. An ex-Communist, Koucher was three times Minister of Health in leftist French governments. He is now France's Minister of Foreign and European Affairs in the right-wing government of Prime Minister François Fillon, and was expelled from the Socialist Party in 2007 for accepting the position. Kouchner is notorious for his endorsement of military interventions for "humanitarian reasons." He is also a regular at every Bilderberg conference, where "left" and "right" are but techniques of deception and control.

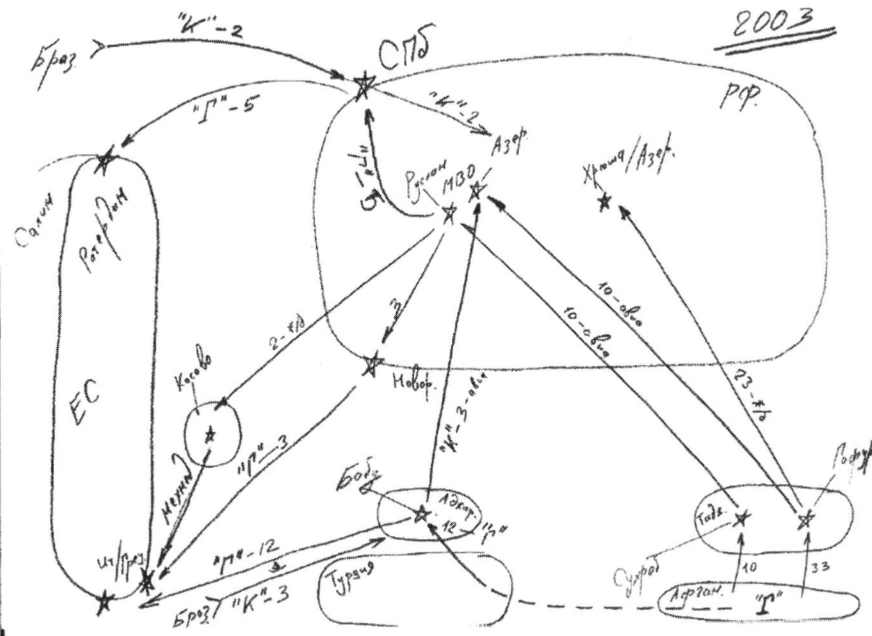

Above: A Russian mafia diagram of a typical opium route into Europe. Eighty percent of the drug enters Europe through Kosovo. Because of the Kosovo war, the United States, the United Nations and NATO are wholly responsible for the creation of the first narco-state in Europe

Below: A 20th century opium den in Manilla, Philippines.

Supreme Court of The State of New York
County of New York

02125895

Jason Torrente and Genevieve Torrente, on behalf of themselves individually and the Estate of Vivian Torrente,
Plaintiffs,

-against-

The Estate of Edmund J. Safra, Lily Safra, Spotless and Brite, Inc., Zurich Insurance Company, Chubb Group of Insurance Companies. Lloyds of London and John and Jane Does #1-10,
Defendants.

COMPLAINT

JURY TRIAL DEMANDED

FILED
DEC 02 2008
NEW YORK
COUNTY CLERK'S OFFICE

Plaintiffs Genevieve and Jason Torrente, through their undersigned attorneys bring this complaint for wrongful death, civil conspiracy and fraud relating to the death of their mother, Vivian Torrente.

Parties

1. Genevieve and Jason Torrente are the children of Vivian Torrente. Both Genevieve and Jason Torrente were the victims of a civil conspiracy and fraud perpetrated by the defendants which was designed to withhold from them critical information relating to the circumstances of their mother's death, including but not limited to the contents of the autopsy report indicating that the death of Vivian Torrente was caused by Edmund J. Safra.

2. Edmund J. Safra was, until his death on December 3, 1999, the founder and principal owner of Republic Bank of New York.

3. Defendant Lily Safra is the widow of Edmund J. Safra and, upon information and belief, is the sole heir to his estate, which is believed to worth billions of dollars. Lily Safra, along with the other defendants, conspired to withhold critical information from the Plaintiffs regarding the circumstances relating to the death of their mother.

Wrongful death complaint by the survivors of Vivian Torrente, the nurse of Edmund Safra, who died with him in a fire at his Monaco penthouse. Like almost everything else in the life of Safra, the circumstances of his death are steeped in mystery. Rumor has it that Safra was the greatest clandestine gold trader in the history of mankind, suspected at the time of his death by the FBI and Interpol of being the principal conduit for Russia's criminal money laundering.

4. Defendant Spotless and Brite, Inc., a New York corporation, was, upon information and belief. the company that arranged for Vivian Torrente to provide nursing services to Edmund J. Safra, Monte Carlo, Monaco and elsewhere.

5. Upon information and belief, defendants Zurich Insurance Company, Chubb Group of Insurance Companies and Lloyds of London issued various insurance policies to Edmund J. Safra and his various enterprises including coverage for the building located in Monaco where both Mr. Safra and Vivian Torrente died.

6. Defendants John and Jane Does #1-10 are persons unknown at this time who conspired with the named defendants to deceive the plaintiffs and to withhold critical information indicating that Edmund J. Safra was responsible for the death of Vivian Torrente.

Relevant Facts

7. In or about 1999 Vivian Torrente was employed by Spotless and Brite, Inc. and Edmund J. Safra to provide nursing services to Mr. Safra.

8. On Dec. 3, 1999, in Monte Carlo, Monaco, Edmund J. Safra and Vivian Torrente died in a locked bathroom located in Mr. Safra's duplex penthouse located atop a building where the Monaco branch of the Republic National Bank of New York was located.

9. Unknown to the Plaintiffs until recently, and upon information and belief, the autopsy report shows that it was Mr. Safra who was responsible for the death Vivian Torrente on December 3, 1999. Among other things, the autopsy revealed that there were "combat-like" marks on the neck of Vivian Torrente and blood in her thyroid, indicating that Vivian Torrente had struggled to escape the bathroom where she and Mr. Safra were located, and that Mr. Safra restrained her and prevented her escape. Vivian Torrente also had bruises on her knees and Mr. Safra's DNA under her fingernails, further confirming that Mr. Safra's efforts to restrain her were the direct and proximate cause of her death.

Central Asia's major drug producing regions. Afghanistan has joined Colombia as the world's major powerhouses. If NATO truly wanted to eradicate drugs, instead of protecting their shipment, it could have interdicted the shipments and not allowed the drugs to leave. That would greatly displease the Shadow Masters. The only reason we have a drug problem is that governments like it that way, as it provides enormous wealth-building opportunities in addition to a means of managing the populace. US troops are dying and being maimed in the cause of the nefarious drug trade. Vietnam, Kosovo and Afghanistan all provide illustrations of wars for drugs. The global financial system is imploding, and drug barons are moving to take over the entire world economy.

Tuesday,
July 27, 2004

Part IV

The President

Exeuctive Order 13348—Blocking Property of Certain Persons and Prohibiting the Importation of Certain Goods from Liberia
Executive Order 13349—Amending Executive Order 13226 To Designate the President's Council of Advisors on Science and Technology To Serve as the National Nanotechnology Advisory Panel

In July 2004, the Bush administration issued Executive Order 3348, directing the Office of Foreign Assets Control (OFAC) to freeze any US assets of former Liberian President, Charles Taylor and a number of his supposed associates, including Victor Bout (p. 305), and also forbidding American firms from doing business with any of them. Bout denies any relationship with Taylor. Interestingly, Bout never had any assets in the United States, something that everyone from President Bush to the mainstream media knew perfectly well. Note also that the notorious Leonid Minin made the list (p. 306), probably with considerably more justification.

44885

Federal Register
Vol. 69, No. 143
Tuesday, July 27, 2004

Presidential Documents

Title 3—

The President

Executive Order 13348 of July 22, 2004

Blocking Property of Certain Persons and Prohibiting the Importation of Certain Goods from Liberia

By the authority vested in me as President by the Constitution and the laws of the United States of America, including the International Emergency Economic Powers Act (50 U.S.C. 1701 *et seq.*) (IEEPA), the National Emergencies Act (50 U.S.C. 1601 *et seq.*) (NEA), section 5 of the United Nations Participation Act, as amended (22 U.S.C. 287c) (UNPA), and section 301 of title 3, United States Code, and in view of United Nations Security Council Resolutions 1521 of December 22, 2003, and 1532 of March 12, 2004,

I, GEORGE W. BUSH, President of the United States of America, note that the actions and policies of former Liberian President Charles Taylor and other persons, in particular their unlawful depletion of Liberian resources and their removal from Liberia and secreting of Liberian funds and property, have undermined Liberia's transition to democracy and the orderly development of its political, administrative, and economic institutions and resources. I further note that the Comprehensive Peace Agreement signed on August 18, 2003, and the related ceasefire have not yet been universally implemented throughout Liberia, and that the illicit trade in round logs and timber products is linked to the proliferation of and trafficking in illegal arms, which perpetuate the Liberian conflict and fuel and exacerbate other conflicts throughout West Africa. I find that the actions, policies, and circumstances described above constitute an unusual and extraordinary threat to the foreign policy of the United States and hereby declare a national emergency to deal with that threat. To address that threat, I hereby order:

Section 1. (a) Except to the extent provided in section 203(b)(1), (3), and (4) of IEEPA (50 U.S.C. 1702(b)(1), (3), and (4)), or regulations, orders, directives, or licenses that may be issued pursuant to this order, and notwithstanding any contract entered into or any license or permit granted prior to the effective date of this order, all property and interests in property of the following persons, that are in the United States, that hereafter come within the United States, or that are or hereafter come within the possession or control of United States persons, are blocked and may not be transferred, paid, exported, withdrawn, or otherwise dealt in:

(i) the persons listed in the Annex to this order; and

(ii) any person determined by the Secretary of the Treasury, in consultation with the Secretary of State:

(A) to be or have been an immediate family member of Charles Taylor;

(B) to have been a senior official of the former Liberian regime headed by Charles Taylor or otherwise to have been or be a close ally or associate of Charles Taylor or the former Liberian regime;

(C) to have materially assisted, sponsored, or provided financial, material, or technological support for, or goods or services in support of, the unlawful depletion of Liberian resources, the removal of Liberian resources from that country, and the secreting of Liberian funds and property by any person whose property and interests in property are blocked pursuant to this order; or

(D) to be owned or controlled by, or acting or purporting to act for or on behalf of, directly or indirectly, any person whose property and interests in property are blocked pursuant to this order.

(b) I hereby determine that the making of donations of the type of articles specified in section 203(b)(2) of IEEPA (50 U.S.C. 1702(b)(2)) by, to, or for the benefit of, any person whose property or interests in property are blocked pursuant to paragraph (a) of this section would seriously impair my ability to deal with the national emergency declared in this order, and I hereby prohibit such donations as provided by paragraph (a) of this section.

(c) The prohibitions in paragraph (a) of this section include, but are not limited to,

(i) the making of any contribution or provision of funds, goods, or services by, to, or for the benefit of, any person whose property or interests in property are blocked pursuant to this order, and

(ii) the receipt of any contribution or provision of funds, goods, or services from any such person.

Sec. 2. Except to the extent provided in regulations, orders, directives, or licenses that may be issued pursuant to this order, and notwithstanding any contract entered into or any license or permit granted prior to the effective date of this order, the direct or indirect importation into the United States of any round log or timber product originating in Liberia is prohibited.

Sec. 3. (a) Any transaction by a United States person or within the United States that evades or avoids, has the purpose of evading or avoiding, or attempts to violate any of the prohibitions set forth in this order is prohibited.

(b) Any conspiracy formed to violate any of the prohibitions set forth in this order is prohibited.

Sec. 4. For purposes of this order: (a) the term "person" means an individual or entity;

(b) the term "entity" means a partnership, association, trust, joint venture, corporation, group, subgroup, or other organization;

(c) the term "United States person" means any United States citizen, permanent resident alien, entity organized under the laws of the United States or any jurisdiction within the United States (including foreign branches), or any person in the United States; and

(d) the term "round log or timber product" means any product classifiable in Chapter 44 of the Harmonized Tariff Schedule of the United States.

Sec. 5. For those persons whose property and interests in property are blocked pursuant to section 1 of this order who might have a constitutional presence in the United States, I find that because of the ability to transfer funds or other assets instantaneously, prior notice to such persons of measures to be taken pursuant to this order would render these measures ineffectual. I therefore determine that for these measures to be effective in addressing the national emergency declared in this order, there need be no prior notice of a listing or determination made pursuant to section 1 of this order.

Sec. 6. The Secretary of the Treasury, in consultation with the Secretary of State, is hereby authorized to take such actions, including the promulgation of rules and regulations, and to employ all powers granted to the President by IEEPA and UNPA as may be necessary to carry out the purposes of this order. The Secretary of the Treasury may redelegate any of these functions to other officers and agencies of the United States Government, consistent with applicable law. All agencies of the United States Government are hereby directed to take all appropriate measures within their authority to carry out the provisions of this order and, where appropriate, to advise the Secretary of the Treasury in a timely manner of the measures taken.

Federal Register / Vol. 69, No. 143 / Tuesday, July 27, 2004 / Presidential Documents **44887**

Sec. 7. The Secretary of the Treasury, in consultation with the Secretary of State, is hereby authorized to submit the recurring and final reports to the Congress on the national emergency declared in this order, consistent with section 401(c) of NEA, 50 U.S.C. 1641(c), and section 204(c) of IEEPA, 50 U.S.C. 1703(c).

Sec. 8. The Secretary of the Treasury, in consultation with the Secretary of State, is hereby authorized to determine, subsequent to the issuance of this order, that circumstances no longer warrant the inclusion of a person in the Annex to this order and that the property and interests in property of that person are therefore no longer blocked pursuant to section 1 of this order.

Sec. 9. This order is not intended to, and does not, create any right or benefit, substantive or procedural, enforceable at law or in equity by any party against the United States, its departments, agencies, instrumentalities, or entities, its officers or employees, or any other person.

Sec. 10. This order is effective at 12:01 a.m. eastern daylight time on July 23, 2004.

Sec. 11. This order shall be transmitted to the Congress and published in the *Federal Register.*

THE WHITE HOUSE,
July 22, 2004.

Billing code 3195–01–P

44888 **Federal Register** / Vol. 69, No. 143 / Tuesday, July 27, 2004 / Presidential Documents

ANNEX

1. ALLEN, Cyril
DOB: 26 JUL 1952
Former Chairman, National Patriotic Party; nationality Liberian; alt. nationality Nigerian

2. BOUT, Viktor Anatolijevitch
aka BUTT
aka BONT
aka BUTTE
aka BOUTOV
aka SERGITOV, Vitali
DOB: 13 JAN 1967; alt. DOB: 13 JAN 1970
Businessman, dealer and transporter of weapons and minerals; Passport No. 21N0532664; alt. Passport No. 29N0006765; alt. Passport No. 21N0557148; alt. Passport No. 44N3570350

3. BRIGHT, Charles R.
DOB: 29 AUG 1948
Former Minister of Finance

4. CISSE, M. Moussa
aka KAMARA, Mamadee
DOB: 24 DEC 1946; alt. DOB: 26 JUN 1944
Former Chief of Presidential Protocol; Chairman, Mohammed Group of Companies; Diplomatic Passport No. D-001548-99 <Liberia>; Passport No. 0058070 <Liberia>

5. COOPER, Randolph
DOB: 28 OCT 1950
Former Managing Director, Roberts Intl. Airport

6. DARRAH, Kaddieyatu
aka DARAH, Kadiyatu
aka DARA, Kaddieyatu
aka DARA, Kadiyatu
Special Assistant to Charles Taylor

7. DUNBAR, Belle Y.
DOB: 27 OCT 1967; alt. DOB: 27 OCT 1963
Former Managing Director, Liberian Petroleum Refining Company

8. DUNBAR, Jenkins
DOB: 10 JAN 1947
Former Minister of Lands, Mines, Energy

9. FAWAS, Abbas
President, Maryland Wood Processing Industries; President, United Logging Company; nationality Lebanese

10. GIBSON, Myrtle
DOB: 03 NOV 1952
Former Senator; advisor to Charles Taylor

11. GOODRIDGE, Reginald B. (Senior)
aka GOODRICH, Reginald B. (Senior)
DOB: 11 NOV 1952
Former Minister for Culture, Information, Tourism

12. JOBE, Baba
Director, Gambia New Millenium Air Company; Member of Parliament of Gambia; nationality Gambian

Federal Register/Vol. 69, No. 143/Tuesday, July 27, 2004/Presidential Documents **44889**

2

13. KIIA TAI, Joseph Wong
Executive, Oriental Timber Company

14. KLEILAT, Ali
DOB: 10 JUL 1970; POB: Beirut, Lebanon; nationality Lebanese
Businessman

15. KOUWENHOVEN, Gus
aka KOUVENHOVEN, Gus
aka KOUENHOVEN, Gus
aka KOUENHAVEN, Gus
DOB: 15 SEP 1942; nationality Dutch
President, Oriental Timber Company; Owner, Hotel Africa;
Villa # 1, Hotel Africa Virginia, Monrovia, Liberia
P.O. Box 1522, Monrovia, Liberia

16. MININ, Leonid
aka BLAVSTEIN
aka BLYUVSHTEIN
aka BLYAFSHTEIN
aka BLUVSHTEIN
aka BLYUFSHTEIN
aka KERLER, Vladimir Abramovich
aka POPILOVESKI, Vladimir Abramovich
aka POPELAVESKI, Vladimir Abramovich
aka POPELOVESKI, Vladimir Abramovich
aka POPELA, Vladimir Abramovich
aka POPELO, Vladimir Abramovich
aka BRESLAN, Wolf
aka BRESLAN, Wulf
aka OSOLS, Igor
DOB: 14 DEC 1947; alt. DOB: 18 OCT 1946; Owner, Exotic Tropical
Timber Enterprise; nationality Ukrainian; Passport No.
5280007248D <Germany>; alt. Passport No. 18106739D <Germany>;
Passport No. 6019832 (6/11/94-5/11/99) <Israel>; alt. Passport
No. 9001689 (23/1/97-22/1/02) <Israel>; alt. Passport No.
90109052 (26/11/97) <Israel>; Passport No. KI0861177 <Russia>;
Passport No. 65118 <Bolivia>

17. NASR, Samir M.
aka RUPRAH, Sanjivan
DOB: 09 AUG 1966
Businessman; Former Deputy Commissioner, Bureau of Maritime
Affairs; Passport No. D-001829-00 <Liberia>; nationality Kenyan

18. NEAL, Juanita
DOB: 09 MAY 1947
Former Deputy Minister of Finance

19. SALAMI, Mohamed Ahmad
aka SALAME, Mohamed Ahmad
DOB: 22 SEP 1961
Owner, Mohamed Group of Companies; Taylor's informal diplomatic
representative; nationality Lebanese

20. SANKOH, Foday
Deceased

21. SHAW, Emmanuel (II)
DOB: 26 JUL 1946; alt. DOB: 26 JUL 1956; alt. DOB: 29 JUL 1956
Advisor to Charles Taylor

3

22. TAYLOR, Charles Ghankay
aka TAYLOR, Charles MacArthur
aka SOME, Jean-Paul
aka SONE, Jean-Paul
DOB: 01 SEP 1947
Former President of Liberia

23. TAYLOR, Charles (Junior)
aka "Chuckie"
DOB: 12 FEB 1978
Advisor and son of former President Taylor

24. TAYLOR, Tupee Enid
DOB: 17 DEC 1962
Ex-wife of former President Taylor

25. REEVES-TAYLOR, Agnes
aka TAYLOR, Agnes Reeves
aka REEVES-TAYLOR
DOB: 27 SEP 1965
Ex-wife of former President Taylor; ex-Permanent Representative to the International Maritime Organization; nationality Liberian

26. TAYLOR, Jewell Howard
DOB: 17 JAN 1963
Wife of former President Taylor

27. UREY, Benoni
DOB: 22 JUN 1957
Former Commissioner of Maritime Affairs; Diplomatic Passport No. D-00148399 <Liberia>

28. YEATON, Benjamin
aka YEATEN, Benjamin
Former Director, Special Security Services; Diplomatic Passport No. D-00123299 <Liberia>

Note: The identifying information with respect to each person listed in this Annex reflects information currently available and is provided solely to facilitate compliance with this order. Each individual listed in this Annex remains subject to the prohibitions of this order notwithstanding any change in title, position, or affiliation.

[FR Doc. 04–17205
Filed 7–26–04; 8:45 am]
Billing code 4810–25–C

Top row: Some of Bout's air-cargo fleet, amongst them an Ilyushin-76.
Lower row: UN peacekeepers transported by Bout in April 2000.

EMBASSY
OF THE RUSSIAN FEDERATION
IN THE KINGDOM OF THAILAND
Consular Section

78 Sap Rd., Bangkok, Thailand 10500
Tel/Fax: (662) 234-2012/268-1166

No. 559
September 22, 2009

Mr. Songvuthi Patanakul
Director, Bangkok Remand Prison
Fax: 02-588-4023

Dear Mr. Patanakul,

I hereby request Your kind permission to visit Russian detainee **Mr. Victor But** this Thursday, September 24, 2009 and this Friday, September 25, 2009 by his spouse Alla But and his translator Mr.Daniel Estulin.

It would be highly appreciated if such permission were granted.

Looking forward to Your anticipated cooperation on this matter.

Respectfully Yours,

Popov S.V,
vice-consul,
Embassy of the Russian Federation

In the guise of translator, I managed to be the only journalist in the world to obtain interviews with Victor Bout in Bangkok. My thanks to the Russian embassy, whose support also led to my access to Bout's files and other personal materials. Officially, visitors are only allowed twenty minutes per day with prisoners, but I was able to spend over two hours with Bout during each of my many visits.

Above: Welcome to Hell. Southeast Asia's worst prison, KlongPrem, known locally as the "Bangkok Hilton." Below: Victor Bout (center) waiting for his court appearance behind a quadruple fence, shackled in leg irons and handcuffed.

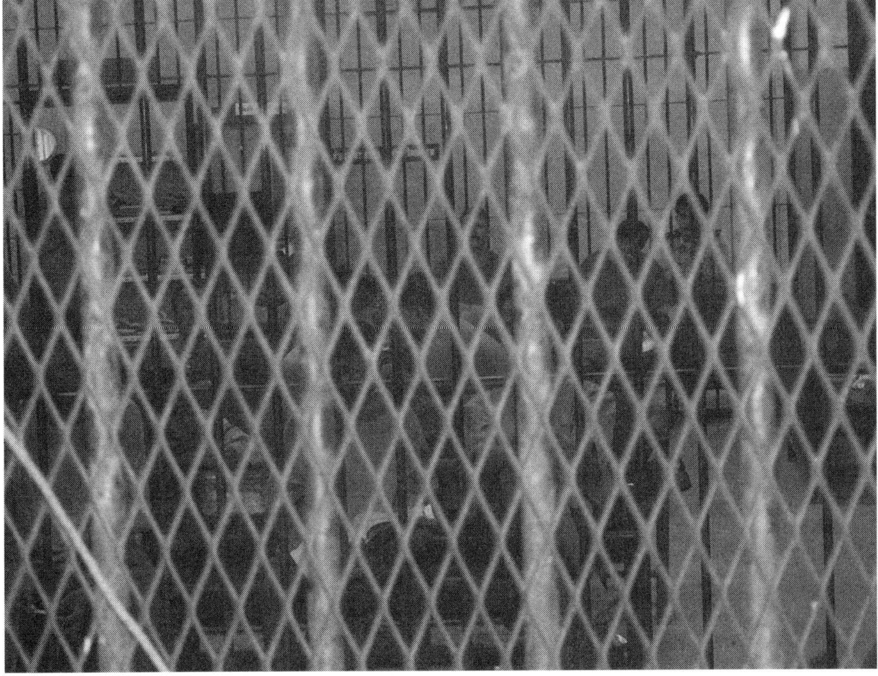

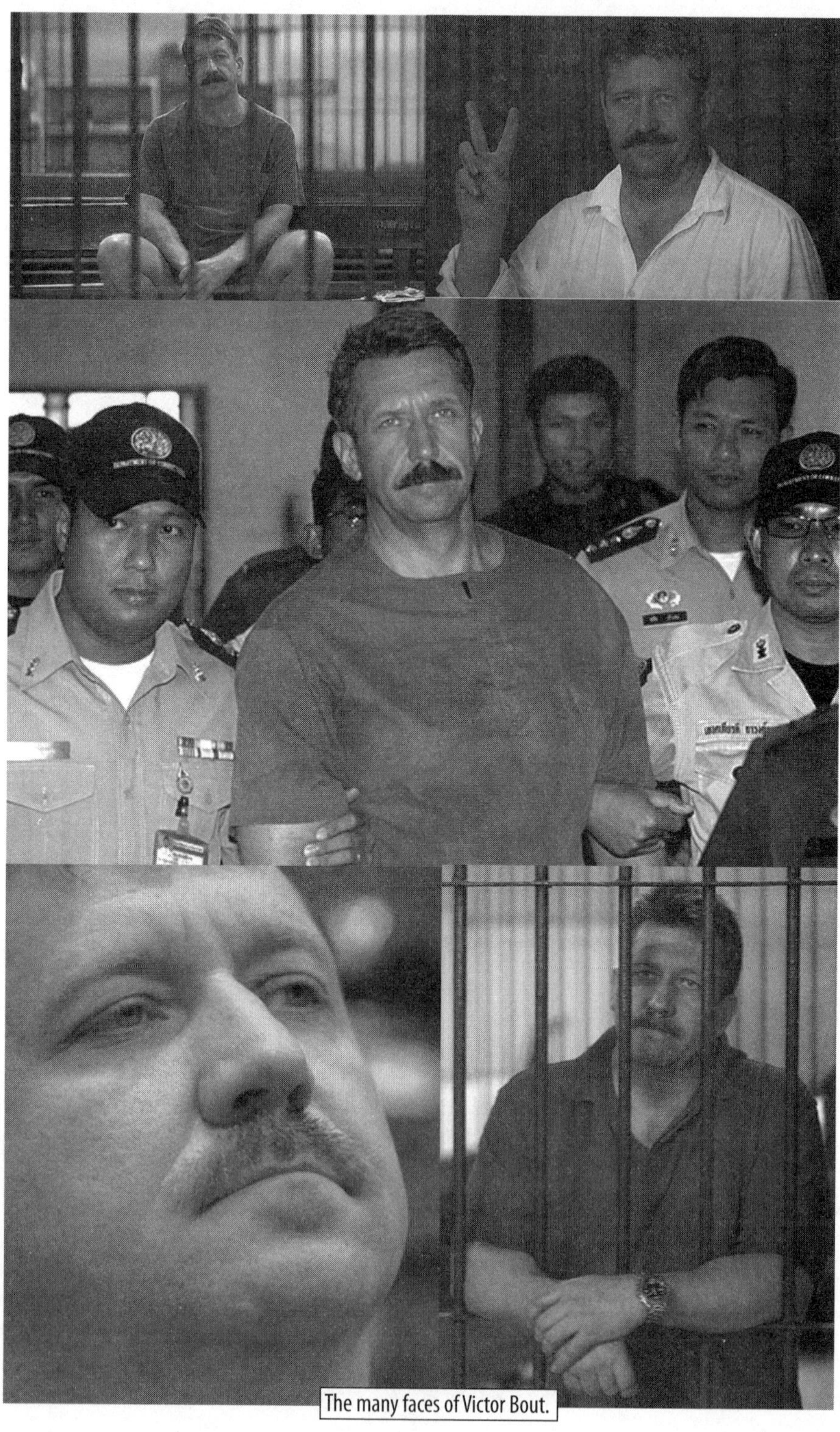

The many faces of Victor Bout.

(Translation)

Memorandum of Search / Confiscation

Written at Room 1420,
Sofitel Silom Hotel

Date : 6 March 2008

This memorandum is made to show that, today (6 March 2008) at approximately 15.30 hours, the police officers of Crime Suppression Division and the officers of U.S. Drug Enforcement Administration, led by Pol.Col. Phetcharat Saengchai, Deputy Commander of Crime Suppression Division, Pol.Lt.Col. Nontawat Amaranon, Investigating Officer (SB 2) of Crime Suppression Division, Pol.Maj. Akarawut Limrat, Inspector KK.PP. of Crime Suppression Division, together with the Special Investigators of U.S. Drug Enforcement Administration in Thailand, Mr. Scott Hacker and Mr. Derek Odney, jointly searched the Room No. 1420, Sofitel Silom Hotel. Mr. Victor Analtojevic Bout was arrested under the Warrant of Arrest, issued by the Criminal Court, No. , dated 5 March 2008. Mr. Prommin Suwannagot, a security officer of Sofitel Silom Hotel, was present. The search started at 15.30 hours and finished at 16.00 hours, and no illegal article was found.

List of items confiscated from a man who is reportedly worth $6 billion. Note the amount of money in Bout's possession: 112 dollars and 660 rubles (a bit over 20 dollars).

The officers conducting search confiscated the properties of Mr. Victor Analtojevic Bout, which were found in the Room No. 1420, Sofitel Silom Hotel, for examination purpose, with the consent of Mr. Victor Analtojevic Bout, as follows :

1. Nokia E90 cell phone, q'ty 1
2. Nokia cell phone, q'ty 1
3. Samsung DUOS cell phone, q'ty 1
4. Passport of Russian Federation of Mr. Victor Analtojevic Bout
5. Light blue note paper
6. Copy of Passport of Russian Federation of a Russian man
7. Euro Locks with Number 25
8. White note paper
9. Black wallet containing 12 bank notes, as per the details of bank notes in this memorandum.

10. U.S. bank notes	US$100	q'ty 1
11. "	10	" 1
12. "	1	" 2

13. JEFF Vehicle document, 1 sheet
14. Pink note paper, 1 sheet
15. White note papers, 2 sheets

16. Russian bank notes	Ruble 500	q'ty 1
17. "	100	" 1
18. "	50	" 1
19. "	10	" 2

20. Air-ticket of Aeroflot Airlines, Flight No. SU 553 and SU 554 q'ty 1
21. Suitcase, q'ty 1

Therefore, the above items were confiscated and recorded as evidence.

(Signature) Mr. Victor Analtojevic Bout	Leading search/co
(Signature) Pol.Col.	Conducting search
(Signature) Pol.Lt.Col. Illegible	Conducting search
(Signature) Pol.Maj.	Conducting search
(Signature)	Conducting search
(Signature)	Conducting search
(Signature) Prommin S.	Leading search/co

IN RESIDENCE AT SOFITEL SILOM BANGKOK

APPROVED: [signature]
BRENDAN R. MCGUIRE / ANJAN SAHNI
Assistant United States Attorneys

BEFORE: HONORABLE THEODORE H. KATZ
United States Magistrate Judge
Southern District of New York

08 MAG 0386

- x

UNITED STATES OF AMERICA :

- v - : **SEALED COMPLAINT**

VIKTOR BOUT, :
a/k/a "Boris,"
a/k/a "Victor Anatoliyevich Bout," :
a/k/a "Victor But,"
a/k/a "Viktor Budd," :
a/k/a "Viktor Butt,"
a/k/a "Viktor Bulakin," :
a/k/a "Vadim Markovich Aminov," and
ANDREW SMULIAN, :

Defendants. :

Violations of Title 18, United States Code, Sections 2339B & 3238

- x

SOUTHERN DISTRICT OF NEW YORK, ss.:

ROBERT F. ZACHARIASIEWICZ, being duly sworn, deposes and says that he is a Special Agent of the Drug Enforcement Administration ("DEA"), and charges as follows:

COUNT ONE: CONSPIRACY TO PROVIDE MATERIAL SUPPORT TO A FOREIGN TERRORIST ORGANIZATION

1. From in or about November 2007 up to and including in or about February 2008, in an offense that occurred in and affected interstate and foreign commerce, VIKTOR BOUT, a/k/a "Boris," a/k/a "Victor Anatoliyevich Bout," a/k/a "Victor But," a/k/a "Viktor Budd," a/k/a "Viktor Butt," a/k/a "Viktor Bulakin," a/k/a "Vadim Markovich Aminov," and ANDREW SMULIAN, the defendants, who will be first brought to and arrested in the Southern District of New York, and others known and unknown, unlawfully and knowingly did combine, conspire, confederate and agree together and with each other to provide "material support or resources," as that term is defined in Title 18, United States Code, Section 2339A(b), to a foreign terrorist organization, to wit, Fuerzas Armadas Revolucionarias de Colombia-Ejército del Pueblo ("the FARC"), which was designated by the United States Secretary of State as a foreign terrorist organization in October 1997, pursuant to Section 219 of the Immigration and Nationality

Here and next page, first and last pages of the sealed complaint in US v. Bout and his alleged accomplice, Andrew Smulian . Bout is accused of providing material support to Colombian FARC terrorists, including guided ballistic missiles. By implying Bout's role in arming terrorists, New-World-Order enthusiasts also implicated Russia as a potential supplier of the materiel. The complaint is co-signed (top) by Assistant US Attorney, Brendan McGuire. Mcguire failed to answer even one of more than two dozen questions I asked him about the case. The deponent before the US Magistrate issuing the complaint was DEA special agent Robert Zachariasiewicz, who has been charged (along with Derek Odney, DEA station chief in Bangkok) in Thailand with Bout's illegal arrest. Rather than face trial for what Thai judges have acknowledged to be an illegal arrest, Zachariasiewicz has left the country. The US embassy in Bangkok announced that Derek Odney has a diplomatic passport and thus can't be tried in a foreign court. Just in case, Odney too has left Thailand.

March 6, 2008. BOUT then asked whether the meeting will be in the same place, which, based on paragraphs 23 through 25 above, I believe was a reference to Thailand. CS-2 replied that it would be in the same place. CS-2 asked BOUT whether he would have any problems with that date, and BOUT replied that he would not. After CS-2's telephone call with BOUT, CS-2 called ANDREW SMULIAN, the defendant. During that call, which CS-2 recorded, CS-2 stated that he had spoken with "your friend" -- which I believe refers to BOUT -- and we are "going to the place" next month on the sixth (i.e., Thailand on March 6, 2008). SMULIAN replied, "yes, okay." CS-2 then stated, "get ready for travel."

WHEREFORE, your deponent respectfully requests that arrest warrants be issued for VIKTOR BOUT, a/k/a "Boris," a/k/a "Victor Anatoliyevich Bout," a/k/a "Victor But," a/k/a "Viktor Budd," a/k/a "Viktor Butt," a/k/a "Viktor Bulakin," a/k/a "Vadim Markovich Aminov," and ANDREW SMULIAN, the defendants, and that they be imprisoned or bailed as the case may be.

ROBERT F. ZACHARIASIEWICZ
Special Agent,
Drug Enforcement Administration

Sworn to before me this
____ day of February, 2008

S/ Theodore H Katz FEB 27 2008
UNITED STATES MAGISTRATE JUDGE

THEODORE H. KATZ
UNITED STATES MAGISTRATE JUDGE
SOUTHERN DISTRICT OF NEW YORK

A handcuffed Victor Bout being led from a Bangkok hotel room after his arrest. Over forty Thai commandoes guarded Victor Bout and Andrew Smulian. Then Smulian "somehow" escaped, and he "somehow" headed straight to the USA, where he faced federal charges that might lead to life in prison. This is essentially the official account, which doesn't merely stretch credulity: it obliterates it.

COURT OF 1st INSTANCE

Of

BRUSSELS

COUNCIL CHAMBER

ORDER

Report n°: BR 27.97.2780/97

Investigation Judge: FREYNE

File n°: 01/97

CONCERNING : 1. BOUT Victor Alias Victor ANATOLIEVITSH(SDF)

2. DENIS Olivier (SDF = Without known Domicile)

3. DE SMET Roland

4. PIRET Nathalie

5. PIRET Olivier

6. VAN POYER Roger

7. XXX

The Council Chamber of The Court of 1st Instance of Brussels:

Concerning the pieces of (the administration of) justice, and the claim (request / demand) of the public prosecutor;

(Concerning) the evidence of forwarding of the recorded delivery, sent by the clerk of the court on March 16th of 2007

to the suspects sub 3 to sub 6

even as to Mr. SCHEERS Johan (JOTS Dirk)

Mr. DESMET Raf (YUBERO DIAMONDS BVBA)

Due to the fact that the suspects sub 1 and sub 2 haven't got an official (permanent) residence or place of contact in our country, it is therefore impossible to forward them the recorded delivery (registered writing) as predicted by the law.

Due to the fact that suspect sub 7 (X) is unknown, it is impossible to forward him the recorded writing as predicted by the law,

Heard, Mr. FREYNE

Investigation Judge, in his report;

Present Mr. SCHEERS Johan, lawyer, acting for and on behalf of Mister JOTS Dirk

Heard, Mr STEPPE

First substitute-Crown prosecutor,

In his claim;

In 2007, the Belgian court of 1st Instance passed down a "not guilty" verdict in Bout's case. Two years later, the Thai court of 1st Instance, followed suit, but a US appeal is pending.

Heard, suspect sub 5

In his defense,

Considering that suspects sub 1, sub 2, sub 3, sub 4 are not present ,

Considering that suspect sub 7, non identified, not present;

Enrolling (taking over) the motive of the claim;

Applying the legal decision, indicated by the chairman ,

Namely the following articles:

- 127 of the Criminal Prosecution Code (Penal Code= strafwetboek)
- 11.12.13.16.21.31à37.40à42 of the law of June 15th 1935 on the use of languages in courtcases, modified by the law of March 24th 1980,
- 94 of the Judicial Code
- 21 Previous Title of the Criminal Prosecution Code

Says that the Criminal Procedure is expired by prescription of claims

Says that the trial costs until today amounts to 109 665,01€ and are at expense of the Belgium Nation;

Dutch was used as official language for the Administration of Justice, for the claim of the Public Prosecutor and for the pleas.

Pronounced on May 29th 2007

In the Council Chamber,

Where were seated:

M. VAN BOSTRAETEN H.	Singleseated, added judge
M. STEPPE E.	1st substitute Crown Prosecutor
Ms. GOOSSENS K.	Dep. Assistant clerk of Justice

Approved the strikethrough of 0 lines and 0 words.

GOOSSENS K. VAN BOSTRAETEN H.

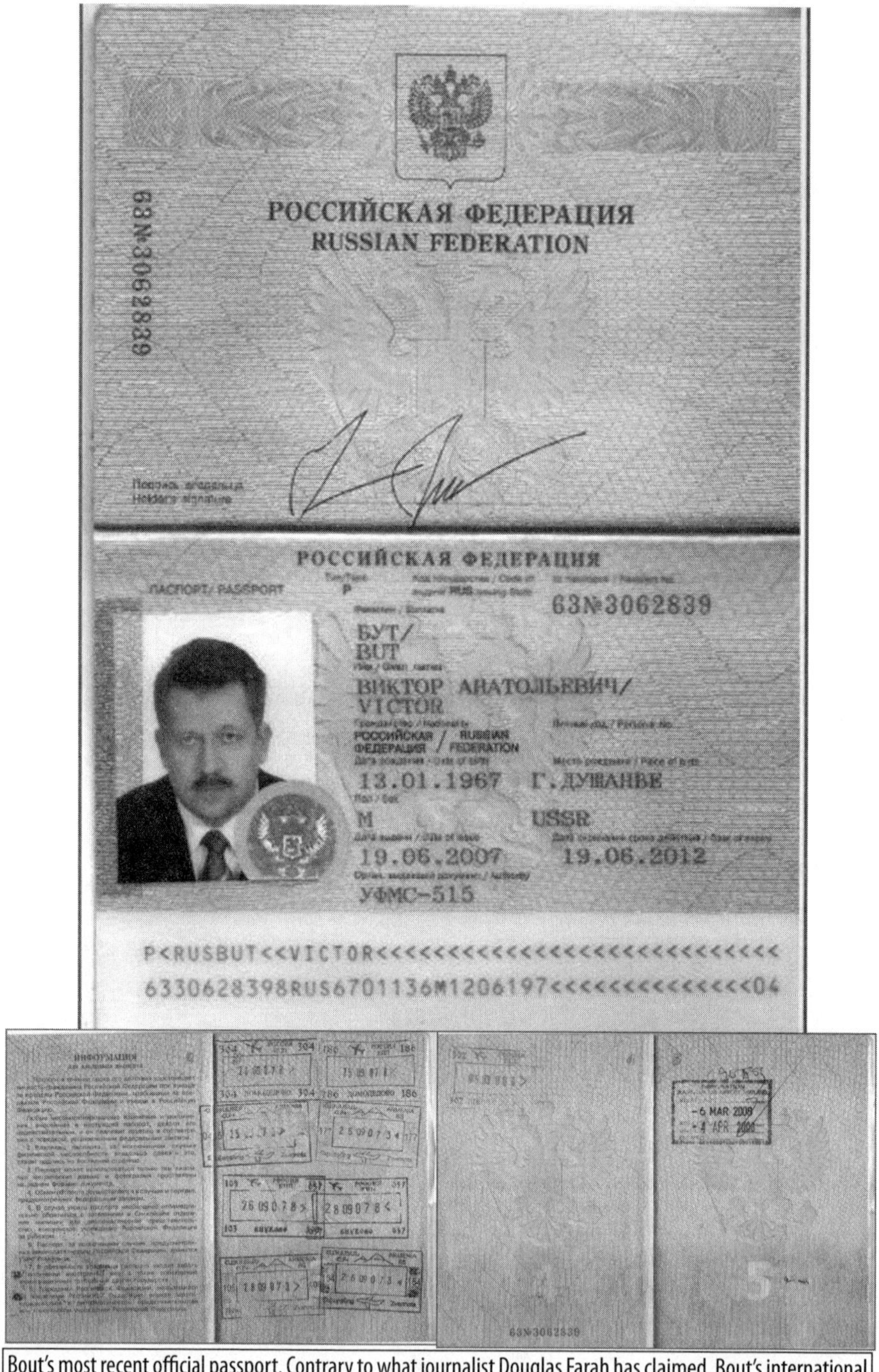

63№3062839

РОССИЙСКАЯ ФЕДЕРАЦИЯ
RUSSIAN FEDERATION

РОССИЙСКАЯ ФЕДЕРАЦИЯ

P

63№3062839

БУТ/
BUT

ВИКТОР АНАТОЛЬЕВИЧ/
VICTOR

РОССИЙСКАЯ / RUSSIAN
ФЕДЕРАЦИЯ / FEDERATION

13.01.1967 Г.ДУШАНБЕ

M USSR

19.06.2007 19.06.2012

УФМС-515

P<RUSBUT<<VICTOR<<<<<<<<<<<<<<<<<<<<<<<<<<<<<<<<

6330628398RUS6701136M1206197<<<<<<<<<<<<<<04

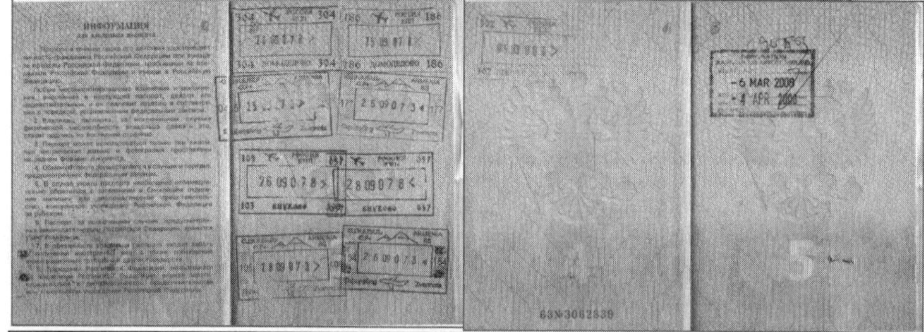

Bout's most recent official passport. Contrary to what journalist Douglas Farah has claimed, Bout's international travel in the nine months prior to being caught in Bangkok was limited to Armenia. The entry stamp on March 6, 2008 was made upon his arrival in Bangkok. Will there be an exit stamp?

Wanted

BOUT, Viktor

Legal Status	
Present family name:	**BOUT**
Forename:	**VIKTOR**
Sex:	MALE
Date of birth:	13 January 1967 (41 years old)
Place of birth:	DUSHANBE, Tajikistan
Language spoken:	English, French, Portuguese, Russian, Spanish Castilian, Uzbek
Nationality:	Russia

Physical description	
Height:	1.83 meter <-> 72 inches
Colour of hair:	BROWN

Offences	
Categories of Offences:	TERRORISM CONSPIRACY
Arrest Warrant Issued by:	SOUTHERN DISTRICT OF NEW YORK / United States

IF YOU HAVE ANY INFORMATION CONTACT
YOUR NATIONAL OR LOCAL POLICE
GENERAL SECRETARIAT OF INTERPOL

Last modified on 12 Mar 2008

Interpol arrest warrant for Victor Bout. Until his spectacular arrest in Bangkok in March 2008, few people knew what Bout looked like . . . at least that's what the intelligence community wants us to believe. One super-villain against a world powerless to stop him.

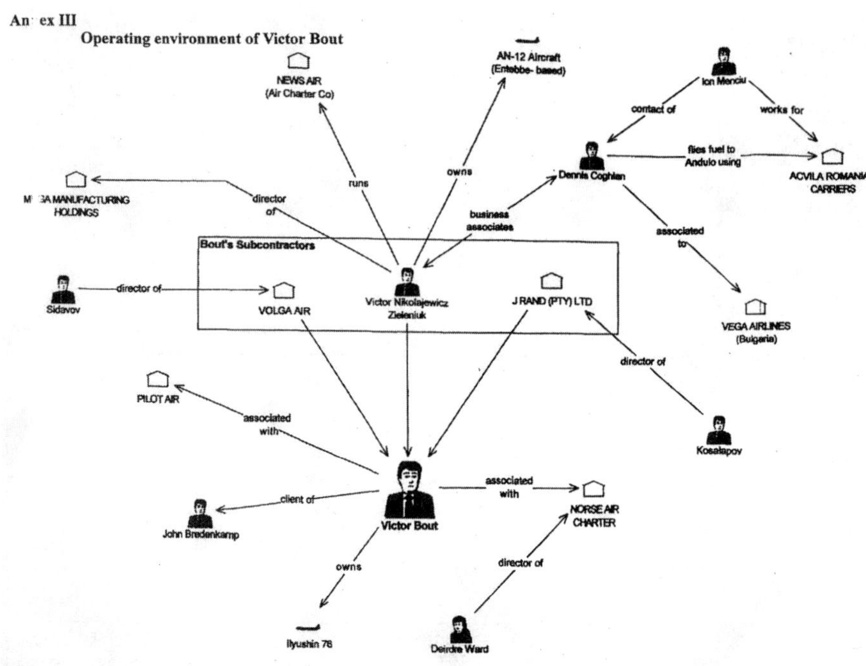

LIBERIA/CHARLES TAYLOR E.O.

VIKTOR BOUT
BUSINESS EMPIRE

April 2005

U.S. Department of Treasury
Office of Foreign Assets Control

VIKTOR BOUT
DOB: 13 JANUARY 1967
Currently resides in Russia
(designated 23 July 2004)

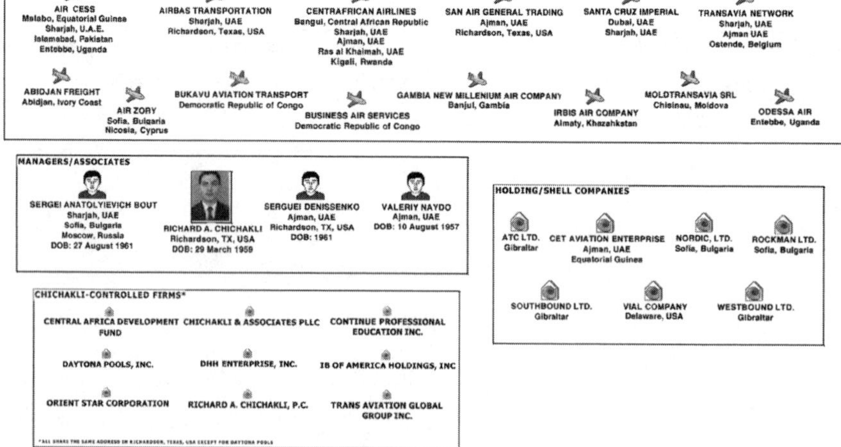

Organizational diagram of Bout's alleged "business empire." US authorities consider this evidence.

(Translation)

(Official Emblem)

(Petition)
1st Detention

Black Case No. P. 585 /2551
Red Case No.

Certified Correct Translation
รับรองคำแปลถูกต้อง
บัญญัติ วงศ์กลึคนาค
(Banyat Vongklednak)
LICENSED QUALIFIED LAWYER LL.B.
World Translation Center Institute (Registered Lawyer/Solicitor)
Goverment-Approved Law Office
12 MAR 2008
Tel. 02-2334267, 2330584, 2526345
02-2545731, 2580502, 2546340

Criminal Court

Date : 8 March 2008

Criminal Lawsuit

Between Investigating Officer, Crime Suppression Division (Lt.Col. Pairin Jaemjamrat) — Petitioner

Mr. Viktor Analtojevich Bout or BUTT or BOUTOV or SERGITOV, 41 years of age, holding Passport of Russian Federation, 63 NO 3062839 — Suspect

I, the investigating officer, Crime Suppression Division, hereby submit a petition as follows :

1. On 6 March 2008, at approximately 15.30 hours, the police officers arrested Mr. Viktor Analtojevich, suspected of "supplying properties for terrorism" and he was sent to the investigating officers on 6 March 2008, at 18.00 hours.

On 3 March 2008, Mr. Derek S. Odney, the investigating officer, Drug Enforcement Agency, the United States of America, requested the investigating officers, Crime Suppression Division, to charge Mr. Viktor Analtojevich with committing crime under the Criminal Code of Thailand relating to terrorism act, and requesting the investigating officers, Crime Suppression Division, to investigate and arrest Mr. Viktor Analtojevich for terrorism act. On 4 March 2008, the investigating officers, Crime Suppression Division, gathered evidences and submitted the petition to the Criminal Court requesting the issuance of Warrant of Arrest for the apprehension of Mr. Viktor Analtojevich and it was approved by the court under the Warrant of Arrest No. 893/2551, dated 4 March 2008.

On 6 March 2008, at approximately 15.30 hours, the arresting team found that Mr. Viktor Analtojevich was traveling to Thailand and staying at Room No. 1420, Sofitel Hotel, Silom Road, Silom Sub-district, Bangrak District, Bangkok. Then, the arresting team and U.S. special investigating officers from DEA waited in ambush until Mr. Viktor Analtojevich, the Russian suspect, was arrested and sent to the investigating officers for legal proceedings. The investigating officers, Crime Suppression Division, informed the charge to Mr.

First page of a report by the Thai investigating officer overseeing Bout's arrest. This report was added to the evidence presented against Bout in the Thai court. The second paragraph clearly states that Bout was charged under the criminal code of Thailand on March 3. As Bout didn't enter Thailand until March 6, the absurdity of the charge is obvious on its face. I find it hard to believe that this can be chalked up to mere incompetence. But if not, then what?

Ironically, Bout's arrest led to Thai criminal charges for unlawful arrest against three US DEA officers. All three have since left the country, and, according to a submitted statement to the court by the US Embassy, the US government has no idea of their whereabouts.

(Translation)

(Official Emblem)

(31)

For Court Only

JUDGMENT

Black Case No. Por. 3 /2551
Red Case No. /2552

Certified true copy.
(Signed)
(Mrs. Kanlaya Ratanachuen)
Justice Court Officer 5

In the Name of H.M. the King

Criminal Court

Date : 11th August 2009

Criminal Lawsuit

Between *Public Prosecutor, Office of the Attorney General* Prosecutor

Mr. Viktor Bout or Boris or Victor But or Viktor Budd or Viktor Bulakin or Vadim Markovich Aminov Alleged Offender

Re : Offense against the Act on Extradition

1. The prosecutor filed the lawsuit that in accordance with the Act on Extradition between the Kingdom of Thailand and the United States of America, B.E. 2533, stipulating the extradition between the government of the Kingdom of Thailand and the government of the United States of America, Article 2, stating that an offense shall be an extraditable if the conduct on which the

Certification Fee : 50 baht
Receipt : Book No. 19986 Serial No. : 83
Date : 13th August 2009
Signed : Illegible Court Officer

The judgment of the Thai court was issued 533 days after Bout's arrest. It denied the US request for extradition and ordered his release. Bout has remained incarcerated pending a US appeal.

(31 bis) For Court Only

- 49 -

duties and never has problems or has benefits with any party. There is no doubt that he would testify to help or incriminate the accused or prosecutor. It is credible that what testified by the witness is true. Although the prosecutor's witness, Mr. Robert Sahari Vazevit, the head of investigation and inquiry who collected evidence connected with the accused's trade of war weapons, came to testify for confirmation, it is found that the witness is the officer of the United States who testified without any documentary evidence containing photographs or materials. Based on the prosecutor's documentary evidence, it is credible that FARC is a group of patriots whose opinions of administration differ from the government and has fought against the Colombian Government for decades which it is a political fight. Consequently, the conspiracy is considered as the political support and it is the case of exception not to extradite the accused to the government of the United States.

(31 bis) For Court Only

- 50 -

Therefore, the petition made by the prosecutor shall be rejected and the accused shall be released at the end of 72 hours after reading this order of release, except within such period, the public prosecutor shall notify the Court of the appeal, and then the accused shall be detained during the appeal.

Mr. Jittakorn Pattanasiri -Signed-

Mr. Peera Jungpiwat -Signed-

(Translation)

CONFIDENTIAL
(Official Emblem)

TOP URGENT
No. Kor Tor 1102/ 1001

Confidential

Receipt No.: 453
Date : 31st August 2009
Time : 13.03 hours

To : The Office of the Attorney General

International Affairs Department
Date : 3rd September 2009
Time : 13.43 hours
Receipt No.: 1248

With reference to our Letter No. Kor Tor 1102/977, dated 24th August 2009, informing you of the additional information about Mr. Viktor Bout.

We would like to inform you that, on 26th August 2009, the Colombian Ambassador in Peru met with Mr. Udompon Ninnart, Thai Ambassador in Lima, to inform him that the Colombian Minister of Foreign Affairs has sent a letter to Thai Minister of Foreign Affairs about the ruling uttered by Thai Court concerning the refusal to the extradition of the Russian citizen, Mr. Viktor Bout, for prosecution in the United States of America, which the Court considered that the group of Colombian left-wing guerrillas (FARC) intended to overthrow the Colombian government to change the administration, therefore, FARC was a political group and was not a terrorist organization.

In this respect, we would like to inform you of the main points of the letter of the Colombian Minister of Foreign Affairs as follows :

1. FARC is known worldwide for the cruelty and drug trafficking network. FARC was considered to be the world's largest drug dealer. The systematic attacks against the Colombian population, including teachers, mayors, councilmen, union members and indigenous population. In addition, FARC engaged in the forced recruitment of children and long-term kidnappings. Therefore, FARC is on the list of terrorist organizations of the United States and the European Union. Moreover, the majority of the kidnappings and landmine victims in Colombia were caused by FARC operations, and between 2002 – 2009, there were 8,998 kidnapped people and there were 2,229 landmine victims.

2. Today, the FARC are not able to produce any mass support in Colombia. In the framework of the Democratic Security Policy, the Armed Forces and the National Police of Colombia continue to establish territorial control over the great majority of the territory. Since 2002, more than 10,000 members of the FARC have voluntarily laid down their weapons and are returning to society with the support of the program of troop withdrawal, disarmament and society return of Colombia.

3. Given the aforementioned context, the Colombian Minister of Foreign Affairs requested Thai government that, in the frame of the independency of power, illustrated to the judge in charge of the case, the nature and extent of the terrorist activities undertaken by FARC, so that these elements could be taken into account in the correspondent judicial process, that was hoped to avoid the release of a very dangerous arms trafficker to the world such as Viktor Bout.

4. The Colombian government was willing to promote an exchange of information with the United States' authorities that would allow the judicial authorities to cooperate effectively so that these damaging activities of arms trafficking undertaken by this individual will be investigated and punished, as per the copy of the letter of the Colombian Minister of Foreign Affairs, dated 26th August 2009, copy of unofficial translation, document explaining reasons why the FARC is on the international lists of terrorist groups.

5. The Colombian Ambassador in Thailand who is residing in Kuala Lumpur informed the Embassy in Kuala Lumpur that he would like to meet with Thai Minister of Foreign Affairs to discuss this matter, and it is under the schedule coordination.

Please be informed accordingly.

Office of the State Attorney Special,
International Affairs 3 Section
Date : 4th September 2009
Time : 11.00 hours
Receipt No.: 165

-Signed-
The Ministry of Foreign Affairs
28th August 2009
(Official Seal)

To submit to the Office of International Affairs 3 for further proceedings.
-Signed-
Mrs. Somsook Meewutsom
Deputy Director-General,
International Affairs Section.
For Deputy Director-General
3rd September 2009

Certified true copy.
-Signed-
Pol.Capt. Sopon Kasempibooncai

- To submit to the Office of the International Affairs urgently.
-Signed-
(Mr. Chaikasem Nitisiri)
Attorney General
1st September 2009

America and South Pacific Department
North America Division
Tel. 0 2643 5000 ext. 3055
Fax. 0 2643 5124

-Signed-
(Mr. Chatchom Akkapin)
Special Attorney, the Office of the International Affairs,
For the Special Attorney, the International Affairs Section.
4th September 2009.

In the event that Thai officials had bogged down in the several-hundred-point indictment of the FARC sent by the Colombian Ministry of Foreign Affairs in support of the US request for Bout's extradition, this summary underlined its main points. In the weeks after the Thai court's ruling, reports claimed that the Thai judiciary was leaning toward granting the US appeal. If so, the Colombian intervention has apparently had a contrary effect, and is yet another baffling event in the strange proceedings against Victor Bout, "Merchant of Death."

Because of this, Taylor issued airplane registrations to Victor Bout, one of the world's largest illegal weapons dealers. Bout was later discovered not only to be selling weapons to most sides of most civil wars in Africa, but also to the Taliban AND the Northern Alliance in Afghanistan. He often took his payment in diamonds. Until very recently he was also flying for the U.S. military in Iraq.[4]

The documentary and anecdotal evidence point to two distinct phases in al Qaeda's diamond activities. The first started sometime before 1996, when bin Laden lived in the Sudan, and was aimed at helping finance the organization. The latter years overlap with the large-scale, al Qaeda dominated purchase of tanzanite in East Africa.

Wadi el Hage, bin Laden's personal secretary until he was arrested in September 1998, spent a great deal of time on gemstone deals. During his trial in New York, El Hage's file of business cards, personal telephone directory and handwritten notebooks were introduced as evidence. He was sentenced to life in prison for his role in the East Africa bombings. The notebooks contain extensive notes on buying diamonds, attempts to sell diamonds, and appraising diamonds and tanzanite. There is a page on Liberia, with telephone numbers and names. His address book and business

5

An excerpt from Douglas Farah's submitted testimony before the US House subcommittee on the role of commodities in terrorist financing, February 16, 2005, which appears to link Bout to Osama bin Laden via their supposed common interest in African diamonds.

JUDGE SULLIVAN

UNITED STATES DISTRICT COURT
SOUTHERN DISTRICT OF NEW YORK
- - - - - - - - - - - - - - - - - - X
:
UNITED STATES OF AMERICA :
:
v. : 08 Cr. (RJS)
:
ANDREW SMULIAN, : 08 CRIM 711
:
Defendant. :
:
- - - - - - - - - - - - - - - - - - X

The above-named defendant, who is accused of violating Title 18, United States Code, Sections 1114, 1117, 2332(b), 2332g, and 2339B, being advised of the nature of the charges and of his rights, hereby waives, in open Court, prosecution by indictment and consents that the proceeding may be by Information instead of by Indictment.

ANDREW SMULIAN
Defendant

Witness

Mary Mulligan, Esq.
Counsel for Defendant

USDC SDNY
DOCUMENT
ELECTRONICALLY FILED
DOC #: ______
DATE FILED: JUL 30 2008

Date: New York, New York
July 30, 2008

0202

Andrew Smulian's waiver of indictment, eliminating any need for testimony in the matter. There can be little doubt that Smulian was working for the US.

Fuel Purchase Agreement

ABY ✓

Air BAS Transportation, Inc.
P.O.Box 8299
Sharjah, U.A.E.

DESC-RRF
Attn: Mr. Tom Blann
Building 1621-K
2261 Hughes Ave Suite 128
Lackland AFB TX 78236-9828

Subject: Authorization to Purchase Department of Defense (DoD) Aviation Fuel Other Than Cash

1. The Defense Energy Support Center (DESC), Ft. Belvoir, VA, provides fuel to U.S. Military facilities. DESC owns all DoD bulk petroleum product from point of purchase until it is used to power aircraft, vehicles and ships. **Air BAS Transportation, Inc.**, (hereinafter "Purchaser") wishes to purchase aviation fuel from DESC at United States (U.S.) Military facilities. Purchaser is required to land at U.S. Military facilities to charter flights.

2. Purchaser requires 4 (four) DD Forms 1896, Jet Fuel Identaplates. Our billing and operating location addresses are:

Billing Address	**Operating Location Address**
Air BAS Transportation, Inc. P.O.Box 8299 Sharjah, U.A.E.	Same

Types of aircraft and tail numbers are: **(see note 2)**
AN12 No UN11007
IL18 Nos. UN75003 and UN75005
YAK42 No UN42428

3. Purchaser agrees to present the appropriate landing permit number (if requested) when requesting fuel at a U.S. Military facility.

4. Purchaser agrees to provide appropriate tax exemption information, including all pertinent tax exemption certificates, to DESC-RRF in advance of any fuel purchases. Failure to provide a tax exemption certificate(s) will result in the addition of applicable taxes to the fuel price.

5. Purchaser agrees that fuel purchased from DESC will be utilized **for official government purposes as defined in note 1 only.** Failure to abide by this requirement may result in cancellation of this Purchase Agreement. Purchaser further agrees that fuel it purchases from DESC will not be resold without express authorization from DESC.

6. Purchaser agrees that when it purchases fuel at a U.S. Military facility, it will receive a copy of the sales form. An electronic file with the data obtained from the sales form will be forwarded to Defense Finance and Accounting Service Columbus Ohio, (DFAS-CO) for billing purposes. Purchaser agrees that the invoice generated as a result of the fuel purchase is due and payable within 30 days of the invoice date.

7. Purchaser agrees that if it does not remit payment for each invoice in sufficient time to reach the billing office within 30 days from the invoice date, its account will be delinquent. If Purchaser's account becomes delinquent Purchaser will be in violation of this agreement. Purchaser agrees that such delinquency is grounds for permanent revocation of Purchaser's credit fuel purchase privileges at U.S. Military facilities. Once credit authority has been permanently revoked, purchase of aviation fuel at a U.S. Military Facility can only be made by cash, company check or wiring payment for the fuel prior to arrival at the facility.

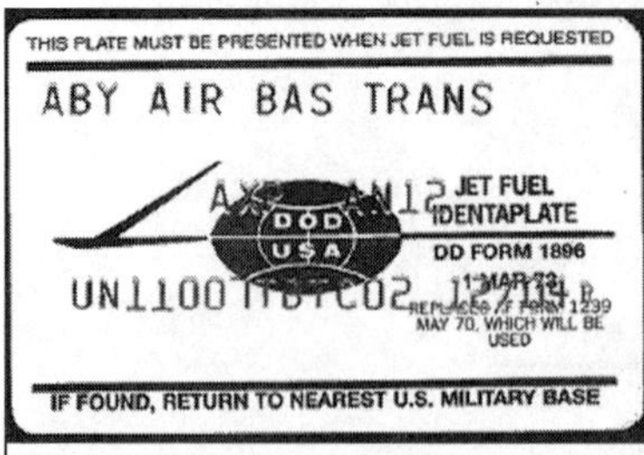

THIS PLATE MUST BE PRESENTED WHEN JET FUEL IS REQUESTED
ABY AIR BAS TRANS
JET FUEL IDENTAPLATE
DOD
USA
DD FORM 1896
MAY 70, WHICH WILL BE USED
IF FOUND, RETURN TO NEAREST U.S. MILITARY BASE

After his honorable discharge from the US Army, Richard Chichakli was responsible for liaison with commercial flights at the airport in Sharjah, United Arab Emirates, where Victor Bout's air-cargo business operated. He has stated on the record several times that he considers Bout a "friend and brother." This association with Bout has earned him considerable grief, especially after various reports labeled Air Bas to be a Victor Bout company and UN actions led to the freezing of Air Bas assets. While there is no real evidence that Air Bas was ever a Bout operation, there is no lack of evidence of Chichakli's involvement. Note his signature on document.

8. Purchaser agrees and understands that DESC-RRF will take all available measures to obtain payment for fuel purchases in the event Purchaser's account becomes delinquent. This includes, but is not limited to, offsetting delinquent payments against payments due to Purchaser from any U.S. Government agency.

9. Purchaser agrees that any delinquent accounts shall bear interest on the delinquent amount from the date payment is due until the delinquent amount is paid, offset or otherwise collected at a rate determined by the United States Department of Treasury.

10. Purchaser agrees that its accounting department is fully aware of all the payment conditions which must be met to maintain a current purchase account with DESC. Purchaser's point of contact for financial matters is:

Office +9716 558 17 58, Duty's Cell (24H) +97150 631 05 35

11. Purchaser represents and warrants:

a. That it is a corporation duly formed, validly existing and in good standing under the laws of Texas, U.S.A.

b. That execution, delivery and performance of this agreement are within Purchaser's legal powers, have been duly authorized by all necessary principals of the company, and do not contravene (i) any charter or by-laws or (ii) any law or any contractual restriction binding on or affecting Purchaser or any of its assets.

c. This Agreement is a legal, valid and binding obligation of Purchaser enforceable against Purchaser in accordance with its respective terms.

Signed and Agreed

AIR BAS Transportation, Inc.

By: ______________________

Victor Bahudev, General Manager

Date: 9th March, 2004

NOTES:

1. Include the type of business you are conducting (for example, contract, charter, or civil aircraft operations). Be specific: cite contract numbers, charter agreements, specific type of civil operations, etc. Insufficient information may delay approval or result in disapproval to purchase fuel from DESC. "Contract" refers to carriers under contract to the U.S. Government to transport passengers or cargo or as authorized by the US Government or DESC. Civil aircraft operations includes emergency landings for medical evacuations, weather or mechanical problems, fire fighting operations, etc. **Further clarification is available by contacting DESC-RRF at the above address or phone (210) 925-4887.**

2. The information is utilized for further identification of the customer for billing purposes. Identaplates will be embossed with the aircraft tail number on the card. There is no charge for the cards. In the event that the billing and operating location addresses are the same, type "SAME" under the heading "Operating Location Address". If you desire to have the identaplates and/or future purchase renewal correspondence sent to a different address insert a third address as **Other Correspondence**.

3. The person signing the Fuels Purchase agreement must be someone who can financially bind the company or agency submitting he agreement.

11/09/2005 02:06 FAX OCRS Crim Div 002/(

U.S. Department of Justice

Criminal Division

Washington, D.C. 20530

November 9, 2005

If Mr. Chichakli agrees to be re-interviewed, I have been advised that the Northern District of Texas would extend the standard limited use immunity protections afforded those cooperating in criminal investigations. I can provide a sample letter including those provisions if Mr. Chichakli wishes. I cannot, as your letter requests, extend blanket or transactional immunity to Mr. Chichakli in exchange for his re-interview.

If at that time, as Mr. Chichakli suggests, Victor and Sergei Bout wish to be interviewed as well, we would make every effort to accommodate their requests.

The US has twice offered Richard Chichakli immunity from prosecution in return for his testimony against Victor Bout. In September 2005, an initial offer was made, which led to a counter offer by Chichakli to testify without immunity, leading to another offer (above), which was refused. Chichakli has redacted sensitive information that may pertain to legal proceedings involving him or Victor Bout. As you can see (right), even after renditioning him to Syria, the US in 2008 was taking a let-bygones-be-bygones approach, offering Chichakli another immunity agreement, which he also refused. His offers to testify without immunity get no takers.

U.S. Department of Justice

United States Attorney
Northern District of Texas

Christopher Stokes
Assistant United States Attorney

1100 Commerce St., 3rd Fl.
Dallas, Texas 75242-1699

Telephone 214. 659.8676
Fax 214.767.2846

November 21, 2008

Mr. Clay C. Scott, Jr.
Attorney at Law
4304 Druid Lane
Dallas, Texas 75205

Re: Richard Chichakli

Dear Mr. Scott,

The Government proposes to interview Mr. Chichakli beginning on or about December 8, 2008 in the U.S. embassy in Moscow concerning his full knowledge of his activities and that of other persons, which may or may not be criminal in nature. In exchange for truthful and complete information this office is extending "use"immunity as described below.

It is agreed that no statements made by Mr. Chichakli during this meeting will be used against him in any criminal proceeding <u>except that such statements may be used for impeachment purposes in the event he testifies in a legal proceeding and such testimony is inconsistent with statements made in the interview</u>. The government may make derivative use of any information provided, that is, it may pursue any investigative lead suggested by any statement or other information he provides.

Mr. Chichakli's complete truthfulness and candor are express material conditions to this agreement and the undertakings of the government set forth in this letter. Therefore, if the government should ever conclude that Mr. Chichakli knowingly withheld material information from the government or otherwise has not been completely truthful and candid, this agreement shall be rendered null and void and the government may use against you for any purpose (including sentencing) any statements made or other information provided by you during the interview.

Other than those expressly set forth in this agreement, no understandings, promises, agreements and/or conditions have been entered into with respect to any potential charges against Mr. Chichakli.

Sincerely,

RICHARD B. ROPER
United States Attorney

Christopher Stokes
Assistant United States Attorney

The Honorable Congressman Ed Royce
2185 Rayburn House Office Building
Washington, DC 20515
Via Facsimile: (202) 226-0335

February 17, 2009

Dear Congressman Royce:

My name is Richard Chichakli; I am an American citizen, an honorably discharged disabled US Army veteran, a husband, a father, college lecturer, and a CPA serving taxpayers and small businesses in North Texas community. I am writing to you concerning your statement made in regards to the extradition of Viktor Bout.

On April 26, 2005 I was included in OFAC SDN list on allegation that I was an employee of the alleged world-spanning empire of Victor Bout. An empire that I was allegedly managing its day-to-day operations while I was a soldier in the US Army, an Employee of the US DOJ, a lecturer in US universities, a full-time student, and a CPA managing 500 client practices in Texas. **Congressman, I wonder how awkward your call for justice may sound when people know that you were one of those aborted the US constitution by denying me my constitutional right to stand trial.**

Congressman is it possible that you have been listening to one side only, and I wonder, for you being a man of fairness, principles, and conviction, if you are ready to hear the complete story. I was sanctioned without being given a chance to speak or to defend myself, that is what the WORLD and Russia sees and I wonder how you would expect them to react to your call for the extradition of Bout. **Congressman, EVERYTHING you know about Bout's operations came from sources and persons who never personally knew Victor Bout or seen much of his operations!** Is that strange coincidence or is something planned? Your subcommittee heard from people who invented the Bout story and is benefiting from it, but you never called anyone who actually saw, spoke to, and seen the records of Viktor Bout?

Congressman, if you are interested in getting the facts and seeing the entire picture, I can help. However, if this is just politics and the fallacious version is something should remain despite that you are fully aware of its possible falsity, then that will explain why the Congress in 2005 invited witnesses like Douglas Farah to testify about persons he has never seen, and a matter he is not qualified for while neglecting to summon me to testify, after all you alleged that I am the most knowledgeable about Viktor Bout. I am writing you asking for a hearing, a trial in a US court of law under the US constitution, a chance to be heard without the politics and a chance to clear my name.

Respectfully

Richard A. Chichakli
C/o: Clay Scott, Jr., 4304 Druid Ln, Dallas, TX 75205, Tel. (214) 358-0341
Richard@chichakli.com Mobile: 01179166404012 and 01179267534384

Citizen Chichakli's frustration with the US administration of justice is apparent.

The Honorable President Barak Obama
The White House
1600 Pennsylvania Ave. NW
Washington, D.C. 20500

January 23, 2009

Dear Mr. President:

My name is Richard Chichakli, I am an American citizen, an honorably discharged disabled US Army veteran, a husband, a father, and a CPA serving taxpayers and small businesses in North Texas community. On April 26, 2005 I was included on OFAC SDN list on allegation that I was an employee of Victor Bout, a person sanctioned by the US government in July 2004 by Executive Order 13348. In a press release on that day OFAC, the DOJ, and the State Dept. indicated that my designation was subsequent to a two-year investigation. The said investigation was closed in 2008 without bringing charges for any wrongdoing on my part, and without asserting the justification used by OFAC for designating me.

Upon my inclusion in the SDN list my businesses were closed, my assets were confiscated, my bank accounts were frozen, my car was taken, and I was kicked out of my house. I was effectively executed without a trial, without charges, without being questioned, and without having the opportunity to defend myself. All my constitutional and legal rights were terminated immediately and all I was permitted to do is to leave the US and go into exile. Furthermore, and at the request of the US State Department, the United Nations Security Council issued added me to the lists of worldwide travel ban and assets freeze. I have no assets outside the United States.

On August 25, 2006 I filed a law suit demanding trial against OFAC's action; 10 months later on June 04, 2007 Judge David C. Godbey of the Federal Court in North Texas granted the government a summary judgment without meeting or talking to my lawyer. The government filed 1,212 pages in response to my complaint, nearly 1,000 of which were about Victor Bout, and it did not make any reference to me. I asserted to the court that the trial is about Richard Chichakli not Victor Bout, and I asserted that I did not have any business with Mr. Bout since he was designated by the US government in July of 2004, and therefore; there was no justification for OFAC action against me. OFAC agreed that I had no business with Mr. Bout after he was designated; however, stating that my relation to him, 10 years earlier in 1995 is sufficient cause for designation. In 1995 I was an employee of the government of Sharjah in the United Arab Emirates and I was responsible for creating a free trade and industrial zone in the state of Sharjah. Mr. Bout was one of the 170+ clients the zone had and my relation to him was part of my duties as the Commercial Manager of that Free Zone. In 1995 there was not any derogatory information or any accusations pertinent to Victor Bout and his operations. The first questionable information about this person was made available to the public in 2001 after he was mentioned in the UN report S/2000/1225.

Mr. President, OFAC was either penalizing me because I could not predict in 1995 what will be of Victor Bout 10 years later in the future, or simply because they needed a scapegoat for a political objective beyond my knowledge or understanding. All I know is that I was to be sacrificed outside the reach of the US legal system and I was not permitted to ask why.

Another request, this time to the President of the United States, Barak Obama, asking for a chance to clear his name after an unjust decade-long persecution. The same letter was sent to Secretary of State Hillary Clinton.

OFAC stated in my designation that I have been an employee of Victor Bout for more than a decade; that is impossible and untrue because during the time OFAC stated that I was working for Viktor Bout, I was either an employee of the United States federal government, in the United States Army, A Co. 1/58th AVN, RGMT (FWD), The 18th Avn. Corp; or the United States Department of Justice, INS - Dallas Finance Center. After separation from government service and while I was in process for gaining certification in the State of Texas as a Certified Public Accountant (CPA), I worked as an accountant in several companies through the US-based employment agency "Robert Half Account Temps" and my employment records clearly indicate that I was working in excess of 8 hours per day.

Guilty

Besides working full-time to support my wife and children, and in addition to coaching the Richardson Independent School District Soccer squad, I was also attending two universities; full-time, and my academic records support my statement. I had done all of that while I was in the United States, *so how can I be the CFO handling the day-to-day operations of a company on the other side of the earth?* OFAC mentioned that my resume indicated that I was Bout's employee in 1998 in South Africa – that is not true and it also dated seven years before he was designated. In 1998, I was an employee of the US-DOJ, and I had a swimming pool cleaning business where I performed the work, and the business records testify to that. In 1998 I visited South Africa for 15 days, and was never an employee there, the immigration, travel, government, and tax records all prove that I was in the United States not anywhere else. I was not an employee of Victor Bout and I never received salary or employees' benefits from the Bout's organization, is it possible that I worked more than 10 years for free? How could I be a senior employee and no one knew me, met me, or heard of me, not bank, not a customer, or even a coworker?

How can I be a CFO of a conglomerate, a very busy organization as OFAC alleged while I was a full-time practicing CPA in the US, and a part-time faculty teaching accounting or information systems in Texas universities? My 500 tax and accounting clients, and hundreds of students I taught are willing to testify that my work day started at 7 am and ended with my classes' ending at 10 pm. OFAC's stated justifications for designation cannot possibly be true, it simply defy the boundaries of logic and stretches the impossible. Guilt and innocence should be determined in a court of law by jury of one's peers; this is a constitutional right should not be denied.

I am writing you asking for your help to be removed from OFAC's SDN list and the UN sanctions lists in the name of justice and fairness. If that is too much to ask, would a trial in a US court of law in accordance with the US constitution would also be too much to ask. I am a law abiding citizen, a decorated and honorably discharged, disabled war veteran of the United States Army, and all I am asking for is justice. Please relief me or let me be tried in a court of law.

Respectfully

Richard A. Chichakli
C/o: Clay Scott, Jr., 4304 Druid Ln, Dallas, TX 75205, Tel. (214) 358-0341
Richard@chichakli.com Mobile: 01179166404012 and 01179267534384

Above: Richard Chichakli's wedding on July 14, 1983. Behind him is Saad bin Laden, Chichakli´s university friend and Osama bin Laden's half brother.
Below: A record of Chichakli's university attendance.

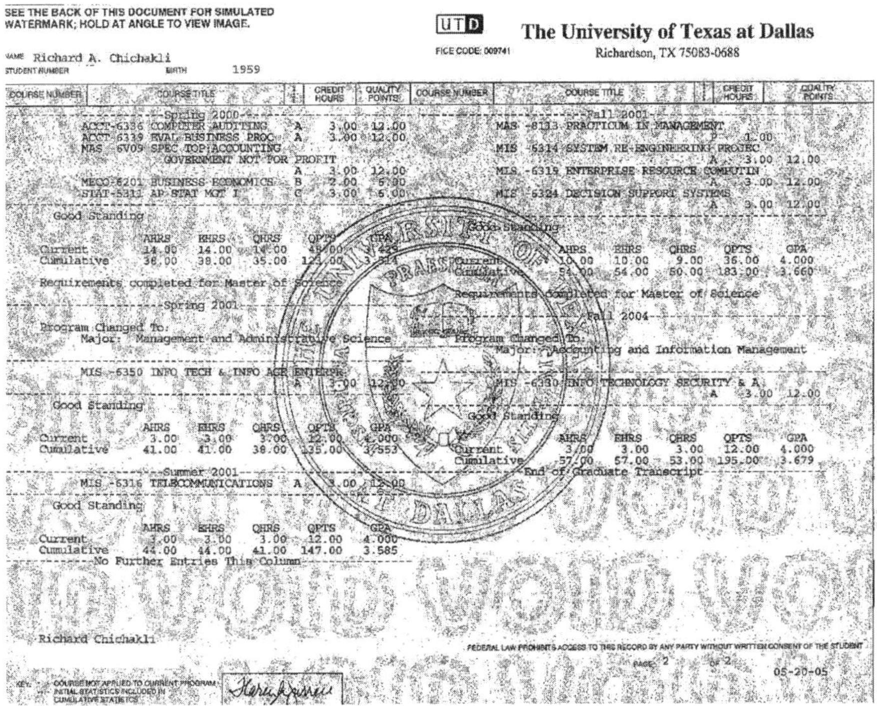

SEE THE BACK OF THIS DOCUMENT FOR SIMULATED WATERMARK; HOLD AT ANGLE TO VIEW IMAGE.

UTD **The University of Texas at Dallas**
FICE CODE: 009741 Richardson, TX 75083-0688

NAME Richard A. Chichakli
STUDENT NUMBER BIRTH 1959

COURSE NUMBER | COURSE TITLE | CREDIT HOURS | QUALITY POINTS

Spring 2000
ACCT-6336 COMPUTER AUDITING A 3.00 12.00
ACCT 6339 EVAL BUSINESS PROC A 3.00 12.00
MAS 6V09 SPEC TOP:ACCOUNTING GOVERNMENT NOT FOR PROFIT A 3.00 12.00
MECO-6201 BUSINESS ECONOMICS B 2.00 6.00
STAT-5311 AP STAT MGT I C 3.00 6.00

Good Standing

	AHRS	EHRS	QHRS	QPTS	GPA
Current	14.00	14.00	14.00	48.00	3.429
Cumulative	38.00	38.00	35.00	123.00	3.514

Requirements completed for Master of Science

Spring 2001
Program Changed To:
Major: Management and Administrative Science

MIS -6350 INFO TECH & INFO AGE ENTERPR A 3.00 12.00

Good Standing

	AHRS	EHRS	QHRS	QPTS	GPA
Current	3.00	3.00	3.00	12.00	4.000
Cumulative	41.00	41.00	38.00	135.00	3.553

Summer 2001
MIS -6316 TELECOMMUNICATIONS A 3.00 12.00

Good Standing

	AHRS	EHRS	QHRS	QPTS	GPA
Current	3.00	3.00	3.00	12.00	4.000
Cumulative	44.00	44.00	41.00	147.00	3.585

No Further Entries This Column

Fall 2001
MAS -8133 PRACTICUM IN MANAGEMENT P 1.00
MIS -6314 SYSTEM RE-ENGINEERING PROJEC A 3.00 12.00
MIS -6319 ENTERPRISE RESOURCE COMPUTIN A 3.00 12.00
MIS -6324 DECISION SUPPORT SYSTEMS A 3.00 12.00

Good Standing

	AHRS	EHRS	QHRS	QPTS	GPA
Current	10.00	10.00	9.00	36.00	4.000
Cumulative	54.00	54.00	50.00	183.00	3.660

Requirements completed for Master of Science

Fall 2004
Program Changed To:
Major: Accounting and Information Management

MIS -6330 INFO TECHNOLOGY SECURITY & A A 3.00 12.00

Good Standing

	AHRS	EHRS	QHRS	QPTS	GPA
Current	3.00	3.00	3.00	12.00	4.000
Cumulative	57.00	57.00	53.00	195.00	3.679

End of Graduate Transcript

Richard Chichakli

FEDERAL LAW PROHIBITS ACCESS TO THIS RECORD BY ANY PARTY WITHOUT WRITTEN CONSENT OF THE STUDENT
PAGE 2 OF 2
05-20-05

KEY: COURSE NOT APPLIED TO CURRENT PROGRAM; INITIAL STATISTICS INCLUDED IN CUMULATIVE STATISTICS

Happier days? Chichakli and Bout during the 2007 Christmas season in Moscow. After escaping from Syria, Chichakli married a Russian woman, in the process becoming a Russian citizen. He resides in Moscow.

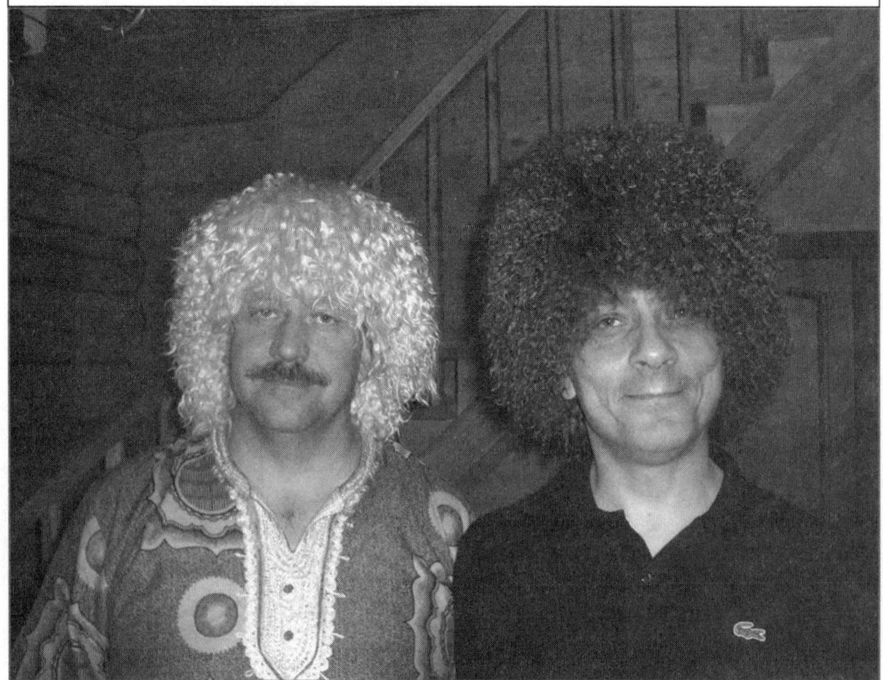

Year	Place of Work/Employment	Type of evidence
1990	United States Armed Forces	US Gov. Records
1991	United States Armed Forces	US Gov. Records
	Embry-Riddle Aeronautical University, FL	School Records
1992	United States Armed Forces	US Gov. Records
	Embry-Riddle Aeronautical University, FL	School Records
1993	United States Armed Forces	US Gov. Records
1994	Al-Agroobi General Trading - Dubai, UAE	US Travel and Tax records. US Passport
1995	Sharjah Government - Sharjah, UAE	US Travel and Tax records. US Passport
1996	Sharjah Government - Sharjah, UAE	US Travel and Tax records. US Passport
1997	Account Temps - Dallas, TX	Telephone, banking, attendance, tax, medical, and insurance records
	Collin County Community College, Plano, TX	School Records
	Dallas County Community College, Dallas, TX	School Records
	University of Texas at Dallas, Richardson, TX	School Records
1998	US Dept. of Justice - INS, Dallas, TX	US Gov, Medical & insurance records
	Daytona Pools, Inc. Arlington, TX	Tel, Bank, attendance, and tax records
	Account Temps - Dallas, TX	Tel, Bank, attendance, and tax records
	Dallas County Community College, Dallas, TX	School Records
	University of Texas at Dallas, Richardson, TX	School Records
1999	Chichakli, Hickman-Riggs & Riggs. Plano, TX	Tel., Bank, attendance, and tax records
	University of Texas at Dallas, Richardson, TX	School Records
	Dallas County Community College, Dallas, TX	School Records
2000	Chichakli, Hickman-Riggs & Riggs. Richardson, TX	Telephone, banking, attendance, tax, medical, and insurance records
	University of Texas at Dallas, Richardson, TX	School Records
	Dallas County Community College, Dallas, TX	School Records

Summary of Richard Chichakli's employment from 1990 to 2000, with list of evidence he can provide as corroboration.

Criminals are not welcome

The arrest in Bangkok last week of the internationally infamous Viktor Bout is at once both reassuring and troubling. The arrest by Thai police after a US-directed sting operation showed that with determined, imaginative effort, a cross-border effort can succeed. Taking the world's best-known arms trafficker off the street was good for Thailand and the world. It is unknown why the notorious "Lord of War" and others of his ilk pick Thailand to do their dirty business.

Thailand was in the world news for two other unpleasant reasons last week. In the United States, a woman known as the "ponytail bandit" appeared in a California court. Morgan Michelle Hoke, 21, was charged with multiple bank robberies. On the run from American authorities, she fled to Thailand in the belief she could disappear here. Hardly the brightest robber in the gang, she kept her ponytail and made it easy for Immigration Division police to arrest her. Her alleged accomplice, Stuart Michael Romine, 26, is still on the run, probably in Thailand. Meanwhile, in Exeter, England, a court put paedophile Sean McMahon in prison after he was captured in Thailand and extradited.

The McMahon case was part farce, part incompetence, and all danger to Thais. He fled British justice in 1999, figuring he could find shelter in Thailand — and he was right. For five years, he was free and clear. He was finally tracked and was due to be arrested in Phuket on Dec 27, 2004. But the tsunami foiled those plans, giving McMahon another three years-plus of freedom. During that time, he taught Thai children. It remains unclear whether he harmed anyone during his seven years of free rein in this country.

It is time for authorities to ask why the terrorists, traffickers, gangsters, thieves and paedophiles pick Thailand as their refuge. It is not enough to shrug off this question with the facile claims that our open borders and robust tourism industry means Thai society must play host to repellent criminals as well. Thailand has both the right and the duty to protect its own people from foreigners who wish to do harm here or hide here while planning to harm others.

Mr Bout is credibly charged with trying to sell advanced war weapons — anti-aircraft missiles included — to one of the world's leading terrorist gangs. The Revolutionary Armed Forces of Colombia, or Farc, was in the middle of an international dispute last week that came within a hairsbreadth of a major South American war. In 2000, al-Qaeda members and two of the eventual hijackers chose Bangkok as their meeting place to help plan the Sept 11, 2001 attacks on New York and Washington. In 2003, using a fake Spanish passport, the top Jemaah Islamiyah planner Hambali felt — wrongly, thank goodness — that he could find dependable shelter from an international manhunt in Thailand.

The whole world watched as a creative Thai-American team took down Mr Bout. To work the sting that led to the Russian's downfall required time, trouble and trust. Too often, criminals and odious individuals operate in Thailand because of a lack of cooperation and, especially, communications. Thailand should and can continue to welcome men, women and children from around the world. Far more must be done, however, to weed out the few rotten apples from the millions of people who want to see and to enjoy Thailand. A strong, diplomatic push is needed for better international cooperation.

When criminals and terrorists flee their own country, Thailand must be alert and on guard to stop them from entering this country. Men like Mr Bout should be welcome nowhere, but, in particular, they should be unwanted in Thailand.

Moscow, US and Thailand want Russian

WASSAYOS NGAMKHAM

Moscow and Washington have moved to compete for the extradition of Viktor Bout, one of the world's most wanted arms traffickers, but Thailand says the Russian suspect will have to be prosecuted in Bangkok first.

Pol Lt-Gen Adisorn Nonsi, chief of the Central Investigation Bureau (CIB), said the suspect will be charged and put on trial for the procurement of weapons or assets to assist terrorist training or operations. He faces 2-10 years in jail and/or a fine of 4,000-200,000 baht.

According to Pol Lt-Gen Adisorn, Thai police are in charge of the investigation and will today seek to detain Mr Bout for 12 days of further questioning.

The Crime Suppression Division (CSD) has set up an investigation team headed by CSD deputy chief Pol Col Petcharat Saengchai to look into the suspect's alleged arms dealing activities.

He said the CSD will jointly expand the investigation with the United States Drug Enforcement Administration (DEA) for the time being. Pol Lt-Gen Anusorn said negotiations on Mr Bout's extradition would need to await the outcome of any prosecution here.

The US Department of Justice said in a statement yesterday the US plans to pursue the extradition of Mr Bout from Thailand.

Yevgeny Afanasiev, ambassador of the Russian Federation, yesterday met Foreign Minister Noppadon Pattama.

Mr Noppadon said after the meeting that the ambassador also discussed cooperation between the two countries in the possible extradition of Mr Bout despite the fact that the ambassador had not yet decided how to move forward with the case.

The suspect has so far refused to give any statements to police, he added.

CSD chief Pol Maj-Gen Pongpat Chayaphan said police will have Mr Bout's assets examined.

"Besides criminal prosecution, investigators will ask the Anti-Money Laundering Office [Amlo] to look into his assets. Terrorism is one of the charges [which call for assets examination]," the CSD chief said.

Mr Bout, 41, dubbed the "Merchant of Death", was arrested at a conference room on the 27th floor of the Sofitel hotel on Silom road on Thursday.

The Russian was silent throughout a press conference yesterday after he was paraded before the press following lengthy questioning by Thai investigators and Thomas Pasquarello, special agent in charge of East Asia for the DEA.

Victor Bout was the topic of conversation in Thailand for months after his arrest. Here are two articles from the *Bangkok Post.*

Young diamond hunters in Congo. The mainstream media has gone out of its way to link Liberia's former strongman Charles Taylor and blood diamonds to Victor Bout. Diamonds are easy to transport and hard to trace. There is nonetheless plenty of evidence linking international terrorist groups such as al-Qaeda, and even Osama bin Laden himself, to illicit diamond trading. On the other hand, despite heroic efforts by US operatives, only the pronouncements of Douglas Farah and associates provide any "evidence" linking Bout to illicit diamond trading

(Translation)

(Official Emblem)

O

APPEAL

Black Case No. Or Por. 3 /2551
Red Case No. Or Por. 8 /2552

Certified true copy.
(Signed)
(Illegible)

Criminal Court

Date : 26th August 2009

Criminal Lawsuit

Between *Public Prosecutor, International Affairs Department, Office of the Attorney General* Prosecutor

Mr. Viktor Bout or Boris or Victor But or Viktor Budd or Viktor Bulakin or Vadim Markovich Aminov Alleged Offender

Charge/Offense Extradition

I, the public prosecutor, International Affairs Department, Office of the Attorney General, hereby appeal the judgment to this Court which it was judged on 11th August 2009, as follows :

1. In this case, the prosecutor filed a lawsuit stating that, pursuant to the Act on Extradition between the Kingdom of Thailand and the United States of America, B.E. 2533, prescribing that the extradition between the government of the Kingdom of Thailand and the government of the United States of America in the Article 2 - An offense shall be extraditable if the conduct on which the offense is based is punishable under the laws in both States by deprivation of liberty for a period of one year or more or by a more severe penalty.

-Sheet 2-

2. In/about November 2007 to March 2008, the accused and his conspirator(s) conspired to provide, compile weapons and train terrorism to FARC group with the purpose of intimidating or forcing the U.S. government not to disrupt cocaine manufacturing and distribution activities by agreement to provide the millions of U.S. dollars worth of war weapons to be used to attack the officers of the U.S. government.

3. In/about November 2007 to March 2008, the accused and his conspirator(s) conspired to provide, supply and train the use of war weapons such as surface-to-air missiles, guided ballistic missiles, including devices and components for assembly, installation and modification to FARC group, in order to use against the U.S. government with the purpose of intimidating or forcing the U.S. government not to disrupt cocaine manufacturing and distribution activities by agreement to provide the millions of U.S. dollars worth of war weapons to be used to attack the nationals and properties of the United States in Colombia.

For the acts stated in No. 1 to No. 3 from 10th January to 6th March 2008, the accused and his conspirator(s) discussed about providing and delivering surface-to-air missiles including devices and components several times through phone calls, meetings and electronic mails. Finally, on 6th March 2008, the accused was arrested in Thailand.

Above and the preceding page: The US Public Prosecutor's appeal of the Thai court's denial of the US request for Victor Bout's extradition. The inclusion of "guided ballistic missiles" (paragraph 3) upped the stakes, implicitly accusing Bout of involvement in nuclear terrorism.

FROM :RUSSIAN EMBASSY BANGKOK CONSUL FAX NO. :6622681166 14 Jan 2010 11:03AM P1

EMBASSY
OF THE RUSSIAN FEDERATION
IN THE KINGDOM OF THAILAND
Consular Section

78 Sap Rd., Bangkok, Thailand 10500
Tel/Fax: (662) 234-2012/268-1166

No. 12
January 14, 2010

Mr. Sophon Thitithammapruek
Director, Bangkok Remand Prison
Fax: 02-588-4023

Dear Mr. Thitithammapruek,

I hereby request Your kind permission for **Mr. Lak Nitiwat-Vicharn (lawyer)** and **Mr. Daniel Estulin (interpreter)** to visit Russian detainee **Mr. Victor But** next Wednesday and Tuesday, January 20 and 21, 2010.

It would be highly appreciated if such permission were granted.

Looking forward to Your anticipated cooperation on this matter.

Respectfully Yours,

Sergey V. Popov
First Secretary, Vice-Consul

ส่ง ส่วนทัณฑปฏิบัติ
☑ ดำเนินการ
☐ เพื่อทราบ
☐ อื่นๆ..........

14 มค 53

(นายโสภณ ธิติธรรมพฤกษ์)
ผู้เชี่ยวชาญเฉพาะด้านทัณฑวิทยา รักษาราชการแทน
ผู้บัญชาการเรือนจำพิเศษกรุงเทพมหานคร

ฝ่ายทัณฑปฏิบัติ
ดำเนินการ

15 มค 53

แบบฟอร์มแจ้งเยี่ยมญาติ (เรือนจำพิเศษกรุงเทพมหานคร)
Visiting Application Form (Bangkok Remand Prison)

รอบ 2 ห้อง 1 — วันที่ 21 เดือน 01 พ.ศ. 2010 (Day / Month / Year)

1. ขอเยี่ยมผู้ต้องขัง (ชื่อ-นามสกุล) Prisoner's First name and Last name: VICTOR BOUT — แดน Building/Section: SECTION 8

2. ต้องหาคดี Case: EXTRADITION — 3. ญาติเข้าเยี่ยม จำนวน ... คน ดังมีรายชื่อต่อไปนี้ Number of visitor

ลำดับ Visitor on	ชื่อ-นามสกุลผู้มาติดต่อเยี่ยม First name - Last name	ความสัมพันธ์กับผู้ต้องขัง Relationship to Prisoner	หมายเลขบัตรประจำตัวประชาชน ID.card/Passport No.
1	DANIEL ESTULIN	FRIEND	JX265404
2			
3			
4			
5			

4. ที่อยู่ของผู้ที่เข้าเยี่ยมลำดับที่ 1 ตามบัตรประชาชน First visitor's address
บ้านเลขที่ House No./Name's hotel in Bangkok: HERITAGE HOTEL — หมู่ที่ 19 — ถนน Road: SILOM RD
ตำบล/แขวง Sub District — อำเภอ/เขต District: BANGRAK
จังหวัด Province: BANGKOK

-Staf Only-

Above: As this book was going to press, and directly after a few advance "galleys" were sent out, the author was suddenly denied entry to visit Victor Bout after many previous visitations without any problems. This prompted an official request from the Russian embassy in Thailand to allow the author to visit Bout.
Below: Form the author must fill out every time he visits Bout.

A special edition of a Colombian right-wing weekly magazine.
On the cover is a photo of FARC's dead second-in-command, Raul Reyes, with laptop alleged to contain highly incriminating evidence against the usual potpourri of anti-US forces there and elsewhere. Widely discredited, the story was prominently reported in the mainstream US media, but not its subsequent debunking.

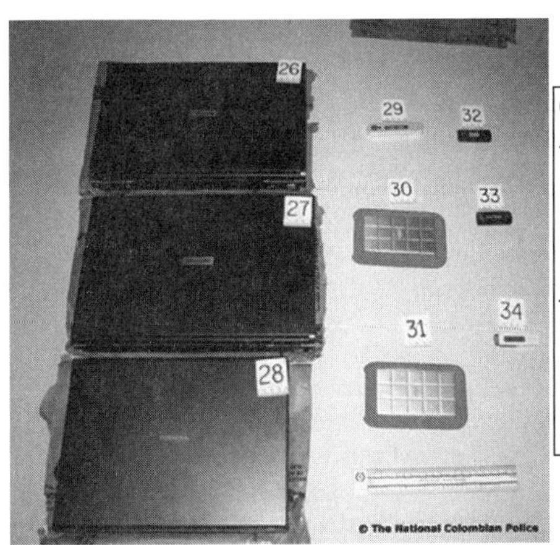

ComputadorasFARC – three alleged FARC computers, flash drives and external storage disks that survived unscathed a scorched-earth overkill of US smart bombs dropped on less than half an acre of Ecuadoran jungle. Bodies found at the scene were mere mangled remains of flesh, but we are supposed to believe that computers reportedly filled with key evidence against Victor Bout miraculously survived intact.

The Americas - WSJ.com

March 10, 2008

THE AMERICAS
By MARY ANASTASIA O'GRADY

This *Wall Street Journal Online* article helped spread disinformation regarding the supposed discovery in Raul Reyes' computer files of evidence incriminating the FARC in a variety of heinous acts.

The FARC Files

March 10, 2008

Colombia's precision air strike 10 days ago, on a guerrilla camp across the border in Ecuador, killed rebel leader Raúl Reyes. That was big. But the capture of his computer may turn out to be a far more important development in Colombia's struggle to preserve its democracy.

- See a sample reprint in PDF format.
- Order a reprint of this article now.

Reyes was the No. 2 leader of the Revolutionary Armed Forces of Colombia, or FARC, which has been at war with the Colombian government for more than four decades. His violent demise is a fitting end to a life devoted to masterminding atrocities against civilians. But the computer records expose new details of the terrorist strategy to bring down the government of Colombian President Álvaro Uribe, including a far greater degree of collaboration between the FARC and four Latin heads of government than had been previously known. In addition to Venezuelan President Hugo Chávez, they are President Rafael Correa of Ecuador, Nicaragua's President Daniel Ortega and Bolivian President Evo Morales.

Mr. Chávez is said to have been visibly distressed when told of the death of Reyes, a man he clearly admired. He also may have rea[...] was later reported that the Colombian [...] call to Reyes from the Venezuelan pre[...]

Note the association of leftist Latin American presidents with the FARC terrorists: yellow journalism pure and simple.

Mr. Chávez rapidly ordered 10 battalions to the Colombian border. Should the Colombian military cross into Venezuela in search of FARC, he warned, it would mean war. That may have seemed like an unnecessary act of machismo. But the Colombia military has long claimed that the FARC uses both Ecuador and Venezuela as safe havens. Now it had shown that it wasn't afraid to act on that information.

There is a third explanation for Mr. Chávez's panic when he learned of the strike: He was alarmed about the possibility that his links with Reyes would be exposed. Sure enough, when the Colombian national police retrieved Reyes's body from Ecuador, it also brought back several computers from the camp. Documents on those laptops show that Mr. Chávez and Reyes were not only ideological comrades, but also business partners and political allies in the effort to wrest power from Mr. Uribe.

The tactical discussions found in the documents are hair-raising enough. They show that the FARC busies itself with securing arms and explosives, selling cocaine, and otherwise

http://online.wsj.com/public/article_print/SB120510858118323265.html 20/03/200[illegible]

The Americas - WSJ.com

financing its terrorism operations through crime. In a memo last month, for example, a rebel leader discussed the FARC's efforts to secure 50 kilos of uranium, which it hoped to sell to generate income. In the same note, there is a reference to "a man who supplies me material for the explosive we are preparing, his name is Belisario and he lives in Bogotá . . ."

Though it is far from clear, Colombian national police speculated from this that a dirty bomb could be in the making. An April 2007 letter to the FARC secretariat lays out the terrorists' effort to acquire missiles from Lebanon. When Viktor Bout, allegedly one of the world's most notorious arms traffickers, was arrested in Thailand on Thursday, the Spanish-language press reported that he was located thanks to the Reyes computer files.

The maneuvers of thugs seeking power are r
relationship between the FARC and Mr. Chá
All four, it turns out, support FARC violenc

Here, the *Journal*, citing "the Spanish-language press," attributes Victor Bout's arrest in Thailand to information found on Reyes' computer. We know of course that it resulted from a sting operation that had been going on long before the attack on the FARC encampment.

According to the documents, Mr. Chávez's f
far as 1992, when he was in jail for an attem
him $150,000. Now he is returning the favor,
much as $300 million. But money is the least important of the Chávez gifts. He is also using his presidential credentials on behalf of the FARC.

The FARC puts a lot of effort toward discrediting Mr. Uribe in the court of world opinion. A September letter from a rebel commander to "secretariat comrades" reads: "As to the manifesto, I suggest adding the border policy and making it public by all means possible to see if we can stop all the world from supporting *uribismo* [the agenda of Mr. Uribe] in the October elections." He then proposes a "clandestine" meeting between one rebel and Mr. Chávez in Caracas to discuss "our political-military project." Mr. Chávez, the rebels say in a later document, suggested that the FARC videotape any Colombian military strikes in the jungle for propaganda purposes.

In January, FARC leader Manuel Marulanda (aka "Sureshot") wrote to Mr. Chávez: "You can imagine the happiness that you have awoken in all the leaders, guerrillas, the Bolivarian Movement of New Colombia [and] the Clandestine Communist Party with the plan you put forth . . . to ask for the analysis and approval of recognizing the FARC as a belligerent [therefore legitimate] force."

The documents also show why it was a good idea for Colombia not to ask Ecuador for permission before moving against the FARC camp -- even though in the past it had done so when tangling with the rebels at the border. A January memo reports on a FARC meeting with the Ecuadorean minister of security, who said that Mr. Correa is "interested in official relations with the FARC" and has decided not to aid Colombia against the rebels. "For [Ecuador] the FARC is an insurgent organization of the people, with social and political proposals that it understands," the memo reads.

It also says Mr. Correa plans to increase commercial and political relations with North Korea, and that he requests that one of the FARC's hostages be released to him next time, so as to "boost his political efforts." A Feb. 28 letter from Reyes summarizes a meeting with an emiss

Here the evil Ecuadoran President Correa is linked to axis-of-evil pariah state North Korea, a linkage that would also be applied to Victor Bout in a last-minute US move against him in Thailand.

http://online.wsj.com/public/article_print/SB120510858118323265.html 20/03/2009

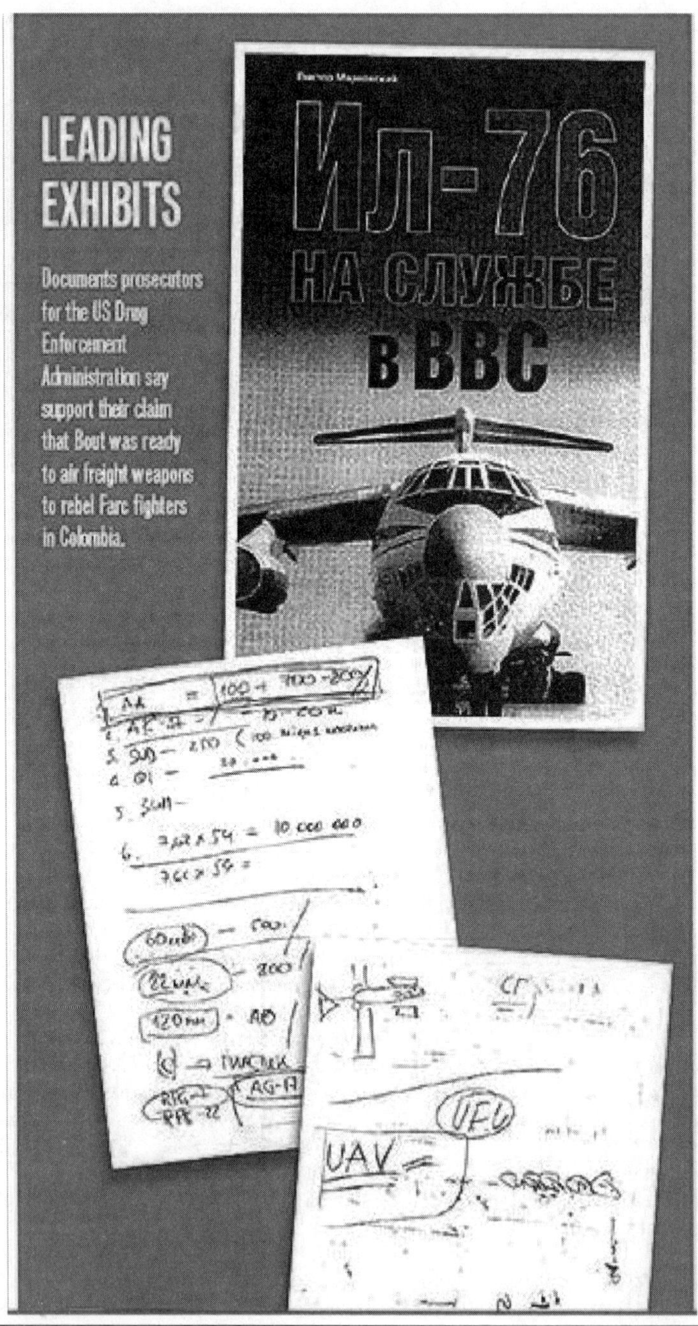

LEADING
EXHIBITS
Documents prosecutors for the US Drug Enforcement Administration say support their claim that Bout was ready to air freight weapons to rebel Farc fighters in Colombia.
Ил-76
НА СЛУЖБЕ
В ВВС
UAV

Doodles, allegedly drawn by Bout during his fateful meeting in Bangkok on March 6, 2008, moments before being apprehended by Thai secret police and DEA agents. Any evidentiary value was severely compromised by the fact that the doodles bear no resemblance to any writing known to come from Bout's own hand. It would appear that the forgery division at the Justice Department is not as capable as it once may have been.

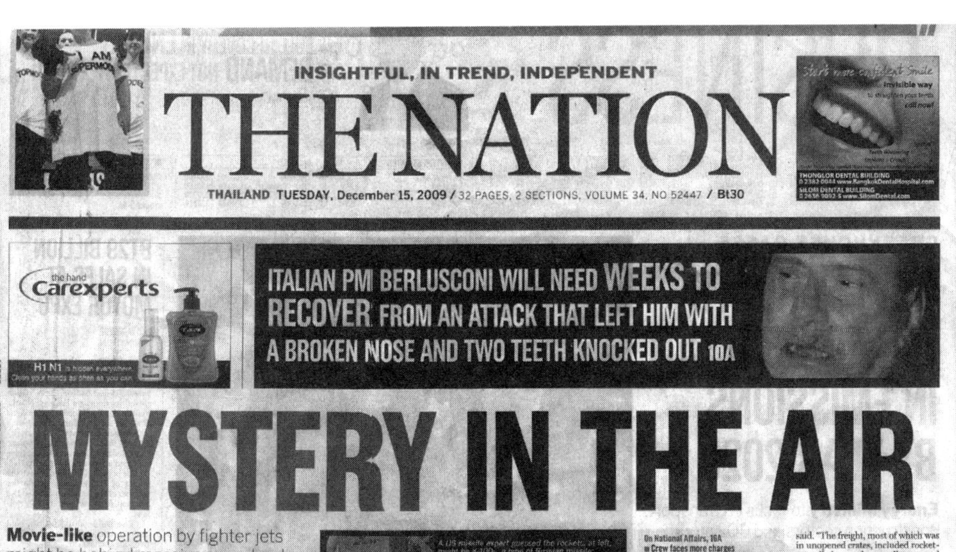

INSIGHTFUL, IN TREND, INDEPENDENT

THE NATION

THAILAND TUESDAY, December 15, 2009 / 32 PAGES, 2 SECTIONS, VOLUME 34, NO 52447 / Bt30

ITALIAN PM BERLUSCONI WILL NEED WEEKS TO RECOVER FROM AN ATTACK THAT LEFT HIM WITH A BROKEN NOSE AND TWO TEETH KNOCKED OUT 10A

MYSTERY IN THE AIR

Movie-like operation by fighter jets might be behind massive arms haul

THE NATION, AGENCIES

"There's much more to this story than what has been made public so far," Bertil Lintner, an author who has written extensively on North Korea, told *The New York Times* when asked about the massive arms seizure at Don Mueang airport over the weekend.

Why would you refuel in Thailand to begin with, while there's a place like Burma, which is more Pyongyang friendly?

It could have been that some fighter jets forced the cargo plane carrying weapons from North Korea to land at Don Mueang, leading to one of the world's largest hauls of illegal arms in violation of a UN resolution.

As the mystery deepens over the arms smugglers' final destination and how such a high-stakes operation was interdicted, US and Thai authorities remain tight-lipped as to how the Russian-made Ilyushin Il-76 cargo aircraft was taken over by Thai officials on Friday, with public information still sketchy and ambiguous if not totally contradictory.

However, one well-placed source indicated the aircraft could have been confronted by a fighter squadron that intercepted the cargo plane in midair almost immediately after it left North Korea and threatened to shoot it down if it failed to obey an ultimatum of landing in Bangkok. When it approached Thailand, the fighter squadron was replaced by another one taking off from the Philippines. Once the cargo plane entered Thai airspace, it was the Kingdom's jet fighters that took over and forced it to land.

"That was how the Thai authorities nabbed the pilots," the source said. "This is the first time illegal weapons weighing about 35 tonnes were seized, because arms smuggling has mostly gone undetected."

In its report yesterday, *The New York Times* quoted a senior White House official in Washington as saying Friday's interception had required "high-level coordination among intelligence agencies" that watched the shipment asis it was loaded in Pyongyang.

The seizuure was evidence the Barack Obamma administration would "aggressively , and rigorously implement" a UN S Security Council resolution passed in June after North Korea set off its second nuclear test.

The US would like to amplify the interception of the illegal arms smuggling as a success in its effort to enforce the UN ban on weapons exports by the North Korean government, an attempt to cut off the country's most profitable export, *The New York Times* said.

On National Affairs, 16A
- Crew faces more charges
- Embarrassing arms seizure
- Georgian firm leased plane

In another scenario of how the plane was seized, a Western diplomatic source told *The Nation* the cargo plane flew from the United Arab Emirates and stopped over in Bangkok for refuelling last Wednesday. At that time, the plane was empty.

When the same plane made a scheduled stopover in Bangkok for refuelling on its way back from North Korea, Thai intelligence officials were tipped off by the US that it was carrying an arms shipment, and they went to search it before uncovering the illegal weapons in the hold, the source said.

Acting Government Spokesman Panitan Wattanayagorn also said that after receiving tips from several intelligence agencies, the plane was boarded when it stopped for fuel before proceeding to Sri Lanka.

"Weapons experts will begin to unpack the cargo tomorrow," Panitan said. "The freight, most of which was in unopened crates, included rocket-propelled grenades, small arms and major weapons components."

Sceptics doubt a plane transporting such an illegal load would have to make a refuelling stop in Bangkok, because the flight time from North Korea is only five to six hours at the most.

They say the plane had enough fuel to fly to Sri Lanka before proceeding to the UAE, without having to land in Bangkok. From Sri Lanka, the plane might have travelled farther to Iran or other spots before unloading the weapons, they said.

The value of the weapons is difficult to estimate at this point.

"Say, it is worth US$1,000 [Bt33,100] a kilo, the total 40 tonnes would have been valued at $40 million," said the first source.

"The weapons, produced in North Korea by Russian technology, are mostly for use in guerrilla warfare, and they could end up in the hands of Hizbollah or Hamas. Most of the US helicopters shot down in Pakistan, Afghanistan and Iraq were fired on by the same type of shoulder- and truck-launched missiles that were loaded on the captured cargo plane."

Here and next page, English-language Thai newspaper coverage of an arms seizure. On Saturday, December 12, 2009, Thai authorities seized 35 tons of missiles and explosives from an Ilyushin-76 aircraft when it landed at Bangkok's Don Muang Airport en route from Pyongyang, North Korea. The weapons were packed into 140 crates, and included surface-to-air missiles, tube launchers with computerized weapon controls, and rocket-propelled grenades. In an the ensuing media circus in Bangkok, no effort has been spared in attempting to link the seized plane to Victor Bout. The US State Department claims that the seized aircraft has previously been registered with three companies identified by the US Treasury Department as being controlled by Bout. With the Thai appeals court only weeks away from deciding Bout's fate, this high-profile incident appears to have been calculated to influence the judges' decision. Sources, including a US State Department official, have told me that the impending release of this book has helped spur actions to both influence the Thai court's decision and discredit the book.

PILOT TO THAI POLICE: WE THOUGHT WEAPONS WERE OIL RIG EQUIPMENT

THE NATION

MYSTERY FLIGHT

An Ilyushin-76 aircraft was found carrying a huge quantity of weapons when it landed at Thailand's Don Mueang Airport on Saturday for refuelling.

Where was it from?

1 The plane left Ukraine for North Korea, stopping by at Azerbaijan, the United Arab Emirates and Thailand to refuel.

2 It was loaded with war weapons in North Korea's capital, Pyongyang.

3 The plane then headed back, making a stop for refuelling at Bangkok, where officials searched it and arrested all those on board. The pilot claimed the plane would be refuelled again in Colombo and the cargo would be offloaded in Ukraine.

UKRAINE
AZERBAIJAN
UNITED ARAB AMIRATES
SRI LANKA
THAILAND
NORTH KOREA (Pyongyang)

On board

Ilyas Isakov · Alexander Zrybnev · Mikhail Petukhov · Vitaly Shumkov · Viktor Abdullayev

Source: The Nation

NATION GRAPHICS

Deputy Prime Minister Suthep Thaugsuban, who oversees security affairs, will today convene a meeting of security agencies to discuss the case with armed forces chiefs.

Intelligence and security officials in various countries were scrambling yesterday to find out the destination of a massive consignment of war weapons found in Bangkok over the weekend in a plane arriving from North Korea.

As the security alert spread across continents, attention was focused on the Thai interrogation of the five foreign suspects, who reportedly claimed they thought they were transporting heavy equipment for oil rigs.

A North Korean dealer was probably responsible for the impounded consignment, weighing more than 35 tonnes, PM's Secretary-General Panitan Watayagorn yesterday quoted intelligence sources as saying.

"But we don't know to whom these weapons will be delivered," he said.

On Saturday, acting on a tip-off, Thai authorities seized the military weaponry, which included rocket-propelled grenades, surface-to-air missiles and ammunition from the military plane after it landed at the Don Mueang Airport for refuelling.

All five crew members are in police detention. They are Alexander Zrybnev, Viktor Abdullayev, Vitaly Shumkov and Ilyas Isakov from Kazakhstan, and Mikhail Petukhov from Belarus.

They denied charges of possessing war weapons and would defend themselves in court, police said.

Petukhov, who was the pilot, reportedly told interrogators that the plane picked up the goods in North Korea and would offload them in Ukraine.

During a six-hour interrogation by the Crime Suppression Division, he insisted that he had no knowledge about the war materials. Petukhov told investigators that he and his four companions were hired to transport goods and that he would only "provide other information in court".

Petukhov also reportedly admitted delivering such consignments three or four times before. The seized weapons are being stored at an air force arms depot at Takhli air base in Nakhon Sawan province.

The Thai government said this case involved many laws and Bangkok had to comply with the United Nations (UN) resolution. A report would be filed with the UN within 45 days.

Deputy Prime Minister Suthep Thaugsuban, who oversees security affairs, will today convene a meeting of security agencies to discuss the case with armed forces chiefs.

Kazakhstan is closely checking developments. "We can neither confirm nor reject this [registration] information so far. We are clarifying the circumstances of the incident through diplomatic channels, and the possibility of the aircraft's affiliation with Kazakh air companies," Kazakh Foreign Ministry spokesman Ilyas Omarov told *RIA Novosti*.

Where the weapons would be delivered also was not clear. Thai police said the plane was bound for a Middle East country. Meanwhile, Sri Lanka yesterday denied it was the destination. The pilot claimed the shipment was bound for Ukraine.

South Korean officials were on high alert.

"If the Thai government's announcement is true that North Korean weapons were on board, measures should be taken against the apparent violation of UN resolutions," an official at Seoul's Foreign Ministry said on condition of anonymity.

En route to Pyongyang, the plane refuelled three times – in Azerbaijan, the United Arab Emirates and Thailand – the pilot reportedly said. The flight plan was to stop for refuelling at Don Mueang and Sri Lanka and drop off the cargo in Ukraine.

Insisting that he had no knowledge about the war material aboard the aircraft, Petukhou told investigators that he and his four companions were hired to transport goods and that he would only "provide other information in court."

Police are scheduled to escort them to the Criminal Court today to seek further detention for interrogation.

As much as the mainstream press tries to portray my investigative journalism as conspiracy fiction, my discussions of the Shadow Masters have been drawing full houses across North America, Europe and Southeast Asia. Over 400 people packed an auditorium in Bologna for my conference on Bilderberg and its historical roots. Above is a press conference in Zagreb in late November 2009 about the Croatian release of *The True Story of the Bilderberg Group*. Joining me at the press conference were numerous political leaders representing anti-European Union interests. I urged Croatians to vote against joining the European Union: "A fascist type of assault on humanity is expressed as the elimination of national sovereignty through the mode of imperialist tyranny known as globalization, which, in itself, is just another word for Empire. Is that what you want for your country?"

Bilderberg has become a worldwide bestseller.

Leading mainstream periodicals and magazines are strarting to take notice. Here I am on the cover of *GeoPolitica*, a leading Serbian political magazine.

Index

A

Abraham, Yehuda 32, 147, 148, 157, 158
Abramovich, Roman 65, 66
Abrams, Elliot 81, 82
Ackerman & Palombo 35
Adelman, Kenneth 27, 192
Adulyadej, Bhumibol 230
Aeroflot 30, 49
African Development Company 180
Air Bas 159, 164, 165, 171, 172, 176, 182, 185, 186, 204
Airbus 164
Air Cess 145, 171, 172, 204
Al Baraka International Foundation 199
Albright, Madeleine 86, 91, 92, 93, 96
Alfred P. Sloan Foundation 167, 231
Alighieri, Dante 6
al-Qaeda 24, 32, 33, 91, 102, 146, 147, 149, 154, 155, 158, 159, 167, 170, 171, 181, 182, 184, 187, 202, 204, 214
al Suqami, Sattam 210
al-Zawahiri, Ayman 26
American Brodcasting Company (ABC) 141, 175
American Committee for Peace in Chechnya (ACPC) 27, 28
American Enterprise Institute 27
Aminov, Vadim Markovich 134, 137, 188
Amnesty International 102
Aquinas, Thomas 6
Arafat, Yassar 26
Arenzana, Pepe 16
Arizona Republic 80
Armitage, Richard 182
Arms and the Man 152, 202, 203
Aslund, Anders 51
Associated Press 23, 70, 120, 202, 213

B

Bank Menatep 48, 56
Bank of Credit and Commerce International (BCCI) 121
Bank of New York (BoNY) 44, 64, 66, 70, 71, 75
Bank of Nova Scotia 120, 123
Bank of Sydney 65
Barak, Ehud 150
Bath, James 165
Bemba, Jean-Pierre 140
Bend Sinister 233, 234
Berezovsky, Boris 27-31, 33, 40, 56, 65, 66, 73, 151
Berliner Zeitung 84
Berlusconi, Silvio 34, 37, 38
Bernays, Edward 215, 216, 231
Bertelsmann 192
Big White Lie, The 93
Bilderberg Group xi, 1, 3-6, 8, 9, 26, 77, 79, 81, 89, 96, 100, 111, 143, 144, 152, 153, 174, 192, 193, 212
bin Laden, Osama 92, 93, 106, 149, 154-158, 160, 165, 166, 184, 188, 202, 212, 220-224, 226, 231, 234
bin Laden, Saad 165, 166
bin Laden, Salem 165
Black, Lord Conrad 6, 88, 175
Blood from Stones 152
Bloomberg News 210
Blumenthal, Max 181
Blum, Jack 111
Blum, Robert 22
Bokeriya, Lev 102, 103
Borovoi, Alexander 40
Boston Globe 92
Bouchard, Lucien 4
Bout, Alla 138, 151
Bout, Sergey (Serguei) 132, 165
Bout, Victor 131-153, 158-219, 227-234
Boyes, Roger 109
Braun, Michael 190-194, 198
Braun, Stephen 147, 159, 170, 172, 177, 178, 183, 190-194, 198, 201-204
British Broadcasting Corporation (BBC) 48, 72, 114, 136, 141-143, 145, 162, 176, 232

Bronfman, Edgar 152
Brown & Root (see KBR, Inc)
Brown Brothers Harriman 71, 94
Brudno, Mikhail 57
Brzezinski, Zbigniew 26-28, 40, 44, 49, 50, 52, 73
Buitenweg, Kathalijne Maria 12
Bulakin, Viktor 134, 137, 188
Bundesnachrichtendienst (BND) 88, 89
Bush administration (GHW) 57
Bush administration 165, 170, 183, 210
Bush, George Herbert Walker 22, 23, 52, 82, 111, 119, 128, 165
Bush, George W. 23, 82, 101, 143, 164, 165, 210, 214
Bush, Neil 151
Bush, Prescott 71

C

Cable News Network (CNN) 136, 137, 141, 145
Calderón, Francisco Santos 213
Carlos the Jackal (Sánchez, Ilich Ramírez) 26
Carrington, Lord (Carington, Peter Alexander Rupert) 89
Carter administration 22
Carter, James Earl 44
Carter, Edwin Redwald 22, 37, 44
Casey, William 22, 23, 81, 122
Casper-Anserme, Loran 66
Ceku, Agim 92, 102
Center for Public Integrity 145, 168, 171, 172, 203
Center for Strategic and International Studies 74, 207, 210
Central Intelligence Agency (CIA) 22, 27, 28, 31, 34-36, 39, 40, 44, 63, 78, 79, 81, 88, 90, 93, 94, 96, 103-105, 111, 114, 120-122, 128, 129, 146, 159, 160, 163, 165, 167, 171, 179, 181, 186, 201, 207, 231
Chandler, Michael 159
Chase Manhattan Bank 94, 120
Chavez, Hugo 209
Cheney, Dick 151, 164, 171, 186, 203
Cherkesov, Viktor 49
Chichakli, Richard 133, 144, 153, 165-167, 172, 176, 178-182, 186
Chossudovsky, Michel 80, 89, 101, 104, 106, 107
Chretien, Jean 4
Christian Science Monitor 87, 202
Chubais, Anatoly 52
Citibank 120
Clark, Neil 41, 77, 101, 104
Clark, Wesley 89, 91- 93, 98, 100, 106
Clarke, Richard C. 163
Cleary, Sean 32
Clifford, Clark 121
Clines, Tom 111
Clinton administration 52, 54, 55, 57, 58, 62, 73, 87, 91, 92, 95, 128, 159, 161, 163, 164, 168
Clinton, William J. 23, 57, 58, 79, 89, 91, 93, 96, 98, 143, 150
Clive, Robert 117
Coalition Provisional Authority (CPA) 183, 186
Cohelo, Tony 71
Coleman, John 128, 204, 216
Collateral (film) 152
Columbia Broadcasting System (CBS) 71, 141, 175
Concordantia Catholica 6
ConsortiumNews 24
Conspirators' Hierarchy: The Story of the Committee of 300 216
Copeland, Miles 166, 167
Correa, Rafael 209
Council on Foreign Relations (CFR) 25, 79, 81, 82, 86, 89, 91, 92, 93, 96, 143, 174, 175, 176, 212, 216
Crossing the Rubicon 94, 95, 129
Cyril, Saint 136

D

Dagens Nyheter 86
da Vinci. Leonardo 7
Dayle, Dennis 111

Dearlove, Richard 215
de Brie, Christian 95, 122, 129
Deep Cover (book) 93
Defense Energy Support Center (DESC) 185
Defense Intelligence Agency (DIA) 90
de Maillard, Jean 95, 122
De Monarchia Mundi 6
Der Kosovo-Konflikt. Wege in einen vermeidbaren Krieg (*The Kosovo Conflict: Road to an Avoidable War*) 86
Der Spiegel 169
DeStefano, Anthony M. 113
Deutch, John 110
Direction Générale de la Sécurité Extérieure (DGSE) 122
Djukic, Djordje 81
Djurdjevic, Bob 80, 104
Dokmanovic, Slavko 80, 81
Donohue, Daniel 35
Donovan, Bill 166
Drug Enforcement Administration (DEA) 93, 104, 109, 111, 135, 138, 148, 159, 188-191, 193, 195, 196, 198, 201, 206-208, 214, 217, 227, 231, 232
Dubov, Vladimir 57
Dulles, Allen 121
D'yachenko, Tatiana 65
Dyncorp 164
Dzerzinski, Felix 48

E

Edicioni 185
Eisenhower, Dwight 122
El Espectador 213
el Hage, Wadih 154
El Tiempo 209
Emery, Frederick 216
Engdahl, F. William 21, 41
Environmental Crime Prevention Program (ECPP) 37, 38
Environmental Security, Inc. (ESI) 38, 39
Ergenekon 126
Erinys 31, 32, 40
Estulin, Daniel x, xi, xii, 1, 10-13, 16, 17, 138, 161, 177, 191-194, 233
Etchegaray, Patricio 210
Evrobank 58
External Intelligence Service (*Sluzhba Vneshnei Razvedki*, SVR) 47, 170

F

Falcon Express (Dubai) 164
Falcone, Pierre 199
Farah, Douglas 137, 138, 145, 151, 152, 159, 166-170, 172, 174-177, 183, 184, 201-204
Farrell, Ellis 58, 74
Federal Bureau of Investigation (FBI) 35, 43, 64, 65, 68, 125, 146, 147, 159, 170, 182, 201, 213
Federal Security Bureau (FSB, Russian Federation) 25, 28, 30, 31, 33, 37, 49, 122
Feingold, Russell 183
Ferguson, Charles 212, 213, 217, 219, 220
Filatov, Sergey 30
Fimaco 58
Financial Times 55, 60, 63, 74, 187, 204
First American Bankshares 121
Fischer, David 26
Fitts, Catherine Austin 119
Flounders, Sara 78, 104, 106
Forbes 57, 151
Foreign Affairs 15, 25, 30
Frankfurter Rundschau 85
Freedom Gold (front company) 181
Freeland, Chrystia 55
Freud, Sigmund 215, 231
Friedman, Robert 45, 72, 192
Frontline 150, 151, 201-203
Fuerzas Armadas Revolucionarias de Colombia – Ejército del Pueblo (FARC) 120, 126, 177, 188-190, 194-198, 207-215, 217-219, 222, 224, 226, 227, 231

G

Gadhafi, Moammar 140, 209
Gaidar, Yegor 30, 52
Garratt, Jonathan 32
Gates, Jeff 24, 25, 41
Gates, Robert M. 23,
Gaydamak, Arkady 41, 199
Geithner, Tim 21
Gelbard, Robert 87
General Electric 94, 120, 152, 153
Gilbert, John William 87
Girard, Renaud 83
Giuliani, Rudolph 151
Global Research 27, 41, 107
Glushkov, Nokolai 30
Godfather of the Kremlin 73, 151
Goebbels, Josef 232
Goldfarb, Alex 31, 33, 41
Golubyev, Valery 49
Gongadze, Heorhiy 31
Gorbachev, Mikhail 22, 49
Gordievsky, Oleg 31
Gore, Al 52, 71, 89, 92, 93
Gotti, John Jr 120
GQ 135
Graham, Katherine x, 175
Grand Chessboard: American Primacy and its Geostrategic Imperatives, The 28, 44, 49, 52, 73
Grasso, Richard A. 120
Greene, Graham x
Grigg, William Norman 82
Grobe, Karl 85
Groot Bijgaarden De Standaard 161
Gryzlov, Boris 49
Guardian 28, 134, 136, 142, 201
Guyatt, David 45, 72

H

Hagon, Christopher 35
Haig, Alexander 27
Halliburton 164, 171, 182, 185, 186, 203
Hamas 154
Hamilton, Alexander 70
Hamilton, Lee 23
Harrison-Kroll Environmental Services, Inc 36
Harwood, Richard 175
Hastings, Warren 117
Helms, Richard 121
Hen, Hazki 32
Heritage Foundation 231
Hezbollah 154, 155, 156, 202, 226
Hitler, Adolph 22
Holbrooke, Richard 79, 80, 89, 93, 96
Hollinger Corporation 175
Homeland Security 179
Hong Kong and Shanghai Bank 120, 123
Hong Kong and Shanghai Corporation (BHSH) 123, 124
Hoover Institute 49
Hudson Institute 174-176, 231
Human Rights Watch 102
Hussein, Saddam 214, 216, 223

I

Illicit: How Smugglers, Traffickers and Copycats are Hijacking the Global Economy 159
Incident Management Group (IMG) 35, 36, 37, 39
Independent 34
India Today 147, 201
Inkombank 70
International Association of Lawyers Against Nuclear Arms (IALANA) 85
International Atomic Energy Agency 40
International Consortium of Investigative Journalists 139, 144, 172
International Crisis Group (ICG) 98, 99, 100
International Monetary Fund 40, 52, 54, 55, 57-68, 74, 77, 78, 100, 112
International Narcotics Control Board 114
International Narcotics Control Strategy Report 125

Interpol 62-66, 70, 90, 92, 93, 106, 137, 139, 146, 159, 164, 182, 201
Investor's Business Daily (*IBD*) 213
Iran-Contra affair 22, 23, 81, 82, 110, 111
ISC Global UK 29
Isikoff, Michael 171, 183, 185, 203
Ivanov, Sergei 49
Ivanov, Viktor 49

J

Jackson, Bruce P. 26
Jacob, Cyril 157
Jane's Intelligence Review 88, 109
Jemaah Islamiya 33
Johnson, Lyndon B. 121
J.P. Morgan Chase 71, 167

K

Karni, Asher 33
Kasianov, Mikhail 64
Kasper-Ansermet, Laurent 66
Kati, Cassin Abdullah 199
KBR, Inc 164, 171, 172, 182, 185, 186
Kellogg Brown & Root (see KBR, Inc.)
Kelly, Martin 29
Kennedy, John F. 5, 42
Kersovic, Tomislav 90
Khalezov, Dimitri 218, 219, 220, 221, 222, 223, 226, 227
Khlebnikov, Paul 57
Khodorkovsky, Mikhail 27, 41, 56, 57
Khomeini, Ayatollah 23
Kichikhin, Viktor 48
Kipling, Rudyard 96
Kirk, Mark 78
Kissinger, Henry 3, 28, 79, 89
Klebnikov, Paul 73, 151
Koevoet 32
Koljevic, Nikola 81
Kolko, Richard 213
Komitet gosudarstvennoy bezopasnost (KGB) 3, 20, 25, 26, 29, 30, 31, 33, 35, 37, 40, 42, 44, 45-49, 56, 63, 71, 103, 137, 231, 233, 234
Korzhakov, Alexander 54
Kosovo Diplomatic Mission (KDOM) 78
Kosovo Foundation for an Open Society (KFOS) 100
Kosovo Liberation Army (KLA) 27, 78, 82-85, 87-96, 99-102, 105, 106, 110, 112, 114, 128
Kouchner, Bernard 100
Kouwenhoven, Gus 198, 199
Kovtun, Dmitri 30
Kozirev, Andrei 30
Kroll Associates 35, 36, 37, 39
Kroll, Jules 36
Kuchma, Leonid 31

L

Lakhani, Hemant 147, 148, 157, 163, 201
Landesman, Peter 137, 151, 152, 153, 163, 187, 202-204
La Razón 14
La Repubblica 34, 35, 37, 40
Larrea, Gustavo 209
La Stampa 35
Last of the Mohicans, The 152
Laughland, John 27, 41, 105
Lazard Frères 13, 152, 152, 192
Lebedev, Platon 57
Ledeen, Michael 27
Leeuw, Ruud 133, 145
Le Figaro 83
Le Monde 83, 95, 121, 122, 129, 204
Leonhart, Michele M. 189
Levine, Michael 90, 93, 94
Lewis, James 210, 211
Libby, Scooter 151
Lieberman, Joe 92, 93
Limarev, Yevgeni 31
Lippmann, Walter 215, 216
Litvinenko, Alexander 25-35, 37, 39-42, 231, 233, 234
Loquai, Heinz 86
Lord of War 188
Los Angeles Times 61, 74, 82, 105, 139, 145, 170, 171, 175, 177, 182, 185, 201, 204, 211, 212
Lugovoi, Andrei 30

M

Madsen, Wayne 36, 150, 151, 187, 201-204
Maher, Ted 67, 181
Makhlouf, Adnan 181
Malone, John C. 71
Malthus, Thomas 118
Mann, Michael 152
Marino, Filippo 35, 36
Marshall, Tim 78
Massoud, Ahmed Shah 140
Matheson, Alexander 117
McGuire, Brendon Robert 194
McVeigh, Timothy 226
Men's Journal 131, 134, 135, 201
Merchant of Death: Money, Guns, Planes, and the Man Who Makes War Possible 131, 132, 134, 137, 141, 143, 151, 164, 166, 170, 172, 177, 184, 188, 192, 194, 197, 201-203, 228, 234
Mercy International Relief Agency 158
Messier, Jean-Claude 152
MI5 63, 72
MI6 31, 33, 63, 90, 91, 122, 164, 215
Miami Herald 209, 210, 211
Middle East Intelligence Bulletin 155, 202
Military Professional Resources Inc. (MPRI) 90
Mill, John Stuart 118
Miloševic, Slobodan 77, 78, 85, 99-104, 106
Minin, Leonid 148-151, 170, 172-174, 202
Mitrokhin Commission 37, 38
Mitrokhin, Vasili 33, 37
Mitterrand, Francois 199
Mitterrand, Jean-Christophe 199
Morgan Stanley 167
Moscow News 31
Moscow Times 158, 159
Mossad 37, 63, 67, 122, 154
Mother Jones 105, 165, 167, 185, 203
Mulligan, Mary Elizabeth 192-195
Mulroney, Brian 4
Music Corporation of America (MCA) 152
Mutschke, Ralf 92, 106

N

Nabokov, Vladimir 233
Naím, Moisés 159
Naranjo, Oscar 210, 213
Nation, The 181
National Broadcasting Company (NBC) 141, 152, 175
National Security Agency (NSA) 36, 104, 105, 142, 143, 157, 159, 187
National Security Council (NSC) 53, 163
Negodov, Nikolai 49
Nemanja, Stefan 97
Nevzlin, Leonid 27, 41, 57
New American (magazine) 90
NewsHawk 217
New Statesman 101, 104, 106
Newsweek 23, 171, 172, 183, 185, 203
New Yorker 45
New York Press 102, 107
New York Times 23, 54, 74, 82, 83, 97, 105, 106, 136, 141, 145, 172, 175, 203, 233, 234
New York Times Magazine 134, 151, 162, 163, 187, 202
Nezavisimaya Gazeta 101
Nicole, Ana 5
North American Union 5
North Atlantic Treaty Organization (NATO) 19, 27, 58, 78-80, 82-87, 89, 91, 92, 94, 96, 98, 100, 105, 110, 125, 170, 232
North, Oliver 81, 105, 1117

O

Obama, Barack 23
Observatoire Geopolitique des Drogues 112, 124
Observer 39, 59, 78, 81, 202
Odney, Derek 191, 192, 195, 196, 219
Office of Foreign Assets Control (OFAC) 176, 178, 179, 182-184

Office of Strategic Services (OSS) 122, 166
Omar, Mullah 168, 223
Operation Blessing 180, 181
Opium, Empire and the Global Political Economy 115
Organization for Security and Co-operation in Europe (OSCE) 82-84, 86
Owen, David 28, 201

P

Palestine Liberation Organization (PLO) 156
Palombo, Louis F. 35, 36
Panorama 38
Parenti, Michael 86, 106
Parry, Robert 23, 24, 41
Pasqua, Charles 199
Patarkatsishvili, Badri 30
Patrushev, Nikolai 49
Paulson, Henry 21
Pavlov, Valentin 45
Peleman, Johan 161, 162, 173, 199
Pellnäs, Bo 86
Penders, Michael J. 38, 39
Peres, Shimon 150
Perle, Richard 27, 81, 98, 164
Permanent Intergovernmental Conference for Environmental Crime Prevention 35
Perry, Curtis 35
Perry, William J. 89
Petras, James 69
Pilger, John 77, 87, 104, 106
Pirani, Simon 58, 74
Plato 7
Popovski, Toni 39
Potanin, Vladimir 52, 55
Powell, Collin 214
Primakov, Yuri 56
Project for a New American Century (PNAC) 27
Propaganda 215
Public Broadcasting Service (PBS) 150, 168, 185, 201-203
Pugachov, Sergei 49
Putin, Vladimir 20, 26-31, 33, 48, 49, 71, 72, 74, 170

Q

Quinn, John 217

R

Rabbani, Burhanuddin 168
Racak (village) 81-84
Radin, Charles A. 92
Reagan, Ronald 20, 22, 23, 81, 122
Reddaway, Peter 54, 73
Regional Environmental Centre for Central and Eastern Europe 39
Republic National Bank of New York 64, 66
Revolutionary United Front (RUF) 149, 155
Reyes, Raul 120, 209, 210, 213, 214, 224, 227
Rice, Condoleezza 187, 190, 208
Rich, Marc 150, 151
Riley, David 59
Robertson, Pat 180, 181
Rockefeller, David 4, 8, 9, 89, 121
Rodriguez, Felix 105, 111
Romodanovsky, Konstantin 49
Roper, Richard 179
Rothschild, Jacob 28, 63
Royal Bank of Scotland 120
Royal Institute for International Affairs 216
Rumsfeld, Donald 164
Ruppert, Michael C. 94, 95, 106, 110, 115, 128, 129
Ruprah, Sanjivan 147-149, 151, 153, 163
Russian Central Bank 58
Russian Federation 54, 58, 71, 72

S

Sabagh, Amal A. 179
Sachs, Jeffrey D. 44, 51, 52
Sackville, Tom 125

Safra, Edmond 64, 66, 67, 68, 113
San Air General Trading 177
San Air UAE 178
San Air USA 178
San Francisco Chronicle 112, 128
SAS 90, 91
Sasoon, David 118
Savimbi, Jonas 32, 139
Scaramella, Mario 34-40
Scarlett, John 33
Scharping, Rudolf 85, 86
Scherer, Michael 165, 203, 204
Schneidman, Whitney 142, 143
Scotland Yard 35
Scotsman 42, 90
Scribner, Yusill 194
SEC 36
Sechin, Igor 49
Secord, Richard 111
Secrecy and Privilege: Rise of the Bush Dynasty from Watergate to Iraq 23
Seko, Mobutu Sese 140
Semenchenko, Andrei 178
Sendero Luminoso (Shining Path) 224
Shackley, Ted 111
Shadowplay 78
Shalom, Avram 37
Shanghai Cooperation Organization (SCO) 20
Shestopalov, Mikhail Yosifovich 56
Shevardnadze, Eduard 101
Shin Beth 37
Shishakli, Adib 165-167
Shutt, Harry 60
Shvets, Yuri 31
Silverstein, Ken 149
Smith, Adam 15, 118, 163
Smith, Gayle 163
Smith, Phillip 320
Smulian, Andrew 188, 189, 191-195, 207, 208, 214
Socrates 7
Sokolenko, Vyachenslav 30
Solana, Javier 83, 96
Solarz, Stephen 98
Solon 7
Soros, George 89, 98, 100-102, 106, 107
SourceWatch 32
Soviet Union ix, 43-46, 48, 49, 52, 57, 77, 78, 100, 125, 127, 133, 138, 139, 145, 146, 232
Special Research Monitoring Centre (SRMC) 35
Spectre Group 190
Stanton, John 36
Stasi 63
Stepashin, Sergei 49
Stephanopoulos, George 89
Stephens, Chris 91, 106
Stewart, William 124, 129
Stiglitz, Joseph 55
Stock, Harley 35
Strategic Research Institute of the United States (SIRIUS) 93
Strydom, Francois 32
Sukhorenko, Stepan 103
Sultanov, Oleg 28, 29
Sunday Express (UK) 158, 202
Sunday Times (UK) 29, 91, 105, 106, 203
Surkov, A.P. 47, 72
Szamuely, George 82-84, 102, 105, 107
Szubin, Adam 176

T

Talbot, Karen 52, 101, 107
Taliban 53, 73, 115, 129, 149, 157-159, 167-172, 182, 184, 187, 214, 222, 223
Talty, Stephan 134, 135, 201
Tavistock Institute of Human Relations 175, 216
Taylor, Charles 72, 139, 149, 150, 152, 180, 181, 184, 187, 199, 201, 204
Thaci, Hashim 27, 92, 96
Time 75, 141, 200
Times (UK) 29, 33, 68, 109
Timmons, Ned 36
Titon International 31, 32, 39, 40
Todorovic, Alex 92

Toronto Star 137
Transnational Threats Update 207
Trepashkin, Michael 31
Trepca (mines) 89, 97, 98, 99, 100, 106
Trist, Eric 216
Trocki, Carl 115, 129
Trud 45
Truth in Media 80, 89

U

União Nacional para a Independência Total de Angola (UNITA) 32
United Nations Mission in Kosovo (UNMIK) 98-100, 106
USSR 20, 37, 39, 44, 45, 134, 136
Ustinov, Vladimir 49

V

Vasiliev, Dmitri 61
Vazevit, Robert Sahari 148
Velrooy, André 139, 144
Ventura, Jesse 1-3, 5, 6, 7, 13, 16
Veterans Today 24, 41
Vivendi SA 152, 153
Volkov, Nickolai 66
von Kirchbach, Hans Peter 85
Vorovskoi Mir (Thieves' World) 49

W

Wager, Robert 36
Wainwright, Philip 43
Walker, William 81- 84
Wall Street Journal 54, 63, 73, 106, 113, 141, 175
Wall Street Journal Europe 63
Washington Monthly 149, 168
Washington Post 32, 42, 82, 84, 105, 141, 145, 159, 172, 175, 201-204, 232
Washington Times 80, 92, 172, 211, 212
Wattanasin, Jittakorn 189
Wayne, Anthony 90, 106
WayneMadsenReport 36
Weishaupt, Adam 315
Williamson, Anne 54, 55, 59, 73, 74
Winer, Jonathan M. 164
WMD Insights 213
Wolfowitz, Paul 26, 98, 172, 182, 183
Wolosky, Lee Scott 143
Woolsey, James 27
Works, Ben 93, 119
World Bank 52, 59, 73, 77, 78, 99, 100, 107

X

X-55 206, 207, 215, 227

Y

Yakunin, Vladimir 49
Yeltsin, Boris 20, 49, 51-59, 65, 71, 72, 231
Yosifovich, Mikhail 56
Yukos 28, 41, 56, 57

Z

Zakayev, Ahmed 29
Zaostrovtsev, Yuriy 49

TrineDay's Featured Titles

The True Story of the Bilderberg Group

BY DANIEL ESTULIN

More than a center of influence, the Bilderberg Group is a shadow world government, hatching plans of domination at annual meetings ... and under a cone of media silence.

THE TRUE STORY OF THE BILDERBERG GROUP goes inside the secret meetings and sheds light on why a group of politicians, businessmen, bankers and other mighty individuals formed the world's most powerful society. As Benjamin Disraeli, one of England's greatest Prime Ministers, noted, "The world is governed by very different personages from what is imagined by those who are not behind the scenes."

Included are unpublished and never-before-seen photographs and other documentation of meetings, as this riveting account exposes the past, present and future plans of the Bilderberg elite.

Softcover: **$24.95** (ISBN: 9780979988622) • 432 pages • Size: 6 x 9

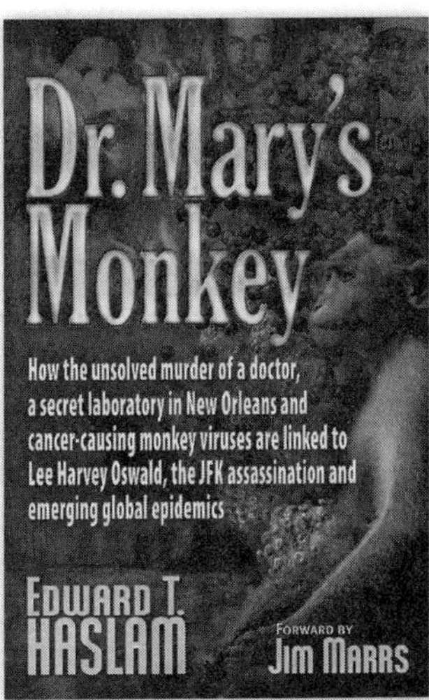

Dr. Mary's Monkey

How the Unsolved Murder of a Doctor, a Secret Laboratory in New Orleans and Cancer-Causing Monkey Viruses are Linked to Lee Harvey Oswald, the JFK Assassination and Emerging Global Epidemics

BY EDWARD T. HASLAM, FOREWORD BY JIM MARRS

Evidence of top-secret medical experiments and cover-ups of clinical blunders

The 1964 murder of a nationally known cancer researcher sets the stage for this gripping exposé of medical professionals enmeshed in covert government operations over the course of three decades. Following a trail of police records, FBI files, cancer statistics, and medical journals, this revealing book presents evidence of a web of medical secret-keeping that began with the handling of evidence in the JFK assassination and continued apace, sweeping doctors into cover-ups of cancer outbreaks, contaminated polio vaccine, the genesis of the AIDS virus, and biological weapon research using infected monkeys.

Softcover: **$19.95** (ISBN: 0977795306) • 320 pages • Size: 5 1/2 x 8 1/2

The Oil Card

Global Economic Warfare in the 21st Century

BY JAMES NORMAN

Challenging the conventional wisdom surrounding high oil prices, this compelling argument sheds an entirely new light on free-market industry fundamentals.

By deciphering past, present, and future geopolitical events, it makes the case that oil pricing and availability have a long history of being employed as economic weapons by the United States. Despite ample world supplies and reserves, high prices are now being used to try to rein in China — a reverse of the low-price strategy used in the 1980s to deprive the Soviets of hard currency. Far from conspiracy theory, the debate notes how the US has previously used the oil majors, the Saudis, and market intervention to move markets — and shows how this is happening again.

Softcover **$14.95** (ISBN 0977795390) • 288 PAGES • Size: 5.5 x 8.5

The Franklin Scandal

A Story of Powerbrokers, Child Abuse & Betrayal

BY NICK BRYANT

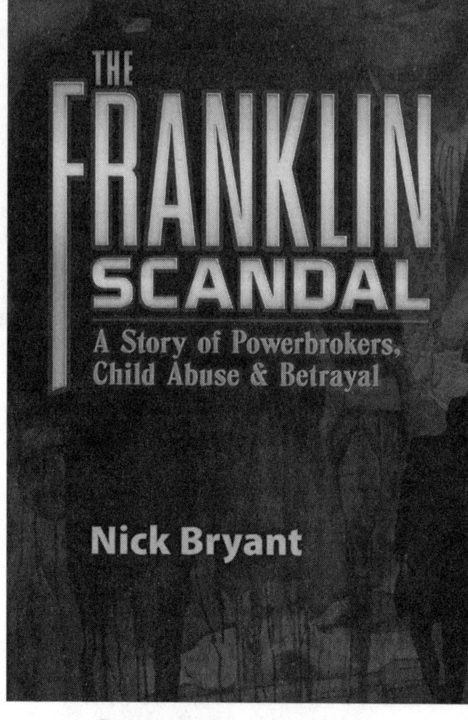

A chilling exposé of corporate corruption and government cover-ups, this account of a nationwide child-trafficking and pedophilia ring tells a sordid tale of corruption in high places. The scandal originally surfaced during an investigation into Omaha, Nebraska's failed Franklin Federal Credit Union and took the author beyond the Midwest and ultimately to Washington, DC. Implicating businessmen, senators, major media corporations, the CIA, and even the venerable Boys Town organization, this extensively researched report includes firsthand interviews with key witnesses and explores a controversy that has received scant media attention.

The Franklin Scandal is the story of a underground ring that pandered children to a cabal of the rich and powerful. The ring's pimps were a pair of Republican powerbrokers who used Boys Town as a pedophiliac reservoir, and had access to the highest levels of our government and connections to the CIA.

Nick Bryant is a journalist whose work largely focuses on the plight of disadvantaged children in the United States. His mainstream and investigative journalism has been featured in *Gear, Playboy, The Reader*, and on Salon.com. He is the coauthor of *America's Children: Triumph of Tragedy*. He lives in New York City.

Hardcover: **$24.95** (ISBN: 0977795357) • 676 pages • Size: 6x9

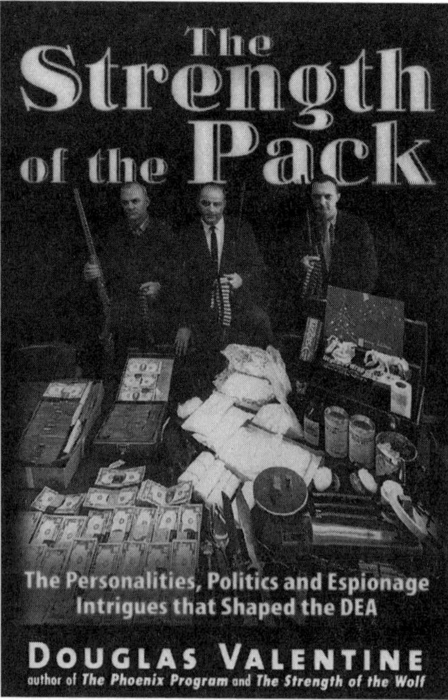

The Strength of the Pack

The Personalities, Politics and Espionage Intrigues that Shaped the DEA

BY DOUG VALENTINE

Through interviews with former narcotics agents, politicians, and bureaucrats, this exposé documents previously unknown aspects of the history of federal drug law enforcement from the formation of the Bureau of Narcotics and Dangerous Drugs and the creation of the Drug Enforcement Administration (DEA) up until the present day. Written in an easily accessible style, the narrative examines how successive administrations expanded federal drug law enforcement operations at home and abroad; investigates how the CIA comprised the war on drugs; analyzes the Reagan, Bush, and Clinton administrations' failed attempts to alter the DEA's course; and traces the agency's evolution into its final and current stage of "narco-terrorism."

Douglas Valentine is a former private investigator and consultant and the author of *The Hotel Tacloban, The Phoenix Program, The Strength of the Wolf*, and *TDY*.

Softcover: **$24.95** (ISBN: 9780979988653) • 480 pages • Size: 6x9

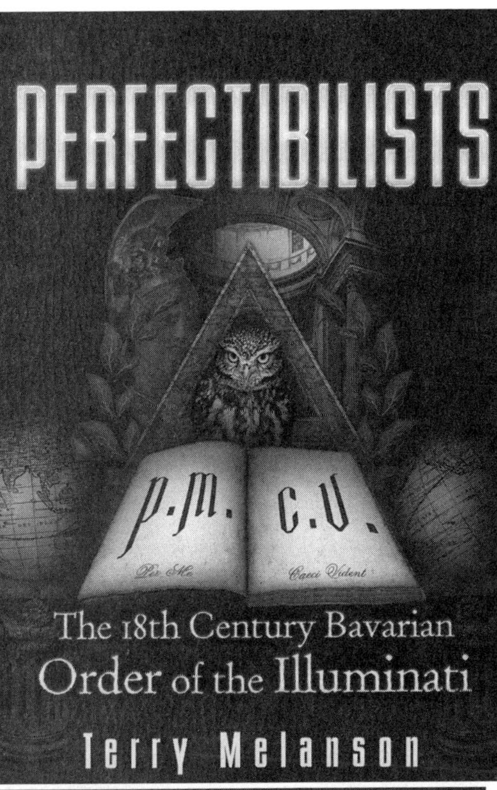

Perfectibilists

The 18th Century Bavarian Illuminati

by Terry Melanson

The shadowy Illuminati grace many pages of fiction as the sinister all-powerful group pulling the strings behind the scenes, but very little has been printed in English about the actual Enlightenment-era secret society, its activities, its members, and its legacy ... until now.

First choosing the name Perfectibilists, their enigmatic leader Adam Weishaupt soon thought that sounded too bizarre and changed it to the Order of the Illuminati.

Presenting an authoritative perspective, this definitive study chronicles the rise and fall of the fabled Illuminati, revealing their methods of infiltrating governments and education systems, and their blueprint for a successful cabal, which echoes directly forward through groups like the Order of Skull & Bones to our own era.

Featuring biographies of more than 400 confirmed members and copiously illustrated, this book brings light to a 200-year-old mystery.

Softcover: **$19.95** (ISBN: 9780977795381) • 530 pages • Size: 6 x 9

ORDER BY ONLINE OR BY PHONE:
TrineDay.com
1-800-556-2012

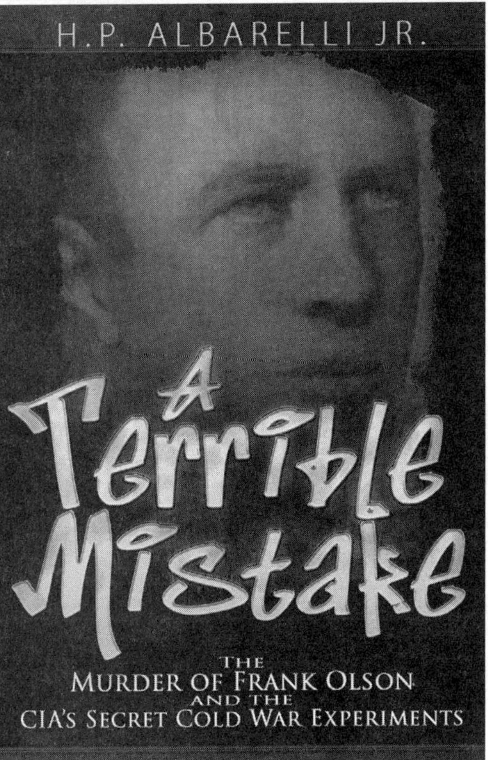

A Terrible Mistake

The Murder of Frank Olson and the CIA's Secret Cold War Experiments

by H.P. Albarelli Jr.

In his nearly 10 years of research into the death of Dr. Frank Olson, writer and investigative journalist H.P. Albarelli Jr. gained unique and unprecedented access to many former CIA, FBI, and Federal Narcotics Bureau officials, including several who actually oversaw the CIA's mind-control programs from the 1950s to the early 1970s.

A Terrible Mistake takes readers into a frequently bizarre and always frightening world, colored and dominated by Cold War concerns and fears. For the past 30 years the death of biochemist Frank Olson has ranked high on the nation's list of unsolved and perplexing mysteries. *A Terrible Mistake* solves the mystery and reveals in shocking detail the identities of Olson's murderers. The book also takes readers into the strange world of government mind-control programs and close collaboration with the Mafia.

H. P. Albarelli Jr. is an investigative journalist whose work has appeared in numerous publications and newspapers across the nation and is the author of the novel *The Heap*. He lives in Tampa, Florida.

Hardcover • $34.95 ISBN 978-0977795376 • 912 pages

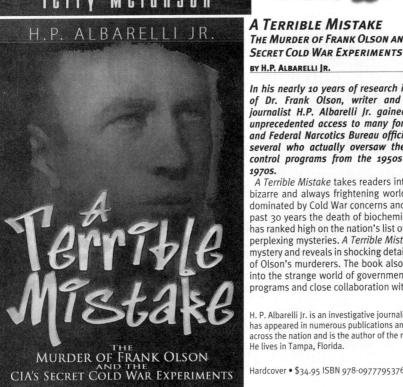

Expendable Elite

One Soldier's Journey into Covert Warfare

BY DANIEL MARVIN , FOREWORD BY MARTHA RAYE

A special operations perspective on the Viet Nam War and the truth about a White House concerned with popular opinion

This true story of a special forces officer in Viet Nam in the mid-1960s exposes the unique nature of the elite fighting force and how covert operations are developed and often masked to permit — and even sponsor — assassination, outright purposeful killing of innocents, illegal use of force, and bizarre methods in combat operations. ***Expendable Elite*** reveals the fear that these warriors share with no other military person: not fear of the enemy they have been trained to fight in battle, but fear of the wrath of the US government should they find themselves classified as "expendable." This book centers on the CIA mission to assassinate Cambodian Crown Prince Nordum Sihanouk, the author's unilateral aborting of the mission, the CIA's dispatch of an ARVN regiment to attack and destroy the camp and kill every person in it as retribution for defying the agency, and the dramatic rescue of eight American Green Berets and hundreds of South Viet Namese.

—NEW SPECIAL VICTORY EDITION— Commemorating our Free Speech Federal Court triumph that allows you to read this book exposing the true ways of war!

—READ THE BOOK,"THEY" DON'T WANT YOU TO!—

DANIEL MARVIN is a retired Lieutenant Colonel in the US Army Special Forces and former Green Beret.

Softcover: **$19.95** (ISBN 0977795314) • 420 pages • 150+ photos & maps

The Octopus Conspiracy

and Other Vignettes of the Counterculture from Hippies to High Times to Hip Hop and Beyond ...

BY STEVEN HAGER

Insightful essays on the genesis of subcultures from new wave and yuppies to graffiti and rap.

From the birth of hip-hop culture in the South Bronx to the influence of nightclubs in shaping the modern art world in New York, a generation of countercultural events and icons are brought to life in this personal account of the life and experiences of a former investigative reporter and editor of High Times. Evidence from cutting-edge conspiracy research including the real story behind the JFK assassination and the Franklin Savings and Loan cover-up is presented. Quirky personalities and compelling snapshots of life in the 1980s and 1990s emerge in this collection of vignettes from a landmark figure in journalism.

STEVEN HAGER is the author of ***Adventures in Counterculture, Art After Midnight,*** and ***Hip Hop.*** He is a former reporter for the New York Daily News and an editor of ***High Times.***

Hardcover: **$19.95** (ISBN 0975290614) • 320 pages • Size: 6 x 9

Fixing America

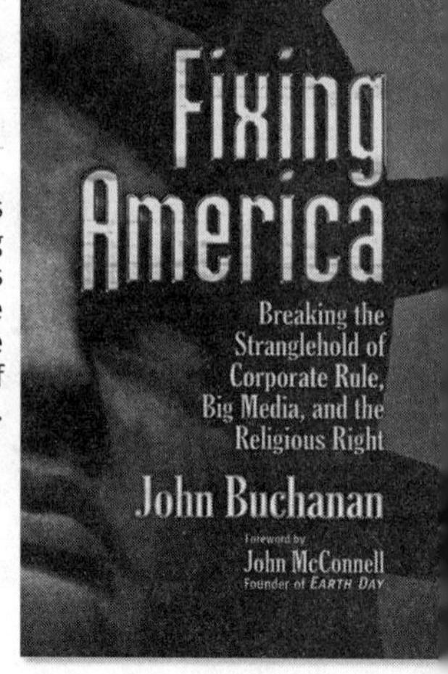

Breaking the Strangehold of Corporate Rule, Big Media, and the Religious Right

BY JOHN BUCHANAN, FOREWORD BY JOHN MCCONNELL

An explosive analysis of what ails the United States

An award-winning investigative reporter provides a clear, honest diagnosis of corporate rule, big media, and the religious right in this damning analysis. Exposing the darker side of capitalism, this critique raises alarms about the security of democracy in today's society, including the rise of the corporate state, the insidious role of professional lobbyists, the emergence of religion and theocracy as a right-wing political tactic, the failure of the mass media, and the sinister presence of an Orwellian neo-fascism.

Softcover: **$19.95**, (ISBN 0-975290681) 216 Pages, 5.5 x 8.5

The 9/11 Mystery Plane
And the Vanishing of America

by Mark Gaffney

Foreword by

Dr. David Ray Griffin

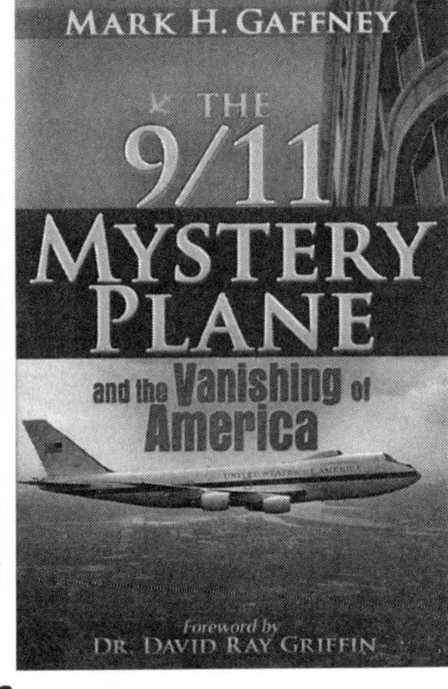

Unlike other accounts of the historic attacks on 9/11, this discussion surveys the role of the world's most advanced military command and control plane, the E-4B, in the day's events and proposes that the horrific incidents were the work of a covert operation staged within elements of the US military and the intelligence community. Presenting hard evidence, the account places the world's most advanced electronics platform circling over the White House at approximately the time of the Pentagon attack. The argument offers an analysis of the new evidence within the context of the events and shows that it is irreconcilable with the official 9/11 narrative.

Mark H. Gaffney is an environmentalist, a peace activist, a researcher, and the author of *Dimona, the Third Temple?*; and *Gnostic Secrets of the Naassenes*. He lives in Chiloquin, Oregon. Dr. David Ray Griffin is a professor emeritus at the Claremont School of Theology, and the author of *The 9/11 Commission Report: Omissions and Distortions*, and *The New Pearl Harbor*. He lives in Santa Barbara, California.

Softcover • $19.95 • ISBN 9780979988608 • 336 Pages

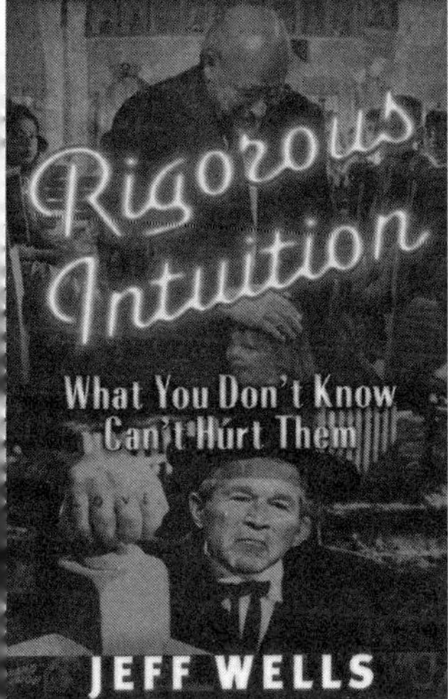

Rigorous Intuition
What You Don't Know, Can't Hurt Them

by *Jeff Wells*

"In Jeff's hands, tinfoil hats become crowns and helmets of the purest gold. I strongly suggest that you all pay attention to what he has to say." —Arthur Gilroy, Booman Tribune

A welcome source of analysis and commentary for those prepared to go deeper — and darker — than even most alternative media permit, this collection from one of the most popular conspiracy theory arguments on the internet will assist readers in clarifying their own arguments and recognizing disinformation. Tackling many of the most difficult subjects that define our time — including 9/11, the JonBenet Ramsey case, and "High Weirdness" — these studies, containing the best of the Rigorous Intuition blog as well as original content, make connections that both describe the current, alarming predicament and suggest a strategy for taking back the world. Following the maxim "What you don't know can't hurt them," this assortment of essays and tools, including the updated and expanded "Coincidence Theorists' Guide to 9/11," guides the intellectually curious down further avenues of study and scrutiny and helps readers feel empowered rather than vulnerable.

Jeff Wells is the author of the novel *Anxious Gravity*. He lives in Toronto, Ontario.

Softcover • $19.95 • 978-0-9777953-2-1 • 505 Pages

Fighting For G.O.D.
(Gold, Oil, Drugs)

by *Jeremy Begin*, *Art by Laureen Salk*

This racehorse tour of American history and current affairs scrutinizes key events transcending the commonly accepted liberal/conservative political ideologies — in a large-size comic-book format.

This analysis delves into aspects of the larger framework into which 9/11 fits and scrutinizes the ancestry of the players who transcend commonly accepted liberal/conservative political ideologies. This comic-book format analysis examines the Neo Con agenda and its relationship to "The New World Order. This book discusses key issues confronting America's citizenry and steps the populace can take to not only halt but reverse the march towards totalitarianism.

Jeremy Begin is a long-time activist/organizer currently residing in California's Bay Area. Lauren Salk is an illustrator living in Boston.

Softcover: **$9.95**, (ISBN 0977795330) 64 Pages, 8.5 x 11

Upcoming Releases

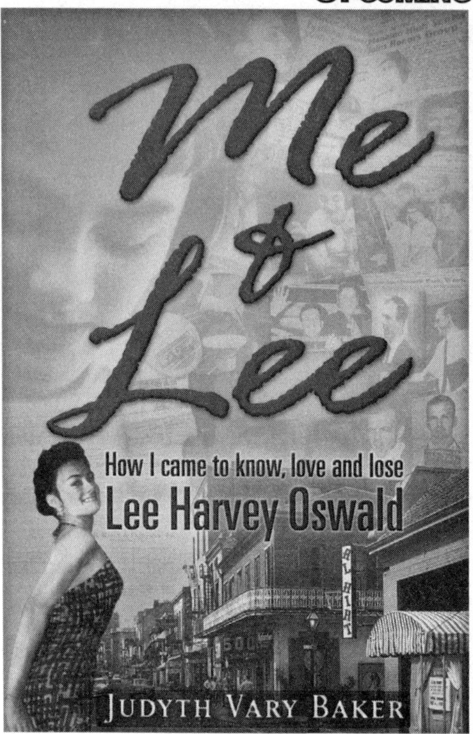

Me & Lee
How I came to know, love and lose
Lee Harvey Oswald
Judyth Vary Baker

Me & Lee

How I Came to Know, Love and Lose Lee Harvey Oswald

By Judyth Vary Baker

Foreword by

Edward T. Haslam

Judyth Vary was once a promising science student who dreamed of finding a cure for cancer; this exposé is her account of how she strayed from a path of mainstream scholarship at the University of Florida to a life of espionage in New Orleans with Lee Harvey Oswald. In her narrative she offers extensive documentation on how she came to be a cancer expert at such a young age, the personalities who urged her to relocate to New Orleans, and what lead to her involvement in the development of a biological weapon that Oswald was to smuggle into Cuba to eliminate Fidel Castro. Details on what she knew of Kennedy's impending assassination, her conversations with Oswald as late as two days before the killing, and her belief that Oswald was a deep-cover intelligence agent who was framed for an assassination he was actually trying to prevent, are also revealed.

Judyth Vary Baker is a former secretary, teacher, and artist. Edward T. Haslam is the author of *Dr. Mary's Monkey*. He lives in Florida.

Hardcover • $24.95 • ISBN 9780979988677 • 480 Pages

Order by online or by phone:
TrineDay.com

Mary's Mosaic

Mary Pinchot Meyer & John F. Kennedy and their Vision for World Peace

By Peter Janney

Foreword by Dick Russell

Challenging the conventional wisdom surrounding the murder of Mary Pinchot Meyer, this exposé offers new information and evidence that individuals within the upper echelons of the CIA were not only involved in the assassination of President John F. Kennedy, but her demise as well. Written by the son of a CIA lifer and a college classmate of Mary Pinchot Meyer, this insider's story examines how Mary used events and circumstances in her personal life to become an acolyte for world peace. The most famous convert to her philosophy was reportedly President John F. Kennedy, with whom she was said to have begun a serious love relationship in January 1962. Offering an insightful look into the era and its culture, the narrative sheds light on how in the wake of the Cuban Missile Crisis, she helped the president realize that a Cold War mentality was of no use and that the province of world peace was the only worthwhile calling. Details on her experiences with LSD, its influences on her and Kennedy's thinking, his attempts to negotiate a limited nuclear test ban treaty with Soviet Premier Nikita Khrushchev, and to find lasting peace with Fidel Castro are also included.

—Available 2010—

Peter Janney is a former psychologist and naturopathic healer and a cofounder of the American Mental Health Alliance. He was one of the first graduates of the MIT Sloan School of Management's Entrepreneurship Skills Transfer Program. He lives in Beverly, Massachusetts. Dick Russell is the author of *Black Genius: And the American Experience*, *Eye of the Whale*, *The Man Who Knew Too Much*, and *Striper Wars: An American Fish Story*. He is a former staff writer for *TV Guide* magazine, a staff reporter for *Sports Illustrated*, and has contributed numerous articles to publications ranging from *Family Health* to the *Village Voice*. He lives in Boston, Massachusetts and Los Angeles.

Hardcover • $24.95 • ISBN 978-0-9799886-3-9 • 480 Pages

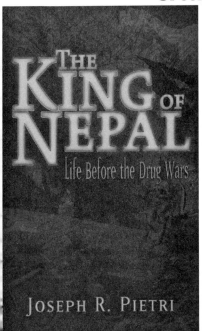

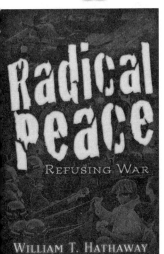

America's Secret Establishment

An Introduction to the Order of Skull & Bones

BY ANTONY C. SUTTON

The book that first exposed the story behind America's most powerful secret society

For 170 years they have met in secret. From out of their initiates come presidents, senators, judges, cabinet secretaries, and plenty of spooks. This intriguing behind-the-scenes look documents Yale's secretive society, the Order of the Skull and Bones, and its prominent members, numbering among them Tafts, Rockefellers, Pillsburys, and Bushes. Far from being a campus fraternity, the society is more concerned with the success of its members in the post-collegiate world.

Softcover: **$19.95** (ISBN 0972020748) 335 pages

Sinister Forces

A Grimoire of American Political Witchcraft

Book One: The Nine

BY PETER LEVENDA, FOREWORD BY JIM HOUGAN

A shocking alternative to the conventional views of American history.

The roots of coincidence and conspiracy in American politics, crime, and culture are examined in this book, exposing new connections between religion, political conspiracy, and occultism. Readers are taken from ancient American civilization and the mysterious mound builder culture to the Salem witch trials, the birth of Mormonism during a ritual of ceremonial magic by Joseph Smith, Jr., and Operations Paperclip and Bluebird. Not a work of speculative history, this exposé is founded on primary source material and historical documents. Fascinating details are revealed, including the bizarre world of "wandering bishops" who appear throughout the Kennedy assassinations; a CIA mind control program run amok in the United States and Canada; a famous American spiritual leader who had ties to Lee Harvey Oswald in the weeks and months leading up to the assassination of President Kennedy; and the "Manson secret.

Hardcover: **$29.95** (ISBN 0975290622) • 396 pages • Size: 6 x 9

Book Two: A Warm Gun

The roots of coincidence and conspiracy in American politics, crime, and culture are investigated in this analysis that exposes new connections between religion, political conspiracy, terrorism, and occultism. Readers are provided with strange parallels between supernatural forces such as shamanism, ritual magic, and cult practices, and contemporary interrogation techniques such as those used by the CIA under the general rubric of MK-ULTRA. Not a work of speculative history, this exposé is founded on primary source material and historical documents. Fascinating details on Nixon and the "Dark Tower," the Assassin cult and more recent Islamic terrorism, and the bizarre themes that run through American history from its discovery by Columbus to the political assassinations of the 1960s are revealed.

Hardcover: **$29.95** (ISBN 0975290630) • 392 pages • Size: 6 x 9

Book Three: The Manson Secret

The Stanislavski Method as mind control and initiation. Filmmaker Kenneth Anger and Aleister Crowley, Marianne Faithfull, Anita Pallenberg, and the Rolling Stones. Filmmaker Donald Cammell (Performance) and his father, CJ Cammell (the first biographer of Aleister Crowley), and his suicide. Jane Fonda and Bluebird. The assassination of Marilyn Monroe. Fidel Castro's Hollywood career. Jim Morrison and witchcraft. David Lynch and spiritual transformation. The technology of sociopaths. How to create an assassin. The CIA, MK-ULTRA and programmed killers.

Hardcover: **$29.95** (ISBN 0975290649) • 422 pages • Size: 6 x 9

ORDER BY ONLINE OR BY PHONE:
TrineDay.com
1-800-556-2012